Informal Groups:

An Introduction

STEPHEN WILSON

Department of Sociology
Temple University

PRENTICE-HALL, INC., Englewood Cliffs, New Jersey 07632

Library of Congress Cataloging in Publication Data

Wilson, Stephen (date)
   Informal groups.

   Bibliography:
   Includes index.
   1. Small groups. I. Title.
HM133.W54   301.18'5   77–13152
ISBN 0–13–464636–3

Prentice-Hall Series in Sociology,
Neil J. Smelser, Editor

© 1978 by Prentice-Hall, Inc., Englewood Cliffs, N.J. 07632

Printed in the United States of America

10 9 8 7 6 5 4 3 2 1

Prentice-Hall International, Inc., *London*
Prentice-Hall of Australia Pty. Limited, *Sydney*
Prentice-Hall of Canada, Ltd., *Toronto*
Prentice-Hall of India Private Limited, *New Delhi*
Prentice-Hall of Japan, Inc., *Tokyo*
Prentice-Hall of Southeast Asia Pte. Ltd., *Singapore*
Whitehall Books Limited, *Wellington, New Zealand*

TO MY PARENTS,
IRENE AND RICHARD

Contents

v

Four

Five

This book was first conceived ten years ago when I began to teach a course entitled "Introduction to Small Groups." It has been written as a text for similar courses in a variety of academic departments. In a real sense, the contents of this book involve my responses to various concerns, complaints and suggestions which my students in this course have raised during the past ten years.

For instance, one of the most frequent difficulties which students encounter is discovering what the results of various experimental group studies have to do with real groups like those to which they belong. This problem is not the result of student ignorance, but, rather, stems from the fact that many researchers have become so concerned with designing experiments to account for the results of earlier experiments, that they have lost sight of how their research relates to "real" or naturally-occurring groups. In fact, the term "small groups" has come to refer to collections of strangers assembled for experimental purposes. This is one of the reasons we have chosen to use the term "informal groups" instead of "small groups." Furthermore, without slighting in the least, the contributions made by experimental research, we have made an effort to include as much information as possible about such naturally occurring groups as work groups, friendship groups, therapy groups, t-groups, gangs, and groups which form among mental patients and prison inmates. In general, the early part of the book is devoted to an examination of some of the general processes which are common to groups of all types. It is here that we rely heavily upon the results of many experimental studies. The latter part of the book is concerned with how groups, including experimental groups, are influenced by the situation or environment within which they form. These later chapters also serve to illustrate how the basic group processes discussed in earlier chapters are manifested in specific kinds of groups. Here the emphasis is on what makes groups differ from one another.

A second concern that students have voiced is that after reading the literature on interaction, conformity, influence, sociometry, leadership, deviance, and so on, they were unsure as to how it all fitted together. In this book we have tried to avoid treating these topics in a disconnected fashion causing the student to lose sight of how the various elements and processes of group life are interconnected. In large part this is accomplished by organizing the material around the concept of "group solidarity." Thus, every topic introduced is discussed in terms of its function in either contributing to or detracting from group solidarity.

Throughout the years many students have also expressed their dissatisfactions with merely reading and talking about informal groups. Some have expressed a desire to learn while participating in a group, while others have wanted to play the role of the researcher. Both of these learning experiences were considered in the writing of this book. Chapter two is devoted to a discussion of six dimensions of solidarity in informal groups. This discussion is intended, in part, to help organize the literature in a meaningful fashion. But, the student is also provided with a series of objective measures which can be used to compare several groups (or the same group at different times) on each dimension. This can aid the student in carrying out research projects using either classroom groups (study groups, self-analytic groups, or experimental groups) or naturally-occurring groups outside the classroom. A student interested in carrying out research will also be aided by the fact that we have devoted considerable space to showing how the investigators in various important studies have gone about obtaining their results.

No text like this one can include a complete literature review, simply because of the large number of studies available. In selecting those to be included here we have used two criterion. One is that we wanted to be certain that the reader was introduced to a wide variety of research procedures and theoretical frameworks.

Secondly, we have included those studies which we felt most clearly illustrated the basic group processes being discussed. In some cases this led to the inclusion of older classic studies rather than more recent studies, dealing with the same topic. Despite this selectivity, most instructors will find that their favorite research program or theory will be mentioned somewhere in the book (if not covered extensively) to serve as a "jumping-off point" for lectures or supplementary reading.

The first chapter begins with three detailed descriptions of the type of groups to be covered in the book. Then, a series of theoretical issues are introduced to show the student what questions have been asked about groups in the past and what will be considered important in this book. Chapter two covers the six dimensions of solidarity, while Chapter three presents a systems approach to informal groups. Chapters four and five review some of the literature dealing with the process by which norms and statuses emerge within informal groups, and Chapter six is devoted to the function of leaders in informal groups.

With Chapter seven, the focus of the book shifts to the environments of groups. This chapter contains an analysis of gangs and their environments. Chapter eight deals with informal groups which form within larger formal organizations, while Chapter nine deals with problem-solving groups such as laboratory discussion groups and committees. In Chapter ten, the final chapter, we show how changes in groups over time can be understood by analyzing the group's relationship to its environment.

I would like to express my gratitude to the reviewers (Professor Ronald E. Anderson, Professor Andrew Effrat, Professor Alan Kerckhoff, Professor John Kinch, Professor Malcolm Klein, Professor Andrew Michener, and Professor Theordore Mills) who read and offered constructive suggestions for the manuscript at various stages of its development. Also deserving mention are Cherie, Carmen, and Andrew, who kept our group solidified while I tackled this project.

Stephen R. Wilson

one

The Study of Informal Groups

INTRODUCTION

Take notice some evening when you are reviewing the events of the day before going to sleep of how many have taken place in groups. While you are a member of a society, a city, or a university, it is likely that the events you recall most vividly are those which occur in smaller groups. Your friends at school, the people with whom you work, the committee on which you serve, your club or fraternity, the therapy group you attend, or the people in your unit of the dormitory are some examples of such small groups. It is groups like these which will be of interest to us in this book.

It is customary in introductory books like this one to begin with a formal definition of the topic. We, however, have chosen to reserve this for later. The reason for this is that any definition of "informal group" presented now would have to be so general, vague, and oversimplified that it would not be very helpful. Instead of providing a definition that we would have to qualify and comment upon throughout the book, we have chosen to wait until the reader has been exposed to some preliminary material in this chapter and then devote much of the second chapter to answering the question, "What is an informal group?" The first part of this chapter presents actual groups in three very different settings. The information about these groups was gathered by social scientists, and each study is now considered a classic. We shall use the results of these studies as examples throughout the remainder of the book.

Later on in this chapter we call the reader's attention to several major themes and issues. Any book that brings together many facts and theories must reflect the viewpoint of its author, but the perspective developed here is closely tied to the way others working in the past have talked about and analyzed groups. To help the reader understand why certain concepts and issues are emphasized and what the author hopes to accomplish we have tried to show briefly how this book is an extention of earlier theory and research. Not all of the social scientists to be mentioned have been interested in informal groups *per se,* but what they have said about them has been useful in organizing this book.

THREE GROUPS

The Bank Wiring Room Study

During the late 1920s and early 1930s a series of studies was carried out within the Western Electric Company's Hawthorne Works near Chicago (Roethlisberger and Dickson, 1947). In the particular study of interest to us, fourteen men who comprised a section of the factory were removed from their usual place and put in a special room for observation. The purpose was to make detailed observations of their day-to-day behavior. Since the men in this section manufactured pieces of equipment for central telephone offices called "banks," this room became known as the bank wiring observation room.

A bank is a piece of plastic about one and a half inches high and four inches long with either 100 or 200 terminals attached, depending upon the type of bank. A finished piece of equipment consists of a series of banks placed adjacent to one another. The terminals of the banks are interconnected in a special pattern by wire and then soldered. There were nine men in the room who connected the terminals with wire (wiremen) and three (soldermen) who soldered the connections after they were wired. There were also two inspectors who tested the pieces of equipment after they were finished.

Two types of equipment were manufactured in the bank wiring room—connectors and selectors. Connectors consisted of more banks but weighed less than selectors. Three wiremen worked on the selectors and were called selector wiremen while the others were connector wiremen. Men started out in the department as soldermen, moved up to selector wiremen with a raise in wage, and as they became more skilled would move up to connector wiremen. (The move from selector to connector wiremen was considered a promotion even though there was no increase in salary.)

Each man in the room was assigned an hourly wage rate depending upon his position and the efficiency of his past performance. His base wage was determined by the hourly wage rate times the hours worked during the week. However, each man could earn more than his base wage because of the group-oriented incentive plan. If the output of the department exceeded a certain level, each man in the group would receive a bonus regardless of his own contribution. The idea behind this was that not only would each man be induced to work harder but each would encourage the others to work harder since the higher the departmental productivity the more they would all benefit.

The observer, who sat at a desk at the rear of the room so as to not appear in authority, kept records on the workers' productivity and other aspects of their behavior on the job over a period of six and a half months. Although most of a worker's time was spent carrying out the requirements of his job, the observer was especially interested in noting those events that revealed the nature of the social relationships among the men. For instance, he recorded such things as which workers helped each other in their work and which played games together. Since mutual help and recreation were not part of the company policy (in fact the company discouraged helping) and all the men did not equally enter into these activities, it was assumed that observing these practices would provide information about the social relationships in the room. Many of the observations can best be summarized by examining diagrams drawn up by the investigators to illustrate their findings (Figures 1.1, 1.2, and 1.3). In these figures, a *W* stands for a wireman, an *S* for solderman, and an *I* for an inspector; the smaller numbers refer to specific workers; and the arrows indicate the

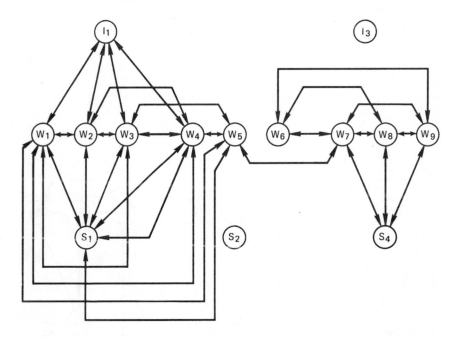

Figure 1.1. Participation in games: Bank wiring observation room. (Roethlisberger and Dickson, 1947, p. 501.)

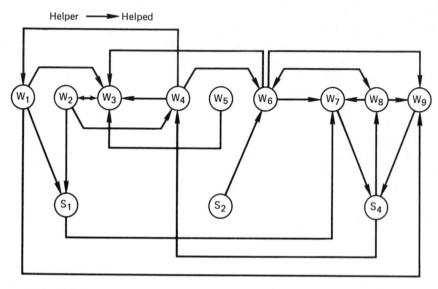

Figure 1.2. Participation in helping: Bank wiring observation room. (Roethlisberger and Dickson, 1947, p. 506.)

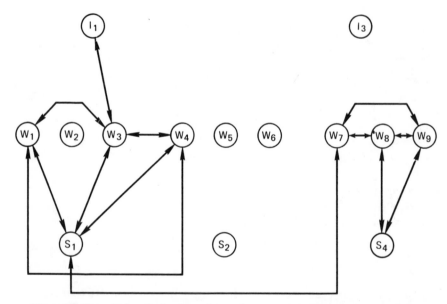

Figure 1.3. Friendships: Bank wiring observation room. (Roethlisberger and Dickson, 1947, p. 507.)

relationships among the various workers. From these and other observations, the investigator identified two cliques in the larger group.

The boundaries are fuzzy, but the subgroup identified by the investigators as clique A consisted of W_1, W_3, W_4, S_1, and I_1. Clique B was said to consist of W_7, W_8, W_9, W_6, and S_4. In general, members of clique A were located at the front of the room while members of clique B were located in the rear. The remainder of the workers seemed not to be a part of either clique. However, this does not mean that the members of clique A did not talk to those of clique B or to the nonclique members but rather that there was more communication between those in the same clique and that this communication tended to be more friendly.

Productivity. In addition, the investigators were interested in determining whether these social relationships affected the productivity of the workers. The immediate supervisor of the workers kept records on their productivity and was supposed to take an accurate count of the number of connections made by each wireman everyday. Because it was easier, however, he allowed each wireman to report his own output. The observer on the other hand made an actual count of the number of terminals wired per day and found that there was often a discrepancy between what a man produced and what he said he produced. In some cases the men produced more than they reported, in other cases less. Productivity could be overreported either by exaggerating the work actually accomplished or by exaggerating the time not spent in actually working due to a shortage of materials or to making repairs. The observers found that the reported output of the men remained relatively constant from day to day and week to week while their actual work behavior was erratic. Sometimes the men would work hard and at other times they would coast. The observer found that the men, regardless of what they put in their daily reports, knew exactly how many terminals they had actually wired. Although the wiremen's productivity fluctuated from day to day, these differences canceled each other out so that the actual output closely matched the reported output at the end of the week. In interviews the men expressed the view that their daily reports should be consistent because management would respond to low output rates with demands for higher productivity and that it might fire men or raise the quotas if it learned that the men were actually capable of higher rates of productivity. The immediate supervisor of the workers knew about the discrepancy between reported and actual levels of output, but he accepted this and his records were never examined by his own superiors.

Interviews with the wiremen and the observer's accounts of conversations in the bank wiring room showed that the majority shared a common notion of what constituted a fair day's work. Although not all wiremen consistently produced at this level, wiring 6,600 connections (two pieces of equipment a day) was the level most men said should be attained. Since the daily and weekly records showed that most men produced at this level, the management considered it to be the limit of the men's physical capabilities. Of course, what management did not know was that on some days some of the men would attain levels much higher than 6,600 connections. Thus the informal goal of 6,600 connections a day which the men shared necessitated that they restrict their daily output to a point well below what was physically possible.

Of special importance was the discovery that the ideal of 6,600 connections was not one that most of the wiremen just happened to share but was the result of group processes. Those wiremen who consistently worked faster than this level were often ridiculed and called names such as "rate buster" or "speed king." On the other hand, those who consistently worked at a level below the accepted level were exposed to the hostility of the others and labeled as "chiselers." Another pressure to conform came in the guise of a game called "binging." The idea of this game was for two men to take turns striking each other on the arm to see who could hit harder. Often, however, the rules were not strictly followed and some workers got "binged" more than they were allowed to bing the others and usually these were the wiremen who strayed too far from the proper level of productivity. Therefore the ideal productivity level of 6,600 was not held by separate individuals nor imposed by management but rather was maintained as a group standard. In addition to prohibiting too much or too little work, the members of the Bank Wiring Room group also felt that no one should tell anything to superiors that would get another man in trouble and that one should not act "uppity or bossy."

At one point during the research the investigators tried to see whether there was any connection between the average output of the wiremen and their scores on both intelligence and dexterity tests. Neither of these factors was found to be related to how many wires a man wired in an hour. However, a man's position in the group did have something to do with his output. In general, clique *A* produced at an acceptable level while clique *B* produced below this level. The worker in clique *A* who most consistently produced at 6,600 was the most popular person in the group (W_3 in Figures 1.1, 1.2, 1.3). He often produced too much but either did not report it or overreported the hours he worked so as to keep his output at the acceptable level. By and large, the men in clique *B* consisted of selector wiremen, and the investigator felt that this was responsible for their low level of productivity. According to Roethlisberger and Dickson, members of clique *B* expressed their resentment and opposition toward the higher ranking connector wiremen by "chiseling." This of course annoyed the connector wiremen who then directed personal criticism at the men in the back of the room. These outside attacks subordinated clique *B* even further but at the same time increased its "internal solidarity," which they expressed by continuing their low productivity.

Two men who were not really a part of either of the cliques consistently went against both groups' ideas of appropriate behavior. W_2 (see Figure 1.3) became an outsider because he did not relate well to the others and did not conform; he consistently produced above the acceptable level. Another wire-man (W_6), produced at an acceptable level but violated other ideals by horsing around too much, telling others what he thought of them, and overtly striving for leadership in the group.

The investigators in this study confirmed their original hunch that workers do not relate to management as individuals but as members of informal groups. Although the result of this study has had tremendous implications for those who manage workers, it has also pointed to some basic processes that occur in groups of all types.

William Whyte: Street Corner Society

At about the same time of the bank wiring room study, one sociologist, William F. Whyte, working alone, set out to study an Italian slum in Boston. His intent was to learn more about the social organization of this area, which was referred to as Cornerville. Although he analyzed powerful organized rackets and the political structure, he also observed the social organization among the "little guys," the common citizens of Cornerville. He was especially interested in the younger men because they had built up a society that was relatively indepen-dent of the older generation. The younger men in Cornerville could be classified into two categories. The first were "college boys," who were attempting to move themselves out of Cornerville; but the majority of young men were in the second category, "corner boys," whose social activities were confined to particular street corners and the surrounding bars, shops, and poolrooms. Whyte's informa-tion concerning the "little guys" in Cornerville came mainly from his close observation of one particular group called the Norton Street Gang. Although Whyte examines how these corner organizations interrelate with rackets and local politicians to form the overall social structure of Cornerville, he also pro-vides many insights about the internal organization of the groups themselves.

Whyte went to live in Cornerville and soon became acquainted with "Doc," the leader of the Norton Street Gang. This group of men were all in their twen-ties, and most were unemployed due to the Depression. Because of his friend-ship with Doc, Whyte became a member of the gang and therefore was able to observe the relationships among the various members for a period of three years. Much of his book, *Street Corner Society* (1965), deals with the effects of group position and prestige (especially the leader's) on each member's behavior.

Whyte diagrammed the relative positions of the men in the gang (see Figure 1.4). Doc had been the recognized leader of the gang (although the membership had changed) since he was thirteen or fourteen at which time he had beaten up the previous leader. Although he retained his reputation for toughness, he was intelligent and performed well in social situations. Doc had been employed, but with the coming of the Depression he lost his job and began to hang out on the corner again. Prior to Doc's return, the members were formed into small clusters

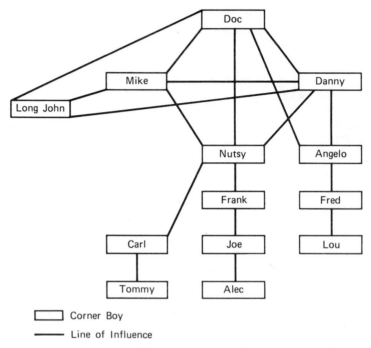

Figure 1.4. Social organization of the Norton Street Gang. (Whyte, 1965, p. 13.)

of friends; but when Doc reappeared, these clusters came together to form the Norton Street Gang as Whyte knew them.

As seen in Figure 1.4, Doc had highest ranking status in the group with Mike, Danny, and Long John following after. Mike and Danny were close friends of Doc's, and along with Doc they were the oldest members except Nutsy. They, like Doc, had many friends in outside groups and had reputations throughout Cornerville. Danny and Mike ran a crap game and therefore spent less time on the corner than some. Long John's superior position was due to his friendship with the top three leaders. He was younger and his bad habits of gambling did not give him prestige in the group. Although Long John had high rank, he was not considered to have any influence over the other members. Many of the other lower ranking members had jobs and were members of other clubs, which gave them a rather marginal status in the Norton gang. How these outside loyalties affect a member's status can be seen in the story of Nutsy:

> In the spring of 1937, Nutsy was recognized informally as the superior of Frank, Joe, and Alec, but his relations with a girl had already begun to damage his standing. A corner boy is not expected to be chaste, but it is beneath him to marry a girl who is "no good." Nutsy was going so steadily with this girl that marriage seemed a distinct possibility, and, reacting to the criticism of his friends, he gradually withdrew from the gang (Whyte, 1965, p. 13).

The relative positions of the men and their lines of influence in Figure 1.4 is Whyte's way of summarizing several years of observation based upon what went on between the members in many different situations. He could draw such a diagram only because he noticed a certain consistency in the behavior of the members over time. Social scientists are always pleased to have some objective evidence to support their observations of such consistencies. For instance, in the bank wiring room, the measures of the workers' output provided evidence of a group norm favoring the restriction of productivity and were related to worker status in the group. Whyte was fortunate to find such an objective index of status in, of all things, the Norton gang's bowling scores.

Bowling and social ranking. Bowling was one of the primary social activities of the Norton Street Gang. Saturday nights especially were devoted to individual and team matches among the members. During the week much of the conversation among the members was devoted to the bowling performances of the previous Saturday and to what would happen the following Saturday. At one point Doc chose a five-man team to bowl against other groups. When the Nortons beat the community club, this was a source of satisfaction. But after that when they bowled other teams, the Norton team consisted primarily of high ranking members. This led to complaints from the low ranking members. Alec, who was a marginal member was especially insistent in his claim that his bowling was underrated. He had the highest bowling score of the group for the season and performed very well when bowling during the week with individual members. When the whole group was assembled on Saturdays, however, he usually had, in his own words, "an off night." When Doc set up a match at the end of the season, Alec boasted that he would do well. The following is Whyte's account of the match.

> After the first four boxes, Alec was leading by several pins. He turned to Doc and said, "I'm out to get you boys tonight." But then he began to miss, and, as mistake followed mistake, he stopped trying. Between turns, he went out for drinks, so that he became flushed and unsteady on his feet. He threw the ball carelessly, pretending that he was not interested in the competition. His collapse was sudden and complete; in the space of a few boxes he dropped from first to last place (1965, p. 20).

It can be seen in Table 1.1 that, with the exceptions of Whyte who held an unusual position in the group and Mark who was an outsider, the rank order of

Table 1.1
Rank Order for Bowling (Whyte, 1967, p. 2.)

1 – Whyte	6 – Joe
2 – Danny	7 – Mark
3 – Doc	8 – Carl
4 – Long John	9 – Frank
5 – Mike	10 – Alec

bowling scores corresponded very closely to the status of the various members in the group (see Fig. 1.4). Whyte was interested in determining the reason for this correspondence. It is worth quoting at some length from *Street Corner Society* to get Whyte's explanation.

> There are many mental hazards connected with bowling. In any sport there are critical moments when a player needs the steadiest of nerves if he is to "come through;" but, in those that involve team play and fairly continuous action, the player can sometimes lose himself in the heat of the contest and get by the critical points before he has a chance to "tighten up." If he is competing on a five-man team, the bowler must wait a long time for his turn at the alleys, and he has plenty of time to brood over his mistakes. When a man is facing ten pins, he can throw the ball quite casually. But when only one pin remains standing, and his opponents are shouting, "He can't pick it up," the pressure is on, and there is a tendency to "tighten up" and lose control (p. 17).
>   . . . When Doc, Danny, Long John, or Mike bowled on opposing sides, they kidded one another good-naturedly. Good scores were expected of them, and bad scores were accounted for by bad luck or temporary lapses of form. When a follower threatened to better his position, the remarks took quite a different form. The boys shouted at him that he was lucky, that he was "bowling over his head." The effort was made to persuade him that he should not be bowling as well as he was, that a good performance was abnormal for him. This type of verbal attack was very important in keeping the members "in their places." It was used particularly by the followers so that, in effect, they were trying to keep one another down. While Long John, one of the most frequent targets for such attacks, responded in kind, Doc, Danny, and Mike seldom used this weapon. However, the leaders would have met a real threat on the part of Alex or Joe by such psychological pressures (p. 24).

The above passages show that the low status members reinforce their poor performances by tightening up and heckling each other and that their poor performances in turn keep them in low status positions. Whyte also points to several external forces that maintained the status and bowling score hierarchy. Whyte received the following answer from Doc when he asked him what would happen if the second team outbowled the first, which consisted mainly of high status members:

> Suppose they did beat us, and the San Marcos would come up and want a match with us. We'd tell them, those fellows are really the first team, but the San Marcos would say, "We don't want to bowl them, we want to bowl you." We would say, "All right, you want to bowl Doc's team?" and we would bowl them. . . . I want you to understand, Bill, we're conducting this according to democratic principles. It's the others who won't let us be democratic (p. 25).

The Norton gang and the Aphrodite Club. The following episode, in which the Norton gang become friendly with a girls' social club, illustrates the effects of status and the functions of a leader in groups. It began when Doc arranged for a night of mixed bowling with the Nortons and the girls in the rather exclusive Aphrodite Club. Although the men looked at these girls before with awe and disdain, the night proved to be a success and the two groups saw each other frequently for a period of several weeks. Everything went well as long as the groups met *en masse* and no pairing-off occurred. However, at one point this did happen, some members were left out, and friendships among the men were strained. After this crisis many members became disenchanted with the Norton gang's alliance with the girls' club. Whyte reports:

> Long John said that he never had cared much for bowling with the girls in the first place. Frank said that he had enjoyed it at first but that now all the fun was gone out of it. Mike said that he and Danny would form a "grievance committee" and would readmit some of us to membership in the Cornerville Bears (this being the name of a championship baseball team on which he had once played) if we would swear not to bowl with the girls anymore.

Later Doc had this to say about the whole affair:

> I enjoyed bowling with the girls at first. I hoped that Mike and Danny would fall in. When they didn't, I didn't enjoy it so much anymore. . . . I knew they didn't like it. They said to me, "It isn't right. The girls are taking all the alleys." . . . You might say that there was a little clash between us about bowling with the girls, but you saw how it worked out. It wasn't really serious. We got together again right away (pp. 31–32).

After this, social contact between the two groups decreased. Several of the Nortons, including Alec, continued to see girls in the club, and this contributed to their marginal status in the gang. Alec became a problem, however, because he insisted on boasting about his prowess with the women. At one point he challenged Doc to prove that he was a better lover than himself. Prodded by Danny, Doc had to demonstrate his success by making an impression on the most desirable of the Aphrodites. When this had no effect on Alec's boasting, Doc offered to take Alec's favorite girl away from him and Alec protested that it could not be done. Later Doc commented to Whyte:

> I didn't think I could do it, but I said it anyway. I was all steamed up. . . . After, Alec called me aside, and he told me he loved Mildred and wanted to marry her, so I should lay off. . . . I said, "All right, Alec, I just wanted to hear you say that." . . . I don't think he really loves her, but that's the screwy code around here. If he says he loves her, I have to leave her alone (pp. 32–33).

It was Doc who initiated the original relationship between the Norton gang and the Aphrodite Club. According to Whyte, one of the most important functions of a leader in such groups is to relate his own group to others:

> Whether the relationship is one of conflict, competition, or cooperation, he is expected to represent the interests of his fellows. The politician and the racketeer must deal with the leader in order to win the support of his

followers. The leader's reputation outside the group tends to support his standing within the group, and his position in the group supports his reputation among outsiders (p. 260).

In spite of his freedom to initiate action for the gang, Doc was not completely immune to the feelings of his followers. For instance, he was sensitive to other members' feelings about bowling with the Aphrodites, especially when they had the support of Mike and Danny, those closest to him. Similarly it was Doc who was expected to deal with Alec's boasting. Alec was not behaving consistently with his status in the group, and this was disquieting to the other members. Doc ignored his boasting until pressed into action by Danny. According to Whyte:

> As in bowling, Alec had to be kept in his place. It was essential to the smooth functioning of the group that the prestige gradations be informally recognized and maintained (p. 35).

The group as a system of mutual obligations. Whyte demonstrates that the primary norm in groups such as the Norton Street Gang is that members should help and not harm one another. When group life is running smoothly, these mutual obligations are not recognized or mentioned. If a conflict should arise, members may then explicitly blame each other for not having lived up to these unspoken obligations. In such cases it was the function of the leader to arbitrate and smooth things out.

One's status in the group is associated with the way he handles his obligations to others. As Whyte states:

> The man with a low status may violate his obligations without much change in his position. His fellows know that he has failed to discharge certain obligations in the past, and his position reflects his past performances. On the other hand, the leader is depended upon by all the members to meet his personal obligations. He cannot fail to do so without causing confusion and endangering his position (p. 257).

The obligations of a leader are extensive. For instance the leader tends to spend more money on lower status members than vice versa. He is obligated to make correct and fair decisions. He is expected to move the group into satisfying activities.

Regardless of status, gang members developed a fixed pattern of relating to each other; and departures from this pattern, according to Whyte, were problematic for both the group and the individual member himself. As with the bowling scores and the incident with the Aphrodites, members became uncomfortable when anyone broke the customary mode of behavior. However, in these cases the group, and as a last resort the leader, acted to put the offending person in his place. When, for whatever reason, this did not occur, the group faced possible disintegration. In fact, this is what happened to the Nortons toward the end of Whyte's stay in Cornerville.

Doc, at the urging of the Nortons, entered the local political race for state representative. Although he was not likely to win, he did have a chance of becoming an important political figure. One day, however, he withdrew without consulting anyone and rationalized that there were too many candidates running. When pressed by Whyte, he explained that, because he had no job, he could not afford to act like a candidate was expected to by the members of the community (i.e., providing stickers, buying tickets for local affairs, attending dances, and so on). The Nortons were tremendously disappointed at Doc's withdrawal and his influence among them began to wane. Doc found a temporary job which kept him away from the corner and when he was through with this he began to hang out with Spongi, a racketeer who ran a gambling place. This further undermined Doc's position in the group. Long John spent his time both on the corner and at Spongi's with Doc. But, he was not considered to be a part of the inner circle by Spongi and with Doc absent from the corner, Long John's status in the Norton's was even more marginal than before. During this time Long John's bowling scores declined and he began to have nightmares. These problems were later overcome when Doc, at Whyte's suggestion, began to support Long John during bowling matches and fitted him into the inner circle which hung around Spongi's and by consciously encouraging his bowling performances.

Another example of how individual members were affected during the period of the Norton's disintegration is seen in a story told by Doc.

> One night Angelo and Phil went to the Tivoli to see a picture. They didn't have enough money for Frank, so they had to leave him behind. You should have seen him. It's a terrible thing to be left behind by the boys. You would have thought Frank was in a cage (p. 264).

Since Angelo had become the street corner leader, Frank had become accustomed to spending a great deal of time with Angelo and Phil. When, because of his financial situation, he was prevented from following his regular course, the incident reported above occurred.

Long John and Frank were not the only men to suffer during that period. During his unemployment, especially during the campaign, Doc reported having dizzy spells when in the company of others. Doc talked about his condition in the following way:

> When I'm batted out, I'm not on the corner so much. And when I am on the corner, I just stay there. I can't do what I want to do. If the boys want to go to a show or to Jennings or bowling, I have to count my pennies to see if I have enough. If I'm batted out, I have to make some excuse. I tell the boys I don't want to go, and I take a walk by myself. I get bored sometimes hanging in Spongi's, but where can I go? I have to stay there. Danny offers me money, and that's all right, but he's been getting tough breaks. Last week he was complaining he was batted out and a couple of days later he offered me two dollars. I refused. I don't want to ask anybody for anything (p. 267).

It was mentioned earlier that the leader is expected to provide money and not to borrow. He is also expected to participate in group events such as bowling. As his resources dwindled, Doc was prevented from behaving in his accustomed pattern. This was even more apparent during the political campaign where he was not able to act as an outside representative for his group. Also, during this time, Mike, acting as his campaign manager, was telling him what to do and Whyte was directing him to job interviews. Having action originated for him rather than being the originator was not a part of Doc's pattern of behavior, and this probably contributed to his psychological problems. When Doc started his job at the recreation center, his dizzy spells ceased. Some time after Whyte left Cornerville, Doc once again became unemployed and the dizzy spells returned. He also had what his friends called a "nervous breakdown," which a reputable doctor said could not be attributed to organic causes. When he later got a WPA job, his difficulties again disappeared.

Due to a decline in the national economy, of which Cornerville was a part, the relationships among the men around Norton Street changed fairly rapidly. Whyte talks about all this in terms of "equilibrium" as a way of summarizing his various findings. "Equilibrium" may be thought of as a state of relatively little change. In Whyte's view, the group is in equilibrium when the interactions of its members fall into a customary regular pattern that organizes the group's activities. Any drastic changes, such as the worsening of the Depression in the Norton's case, can destroy group equilibrium. According to Whyte, the behavior of each group member may also be thought of in terms of equilibrium:

> Each individual has his own characteristic way of interacting with other individuals. This is probably fixed within wide limits by his native endowment, but it develops and takes its individual form through the experiences of the individual in interacting with others throughout the course of his life. . . . The more limited the individual's experience the more rigid his manner of interacting, and the more difficult his adjustment when changes are forced upon him (p. 263).

In Whyte's view, then, a group consists of individuals (high or low in status) whose behavior is determined in large part by the expectations of other members. As long as all individuals follow the expected pattern of behavior, the group is in equilibrium. If, for whatever reason, individuals are forced or allowed to deviate from their accustomed pattern, equilibrium breaks down—which is to say that the group no longer exists as a group.

Allport's Social Facilitation Experiment

The setting for the last study to be discussed was an experimental laboratory at Harvard University. Rather than one group, this study involved the observation of several groups of students meeting under special conditions set up by the experimenter, Floyd Allport (1924). At one point during the experiment the students performed a series of tasks while sitting alone in a room, at another point they performed the same tasks while seated around a table in groups of four or five. The students, when working in groups, were instructed not to communicate with each another. Since they were all performing the same tasks simultaneously, Allport referred to them as *co-acting* groups. The purpose of the experiment was to compare the performances of the subjects when working alone with their performances in the co-acting groups. Allport began the experiments with the hypotheses that students would perform better in co-acting groups than alone, an effect referred to as *social facilitation.*

The tasks Allport gave his subjects were of three types. The first was what will be referred to as *mechanical.* These were tests which measured how rapidly a person could perform routine mental and physical actions. For example, in one such test the subjects were given a series of multiplication problems to perform. In another, the subjects were instructed to cross out vowels in newspaper stories. The second task was a *problem-solving* test where the subjects were asked to write statements disproving didactic passages taken from two ancient philosophers. The third task was a *judgment* task where subjects judged the relative pleasantness of a series of odors (ranging from the floral to the putrid) and the relative weight of a series of objects.

On the *mechanical* tests, Allport found that most subjects performed much more rapidly when with others than alone. On the *problem-solving* test, the subjects wrote longer arguments when in groups than when alone. However, the quality of the arguments was found to be higher when subjects wrote alone. On both the odor test and the weight-judging test, subjects made fewer extreme ratings when with other subjects. Unpleasant odors were judged as less unpleasant and pleasant odors judged as less pleasant, while heavy objects were judged as lighter and light objects as heavier in the group situation.

The behavior of the subjects was certainly affected by being in a group, but the experiment showed that the effects of social facilitation varied according to the type of activity being performed. A number of similar experiments have produced results quite similar to Allport's results, since in some cases the subjects' performances were superior in the group while in other cases they were superior when alone. More recent studies (Zajonc 1966) have suggested that the presence of others may facilitate or inhibit task performance depending upon whether or not the task requires learning. On tasks such as Allport's mechanical task where no new skills had to be developed, performance was enhanced in the presence of others. In problem-solving tasks where one must arrive at the solution by trial-and-error, the presence of others inhibits performance. In these cases, errors become frequent and are facilitated by the group. One implication of this line of research is that one should study alone for a test but take the test with others present.

MAJOR ISSUES IN THE STUDY OF INFORMAL GROUPS

From the foregoing the reader has seen that informal groups can take a variety of forms. Any analysis of informal groups must account not only for the common features found in all such groups but for the differences between them. That is the purpose of this book. To accomplish this however, requires that we isolate those aspects of group life we consider to be important. In the sections that follow we outline some of the major problems and issues that have been of interest to past researchers. As we discuss each we will provide the reader with clues as to how this past work has guided us in the present analysis of informal groups.

Group Size

The bank wiring room contained fourteen men, the street gang had approximately thirteen members, and each of Allport's co-acting groups involved five students at the most. It is easy to understand why the topic of this book has traditionally been called "the small group." However, the use of this label inevitably invites questions. How small is a small group? When does a small group become a large group? Size is not a central criterion for deciding what groups will be covered in this book. However, what we refer to as *informal* groups are characterized by certain qualities, and we do find that, in a general way, the presence or absence of these qualities in groups is related to group size.

The importance of size is not a new discovery. Emile Durkheim (1858-1917), one of the founding fathers of sociology, concluded that societies become more specialized and complex as their populations increase in size and density. His reasoning was that in order to support its increasing population a large society had to find efficient ways of providing and distributing scarce goods, such as food, clothing and so on. According to Durkheim the most efficient type of social organization is specialization (high division of labor).

Ferdinand Tönnies (1957), writing at about the same time as Durkheim, argued that the move toward greater complexity changed the nature of social relationships among members in a society. In a large, complex society the primary type of relationship was the *Gesellschaft*, where each person enters into the relationship because the other can best help him reach some goal. Business, contractual, and barter relationships are examples of Gesellschaft relationships, and generally they tend to be calculative, rational, and impersonal. In a small society with little division of labor, the predominant relationship is the *Gemeinschaft*, which persons enter into because of *who* the other person is (e.g., kin, neighbor, friend). In this case, the relationship is an end in itself and not a means to some external goal as in the Gesellschaft. In other words, Gemeinschaft relationships are based upon emotional and personal considerations.

The works of Durkheim and Tönnies taken together point to size as a determinant of the nature and quality of relationships among members of a society. Georg Simmel, a German sociologist, was more concerned with the smaller subunits found in societies such as unions, political parties, and clubs. Among other things, Simmel is noted for his discussion of the connection between size and other characteristics of smaller groups (1950). For instance, Simmel felt that members of a dyad develop a sense of responsibility and intimacy not found in larger groups. The addition of a third person to a dyad completely changes its form. In the case of disagreement or discord between persons *A* and *B,* the entrance of a third person *C* may help solve the difficulty if he acts as a mediator. But, according to Simmel, no matter how close the members of a triad are, there are always times when one person is felt to be an intruder by the other two. In addition, Simmel observed that relatively small groups require more participation on the part of members and subsequently a greater part of their personality becomes absorbed in the group. While the unity of small groups is based on the interaction among members as it emerges naturally, larger groups must institute official rules and duties to assure their unity.

This distinction can be seen in the bank wiring room study. Here the workers were members of the larger Hawthorne plant; and because of this, much of their behavior on the job was determined by formal rules and regulations. Where they would work, what they would do, when they would eat lunch, and who they could talk to was in large part determined by the officials of the Hawthorne plant. The reason for this is that specialization, formalization, and regimentation are necessary to run such a large organization efficiently. On the other hand, within the bank wiring room the workers themselves also determined certain aspects of their behavior. Who traded jobs, who helped whom, who played games together, how much the men produced, were all activities which the men settled among themselves.

Sociologists generally refer to large organizations like the Hawthorne plant as formal organizations while smaller groups like those in the bank wiring room are called informal groups. In formal organizations a member's behavior is determined by written expectations (rules and regulations) that are formulated by higher officials before he even becomes a member. In informal groups, these expectations are unwritten (often not verbalized), are determined by the members themselves and are easily changed. In this case the expectations emerge spontaneously as the members associate with one another over time. While there are exceptions, *most* informal group are relatively small. Recognizing this fact, we have chosen to use the term "informal group" in this book.

Primary groups. While we are discussing types of groups, we should mention one other label which we could have attached to the subject—namely *primary groups.* This term was coined by the early American sociologist, Charles Horton Cooley.

By primary groups I mean those characterized by intimate face-to-face association and cooperation. They are primary in several senses, but chiefly in that they are fundamental in forming the social nature and ideals of the individual. The result of intimate association, psychologically, is a certain fusion of individualities in a common whole, so that one's very self, for many purposes at least, is the common life and purpose of the group. Perhaps the simplest way of describing this wholeness is by saying that it is a "we"; it involves the sort of sympathy and mutual identification for which "we" is the natural expression. . . . It is not to be supposed that the unity of the primary group is one of mere harmony and love. It is always a differentiated and usually a competitive unity, admitting of self-assertion and various appropriate passions; but these passions are socialized by sympathy and love, and tend to come under the discipline of a common spirit (1909, p. 23).

The essence of the primary group is the feeling of "we-ness" which develops among members (Faris, 1937). In most cases this results from the face-to-face communication that is possible only in smaller groups. Many informal groups are indeed primary groups as described by Cooley; but Cooley included the family in his definition, which is outside the scope of this book because most of the behavior and communication found among family members is determined by traditional norms shared by all members of the same society. Also, the term primary group is problematic because not all informal groups involve a highly developed sense of "we-ness." In fact, some informal groups have a very low sense of "we-ness" among their members.

The External and Internal Approaches

According to Olmstead (1959), those doing research on informal groups can be sorted into one or the other of two traditions. Researchers working within the external tradition have been interested in the group as a whole, as well as the group's relationship to the total society and other groups. Speaking of the external approach, Olmstead states:

> The group is viewed from outside externally, as a cell in the social organism. The major concern is not the internal operation of these cells but their basic characteristics and function in larger social entities (p. 16).

The external approach to small groups is consistent with the way sociologists have traditionally approached societies and larger groupings within society, but relatively few social scientists have actually applied this approach to the study of small groups.

Most of the information about small groups comes from research carried out by social psychologists working within the internal tradition. According to Olmstead, "Groups are conceived of as worth studying because they are relevant environments for individual behavior—they are the subsocieties in which social interaction and the individual's part can be observed and tested" (p. 20). Here the emphasis is upon the individual in groups rather than the group itself as in the external tradition.

Underlying each of these approaches are two different philosophical positions. Those adhering to the external approach have tended to be influenced by the *realist* position, which has been aptly summarized by Warriner (1956) as follows:

> This doctrine holds that (1) the group is just as real as the person, but that (2) both are abstract, analytical units, not concrete entities and that (3) the group is understandable and explicable solely in terms of distinctly social processes and factors, not by reference to individual psychology (p. 550).

The realists hold that the social scientist can analyze and compare groups in much the same way as the psychologist analyzes and compares individuals. We have already seen this approach manifested in the work of Durkheim who compared societies in terms of complexity, population size, and population density— factors that describe total societies, not the individuals who comprise them.

While Durkheim's realist approach has been influential among modern sociologists, the majority of researchers interested in small informal groups have been trained in psychology departments where a different perspective has prevailed. This opposing view, usually referred to as *nominalism,* holds that we use the term "group" only to refer to "an assemblage of individuals," individuals being the only real entity. The differences between these two perspectives can be seen concretely in the three studies cited earlier. The bank wiring room study and Whyte's study of the Norton Street gang fall within the external tradition. In each case, an attempt was made to understand the group as a unit—i.e., how the various aspects of the members' behavior fitted together to comprise a whole. The investigators were also interested in how the informal group served as a subunit of larger social groups—i.e., the Hawthorne plant and the slum community.

On the other hand, Allport's study is a good example of research in the internal tradition. Before Allport's time, social scientists were using concepts like "crowd mind" or "group mind" to explain the fact that persons in groups often seem to lose control and are swept along by the group. Allport, in rejecting the idea of a group mind went to the other extreme maintaining that the groups were not real phenomena and that they could be understood only by examining individual members. This idea was reflected in Allport's research on groups. In the study reviewed earlier, he was really interested in how being in a group setting influenced the behavior of the individual students. Consistent with nominalism, the "groups" in the experiment existed in name only, since they met for only a short period of time and individuals were not allowed to communicate verbally with one another.

Not all research fits neatly into these categories, but, in general, psychologists have taken the internal approach and sociologists the external approach to the phenomena to be studied. In this book we will cover material rooted in both the internal and external tradition. Most of the studies reviewed in Chapters 2, 4, 5 and 6 will be of the internal variety. Our purpose there is to give the reader examples of the type of research which has been most frequently carried out in the past. Most of this has been devoted to the discovery of processes common to all informal groups. Research and theory in the external tradition has not developed as extensively as that in the internal tradition. In Chapter 3 we will cover the two most influential scholars within the external approach. The last four chapters will be devoted to developing more fully the external approach in a manner which is consistent with past work in both traditions. In those chapters emphasis will be upon the factors that contribute to difference between informal groups.

The experimental method. Since many of the studies mentioned in this book follow the internal approach and utilize the experimental laboratory, it is appropriate to say a bit more about this method. While individual subjects placed in a laboratory situation for observation are rarely allowed to become a group in the real sense of the word, studies using this method have the advantage of allowing the investigator to gain some control.

The social scientist is interested in understanding and making predictions about the behavior of people in everyday life. To do this, he attempts to isolate factors or variables that lead to certain events. Suppose that we wanted to test Allport's claim that the presence of co-acting others leads to the heightened performance of a task by an individual. In order to determine whether this hypothesis is correct, we might wander around observing situations where people are either working alone or in co-action with others. In so doing, it is unlikely that we would find everyone working at the same task. Thus, it is possible that by accident all of the individuals that we observe co-acting might have slightly more difficult tasks than all those we observe working alone. It is also quite possible that by chance the average IQ of those working together is lower than those working alone, making them less efficient. If we do not perceive the effect of these other factors (IQ and type of task), we might conclude from our observations that the original hypothesis is incorrect.

Allport did not choose this technique to determine the effects of co-action on individual performance. Rather, he placed individuals in two situations where the conditions were the same except for the presence or absence of co-acting individuals. This meant that he did not have to search for the naturally occurring situations in order to make a comparison. Furthermore, by using the same tasks and people in both solitary and co-acting situations, he could control those factors (task difficulty and IQ) that would affect the efficiency of the individual. This is what is meant by experimental control. Allport controlled the variables to which the subjects were exposed so that if he observed differences in individual performances, he could be reasonably certain that these differences were due to the controlled factors (working alone versus co-acting) and not extraneous factors like task difficulty and IQ.

Social Control and Solidarity

The existence of a group necessarily means that the behavior of each member is influenced by his belonging to the group. Even in the Allport experiment this occurred in a very simple manner. In more highly developed groups, members are pressured to behave in ways favored by the majority. The derogatory names given to the workers who produced too much or little in the bank wiring room are examples of this. The ways in which these pressures are exerted are instances of social control, and it is only through the existence of social control that we can say that a group really exists. Otherwise, we have nothing more than a collectivity of individuals behaving independently of one another or a series of individuals actively opposing one another's attempt to exert social control.

Durkheim (1964) argued that while increasing specialization would not lead to the total disintegration of societies, it would undermine somewhat their solidarity and lead to a condition called *anomie*. Basically, an increase in anomie is the result of a decline in social control. In complex societies the traditionally accepted ways of behaving no longer hold, leaving members with no definite guidelines for behavior. Also, social relationships, being of a Gesellschaft nature, are less intimate and more fragile. When anomie is high, individuals are tied less strongly in stable and predictable social relations with others, a condition that Durkheim felt to be necessary for psychological stability. The lack of strong Gemeinschaft relationships leads to a high rate of various psychological problems, some of which result in suicide. (Durkheim, 1951). Thus when societies no longer exert strong social control over their members, anomie, as manifested in deviant behavior (including high rates of suicide), increases.

It follows from Durkheim's views that societies will fit along a hypothetical continuum such as that shown in Figure 1.5. A society's movement toward greater complexity would be represented by a shift toward the anomie end of the continuum. We will assume that informal groups as well as societies can also be arrayed along the solidarity-anomie continuum. We shall be concerned therefore, with isolating factors that determine the levels of group solidarity and explaining how a given level of solidarity affects group life for the members.

Opposing Social Forces

Simmel (1955) viewed group members as being torn between two alternatives. By belonging to a group an individual must submit to social control and thereby give up some personal freedom. On the other hand, remaining independent of a group deprives the individual of the benefits of membership (e.g.

Figure 1.5. The solidarity-anomie continuum.

economic security, acceptance, prestige and so on). Group members, then, always have a choice between these two alternatives. If a majority of the members seek independence, this may lead to the group's dissolution. But, many groups do not reach such extremes. In most cases, the need for independence that Simmel referred to is reflected in competition antagonism and conflict among members. For example, although the men in the bank wiring room and the Norton gang constituted a group, there were many instances of conflict and hostility among them. Thus, conflict or competition occurs to some extent, in all groups and its magnitude reflects the level of anomie (or conversely solidarity) in the group.

In subsequent chapters we shall develop the idea that members of informal groups are exposed to two conflicting sets of forces, the relative strength of each being determined by circumstances unique to the group in question. One set of forces consists of all of those influences that make it rewarding or advantageous for individuals to form social relationships and strengthen group solidarity. The opposite forces are those factors which induce individuals to avoid social relations and to behave independently of one another. These forces contribute to the development of anomie in groups. The relative strength of these two forces determines where a group will be located on the solidarity-anomie continuum.

Informal Groups and Their Environments

The forces that propel groups toward solidarity and anomie must have a source. In part, they are generated by the characteristics which the individual members carry into the group. For instance, four females in a predominately male school may find that their common sexual status provides a basis for mutual solidarity. Schutz (1955) has found that certain combinations of personality types can lead to either compatible or incompatible groups. However, consistent with the external tradition, we will emphasize those forces that operate on the group as a whole and from the group's social context or environment.

While those working within the external tradition have asked how groups are influenced by the nature of their environments, relatively little has been done to provide systematic answers. However, some clues have been suggested by the classic theorists. For example, Simmel (1955) emphasized the importance of the relationships between group members and outside individuals or groups. The observation made by Simmel which has most often been substantiated by others, is that groups in conflict with another person or group tend to develop unity or solidarity. He also suggested that the common attachment among group members to an outside person like a supervisor would lead either to an increase or decrease in solidarity, depending upon the circumstances.

A similar approach to groups can be found in the works of Sigmund Freud (1960). The essence of his theory was that individuals form groups because of their common attraction to a leader.

According to Redl (1942) who modified Freud's theory, groups form when individuals develop common feelings toward a "central person." One example of a central person is the handsome male teacher who causes all the girls in his class to "fall in love with him." Because highly unprobable that he will return their "love," the teacher becomes not a cause of jealousy, but a common object of attraction who draws the girls together. Another example is the hated teacher who, because he is a shared object of hostility, becomes a source of unity among the students in his class.

The early formulations of Simmel, Freud, and Redl suggest that the orientation of group members toward persons outside their group is an important variable. The last four chapters of the book, examine how the characteristics of groups are influenced by the nature of the environment. As Redl's analysis suggests, the nature of the relationship between group members and authority figures in the environment is of particular importance in analyzing informal groups.

SUMMARY

This chapter began with studies of groups in three very different settings. One group emerged among workers assigned to the same unit in a factory. The second was a street gang which formed in a slum area. The third involved groups that were intentionally set up for experimental purposes. These studies illustrate the wide range of social units that can be considered as informal groups. There is evidence showing that the size of a group determines the quality of the relationships among its members. In general persons in smaller groups have more "say" over what is expected of them than those in large groups and the relationships among members tend to be highly personal. Most small groups are informal groups and most informal groups are small.

The traditional approaches to the study of informal groups were outlined. The external approach is based upon the notion that groups are real phenomena, the emphasis within this tradition is upon the study of groups as a whole. The internal approach holds that groups are only collections of individuals, the latter being the real unit for analysis. Researchers working within the internal tradition tend to see groups as contexts or backgrounds for observing the behavior of individuals. Although there are many exceptions, sociologist interested in informal groups have tended to adopt the external approach and psychologists the internal approach. Most research on informal groups consistent with the internal approach has been based on groups created to be observed under controlled conditions.

The remainder of the chapter raises several issues that have been of interest to past social scientists and that will be taken up in the analysis of informal groups. For example, following Durkheim's analysis of societies, it is argued that all social units, including informal groups, can be placed along a hypothetical solidarity-anomie continuum. It was also pointed out that conflict is a part of any informal group and is related to solidarity. Furthermore, members of informal groups are simultaneously bombarded by conflicting forces. One set "pushes" individuals together increasing solidarity, while the other "pulls" them apart, increasing anomie. The work of Simmel, Freud, and Redl suggests that group members' orientation to an authority outside of the group is an important variable in understanding groups.

Care must be taken in generalizing from the results of experiments with groups where factors are purposely controlled to naturally occurring situations where many factors are at work. For instance, while co-acting groups in experimental situations generally inspired individual performance, the same thing may not occur in natural situations where members know each other and may be reluctant to compete. For this reason, it is important that experimentalists specify the conditions under which they make their observations. For instance, Allport cites the following factors in his description of this experiment: (1) the subjects were college students; (2) they sat around a table; (3) they performed specific tasks; (4) they were instructed not to talk; (5) they were instructed not to compete, and so on. Even though Allport's results can not be expected to hold in situations where some of these factors are different, another scientist should be able to set up the same conditions and get the same results.

two

The Six Dimensions
of Solidarity

INTRODUCTION

In the previous chapter, we used the term "group" to refer to a highly unified gang (the Nortons) as well as a series of individuals merely working at the same table (Allport's experiment). With this concept being applied to such diverse phenomena, it is no wonder that social scientists have found it difficult to agree on what a "group" is. Generally, researchers studying different types of groups (friendship, work, laboratory, gangs, therapy) have formulated definitions which fit the type they have been observing. Cartwright and Zander, who quote an assortment of these specialized definitions in *Group Dynamics* (1968), come to the following conclusion:

> Typically an author selects certain relations or properties that are of special interest to him and then sets these up as criteria for the many apparently conflicting definitions. From our point of view, these various definitions simply identify different kinds of groups, and little is to be gained from arguments over which is the "true" one (p. 46).

Cartwright and Zander offer the following general definition: "a group is a collection of individuals who have relations to one another that make them interdependent to some significant degree." (p. 46). This relatedness, or inter-dependence among individuals, then, is the common feature in all groups. But, we must also account for the ways in which groups differ—more specifically, for the different kinds of *relatedness* or *interdependence* that can be observed in groups.

To categorize a series of individuals as being a group or not being a group is an oversimplification. The fact is that a series of individuals can vary to the extent that they constitute a group. To put it another way, some groups have more togetherness, are more unified or "groupy" than others. To borrow from Cartwright and Zander's definition we can say that the individuals in some groups are more interdependent than those in others. Durkheim and others would say that some groups have higher solidarity than others. Thus, informal groups may be placed along a solidarity-anomie continuum in the same manner as societies (see Figure 1.5). Those located near the solidarity end would be those characterized above as showing togetherness, unity, "groupness" and interdependence.

How does one determine where on the continuum a particular group is located? To help with such an exercise we have chosen six "elements" of group life that various investigators have felt must be present before a collection of individuals can be called a group. The elements most frequently mentioned are as follows: interaction, norms, status structure, goals, cohesiveness, and common perception of membership. However, rather than say that one or more of these elements is *present* or *not present* in a group, it is far more accurate to view each of them as being present in degrees. Therefore we treat each of these elements as dimensions. This way, for example, one group may be said to be highly developed along the interaction dimension, low on the norm dimension, and so on while another group is medium on interaction and high on norms. This approach enables us to compare the degree of development of two groups on any single dimension or any combination of the six dimensions.

Interdependence in a group means that the behavior of one member influences or affects that of others and *vice versa*. The six dimensions to be discussed, all relate to some aspect of interdependence in groups. The more highly developed a group is on one of the dimensions, the greater the interdependence among members. It is not incorrect to say that the more highly developed a group on one or more of these dimensions (i.e. the greater the interdependence) the more the members constitute a group. But, we prefer to say the more highly developed a group, the greater its solidarity. For that reason, we refer to the dimensions as the six dimensions of solidarity.

In the sections to follow, we will discuss some of the classic research and theory dealing with each dimension. We will also show how each can be used as an indicator of the degree of interdependence among group members and therefore as an indicator of group solidarity. We will then go on to show how to establish, through observation, the relative position of groups on each of the six dimensions.

THE DIMENSIONS OF SOLIDARITY

Interaction

There would probably be no disagreement about the fact that interaction is essential before a series of individuals can become a group. Interaction is the process of mutual communication between two or more individuals and is a means by which individuals become interdependent. In the first place, interaction occurs only when two or more people are present, and therefore each person is *dependent* on another for interaction. Second, by definition, the reactions of one participant in an interaction sequence affect the behavior of a second participant and vice versa. These features of interaction are clearly illustrated in a theory by Thibaut and Kelley (1959), which we shall consider in some detail.

Thibaut and Kelley. According to Thibaut and Kelley, a person derives rewards from interaction when his own or the other person's behavior reduces a drive or fulfills a need. For example, for a person to enjoy the rewards of playing cards, he must find another person to join him. However, interacting with another person may also involve punishing behavior, which Thibaut and Kelley call *costs*. Costs in interaction refer to factors that inhibit or deter a person from behaving in a certain way in relation to others. Physical and mental effort, embarrassment, anxiety or the possibility of engaging in more rewarding behavior with another person are examples of costs. The more a given behavior is inhibited, the greater its cost. If interaction is to be repeated, the rewards participants provide one another must outweigh the various costs.

The combination of rewards and costs in a particular sequence of interaction is called an *interaction outcome*.

Interaction is seen by Thibaut and Kelley as a kind of game where each participant tries to maximize his outcomes without minimizing those of others to the point where they leave the relationship. To keep things simple, they deal with interaction between only two people which enables them to use matrices to illustrate the outcomes of various sequences of interaction for any two participants.

Figure 2.1 is a matrix similar to those used by Thibaut and Kelley. The items across the top of the interaction matrix (a, a_1, a_2) indicate different ways person A could behave in response to person B. The matrix contains only several items where in reality a repertoire may contain thousands of items. Down the left-hand side of the matrix are the behavioral alternative for person B. The numbers in the squares refer to the outcome scores, which, as mentioned above, are based on the combination of rewards and costs and reflect the satisfaction value of that alternative.

Let us assume that the person whose point of view we are assuming (we will call him Tom) is person A in the matrix of Figure 2.1. Bill is person B. Let us also assume that a_1 stands for "talking politics," while a_2 stands for "talking about philosophy." Furthermore, b_1 indicates that Bill is behaving in what Tom finds to be an opinionated and dogmatic way. While b_2 indicates that he is behaving in a less dogmatic manner. The remaining items (a_3, a_4, b_3, b_4) represent other possible behavioral items.

The numbers above the diagonal line in each cell of the matrix refer to the

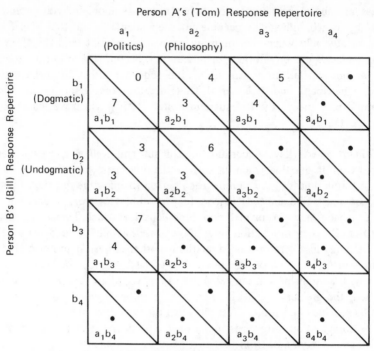

Figure 2.1. Interaction matrix.

outcomes of a particular sequence of interaction for Tom. The numbers below the line are the outcomes for Bill. The matrix tells us that regardless of what Bill does, the outcomes of discussing philosophy (a_2) for Tom (which is *4* in cell $a_2 b_1$ and 6 in $a_2 b_2$) are higher than for discussing politics (cells $a_1 b_1$ and $a_1 b_2$). We can also see that Tom's outcomes are higher when Bill discusses either topic in an undogmatic fashion (cells $a_1 b_2$ and $a_2 b_2$). Looking at the matrix from Bill's point of view, we see that he prefers to discuss politics and that with the exception of cell $a_1 b_1$, Bill's outcomes are similar. It may be, for instance, that he derives particular enjoyment from being dogmatic when discussing politics with Tom because he feels Tom is uninformed about this topic.

If we assume that the outcome scores in this matrix are based on past experiences which Tom and Bill have had discussing politics and philosophy, we can make predictions about what will be likely to happen the next time they get together for a discussion. For instance, if politics comes up as a topic of conversation, it is likely that Tom will attempt to change the conversation to philosophy, especially if Bill begins to get dogmatic. If he is unsuccessful, he may stop associating with Bill altogether. Thus, of all the possibilities $a_1 b_1$ is the least likely to occur. With the exception of dogmatically discussing politics ($a_1 b_1$), the outcomes of the other possibilities are the same for Bill. This suggests that he would be indifferent about which of the other three sequences are followed since they bring the same amount of satisfaction (ie. scores of 3). For this reason we can predict that $a_2 b_2$ will be the sequence most likely to arise because this would be most desirable for Tom.

It should be clear by now that the participants in interaction are dependent upon each other (or interdependent) for attaining rewarding outcomes. What may be less obvious is that because they depend upon one another for rewards, they also control one another. For instance, in our illustration, whether Tom receives a relatively high or low outcome depends upon whether Bill behaves dogmatically or not. So through his behavior, Bill has control over the rewards attained by Tom and *vice versa,* assuming that they both continue to interact with one another. Thus, the more members interact with one another, the more interdependent they become and the greater the solidarity of the relationship. While Thibaut and Kelley's theory analyzes interaction only between two persons, the same principles apply to larger groups as well.

Variations. In concluding this section, let us look at some ways interaction can vary from group to group. To begin with, it is the case that the sheer amount of interaction may be greater in some groups than in others. Groups may also differ in the way interaction is distributed among members. Even if the amount is the same, interaction may be spread fairly equally among the members of one group while being concentrated among a few in another. For instance, unequal distribution will occur in a group consisting of several cliques, as in the bank wiring room. It is also the case that groups may vary widely with respect to the content of interaction. A group of individuals whose interaction is saturated with antagonism and hostility is very different from one whose interaction is essentially positive and friendly. We shall deal with these variations later in this chapter and elsewhere in the book.

Norms

According to George Homans, a norm "is an idea in the minds of the members of a group, an idea that can be put in the form of a statement specifying what the members or other men should do, ought to do, are expected to do, under given circumstances" (Homans, 1950, p. 123). Several additional points should be made to give a clear picture of what norms are. The first is that if a group is said to have a certain norm, it is assumed that a majority of the members have the same "idea" in mind. Unfortunately, it is not possible to specify with any degree of precision how many members must have the same idea before it is considered a group norm. Related to this is the assumption that the members who hold a common idea of a norm in mind actually behave according to this norm. The reader should be reminded that many people may give lipservice to a norm and expect others to behave according to it but do not follow it themselves. Therefore, if a norm is said to exist in a group, we would expect to observe its members acting accordingly. Finally, if a norm exists in a group, we would expect to observe some sort of a reaction from members whenever a member deviated from that norm. Sociologists call such reactions *negative social sanctions;* this refers to behavior ranging from mild scoldings and attempts to embarrass the offending member to more extreme forms of punishment. The use of derogatory names and the "binging" used in the bank wiring room are good examples of negative social sanctions directed at those who deviate from group norms.

To say that a norm exists in a group implies that members behave uniformly—they all wear black leather jackets, use certain words, and so on. A norm then has a constraining or controlling influence in that each member feels pressure, to some degree, to conform to it. This has been clearly demonstrated in experiments by Sherif and Asch, two pioneers in the field of social psychology.

Sherif and Asch. Sherif's 1936 experiment was designed to determine the general psychological processes involved in norm formation. If individuals see a stationary light in complete darkness, the light appears to move. This phenomenon is called the *autokinetic effect.* Sherif placed students who knew nothing about the purpose of the experiment or the autokinetic effect in a dark room and asked them to estimate the amount of movement shown by a small light on the wall. Although subjects were led to believe the light was moving, it was always stationary.

During each session, the light was shown to the subjects 100 times. Some subjects were tested alone in the laboratory on three different occasions. Others were either (1) tested alone first and then tested with two or three others at the same time or (2) tested with others first and then tested individually. When subjects were tested in groups they were able to hear one another's answers but were not permitted to talk among themselves.

One finding was that subjects tested alone developed a stable pattern of estimates over time. For instance, one person might consistently perceive the light moving a quarter of an inch, while another would perceive it to be around two inches. According to Sherif, each subject developed a personal standard, or reference point, for perceiving the situation.

Of more interest for understanding the emergence of group norms were the results when subjects met in groups. Some of these results are illustrated in Figure 2.2. The chart on the left in Figure 2.2 is based on the results for one of the four groups studied where the subjects were first tested alone and then placed in the group situation for three-sessions. In the group represented by the left-hand chart, subject No. 1 (illustrated by dark unbroken line) most frequently answered 7.5 when alone and 4.0 in the second session (the first group session). As can be seen, the three subjects gave quite disparate answers

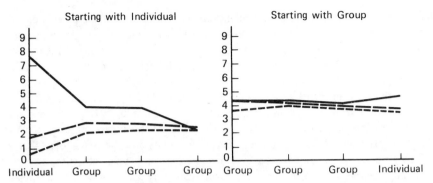

*Adopted from part of Figure 6 in Sherif 1936, p. 103.

Figure 2.2. Medians in groups of three subjects. (Adapted from Sherif, 1936, p. 103.)

alone. However, when these individuals were moved into the group situation, their answers became more similar. During subsequent group sessions, the responses converged even more until they were almost identical in the final group session.

The pattern shown here is representative of what was found in the other three groups, where subjects were initially tested alone and then placed into groups. However, in each group, the answers of the individuals merged to points that were unique to that group. For example, the subjects in the group charted in Figure 2.2 converged to answers slightly higher than two inches while in another group answers converged around a point indicating four and a half inches. Thus, the individual standards developed during the first sessions were overcome and replaced by group standards. To put it another way, in the absence of any external or physical cues to help make judgments concerning the movement of the light, the subjects' estimates were influenced by those of others in the laboratory.

In the case where subjects met for the first three sessions as a group and then were tested individually, a different pattern was found. The chart on the right-hand side of Figure 2.2 shows that the subjects in one such group gave almost identical answers from the beginning. This is understandable when it is remembered that those subjects did not have to overcome individual standards that would have developed if they had first been tested alone. Members of these groups were influenced by hearing others' answers from the very start, and the evidence shows that a stable group standard developed in the first session. In the last session, when the subjects were tested alone, there was some evidence that individual responses deviated somewhat from the earlier group standard, but these variations were slight. In other words, the members of the groups where a group standard had developed carried the effects of this group standard with them even when being tested alone.

Asch (1955) was interested in some of the same issues studied by Sherif, but he approached them differently. His intent was to determine the effects of the group on an individual's responses when the visual stimulus was not ambiguous as it was in the Sherif study. Although he used several variations in his experiments, it is sufficient to describe the common features of his rather simple technique.

In these experiments a subject would arrive at the laboratory to find that he was one of a group of six subjects. Although he did not know it at the time, the other five persons in the room were confederates of the experimenter who were paid to play certain roles. All subjects (confederates and the real subject) were shown a series of cards, two at a time. On one there was a single vertical line and on the other were three vertical lines of different lengths. They were told to pick from the series of three the line which matched the line on the other card. After being shown a pair of cards the subjects announced their answers in order. The real subject in each group was always told that he would be the last to answer. On two-thirds of the cards shown, the confederates all gave incorrect answers. Although the real subject was led to believe that the experimenter was interested in his ability to perceive the correct answer, the experimenter was really interested in whether the subject would go along with the confederates in giving incorrect answers.

Asch found that under normal circumstances, subjects would make errors in matching lines only 1 percent of the time. Under the circumstances described above, subjects made errors approximately 37 percent of the time. In talking with the subjects after the experiment, Asch was able to identify different types of response to the experimental situation. Among those subjects who were not persuaded to give erroneous responses, there were two basic types: the confident and the unconfident. The first type consisted of subjects who never doubted the correctness of the answers they gave. In the second group were subjects who were doubtful and anxious, but who stuck to what they thought were the correct answers. Figure 2.3 shows a sequence of pictures of a subject in the second category. Although he did not yield to group pressure, this subject showed considerable discomfort at being the lone dissenter. Among those subjects who at some point yielded to group pressure were a minority who felt that their own answers were inaccurate—some actually perceived the group's choice as being correct. Most subjects, however, gave erroneous answers because they were concerned about being different from the rest of the group.

Both Sherif and Asch devised ways to observe the most fundamental aspects of pressures toward uniformity in groups. They did this by drawing on their previous knowledge to set up contrived social situations where individuals' responses could be influenced by the responses of others around them. Despite the similarities in the intentions between the two, the situations they constructed were different in some important ways. In Sherif's study, the visual stimuli were ambiguous, although the subjects were not aware of it; and there were no correct answers. In Asch's study, the correct answers were clearly discernible. The subjects in both studies were influenced by the answers of the other group members, but for different reasons.

Informational and normative influences. Most of the information that we use to relate to the world—that is, our conception of reality—is derived through our senses. We know it is daytime because it is light or that an object is soft by feeling it. There are many areas, however, where it is not possible to test reality so simply. The idea, widely held in the past, that tomatoes were poisonous was not likely to be tested by actual tasting, and therefore this myth was perpetuated. Other ideas, such as the existence of God, are not capable of being tested directly through our senses. In these cases we are not able to rely on what Festinger (1950) calls *physical reality*. Instead, we depend on *social reality*, which is information based on the beliefs and opinions of others—that is, whether one believes God exists or that tomatoes are poisonous depends on the beliefs of others around him. The use of the autokinetic effect in Sherif's experiment created conditions where the physical reality was not directly testable. Thus, subjects easily depended upon the social reality which they received from the information provided by the estimates of the other subjects. The primary type of influence in this situation was *informational*, which refers to the acceptance of information from others as evidence about reality (Deutsch and Gerard, 1955).

In Asch's study, there were no barriers to the direct testing of the physical reality, and the subjects were not really dependent upon others for the establishment of reality. We know, for instance, that most of the subjects who were influenced by the answers of others were aware that their answers were incorrect. The type of influence in this situation may be called *normative* (Deutsch and Gerard, 1955), meaning the acceptance of influence so as to gain reinforcement and acceptance (or avoid punishment and rejection) from group members. Although it is helpful in thinking about group processes to distinguish between informational and normative influences, the two are difficult to separate. Both may be at work in any given group. A member may conform to a norm because he believes that it specifies a correct way of behaving, because he wants the other members to accept him, or for both reasons. Whatever the source, the tendency for group members to be influenced by one another and thus become alike in some ways is one of the most frequently observed results of group formation.

Norms provide each individual with guide lines for behavior in the group. Not only does a member know what is expected of him, enabling him to avoid others' disapproval, but he has a basis for anticipating the behavior of others. Thibaut and Kelley (1959) argue that norms function to pattern and coordinate the interaction among group members in order to maximize the outcomes of the participants. When group members accept a norm they, in effect, agree to place

Figure 2.3 Experiment process as follows. In the top first picture the subject (center) hears rules of the experiment for the first time. In the second
picture he makes his first judgement of a pari of cards, disagreeing with
the unanimous judgement of the others. In the third picture he leans
forward to look at another pair of cards. In the fourth he shows the
strain of repeated disagreement with the majority. In the fifth, after 12
pairs of cards have been shown, he explains that "he has to call them as
he sees them." This subject disagreed with the majority on all 12 trials.
Seventy-five percent (75%) of experimental subjects agreed with the
majority in varying degrees. (William Vandivert and Scientific American.)

restraints on their relationships. Norms, then, can be seen as providing a basis for interdependent relationships among members.

Variations. Groups may vary in the number of norms in effect. There will also be variation in the number of members who accept and behave according to group norms—that is, in some cases all members may adhere to a group norm while in others only a slight majority may follow the norm. While the studies by Sherif and Asch show that members of groups often voluntarily conform to the expectations of other members, in many cases they conform only because their deviance will result in negative sanctions. If group members show little concern when a member violates normative expectations, the norm is not strongly established in the group. Therefore, another indication of the extent of norm development in a group is the intensity of the negative sanctions directed against those who deviate from established norms.

Status Structure

For many social scientists, a crucial element of any group is its *social structure*. A structured situation is one in which the participants know what behavior is appropriate and in which their behavior is relatively constant over time. One factor that contributes to social structure is the existence of norms. But norms require uniform behavior from all members of the group, while close observation of any group reveals that not all members behave in the same way. We are not speaking here of random differences between individuals, instead, we mean consistent differences in the behavior of each member which is expected and condoned by a majority of the other members. These patterned differences are referred to as the "statuses" or "roles" of the various members in the group. Although both these terms have been used in the literature, we have chosen to use "statuses."

It is helpful to think of a status as a cluster of expectations that applies to particular people (or particular categories of people) in a group or society. Whyte's account of the Norton Street gang clearly showed how each member was expected by the others to behave in particular ways and how each member held corresponding expectations for his own behavior. What Whyte was describing were the statuses of the various members. It must be emphasized that status differences between members of a group are the product of group processes. A person on a deserted island cannot meaningfully be said to have a status, since more than one person is required.

Status rights and obligations. Sociologists often speak of two kinds of expectations that comprise a social status: *status rights* and *status obligations.* Let us consider the example of an employer and an employee in a small business. Some of the status rights of the employer might be the right to demand that the employee produce at a certain level and that the employee be working at 8:00 A.M. As a part of his status obligations, the employer would probably have to pay the employee an agreed upon salary every week and perhaps provide him with certain fringe benefits. If we reverse the perspective and look at this relationship from the point of view of the employee, we can see that the employer's status rights become the employee's status obligations and the employer's status obligations become the employee's rights. The employee is obligated to produce at a certain level and to be at work on time and it is his right to expect a certain salary from the employer. When two or more persons accept a series of rights and obligations, they place limits on one another's behavior in the group. Thus, the existence of a status structure in a group is a clear sign of interdependence among members.

In smaller groups, status rights and obligations may not be clearly distinguished as in the example above, but they can be observed. For example, in the Norton gang, Doc was obligated to lend money when he had it and to promptly pay back any money he borrowed. On the other hand, he had the right to settle disputes, give commands, suggest new activities, and so forth. The mutually defined statuses in such groups provide the basis for the interdependent relationships among the members.

When looking at total societies or communities, we see that members are ranked according to social class. In a business, the organizational chart will show the relative rank of the various positions. In smaller groups, the ranking system may be less clear-cut than in businesses, but it is nonetheless observable as shown in the diagram of the rank of the various Norton gang members provided by Whyte. As members of informal groups begin to take on distinct statuses, they also begin to evaluate and rank these statuses (and the persons occupying them) along some vertical dimension. Thus, we say some statuses have high rank and others have low rank.

Leadership statuses. Usually in informal groups, the members themselves or anyone observing the group can roughly divide the group into leaders and non-leaders. Even if the members themselves do not think of any particular person as being leader, an observer will usually notice differences in behavior and interaction that set one or two members off from the others. For instance, the men in the bank wiring room did not call W_3 a leader, but they behaved toward him in such a way (and he himself behaved in such a way) that it was appropriate for the investigators to refer to him as the leader of the group. In most cases, when social scientists speak of leaders, they do not mean personalities called "born leaders," but refer only a person's status relative to others in a particular group.

Variations. We can again point to possible variations between groups on this dimension. While any group will have a status structure (interrelated statuses), its development varies from group to group. Since a status structure is a product of shared experience, newly formed groups or those meeting infrequently do not have highly developed structures. Just as members vary in the way they accept and follow norms, they also vary in their acceptance of the group's structure. If members do not agree on the rights and obligations of their own and others' statuses, the structure becomes unstable and the *status consensus* is low. In such cases, there is disagreement and conflict about how particular members should behave, and the group is said to be high on *status conflict.*

Goals

Groups are often described as a series of individuals who have a common goal. A collection of people waiting together for a bus is not a group, but if the bus breaks down and the people cooperate to get it moving, they then become a group. The fact that every person in a collection of people holds a similar goal is not enough to make this collection a group. For example, people waiting for the same bus may not communicate with one another or even be aware of one another's existence. Likewise, several men who wish to be winners of the same contest are not likely to be considered a group. For a group to form, not only must the individuals have a common goal but this goal must be one that requires interdependence among members to be attained.

Group goals and personal goals. Kurt Lewin (1951), the founder of the Research Center for Group Dynamics, and his students have probably done the most to show how individuals become interdependent through the existence of group goals. Lewin initially was interested in the psychology of motivation, but he expanded his theories to account for motivational processes in groups. He conceived motivation to be a process of tension reduction (Lewin, 1951). The way a person sets up tension systems that motivate behavior can be seen in a rather simple experiment carried out by one of Lewin's early students, Zeigarnik (1927). She had subjects work on a series of puzzles. The subjects completed some puzzles, while others were interrupted by the experimenter. After finishing, the subjects were asked to describe the various puzzles. The results, referred to as the *Zeigarnick effect,* were that the subjects could recall a greater number of interrupted than uninterrupted puzzles. According to Zeigarnik, whenever a subject began a puzzle its completion became a goal. The acceptance of this goal set up a tension system in the subjects which was released only when the goal was completed. Unreleased tension remained when the subjects were not allowed to reach this goal and this was manifested in their ability to recall the puzzles not completed. Furthermore, an experiment by Oviankina (1928) found that if given the opportunity, subjects would actually complete interrupted puzzles even though this was not required. These studies demonstrated that the tension produced when a person accepts a personal goals motivates the person to reduce it.

Another of Lewin's students, Lewis (1944), adopted a procedure similar to Zeigarnik's but instead used two subjects working together in cooperation. She found that when one of a pair completed a task, it affected the second as if he had completed it himself. The subjects recalled fewer uninterrupted tasks regardless of whether they themselves or their partners had completed them. This suggests that when an individual has formed an interdependent relationship with another person, he does not actually have to reach the goal through his own effort. Tension reduction will occur if it has been reached by the other person. In other words, a person's acceptance of a group goal has the same effect as his acceptance of a personal goal. Using an experimental design much too complex to describe here, Horowitz (1954) demonstrated more conclusively that members of a group experience tension when the group is prevented from reaching a group goal and tension release when the goal is reached. The results of Lewis' and Horowitz's studies established that once group goals are accepted by the individual members, they have the same effect on their behavior as personal goals.

Cooperative and competitive goals. The next step in establishing the connection between individual and group goals was taken in a study by Deutsch (1949). For Deutsch, a *cooperative social situation* is one where individuals have *promotively interdependent goals*. When everyone in the situation accepts the group goal as his own personal goal, all reach the goal together, regardless of who is most responsible for moving the group toward it. In a *competitive social situation,* the goal is such that only one individual can reach it, and one person reaching the goal effectively prevents others from also reaching it.

Deutsch recognized that any real social situation contains a combination of cooperative and competitive goals; but he wanted to isolate the effects of each type of situation on group processes. To do this, he recruited students in a psychology course to meet in groups instead of attending the regular daily class. Every week for a semester, ten groups were each assigned a puzzle problem to complete and a human relations problem to discuss. Five groups were exposed to cooperative goals. The members of these groups were told that each group in the study would be ranked every week according to their effectiveness in handling the puzzle problem. The weekly ranks were to be averaged and the members of the group with the highest average would be excused from one term paper and would receive an automatic "A" for the course. Likewise, on the discussion problem, the members of the group being rated as having the best discussions were to receive extra credit toward their final grades. The other five groups were made to operate under competive goals. Members of these groups were informed that the various incentives mentioned above would be awarded on the basis of individual effort. That is, the one person in each group (of five members) who attained the highest average would receive these awards. From what is known about college students, it is safe to assume that the opportunity to escape work and still get a good grade is a goal worthy of achievement. It is certain, then that the subjects accepted either the cooperative goal or competitive goals as their own. Deutsch was interested in observing what happened among the members meeting under these two conditions.

While Deutsch measured more variables in the study than can be mentioned here, the results came out as most people would expect. The cooperative groups communicated more ideas, coordinated their efforts, exhibited more friendliness and pride in their group, and were more productive than the competitive groups. In other words the subjects exposed to cooperative goals displayed those characteristics which would lead most observers to say, "Those people are a group." Deutsch demonstrated that groups are likely to form and thrive when individuals must cooperate in order to reach their own personal goals. It is through the common orientation of the members toward the group goal that they become interdependent.

The importance of group goals. The concept of group goals has some problematic aspects because it is an abstraction and is not directly observable. The existence of a group goal must be inferred from other observable phenomena. It is easy to identify the group goal when the members themselves speak about it or refer to it in the group's constitution or charter. However, the members of many groups, especially small informal groups, do not always think in these terms. For instance, if we were to ask a group of friends who meet for lunch frequently what their goals are, they would probably be at a loss to reply. On the other hand, if we were to ask a social scientist observing this group, he might say—depending upon his theoretical orientation—that one of the following was the group goal: (1) to eat lunch together, (2) to receive social satisfactions, or (3) to obtain relief from the impersonality of their jobs. In each case, the goal has been inferred from outside observations and not from the members' awareness.

Thus, groups may vary in the extent to which the members hold and are aware of a clearly defined goal. The greater the extent to which members are aware of and can articulate the group's goals, the greater the interdependence among them. This basic assumption led to Deutsch's experiment on cooperation and competition. The following examples should show why it is true.

It is likely that for the luncheon group, meeting for lunch is a rather haphazard thing. Perhaps whenever the members happen to see each other on the way to work, they decide that they should have lunch together. On other days, however, they normally have lunch with other men in their respective offices. The attitudes or orientation of the members of this group toward each other as group members would be different from a group that decided to meet every Wednesday for lunch. This second group, which members might refer to as the Wednesday Lunch Group, would have a more defined purpose and form in the minds of the members than in the first group. Members would have to arrange their schedules in order to make Wednesday lunch and might even have to give up other satisfying activities to do so. The existence of a definite goal binds the members together into interdependent relationships because each depends upon the other for the accomplishment of the goal.

Groups also vary in the number of defined goals held by the members. Usually, this is reflected in the number of activities that the members carry out together. If, in addition to eating lunch together, the men in the example above, began to plot the overthrow of the existing managerial staff, they would likely become even more independent than they were. In general, the more defined goals a group has the greater the interdependence among the members.

Variations between groups are also found in the extent to which members accept the stated group goals. Disagreement is especially likely in groups with multiple goals over the question as to which goal is of primary importance. The incident related by Whyte where Doc was attempting to get the Norton gang members to bowl with the Aphrodite Club against the wishes of the other members is an example of a temporary state of disagreement over goals. In situations where members cannot agree about group goals, there is little basis for interdependence among them.

Person-oriented and group-oriented motives. In discussing differences between groups in terms of group goals, it is important to remember that while the individual members may derive satisfaction in the group's reaching of the goal, they may have very different individual goals. This is illustrated in Cartwright and Zanders' (1968) story of three boys who are together, yet don't know what to do with themselves. One boy wants to earn some money to buy a baseball glove while the second boy wants to use his new carpentry tools. The third boy is content to do anything as long as he is with the others. After tossing around several ideas, they settle on building a lemonade stand as a group goal. Working toward this goal allows each to fulfill his personal goal whether earning money, using tools, or just being with the others.

Cartwright and Zander feel that it is helpful to conceive of the personal goals of group members as varying along a continuum. At one end of the continuum, goals are based on *person-oriented* motives at the other, they are based on *group-oriented* motives. In the first case, the group is seen as a means to one's individual goal. In the second, the person is motivated more out of loyalty to the group and concern with the consequences for the group of reaching or not reaching the goal. Whether a member is primarily person-oriented or group-oriented may make little difference in terms of whether the group reaches the group goal; both types of members will work toward it. But the personal motives of the members may make a difference in how the goal is reached.

Let us take as a hypothetical case, a community action group. A person might work in this group because of his agreement with the group goals and his desire to contribute to them. This member is attracted to the group out of group-oriented motives. Another member might join this group because he has political ambitions and feels that being associated with the group and helping to accomplish its goals will help his career. While both men contribute to the group goals, their separate motives are likely to have different implications for the group as a whole. The person with group-oriented motives should, like the subjects in Lewis' experiment, be content if the group reaches its goal no matter what the nature of his own contribution. The political aspirant, however, would probably not be content unless he were seen as highly responsible for the group's reaching its goal. That is, he would be likely to strive for high status or leadership in the group as well as strive for its goals. If there were several persons with person-oriented motives, as there usually are, the group may be the scene of conflict and a struggle for leadership. Thus the extent to which group- and person-oriented motives prevail will vary from group to group and influence the nature of the interaction among the members. Of course, the greater the group-orientation, the greater the interdependence among members.

Variations. Groups can vary in the number of defined goals held by members and the extent to which members agree on the goals for the group. Groups can also differ in the number of cooperative versus competitive goals and the degree to which members hold group-oriented as opposed to person-oriented motives.

Cohesiveness

The reader will recall that in the story of the boys building a lemonade stand, each satisfied a very different personal needs sources of satisfaction from group membership for a single member may be numerous. For instance, not only did the boy with tools get to use them in building the stand, but presumably he also received a share of the profit and also derived pleasure from his association with the other boys. In general then, the total of the various sources of satisfaction determines the extent to which a member is attracted to the group. Because satisfaction of belonging to a group depends upon the existence and participation of other members, the greater the degree of attraction by all of the various members, the greater the interdependence in the group.

The variation in the degree to which members are attracted to their group is called *cohesiveness,* a major variable in the small group literature. However, the emphasis in the literature has been on one special type of cohesiveness. In most small groups, a primary source of satisfaction to members is the rewards that come from associating with the others in the group. In some groups such as friendship groups, this may be the only reason for the group's existence. Even in groups that members join primarily to gain money or prestige, they react to one another, evaluate one another and form bonds of attraction and repulsion. Thus, the degree of interpersonal attraction in a group is a particularly important aspect of cohesiveness.

Sociometry. One of the first to point to the importance of interpersonal attraction and measure it in a systematic fashion was J.L. Moreno. His book *Who Shall Survive?* (1934) analyzes the extent to which groups and communities are organized and derives a procedure to measure the degree of organization as it is reflected in the patterns of attraction and repulsion among members. This procedure which he called *sociometry,* was used to restructure groups to increase their therapeutic value, make them more satisfactory to the members, and make them more efficient. Very simply the procedure involves having members of a group or community indicate the individuals in (and some cases outside) the group to whom they are attracted and repulsed. For example, students may be asked to indicate who they would like to sit next to so the teacher can rearrange the seating pattern of the classroom. The goal of this technique is to allow individuals to participate in the formation and reconstitution of their group and the subjects are aware that the information they provide about their orientations to others is used for just this purpose. It should also be pointed out that when group members are asked to provide sociometric information, they are asked to choose or reject according to a specific criterion relevant to the group member. In the above example the criterion was "seating." In some cases students may be asked to name who they would like to work with so that the teacher can assign compatible people to work on the same projects. In large communities like hospitals, camps, and residential youth institutions, authorities may ask members to indicate their choice of roommates in order to assign living spaces.

Moreno provided various methods of analyzing the results of sociometric tests, but the simplest to interpret is a diagram called the *sociogram* which shows the choices made by the subjects. Figure 2.4 is a sociogram adapted from the results of a sociometric test given by Moreno to a class of ten boys and thirteen girls. The students were asked to indicate whom they would like to sit with and were allowed to make up to two choices (or to choose no one). The boys in the diagram are represented by triangles and the girls by circles. A choice is indicated by a line with an arrow drawn from the chooser toward the person chosen. Two people choosing each other is indicated by a line with double arrows.

From the diagram we can derive the following information: (1) there were seven students who were not chosen at all (isolates) (*EK, AS, ER, DHa, FT, RK,* and *GT*); (2) there were five mutual choices or pairs (*JB-TD, EF-LD, LD-DH, DH-NS, NS-MP*); (3) there were three who were chosen by more than five others (*MP, NS, DH*) (sociometric stars); (4) only one choice went across sex lines (*ML-NS*). Besides seating rearrangements, the teacher might use this information to better integrate the isolates into the classroom. Knowing who the stars are, the teacher can use them for starting and carrying out class projects.

While designed as a method for facilitating changes in a particular group, the sociometric test also provides information about groups in general. For

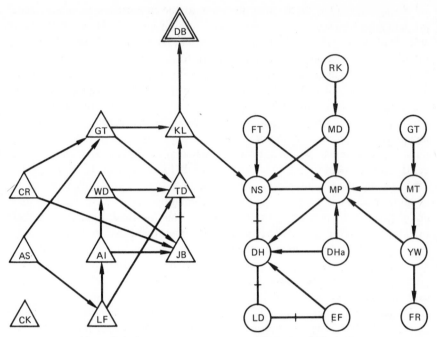

Figure 2.4. Sociogram of a classroom. (Moreno, 1934, p. 163.)

instance, from the sociogram in Figure 2.4 it can be seen that very few members were chosen by more than one person, a pattern that is found in all of the sociograms of various classes provided by Moreno. Consistent patterns of positive and negative feelings like this were important contributions to the study of group life. Furthermore, the sociometric test is a quick method for gathering information that otherwise would require lengthy interviews and detailed observations. For this reason the sociometric test has become widely used by scientists interested in small groups. However, it is usually used today in ways which deviate from Moreno's procedure. One of the important modifications of the sociometric test has involved dropping the requirement that members' choices actually produce changes in group structure. A related modification has involved the type of criterion that group members are given in order to make choices in their groups. They are often asked to respond in a make-believe fashion. For instance, school children might be asked to choose *as if* their choices might result in a changed seating plan. Sometimes criteria such as "seating" or "work" are dropped and members are merely asked to list whom they like or dislike, or whom they consider to be the leaders in the group. In other cases the members are asked to rate how much they like each other on a scale numbered from 0 to 10 where 0 means "dislike very much" and 10 means "like very much." Such procedures indicate the direction of feeling and the intensity between every member in the group without the need for making actual changes.

The measurement of cohesiveness. How a modified sociometric technique can be used to measure cohesiveness is seen in a study by Festinger, Schachter, and Back (1950). This classic study will be described in detail in Chapter 4, but at this point we shall discuss cohesiveness, the major variable in that study. Cohesiveness was defined by the investigators as "the total field of forces which act on members to remain in the group" (p. 164). "Total field of forces" indicates that cohesiveness, very much like Durkheim's concept of solidarity, is a characteristic of the group as a whole. Festinger and his colleagues thought of cohesiveness as a dimension along which groups can be compared. At one extreme are groups whose members receive many rewards from being part of the group and are thus strongly attracted to it. At the other extreme are groups whose members are not highly rewarded and have only a weak attraction to it. Festinger's definition is consistent with the fact that many forces and motives can induce members to remain in a group. According to this definition, a group's cohesiveness is the result of all these positive forces for all its members.

Let us look, however, at the way the investigators actually measured group cohesiveness. In a 1950 study, Festinger, Schachter, and Back asked people who lived in a series of courts in a housing project to provide the names of the three families living in the project whom they saw most frequently socially. Each court contained thirteen apartments. They calculated the proportion of times that people living in a particular court chose others in that same court as opposed to people living in other courts. They reasoned that the greater the number of people within the same court who named each other, the higher the cohesiveness of that court. The investigators were then able to rank order the various courts according to their degree of cohesiveness.

In this study, cohesiveness was operationalized by measuring the degree of interpersonal attraction in each court. Asking people to indicate whom they associate with socially is really a modification of the sociometric technique developed by Moreno, and many subsequent investigators have made cohesiveness synonymous with interpersonal attraction, measuring it by some variation of a sociometric test. Not all researchers consider cohesiveness to be solely the result of *interpersonal attractions* among members, however. It has been demonstrated through research that the satisfaction which members derive from associating with one another is only one reward that binds them to a group and therefore only one dimension of cohesiveness (Gross and Martin, 1952; Eisman, 1959; and Hagstrom and Selvin, 1965.

One distinction that has been made in the literature is that between *social interdependence* and *instrumental interdependence*. The first of these occurs where members are attracted to one another (i.e. interpersonal attraction) simply because of the rewards involved in being with and interacting with them.

Instrumental interdependence occurs where individuals are attracted to one another in order to jointly achieve some goal (i.e. to win a game, stop pollution, play music and so on.) While one or the other type of interdependence may prevail in a group most are based on a mixture of the two types. Currently, there is no single accepted technique for measuring cohesiveness. Measure of interpersonal attraction are most frequently used by researchers but many have avoided this limited technique by asking members to indicate on questionnaire their overall attraction to a group without stating the precise source of their attraction (see Cartwright, 1968). It should be pointed out however that even though interpersonal attraction (or social interdependence) is not the only basis of cohesiveness it is important in almost all groups. Even if a person belongs to a group primarily because of the prestige it offers, his overall attraction to the group will be affected by his evaluations of the other members.

Of the six dimensions, cohesiveness has been used most frequently as a measure of group solidarity. This is because it provides a kind of global description of the nature of the relationship among members. This approach is feasible because many of the dimensions are related to group cohesion. For instance, we will see in Chapter 4 that norms tend to emerge in cohesive groups and that norms can lead to higher cohesiveness. Thus, in many cases, knowledge of a group's cohesiveness will predict how developed the group is on other dimensions. But, this relationship between cohesiveness and the other dimensions is not exact. The members in two friendship groups, for example, may be equally attracted to one another, but if one group meets frequently to plan social gathering, it is not possible to consider both equal in solidarity. Furthermore, as we shall see, groups of prisoners and certain types of gangs develop elaborate norms and status structure but remain very low in cohesiveness. Thus, we consider it more useful to view cohesion as a dimension of solidarity rather than *the* measure of solidarity (see Feldman, 1968).

Variations. The higher the cohesiveness of a group, no matter how it is measured, the more members depend upon one another for various rewards or satisfaction that come from participating in the group. Thus, the level of cohesiveness of a group is indicative of the degree of interdependence among members. In addition to variations in the intensity of the members' attractions, groups may vary in the distribution of these attractions. In some cases, interpersonal attractions may be evenly spread among members while in others they may be concentrated on a few sociometric stars or in cliques. There were several pairs of courts in the MIT study with similar cohesiveness scores (i.e. the same number of in-court choices). However, in some cases the choices were directed evenly throughout the court, while in others several small cliques of residents tended to choose only one another. The existence of cliques means that interdependence among clique members is high but that interdependence of the larger group is relatively low.

Awareness of Membership

It may sound too obvious to state, but members of groups must recognize the fact of their membership. Merton (1957), in discussing the problem of identifying groups, suggests that members come to define themselves as members and are in turn defined as such by other members and by nonmembers. The importance of this is that a sociologist, attempting to determine whether a collection of individuals is indeed a group and what individuals were included in it can find out by asking the individuals involved. This approach is based on the assumption that when individuals are interdependent; that is, when they are influencing one another's behavior, they should be aware of the fact that the greater the interdependence the greater the awareness of group membership.

The subjective aspect of group membership has been observed by scholars we have already cited. Recall that Cooley (1909) stated that a feeling of "we-ness" was a characteristic of primary groups. Deutsch (1949), in his study of cooperation and competition, found that subjects in cooperative groups that were set up to foster their interdependence showed a greater "we" feeling than those in competitive groups and that members of cooperative groups rated themselves higher on this variable. In his discussion of group size, Simmel pointed out that unlike a single person, individuals in a pair relationship had the feeling of being part of a unique unit. Simmel also said that in groups larger than pairs, members develop the feeling of being part of something larger than themselves. Thus, the feeling of being interlinked with, of being part of a larger whole, of sharing a common fate with others, is another aspect of the interdependence among group members. Similar ideas are expressed in Sumner's study of the formation of "primitive" societies. According to Sumner (1960), customs emerge among individuals when they begin to take certain habitual ways of behaving as morally correct. These norms lead to shared feelings of separateness from other groups or individuals not adhering to the same customs. The subjective feeling of belonging to an in-group can in turn reinforce the feeling of the "rightness" of the customs, a condition referred to as ethnocentrism.

As with the other dimensions, members vary in their awareness of membership in a group, their "sense of belonging." Although we commonly speak of individuals as members of a group, we must recognize, in keeping with the idea that groups can vary in interdependence, that membership is a matter of degree. At one extreme, a collection of individuals may be judged by an outsider to be a group because it rates high on one or more dimensions such as interaction, but its members have no sense of being a part of a group or any notion as to who is or is not within the group. As we saw in Whyte's description of the Norton gang, some of the men were considered "marginal members" by the others and saw themselves in this way. Some groups may be comprised almost entirely of "marginal members." At the other extreme are groups in which all of the features discussed by Cooley, Deutsch, Sumner, and Simmel are highly developed. We often talk of *esprit de corps* or morale when describing these groups. High morale usually makes a group more productive, increases teamwork, and makes it more resistant to outside attack. Although the effects of high morale are undeniable, the scientific study of group morale has been rather disappointing. For one thing, there is little agreement as to how the term should be defined and measured (see Golembiewski, 1962, pp. 237–41).

Variations. Groups may vary in the extent to which the members show awareness of their being a part of a group and awareness of who is and who is not a member. Groups also differ in measures of *esprit de corps,* or morale.

MEASURING THE SIX DIMENSIONS

How might a researcher go about determining the relative levels of solidarity of two groups? In Table 2.1, each of the six dimensions has been further broken down into sub-headings. Each of these indicates actual observations or measurement that could be used to determine a group's location on the corresponding dimension. The reader will recall that in the conclusions of our earlier discussions of the dimensions, we listed ways that groups could vary on each. The observations and measurements in Table 2.1 are based on these lists.

Using the information in the figure, a researcher could go down the list, compare groups on each of the six dimensions and determine which group was highest in solidarity on each. Alternatively, he or she could take several measurements on the same group at different points in time to determine whether it is moving toward or away from greater solidarity. For example, under interaction, one might tally the frequency of interaction, measure its distribution, or count the number of antagonistic and friendly remarks made when members are together. The chart shows that one should expect to find frequent, equally distributed interaction in groups high on solidarity, and also a greater proportion of friendly, as opposed to antagonistic, remarks. One could then go on to the variables listed under the next dimension and so forth. He or she could also combine the results for some mixture of measures and observations from several dimensions to form a composite index of group solidarity.

Although it would be ideal to use as many specific comparisons as possible, it is unlikely that this would occur in actual research. For one thing, the nature of any particular group and its circumstances might preclude certain types of comparisons. For example, a researcher may not, for whatever reason, be able to give the group members questionnaires or interview them, thus ruling out certain types of comparisons. Also, because many of these factors are interrelated, the researcher may want to avoid being redundant. For instance, the existence of isolates and cliques identified by sociometric techniques would also be accompanied by an unequal distribution of interaction; low consensus on norms or statuses would be accompanied by the nonsanctioning of deviants; and disagreement on goals would be accompanied by antagonistic interaction and low attraction to the group. In these cases, the researcher would probably choose to compare only a few variables known to be interrelated.

While past researchers have used the various measures listed in Table 2.1, either alone or in combination, as indicators of solidarity, there is no single agreed upon procedure for measuring group solidarity (see Feldman, 1968). This seems to stem from the fact that *all* the variations listed in Table 2.1 can be seen as components of solidarity. While no one doing research need actually measure every single aspect, it is useful to conceive of the overall solidarity of a group as being based upon development along all six dimension (as indicated by the various measures).

Table 2.1
The Dimensions of Solidarity

	Low solidarity	High solidarity
1) Interaction	a low frequency b unequal distribution c much antagonistic interaction	a high frequency b equal distribution c much friendly interaction
2) Norms	a few norms b low concensus on norms c deviants are not negatively sanctioned	a many norms b high concensus on norms c deviants are negatively sanctioned
3) Status structure	a members have low concensus on own and others statuses b many status challenges c deviants are not negatively sanctioned	a high status concensus b few status challenges c deviants are negatively sanctioned
4) Goals	a few defined goals b disagreement on goals c competitive goals d person-oriented motives	a many defined goals b concensus on goals c cooperative goals d group-oriented motives
5) Cohesiveness	a low on various measures of cohesiveness (including interpersonal attraction) b sociometric choices show existence of isolates and cliques	a high on various measures of cohesiveness (including interpersonal attraction) b sociometric choices show existence of no isolates and cliques
6) Awareness of membership	a low awareness b low on measures of morale	a high awareness b high on measures of morale

AN EXAMPLE OF THE DEVELOPMENT OF SOLIDARITY

To provide a better understanding of each dimension and how they relate to one another we shall rely on a study which observed the development of newly formed groups.

The subjects in this study by Sherif and Sherif (1966) were twenty-four boys who were sent to a summer camp sponsored by the Yale Psychology Department. The campers were not aware of it, but the schedule they followed at camp was planned ahead of time to meet the needs of the investigators. The camp session was divided into three stages. Stage I involved having all twenty-four boys live and carry out camp activities together. In Stage II, the boys were divided into two separate groups, each of which lived in separate cabins and engaged in many separate activities. During Stage III, the two groups were placed in competitive and mutually frustrating situations. The camp counselors were trained observers, and the principal investigator was on hand in the role of "Mr. Mussee," the camp caretaker. These observers kept careful records of the behavior of each boy during the entire time he was at camp.

On the first day, the boys arrived at the camp together on a bus and all were housed in one large bunkhouse. During Stage I of the experiment, the boys were interviewed under the pretext of getting suggestions about favored activities and about improving the camp. Among other things, the investigators inquired about each camper's choice of friends at that point in time. When Stage II was instituted, the boys were told that the camp would be divided into two groups in order to make it easier to carry out their favored activities. The two groups were composed so that the boys in each would be similar on several characteristics and so that most of the boys who were close friends were placed in separate groups. The groups were assigned the colors red and blue for purposes of identification and were moved into separate cabins to live. In order to ease the pain of parting, the boys in each group were immediately taken on a group camping trip. From that point on, the reds and blues ate at separate tables, served KP on alternate days, and engaged in separate activities.

During this stage the various observers rated each boy daily on what they called "effective initiative." A boy received a high rating on this dimension to the extent that he was responsible for making decisions and suggestions that were taken up and actualy followed by the other boys in the group. This included actions where one member rewarded or punished another if he had the support of the remaining members. The observers compared their daily ratings of each boy to determine how much consensus there was between observers. Also, during this time, the boys were interviewed again and all were asked to indicate who in their own group usually got things started and accomplished. Using both the observer's ratings and the interview material, each member's status rank was determined. At first there was little agreement between observers, but over time their ratings became more consistent. Agreement developed first about those boys who eventually were seen as having either very high or very low rank in their groups.

The Sherifs later used the diagram reproduced in Figure 2.5 to show how the status structure in these groups and other groups like them emerged over time. The two hypothetical groups (cases *A* and *B*) show that although the processes by which statuses develop are similar, the form of the status structure will vary from group to group. The circles represent individuals about whom outside observers (and presumably the members as well) could not consistently rate in terms of "effective initiative." The triangles represent those members which observers could rate consistently day after day in a variety of activities.

As seen in Figure 2.5, there was little agreement among observers and no distinction in terms of rank (i.e., high versus low status) in the early stages of group development (T_a). As time went on (moving down the diagram), the observers began to agree upon some individuals whom they rated extremely

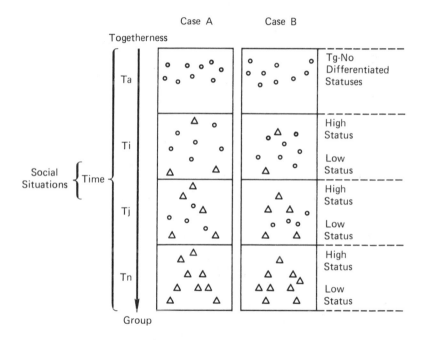

o　Individual Whose Status is not yet Stabilized

Δ　Individual Whose Status is Stabilized

Figure 2.5. Diagram of gradations of organization (structure) in two cases over time, from initial togetherness to hierarchical differentiation of status position. Proceeding from top (Time a), the diagram shows initial stabilization of status at top and bottom (represented by triangles at Ti) and succeeding stabilization of structure on two different patterns. (Sherif and Sherif, 1969, p. 160.)

high or low. Eventually the observers rated all members consistently, and the status structure of the group began to develop. Notice that in Case *A* (as compared to Case *B*) there is a greater distance between the highest and lowest ranking statuses. This indicates that there were more differences in the effective initiative ratings received by members in the first hypothetical group.

Both red and blue groups went through stages similar to that pictured in Figure 2.5. However, the Sherifs' description of the emerging status structure concentrated on the evolution of leaders in the two groups in a manner very similar to Whyte's description of the Norton Street gang. This is easy to understand, considering that the leader's status is one of the easiest to describe and considering the time it would take to describe the status of each boy.

The Sherifs have described some of the events that led the observers and the members themselves to view a boy named Crane as the leader of the blue group.

> At the outset, Crane successfully swung the vote to move to the new bunkhouse. When they arrived at the bunkhouse, a general discussion ensued concerning what could be done to fix it up. One boy, noticing a small picture of a dachshund on a bedpost, said, "Why don't we get some pictures of some animals?" Crane: "Yes, we have the blue and white colors. Let's get a big picture of a bulldog and call ourselves the Bull Dogs." There were shouts of "Yes!", followed by the singing of the Bull Dog song made famous at Yale.
>
> Crane's suggestions for improving the bunkhouse, by putting the letter *B* on the door and by building a chinning bar, for example, were from the first almost always adopted as good ones. He proved to be very effective in leading the group on its first hike and cookout (p. 252).

Evidence of the group's dependence on Crane can be seen in the following incidents. Once during a treasure hunt, Crane got a splinter in his foot and had to discontinue giving directions to the others. While he attempted to remove the splinter, two other high-ranking boys took charge of the hunt. However, according to the observers, the group effort became disorganized and faltered in Crane's absence. With the splinter out, Crane again took charge and the group came together for a successful finish. The investigators report then when one of the lower-ranking members became homesick, Crane made an effort to make him feel better. At another time, when Mr. Mussee, the observer disguised as caretaker, asked the group who their leader was, they replied, "Crane. What Crane says goes" (p. 252). Crane did not make all of the suggestions in the group, but his approval was usually necessary for a suggestion to carry.

In the red group, Shaw emerged with the highest status. He was recognized primarily for his daring, his athletic skill, and his toughness. Although he was described as being good at leading the group in games and darking expeditions into the woods, he was less effective in organizing and coordinating other kinds of activities. For instance, unlike Crane, he did not organize the group to carry out the various work projects the boys were required to do. Lee, the other potential leader in the red group made no effort to become one, and the group often attacked problems and projects in a relatively unorganized manner. Part of this was the result of Shaw's tendency to interact exclusively with several other high-ranking members. Also, Shaw often enforced his commands with threats or actual physical force. One boy, after an encounter with Shaw, wanted to change groups. At one point, in Stage III, Shaw led the members of the red group in throwing apples at several lower-ranking members. The members of the red group respected Shaw, but he did not use this recognition to organize and coordinate the members as Crane did with the blue group.

During the interviews carried out in the second stage, the members were again asked to indicate their friends. This provided additional information for analyzing the development of the two groups. Table 2.2 shows the pattern of friendship choices at Stages I and II; before and after the two groups were separated. The table at the top of Table 2.2 shows the distribution of choices before the boys were actually placed in the two groups. It can be seen that in both cases, the boys had more friends in the groups to which they were not assigned at the beginning of Stage II. The table at the bottom of Table 2.2 shows the distribution of choices toward the end of Stage II. As can be seen, almost all the boys' choices were directed toward members of their own groups.

Figure 2.6 shows sociograms based on the friendship choices within each

Table 2.2
Total Choices of Friends in Red Group and Blue Group
after (Sherif and Sherif, 1953, p. 268)

Total choice of friends, end of stage I

Choices made by: Choices received by:

	Eventual members of red group	Eventual members of blue group
Eventual Members of Red Group	35.1%	64.9%
Eventual Members of Blue Group	65.0%	35.0%

Total choices of friends, end of stage II

Choices made by: Choices received by:

	Members of red group	Members of blue group
Members of Red Group	95.0%	5.0%
Members of Blue Group	87.7%	12.3%

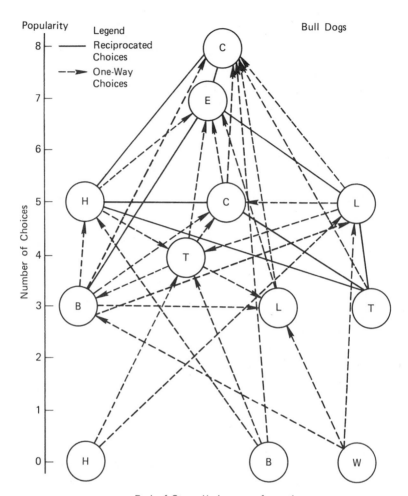

End of Stage II, in-group formation.

Figure 2.6. Sociogram of bull dogs and red devils. (Sherif and Sherif, 1953, pp. 250–251.)

group. Notice in the blue group that Crane (*C*), the leader, received the greatest number of friendship choices, but not Shaw (*S*), leader of the red group. Notice also that the range of choices received in the blue group (0 to 8) was smaller than the range in the red group (0 to 10). In other words, the choices in the blue group were more equally distributed, but those in the red group were directed mainly at two members (*L* and *S*). The reader can also see that there were more reciprocated choices in the blue group.

The investigators reported that throughout Stage II each group developed unique patterns of behavior. For instance, each group made lanyards by different methods and the blues had evolved their own set procedure for clearing

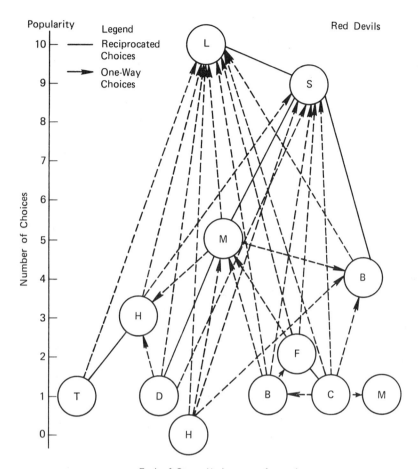

End of Stage II, in-group formation.

the area around their cabin. Each group had its preferred song and each developed standard phrases and nicknames for each other. Members of each group were expected to conform to their group's way of doing things; failure to conform was punished by standardized methods. In the red group, Shaw used physical force, while in the blue group Crane assigned extra KP duty or had the offender remove a certain number of stones from their group's pond.

The boys' identification with their respective groups could be seen in other ways as well. Probably most striking was the development of group names. As already seen, the blue group came to call themselves the Bull Dogs because the nearby Yale team had blue as one of its colors. The red group took the name of Red Devils later when a counselor-observer suggested (contrary to his instructions) it to them. This occurred after the other group already had a name, and even then "Red Devils" did not catch on immediately. The symbolic value of the groups' colors can be seen in the following excerpt.

> Shaw, the Red Devil leader, was placing an order with Mr. Mussee for crepe paper and other supplies needed for craftwork and decoration. He specified that the paper should be red. Mr. Mussee said, "How about some other colors, green, blue, etc.?" Shaw replied with a sneer in his voice, "Not *blue!* Not *that* color. We just want red and white" (p. 252).

Some further examples of group identification by the members are provided by the investigators. When Hall of the blue group asked Crane if he had certain equipment at home, Crane asked him: "Which home?" Hall replied, "Our cabin, I mean." Packages of candy and comic books from home were always shared. The red group set up boundaries around its cabin to designate its own territory. The members of the blue group had to swear not to tell about their secret swimming hole or any other "Bull Dog" secrets.

While Stage II was characterized by considerable in-group loyalty and ethnocentrism, there were no hostile acts between groups until Stage III began. This last stage introduced competitive activities between the two groups. The groups were awarded points for their superior performances in various games and in activities such as keeping their cabins clean. The points accumulated by each group were tallied daily and displayed on a scoreboard for all to see. While all the boys entered the various competitive events with what was described as "considerable good sportsmanship," this did not last long. The dining hall became the scene of much mutual name-calling and threat-trading.

The blue group began accumulating points from the start and this tended to increase their unity even more. The members of the group praised one another's accomplishments, however minor, and the group as a whole was aware that its superiority was due to the fact that it was better organized than the red. On the other hand, the early defeats were devastating for the red group. Shaw berated the other members for not winning, and he retired more into the exclusive company of his clique. Many of the members became resentful of Shaw, and in-group conflict developed along with the hostility directed at the other group.

At one point during the last stage, the experimenters set up a situation where both groups were to attend a party in the dining hall. The blue group was purposely and discretely delayed in attending so that when it arrived, the red group had eaten most of the food. This led to an especially intense bout of name-calling, and at a later meal the boys from the two groups proceeded to throw food at one another. When they began throwing table knives and saucers, the staff had to intervene. After this event, the experimenters, feeling that things had gone far enough, quickly decided to stop Stage III of the experiment.

Despite their efforts to decrease the hostility between groups the boys continued by raiding one another's cabins and engaging in warfare with green apples that they had gathered for ammunition. The investigators reported that during this final phase, Shaw led the red group on raids which raised his prestige again and renewed the "solidarity" of the group.

An Analysis Using the Six Dimensions

The results of this study can be analyzed in terms of the six dimensions of solidarity. We will begin with "interaction." Although the boys in both groups were led into separate activities, they still had opportunities to interact with members of the other group. Because some boys had been separated from friends they had made in the first stage, many of them continued to interact with members of the "out-group" in the second stage. However, as Stage II progressed, the boys interacted more and more with members of their own group. At one point, three members of the red group were branded as traitors and were threatened with punishment unless they saw less of their friends in the blue group. Thus, one observable aspect of the development of each group was the increased level of interaction among members.

The development of norms and status structures in the two groups is quite evident. As the boys began to share common experiences, each group developed characteristic ways of dealing with certain situations. Members who did not follow these prescribed ways often received negative sanctions of some type from the others. Likewise, each member came to have a particular status in the group, which made it possible for both members and outside observers to predict from day to day how each boy would behave in a particular situation. Most distinct in each group were the statuses of those boys who came to be known as the leaders in each group.

Most of the activities carried out by the two groups were in some way imposed upon them by the staff. To the extent that the boys accepted them, we can say that these activities became group goals. However it was not until the third stage, when the hostility between the groups reached its peak, that each group developed goals of its own. The raiding of cabins and the apple warfare were totally unplanned goals; they emerged from the groups themselves and caused the investigators to end the experiment. As mentioned earlier, the emergence of these goals increased group unity or solidarity, especially that of the red group.

As a measure of cohesion, the investigators used the boys' responses to the question concerning their friends in the group. As we have already seen (Table 2.2), the number of friendship choices directed to boys within the same group shifted drastically during the second stage of the experiment. This is only one of several measures of cohesion that could have been used, but it certainly indicates that members became more attracted to their assigned group over time.

Finally, there is evidence that members in both groups developed an awareness of their group membership and identity. The use of group names, group songs, territorial boundaries, and loyalty oaths indicates the development of subjective feelings about being members of an "in-group."

The foregoing shows that the formation of a group, involves what we have referred to earlier as the development of solidarity. But the six dimensions of solidarity can also be used to compare groups. Although it was not the main point of their study, the Sherifs commented that the blue group was more "closely knit" and better organized than the red group. The use of these terms suggests that the investigators were talking about "solidarity" as we have defined it in this chapter. It is therefore helpful to analyze the study once again, using each of the dimensions of solidarity to determine why the authors came to that conclusion.

We are told very little about the sheer amount of interaction in the two groups. In studying groups of this type it would be almost impossible to record every interaction between members. However, the authors report that the red group contained a clique of high status members who interacted with one another frequently. The authors also indicated that the interaction among members of the red group contained a higher level of hostility, especially during the early parts of Stage III. Finally, the fact that some members of the red group had to be threatened with punishment if they interacted with members of the blue group probably indicates that in-group interaction was relatively sparse in the red group.

The authors made no systematic comparison of norm development in the two groups. However, most of the examples of norm development were taken from the blue group, which suggests a somewhat higher degree of standardized behavior in that group. Furthermore, deviants seemed to be more consistently sanctioned in the blue group. In the red group, punishment consisted mainly of "roughing up," which suggests that it was inconsistently applied and that many members did not voluntarily accept the normative expectations in question. In other words, there was probably less consensus about acceptable behavior in the red group.

With respect to the status structures, we are told the most about the leadership statuses in the two groups. Crane seemed to be universally accepted as leader by the members of the blue group, and his leadership extended to all group activities. As we saw earlier, Shaw, Crane's counterpart in the red group, often left the group disorganized and let the group down altogether during the early part of Stage III. As a result, there seemed to be less consensus about the nature of the leadership status in the red group.

The opportunity for adopting group goals was the same for both groups, and we really find little difference in this dimension. However, the fact that Crane organized the blue group to carry out work details and the fact that this group was successful in the various competitive activities against the reds suggests that the blue group accepted goals more uniformly even if they were imposed by the adults running the camp.

The data on cohesion is presented in a form easily used for a comparison of the two groups, but interpreting this comparison is somewhat difficult. Looking again at Table 2.2 the data on friendship choices suggest that the red group was the most cohesive, since 95.0 percent of the members' choices were directed to others in the red group. The comparable figure for the blue group was 87.7 percent; but the difference of 7.3 percent may not be large enough to signify a real difference in the cohesion levels in the two groups. The reader will recall also that the friendship choices were more equally distributed in the blue group. In part, this reflects the existence of the clique in the red group. In fact, it was the more equal distribution of choices in the blue group that prompted the Sherifs to comment upon the greater unity of that group. However, given the data available on friendship choices alone, it is not possible to judge the differences in cohesion between the two groups.

Finally, although the investigators made no systematic attempt to measure differences in the level of the boys' awareness of membership, the anecdotal evidence suggests that the members of the blue group scored higher on this dimension. The fact that this group was the first to adopt a name, had a loyalty oath, and could comment upon the effectiveness of their esprit de corps suggests that the blue group was more highly developed on this dimension of solidarity.

After considering all the dimensions, we can only agree with the Sherifs' conclusion that the blue group was higher in overall solidarity. In many cases there was not really enough evidence available to say with certainty that one group was higher than the other on a particular dimension of solidarity. A social scientist specifically comparing the solidarity of two such groups would have to design measures carefully to determine each group's relative location on each of the six dimensions. To our knowledge, this has never been done, but the Sherifs' study comes the closest of any available to including the kind of data which allows one to make some comparisons on all six dimensions.

Most studies that compare groups usually measure only one or two dimensions. As we have said, it is possible to compare groups on a single dimension of solidarity but, such comparisons are made more meaningful when several dimensions are used. We saw, for instance, that the comparison of cohesion between the red and blue groups in the Sherif's study was not really meaningful by itself. Only when looking at the results of comparisons on other dimensions was it possible to see the overall patterns. Related to this is what Bales (1950) has called the "flip-flop problem," where the results of a comparison on single measure can be interpreted several ways. For instance, an excess of friendly interaction among members in a group may mean either that the group has attained a high level of solidarity or that the relationships are so strained that members dare not disagree or argue because the group might disintegrate. In other words, a social scientist would require information about the group's location on several other dimensions to put this interaction data into context.

SUMMARY

Informal groups vary in the extent to which their members form interdependent relations with one another. The existence of interdependence among members means that the behavior of one influences or affects the behavior of others and *vice versa.* Groups characterized by high interdependence are said to be high in solidarity while those low in interdependence are considered to be low in solidarity (or high in anomie). Interdependence is manifested in informal groups through the development of interaction, norms, a status structure, goals, cohesion and a common awareness of membership.

Interaction is the process of mutual communication between two or more individuals. *Norms* are expectations held by group members about how they and others ought to behave. A *status structure* consists of expectations about how certain members (e.g. the leader) ought to behave in the group. A group *goal* is said to exist when members cooperatively attempt to reach some common goal. The *cohesiveness* of a group is the extent to which members are attracted (or want to remain in) the group. *Awareness of membership* occurs when individuals define themselves as members of a group and are aware of who is and is not a member. The greater the development of a group along each of these six dimensions, the higher its solidarity. There is a series of objective measures that can determine the relative position of actual groups on each of the dimensions (see Table 2.1). Researchers may compare groups along any combination of dimensions to determine their overall solidarity or compare a single group at different points of time.

The six dimensions of solidarity are illustrated in an analysis of the camping groups experimentally created by the Sherifs (1966). In this study two groups of strangers were placed together, and the reseachers observed the emergence of interaction, norms, status structure, goals, cohesiveness, and the perception of membership. The six dimensions of solidarity were used to support the fact that one of the emerging informal groups became more unified than the other.

three

Bales and Homans:
Two Systems Theorists

INTRODUCTION

One theoretical approach growing out of the external tradition is the systems perspective. Those adopting this perspective feel that groups have certain characteristics in common with all types of systems whether they be electrical (i.e. stereo sets) or biological (i.e. living organisms). What qualifies something to be considered a system is the fact that it consists of interdependent parts. (Bertalanffy, 1968). While groups are certainly not the same as stereo sets or biological organisms, they do, as we saw in Chapter 2, consist of interdependent parts. Consistent with Durkheim and others within the external tradition, proponents of this approach view the group as a whole unit and not the simple sum of its parts. In this chapter we will discuss the theories of two men who have chosen to consider informal groups from the systems perspective. Although each utilizes this perspective in a different fashion, both have had a great impact on the study of informal groups. We shall be primarily concerned with those aspects of their work which illustrate how solidarity is attained and lost by informal groups.

BALES'S SYSTEM THEORY

According to Bales, all social systems—including societies, formal organizations, and informal groups—must solve two sets of problems in order to maintain themselves. The first set, called the *instrumental problems* of the social system, refers to those problems arising outside the social system—i.e., in its environment. Instrumental problems are those that a social system faces in reaching its goals.

61

Food and other resources must be distributed to the members of a society. A formal organization must market its product in sufficient quantity in order to pay its employees. To reach these goals requires constant effort and thus constitutes instrumental problems for the social systems. If these problems are not dealt with effectively the social system may disintegrate or have to undergo radical changes. The second set of problems occurs internally in the social system and is called *social-emotional problems*. These problems inevitably arise whenever individuals engage in social relationships. Social-emotional problems include those involved in reducing interpersonal difficulties, coordinating the actions of members, and keeping individuals sufficiently satisfied so that they remain as members of the system.

According to Bales, these two sets of problems need to be balanced if the system is to survive—that is, any system must find some mode of operation that allows it to meet both sets of problems simultaneously. Social-emotional problems require an acceptable level of solidarity for their solution, but this movement toward greater solidarity could undermine the solution of the instrumental problems. On the other hand, the solutions to instrumental problems, while essential for the maintenance of the system, tend to undermine system solidarity. Thus, social systems are caught between two sets of problems, and the way a system solves one set influences the solution of the other. Furthermore, the level of solidarity maintained by the system depends upon how successfully these two sets of problems are solved.

While Bales's theory was intended for social systems of all types, it is difficult to test empirically on large-scale systems. Whether or not the theory applies to smaller groups can best be assessed by examining some of the major studies carried out by Bales and his associates using small groups in laboratory settings.

Interaction Process Analysis

After years of observing and thinking about groups, Bales developed a scheme for classifying interaction and called it Interaction Process Analysis (IPA). This technique classifies all of the interaction observed in a particular group into twelve categories. The categories are based upon Bales' conception of informal groups as being interaction systems that have to solve instrumental and social-emotional problems. By classifying the interaction according to this scheme, the observer can assess the state of the group with respect to the solution (or nonsolution) of these problems at any point in time.

The twelve categories (shown in Figure 3.1) are used to classify the content of group interaction. Bales was not interested in all aspects of the information conveyed during interaction but only in how the interaction affected the solution of the two system problems. The observer breaks down the interaction of the group he is observing into what Bales has called "unit acts." These are identifiable units in the interaction that convey a piece of information or emotion.

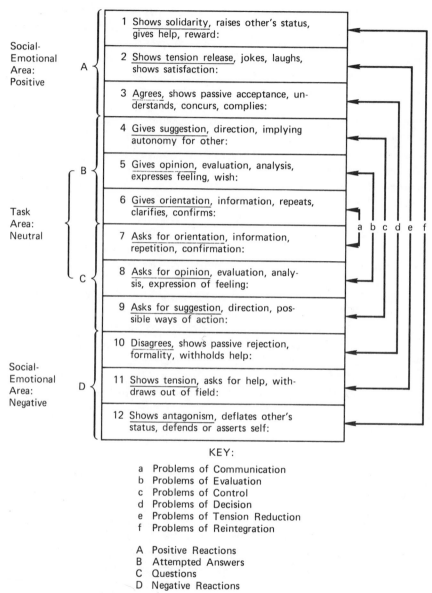

Social-
Emotional
Area:
Positive

A

1 Shows solidarity, raises other's status, gives help, reward:

2 Shows tension release, jokes, laughs, shows satisfaction:

3 Agrees, shows passive acceptance, understands, concurs, complies:

Task
Area:
Neutral

B

4 Gives suggestion, direction, implying autonomy for other:

5 Gives opinion, evaluation, analysis, expresses feeling, wish:

6 Gives orientation, information, repeats, clarifies, confirms:

C

7 Asks for orientation, information, repetition, confirmation:

8 Asks for opinion, evaluation, analysis, expression of feeling:

9 Asks for suggestion, direction, possible ways of action:

Social-
Emotional
Area:
Negative

D

10 Disagrees, shows passive rejection, formality, withholds help:

11 Shows tension, asks for help, withdraws out of field:

12 Shows antagonism, deflates other's status, defends or asserts self:

a b c d e f

KEY:

a Problems of Communication
b Problems of Evaluation
c Problems of Control
d Problems of Decision
e Problems of Tension Reduction
f Problems of Reintegration

A Positive Reactions
B Attempted Answers
C Questions
D Negative Reactions

Figure 3.1. The twelve interaction categories. (Bales, 1950, p. 9.)

In some cases several sentences may be categorized as a unit act, while in other cases several unit acts may be found in one spoken sentence. The observer's job is to keep an accurate account of who in the group says what to whom and how often. For each unit act identified, the observer must record who initiated that unit, to whom it was addressed (either a particular person or the whole group), and within which of the twelve categories it should be placed.

This method of classification is quite difficult and requires a great deal of training for the observers. The observation is facilitated somewhat by the use of a mechanical device. This apparatus, called the Interaction Recorder, consists of a motor that slowly moves a large paper tape across the surface of the box. The twelve categories are listed on the top so that a mark can be made in the appropriate spot on the paper every time a unit act is assigned to a particular category. The movement of the paper immediately provides room for more marks as time passes. After the observation process is completed, the researchers can easily go back over the tape to determine the total number of acts in each category, their sequence, and the number of acts initiated by each person.

Figure 3.1 shows the twelve interaction process categories and some examples of comments that would be placed in each category. It can be seen from the figure that categories 1 to 3 and 10 to 12 are mirror images of each other and pertain to the social-emotional problems of the group. Units of interaction that are classified into any of the first three categories contribute to the solution of social-emotional problems and therefore to solidarity. On the other hand, interaction categorized into any of the last three categories leads to social-emotional problems and thus detracts from group solidarity. Units of interaction that fall into categories 4 to 9 involve solutions to the instrumental problems of the group. For the groups studied by Bales, the primary instrumental problem involved the solution of a specific task provided by an experimenter. Thus, interaction classified into categories 4 to 9 is usually referred to as *task-oriented interaction*.

Although IPA can be used on any group whose members meet and discuss problems face-to-face, Bales made most of his observations on groups of strangers recruited to work in the small-group laboratories at Harvard. The subjects, who were paid for their time, worked in rooms fitted with microphones and one-way mirrors so that they could be observed and recorded by unseen investigators. (The one-way mirror prevented the subjects from being distracted by the observers since the subjects knew they were being observed and recorded.) In most of these experiments the subjects were given a case study to read and told that they were to develop and recommend solutions to the problem as a group. They were given forty minutes for a single problem-solving session.

It is easiest to describe the use of the recorded data by referring to Figures 3.2 and 3.3. Figure 3.2 is an interaction profile for one member of a discussion group observed in Bales's laboratories. This profile illustrates how the interaction initiated by the subject was distributed among the twelve categories. The per-

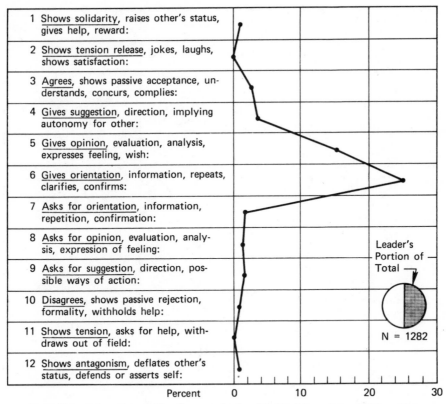

1 Shows <u>solidarity</u>, raises other's status, gives help, reward:			
2 Shows <u>tension release</u>, jokes, laughs, shows satisfaction:			
3 <u>Agrees</u>, shows passive acceptance, understands, concurs, complies:			
4 <u>Gives suggestion</u>, direction, implying autonomy for other:			
5 <u>Gives opinion</u>, evaluation, analysis, expresses feeling, wish:			
6 <u>Gives orientation</u>, information, repeats, clarifies, confirms:			
7 <u>Asks for orientation</u>, information, repetition, confirmation:			
8 <u>Asks for opinion</u>, evaluation, analysis, expression of feeling:			Leader's Portion of Total
9 <u>Asks for suggestion</u>, direction, possible ways of action:			
10 <u>Disagrees</u>, shows passive rejection, formality, withholds help:			
11 <u>Shows tension</u>, asks for help, withdraws out of field:			N = 1282
12 <u>Shows antagonism</u>, deflates other's status, defends or asserts self:			

Percent 0 10 20 30

Figure 3.2. Interaction profile of a group leader. (Modified from Bales, 1950, p. 18.)

centage for each category was calculated by dividing the number of unit acts initiated in each category by the total number of unit acts initiated by that particular group member. In this example the member happened to be designated a leader, but the same procedure could be followed for any member of the group. Figure 3.3 shows an interaction profile for a whole group. In this case the unit acts initiated by the various members are grouped together. To calculate the percentages for each category, the number of units in each category (initiated by all of the members) was divided by the total number of units recorded for the whole group. Among other things, these individual and group profiles enabled Bales and his associates to compare the profiles of members of the same or different groups and to make comparisons between the profiles of different groups.

An example of one such comparison can be seen in Table 3.1, which shows the interaction profiles of two of the many groups Bales and his associates observed. In addition to the profiles of the two groups separately, this table also includes the combined profiles for the two groups. The numbers in this

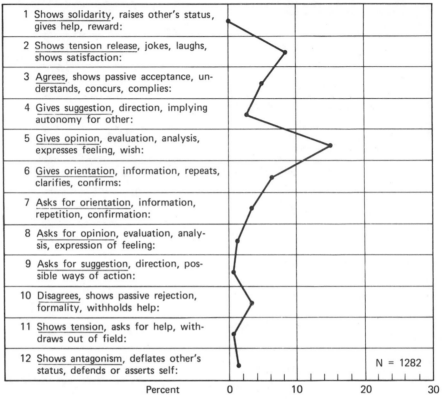

Figure 3.3.   Interaction profile of a whole group. (Modified from Bales, 1950, p. 20.)

column (second from the right) represent the average percentages for the two groups. Also, in the column at the far right we can see the average percentages for each of the four main categories of interaction (Positive Social-Emotional, Attempted Answers, Questions, and Negative Social-Emotional). Let us look at this last column because Bales says that this profile, based on the average of the two groups, is fairly typical of most of the groups observed in his laboratory. It can be seen that most of the interaction was categorized in the "attempted answers" category—much higher than "questions." The reader will also notice that there is more positive than negative social-emotional interaction. Commenting on this, Bales says that, "Intuitively one would feel that the process would surely be self-defeating and self-limiting if there were more questions than answers and more negative reactions than positive" (1953, p. 448). That is, if the group is going to do its job, (1) Task-oriented interaction must be high; (2) more answers must be given than questions asked; (3) there must be more interaction contributing to the solidarity of the group (positive social-emotional) than detracting from solidarity (negative social-emotional). In other words, there

Table 3.1
Interaction Profile of a "Satisfied" and a "Dissatisfied" Group
(Bales, 1953, p. 116.)

Type of act	Meeting profiles in percentage rates			
	Satisfied*	Dissatisfied**	Ave. of the two	Ave. rates by sections
1. Shows Solidarity	.7	.8	.7	
2. Shows Tension Release	7.9	6.8	7.3	25.0
3. Agrees	24.9	9.6	17.0	
4. Gives Suggestion	8.2	3.6	5.9	
5. Gives Opinion	26.7	30.5	28.7	56.7
6. Gives Orientation	22.4	21.9	22.1	
7. Asks for Orientation	1.7	5.7	3.8	
8. Asks for Opinion	1.7	2.2	2.0	6.9
9. Asks for Suggestion	.5	1.6	1.1	
10. Disagrees	4.0	12.4	8.3	
11. Shows Tension	1.0	2.6	1.8	11.4
12. Shows Antagonism	.3	2.2	1.3	
PERCENTAGE TOTAL	100.0	100.0	100.0	100.0
RAW SCORE TOTAL	719	767	1486	

*The highest of sixteen groups. The members rated their own satisfaction with their solution after the meeting at an average of 10.4 on a scale running from 0 to a highest possible rating of 12.

**The lowest of sixteen groups. Comparable satisfaction rating in this group was 2.6.

must be, as Bales's theory suggests, some degree of balance to keep the individuals together as a group. The level of solidarity of the group observed was determined by the relative rates of positive and negative social-emotional interaction (see "Interaction" in Table 2.1). It can be seen from this finding that the solidarity of informal groups is closely linked with the group's success in dealing with its instrumental problems.

Interaction and Cohesion

Let us look for further evidence that these groups are in a state of balance. The two groups whose profiles are displayed in Table 3.1 were administered questionnaires at the end of the discussion period. Bales gave each member a questionnaire that asked him to indicate how satisfied he was with the solution developed by the group. This questionnaire seems to be measuring how attracted members are to the group and can be considered a measure of cohesiveness. All subjects were given a choice of thirteen different levels of satisfaction, ranging from completely dissatisfied to completely satisfied. Depending upon the level, a subject's choice was given a number by Bales: the greater the satisfaction, the higher the number, up to thirteen. Bales then computed a group satisfaction score by taking an average of all the members' satisfaction scores. Of the sixteen groups for which group satisfaction scores were computed, those in Table 3.1 had the highest and the lowest scores.

In comparing the profiles of the most- and least-satisfied groups in Table 3.1 it can be seen that while both had approximately the same number of attempted answers, the dissatisfied group had almost three times as many questions as the satisfied group. It can also be seen that in the dissatisfied group the amount of positive and negative social-emotional interaction was approximately the same, while in the satisfied group the positive interaction was about six times higher than the negative. These results can be interpreted as being consistent with Bales's theory. These groups met only once and were dissolved by the experimenter; there was really no chance for them to break up by themselves. But we can speculate that if these groups had been allowed to meet continuously, the extremely dissatisfied group would have decreased in solidarity to the point that it would have disintegrated of its own accord. The overabundance of questions and the high proportion of negative social-emotional interaction indicates that this group was having difficulties in reaching both instrumental and social-emotional goals. Unfortunately, it is not possible to tell from this data just why or how this occurred. It may be that the subjects placed in this group were incompatible (as evidenced by the high rate of negative interaction), and this made problem-solving difficult (as evidenced by the large number of questions). It could also be that conflict and hostility (negative social-emotional interaction) resulted because of the problems associated with the task. It is most likely, however, that both of these descriptions are correct. Although we don't know the whole story, the data do show us that the two areas of group life are interconnected: groups having social-emotional difficulties are likely to be less efficient in reaching instrumental goals, and groups having problems in reaching instrumental goals will probably have social-emotional difficulties. The data suggest that the groups whose members are satisfied, and thus likely to survive, are in a state of balance or equilibrium, which allows them to deal with both system problems. They also show that two aspects of solidarity—positive social-emotional interaction and cohesion—tend to go hand in hand.

Changes in Solidarity over Time

According to Bales's theory, a group's movement toward the solution of the task should bring about social-emotional problems that threaten solidarity and require members to solve these internal problems. To examine this possibility, Bales decided to examine the changes in interaction that occur at different points of the group meetings. To accomplish this, Bales divided the forty-minute session of a number of groups into three equal periods. He then plotted the relative amounts of the various types of interaction for each of these three periods, as shown in Figure 3.5. Instead of using each of the twelve categories, he grouped them together into five different categories. Two of these five are the familiar *positive* and *negative* social-emotional categories, which bring together categories 1 to 3 and 10 to 12 respectively. Again, the relative frequency of these two types of interaction was taken as an indicator of the current level of solidarity in a group. The category labelled "orientation" consists of interaction such as giving and asking for orientation (categories 4 and 9). The *evaluation* category on the chart consists of giving and asking for opinion (categories 5 and 8); and *control* consists of giving and asking for suggestions (categories 6 and 7).

Let us examine what happens to each of these categories during each of the three time periods. During the first period, asking for and giving orientation is the highest, but this drops off during the latter part of the meeting. As we might expect, one early major problem in Bales's studies was the problem of orientation: What should we do? How should we begin? After the problem of orientation has been solved, it is possible for the group to go on to discussions of their feelings about the problem—asking for and providing information helpful in coming up with solutions. As can be seen in Figure 3.4 evaluation which includes this type of interaction is highest during this second period. Giving and asking for suggestions (control) is relatively low overall but increases consistently as the discussion progresses. According to Bales, this is because suggestions are particularly important when the group is getting down to the business of actually formulating its solution to the task. Negative social-emotional interaction increases throughout the discussion at almost the same rate as the giving and asking for suggestions. According to Bales, as the group progresses on its task, the interaction more and more involves the directive and constrictive interaction (control) involved in developing a group solution. This leads to increased negative social-emotional interaction, which threatened the group's solidarity.

While the chart in Figure 3.4 shows that the positive social-emotional interaction increases over time, it is during the last phase that this type of interaction is recorded as being especially high. It is not possible to tell from the chart, but Bales reports that most of the positive social-emotional interaction occurs during the closing minutes of the discussion, after the groups have accomplished their task. Commenting on this, Bales states:

> We note joking and laughter so frequently at the end of meetings that they might almost be taken as a signal that the group had completed what it considers to be a task effort, and is ready for disbandment or a new problem. This last-minute activity completes a cycle of operations involving a successful solution both of the task-problems and social-emotional problems confronting the group. The apparent incongruity of predicting a peak for both negative and positive reactions in the third phase is thus explained. Negative reactions tend to give way to positive reactions in the final part of the crudely defined third phase (1961, p. 470).

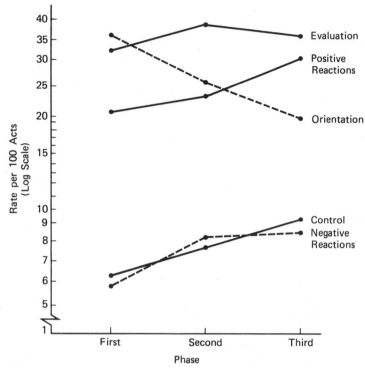

Figure 3.4.   Changes in interaction over time. (Bales, 1953, p. 141.)

As the group members became increasingly involved in meeting the instrumental problems facing them, the solidarity of the group was threatened. However, when the task was successfully completed, there was a brief and intense flurry of social-emotional interaction which apparently functioned to build up this solidarity again to an acceptable level. Again we see some support for the idea that groups as systems tend toward a balance between the types of system problems.

Status Consensus

In the previous chapter we saw that the existence of status consensus in a group indicates a relatively high level of solidarity (see Table 2.1). A study carried out by Heinicke and Bales (1953) measured status consensus in laboratory groups and showed how its development is related to other aspects of group life.

Heinicke and Bales analyzed the data for a total of ten groups comprised either of five or six members. Some groups met for four different sessions, while others met for six sessions. After each session the subjects were requested to rank each other according to who had the best ideas, who did the most to guide the discussion, and other related dimensions. Using this data, the investigators derived a measure of status consensus for each group. This measure was designed to show the amount of agreement among the members of a particular group about the rank order of the members on various dimensions. The full procedure for deriving this measure is too complicated for a detailed discussion, but we can provide some ideas of the basic procedure.

Figure 3.5 illustrates the rankings assigned and received by members of three hypothetical groups. Let us assume that these tables show how members in the three groups responded to a request to rank each other on "best ideas". Let us suppose that in group 1 member *A* thought that member *C* had the best ideas. Since there were five members in the group, member *C* received a score of 5 from member *A*. The fact that member *C* has all 5's in his column indicates that all members, himself included, thought he had the best ideas. A score of 4 means that the member assigning the rank thought the member to be second best. A 3 indicates third best, and so on. To determine a person's total score on "best ideas" we simply add together the scores in his column. Thus, member *C*, in group 1 has a total score of 25 while member *D* is next with a total score of 20. By looking at the sum of the ranks assigned an overall rank order for "best ideas" can be determined. So, for instance, in group 1 member *C* is top ranked, member *D* is second ranked while member *E* ranks third and so on.

The tables for groups 1 and 2 have been set up so that the rank orders are the same for both groups. But look at the differences between them. In Group 1, we see that each member assigned the same rank order to each of the other members. In Group 2, however, there is considerable disagreement among the members as to whom should be assigned what rank. In Group 3, there is no agreement whatever. It is this kind of difference that Heinicke and Bales wanted to capture in their status consensus measure. These differences are reflected in the sum of ranks for the three hypothetical groups. In Group 1, where there was perfect status consensus, there is an interval of five between the sums for each person. In Group 2, the differences are smaller and more uneven. While in Group 3, the sums for each person are the same. These groups represent only three possible patterns, but they illustrate the fact that the greater the disagreement among members on the ranks, the less the differences between these sums. The procedure used by Heinicke and Bales to measure status consensus took into account the difference between the sums of ranks. The larger the differences between the sum scores, the greater the degree of status consensus in the group.

The groups observed by Heinicke and Bales were separated for comparisons on the basis of whether they showed a high or low degree of status consensus. The remainder of the study looks at various characteristics of these two kinds of groups. The first finding of importance was that the groups tended to be either consistently high or low in status consensus over the several group meetings;

Group 1   (Complete Consensus)

Members being assigned the ranks

	A	B	C	D	E
A	2	1	5	4	3
B	2	1	5	4	3
C	2	1	5	4	3
D	2	1	5	4	3
E	2	1	5	4	3
Sum of ranks assigned	10	5	25	20	15
Final rank order	4	5	1	2	3

Members Assigning Ranks (rows A–E)

Group 2   (Low Consensus)

Members being assigned the ranks

	A	B	C	D	E
A	1	2	5	3	4
B	1	3	4	5	2
C	4	1	3	2	5
D	2	1	5	4	3
E	3	2	5	4	1
Sum of ranks assigned	11	9	22	18	15
Final rank order	4	5	1	2	3

Members Assigning Ranks (rows A–E)

Group 3   (No Consensus)

Members being assigned the ranks

	A	B	C	D	E
A	1	2	3	4	5
B	5	1	2	3	4
C	4	5	1	2	3
D	3	4	5	1	2
E	2	3	4	5	1
Sum of ranks assigned	15	15	15	15	15
Final rank order					

Members Assigning Ranks (rows A–E)

Figure 3.5.   Patterns of "Best Idea" ranks for three hypothetical groups.

that is, groups which began with high consensus ended with high consensus and those beginning with low consensus ended with low consensus. Among other things, Heinicke and Bales compared the levels of satisfaction in the two categories of groups. The subjects were given two different satisfaction scales. Heinicke and Bales found that on both of the satisfaction ratings, the members of high consensus groups came out to be more satisfied than those in low consensus groups. For some of the groups, the subjects were asked to provide written solutions to the problems they were solving. Their written solutions were rated by two seprate scorers in terms of "realism," "cogency of expression," and "how many facets of the problem were taken into account in the solution." The scores for the high status consensus groups were significantly higher than for the low status consensus groups.

This study shows that groups having difficulties in solving their social-emotional problems also tend to have difficulties in reaching consensus about the relative rank of the various members. In the previous chapter, we said that one facet of solidarity was the extent to which members develop consensus on their statuses. In the groups studied by Bales, we would not expect to find fully developed status differences because time was so short. The development of consensus about relative rank, however, would be an indication that a group is moving in this direction. Thus, those groups categorized as high in status consensus can be considered relatively successful in solving social-emotional problems and thus higher in solidarity. In fact, Heinicke and Bales provide evidence which indicates that there was prolonged disagreement among the high participators in the low consensus groups and that the members of such groups were more likely to be inconsistent in the amount of interaction they contribute to the groups from session to session. In other words, the low status consensus groups were arenas for constant "status struggles," another indicator of relatively low solidarity (see Table 2.1). Being engaged in such interpersonal difficulties, it is understandable why the members of such groups would find it difficult to agree upon their evaluations of one another.

Specialization and Solidarity

We now turn to a series of studies which made Bales's work both well known and controversial. In one study, Bales (1953) went through all the interaction data from a series of groups and ranked each member of every group meeting according to the total amount of interaction he had initiated (i.e., the total number of unit acts attributed to each member). The members in each of the groups initiating the most interaction were ranked number 1, the members initiating the second most were ranked number 2, and so on. Since some of the groups met more than once, this was done for each of the group meetings or sessions. Therefore, the members of a group that met more than once might be ranked the same on all sessions, or they might have different ranks for each session. The table in Table 3.2 is based upon data collected in eighteen different sessions.

If we look at the last column on the right, we see that although theoretically the strangers brought into the Harvard laboratories were equals, they do not end up this way in terms of their levels of participation. We would expect, by definition, that the lower ranks would have successively lower amounts of total interaction, but the fact that the top participators have about nine times as much

Table 3.2
Who-to-Whom Matrix for 18 Sessions of Six-Man Groups
(Bales, 1953 p. 129)

Rank order of person originating act	Speaking to individuals of each rank						Total to individuals	To group as a whole	Total initiated
	1	*2*	*3*	*4*	*5*	*6*			
1		1238	961	545	445	317	3506	5661	9167
2	1748		443	310	175	102	2778	1211	3989
3	1371	415		305	125	69	2285	742	3027
4	952	310	282		83	49	1676	676	2352
5	662	224	144	83		28	1141	443	1584
6	470	126	114	65	44		819	373	1192
Total Received	5203	2313	1944	1308	872	565	12205	9106	21311

interaction as the lowest participators is an unexpectedly large discrepancy. It is of interest that the largest gap between the total units initiated occurred between those ranked number *1* and those ranked number *2*, with 9,167 and 3,989 units respectively. It is also of interest that it is only the top-ranking men who addressed more to the group as a whole than to separate individuals. It is also clear from Table 3.2 that the top participators tend to stand out by having an inordinately large portion of the interaction from lower ranking members directed to them. Thus, the top participators seem to be clearly distinguished from all of the lower-ranking members in their group.

To learn more about the importance of the amount of interaction initiated in discussion groups, Bales looked at the relationship between a person's participation rank in his group and the way he was evaluated by the other members on certain criteria. The data pertaining to this issue came from twelve different sessions of five-person groups. Each of the four groups met four different times, giving a total of sixteen sessions. For some reason the data for four of these sessions was not usable, and therefore the final analysis was based on twelve sessions. At the end of each session in these groups, Bales administered questionnaires. The quasi-sociometric questions that Bales asked were based upon his theoretical distinction between instrumental and social-emotional problems. It was felt that individuals may differ in the extent to which they contribute to either of these problems, and therefore they may be differentially evaluated in the eyes of the other group members. There were two questions on the questionnaire which were designed to measure the members' perceptions of the degree to which each member contributed to the task, or instrumental problems of the groups. These two questions were worded as follows:

1. Who contributed the best ideas for solving the problem?
2. Who did the most to guide the discussion and keep it moving efficiently?

The subjects were instructed to rank order the other members, including themselves on each of these questions. To determine how the members perceived one another's contributions to the social-emotional problems of the group, they were asked to rank order the members according to how much they liked them and again according to how much they disliked them. Needless to say, they were not asked to include themselves when making these rankings.

As in the status consensus study, the various ranks were reversed. Those members, for instance, who were ranked by others as having the best ideas were given a score of 5. Those ranked next best were given a score of 4, and so on. Bales was interested, then, in how these scores, or what he called "votes," were related to participation rank. Before looking at the results, it is interesting to consider what Bales expected to find. Bales's working hypothesis was that the highest participators would receive the highest number of votes on "best ideas," "guidance," and "liking" and the lowest number on "disliking." In general, it was assumed that in order for a person (e.g., person A) to contribute to the instrumental problems of the group he would have to be a fairly high participator. The members agreeing with person A's contributions would, in a sense, allow him to be the top participator by supporting him and by not participating highly themselves. If they were in agreement with him and he did the most to move the group toward the completion of its task, they would also tend to like him. On the other hand, person B, whose ideas and contributions were judged to be less worthy, would be relatively disliked by the other members, who through their disagreements with him would discourage him from participating highly. Thus, Bales's prediction was that as participation rank goes up, scores on "best ideas," "guidance," and "liking" will also increase.

An examination of Figure 3.6 shows that Bales's working hypothesis was not wholly correct. The numbers across the bottom of the chart refer to participation ranks. Bales added the "best ideas" scores (or votes) for the top participators in the twelve sessions and attained a total score of approximately 230. He followed this same procedure for each of the other ranks. Following the lines depicting the changes in "best ideas" and "guidance" across the chart, we can see that both are very similar and seem to measure the same thing. In general, the changes in these two dimensions follow Bales's working hypothesis because they increase as participation rank increases. However, if there were a really strong correlation between these dimensions and participation, the lines on chart would be much straighter than those shown. As it turned out, the "best ideas" and "guidance" scores for the men ranking second in participation are lower than would be expected from the working hypothesis.

The total scores for "liking" for each participation rank produce a graph that deviates quite a bit from the hypothesis that all evaluations should increase as participation rank increases. While there is an increase in "liking" scores from ranks *5* to *3,* scores for the second-ranking men are the same as for the third, and the scores for the top-ranking men are lower than for ranks *2* and *3*. Thus, the high participators who were also ranked high on "best ideas" and "guidance"

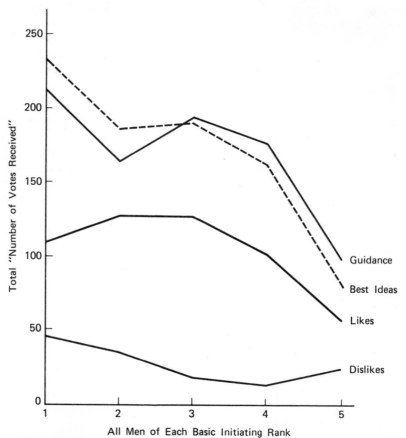

Figure 3.6. Total number of votes received on four sociometric dimensions. (Bales, 1953, p. 146.)

were unusually low on "liking," while the second-ranked participators were unusually low on "best ideas" and "guidance" but relatively high on "liking." How can this be explained? The reader should stop for a minute to examine Figure 3.6 carefully and try to come up with his own interpretation before going on to read about Bales's explanation. It might be helpful in this regard to know that Bales's revised interpretation was more consistent with his view that groups are systems that must solve the two system problems than with his working hypothesis.

According to Bales, the data show that there is something about the combination of high participation and contributing to the solution of the group problem that leads to feelings of hostility and dislike on the part of the other members. This idea is bolstered by the observation that the second-ranking men, who were rated only moderately high on "best ideas" and "guidance," were higher on "liking" than the top participators. In other words, those who, like the top participators, contribute solutions to the instrumental problems facing the group, tend to disrupt the solidarity of the group and raise social-emotional problems. For one thing, those members concentrating on instrumental activities would have little time to help solve the social-emotional problems of the group. In addition, Bales says that those contributing the most to the solution of the group's task tend to alienate themselves from the other members. This occurs because they must do such things as direct the discussion and veto suggestions— activities which threaten the self-esteem of the other members. All of this contributes to their receiving relatively low "liking" evaluations. The second-ranking men have high enough levels of participation to rate them recognition on all the evaluative dimensions, but because they did not go to the extremes that the top participants did, their liking ratings are relatively high.

We must be careful in how we generalize from this study. The data were based on sessions pooled together and there is no guarantee that the relationship between participation rank and the evaluations will be the same in every group. About all we can say is that there is a tendency in that direction. However, these findings prompted Bales and his associates to look further at how differences between members affected group equilibrium.

One attempt to do this was carried out by Slater (1955) under the direction of Bales. Among other things, Slater was interested in changes in groups as they met over several sessions. Slater's analysis was based on twenty groups, ranging from three to seven men, who met for four different sessions. At the end of each session, the subjects were asked to rank each other according to "best ideas" and "liking." Because in the earlier analysis Bales had found that task contributions and "liking" tended not to go together, Slater wanted to determine how "best idea" rankings and "liking" were related over time. His procedure was to add together the rankings given to each member from all the other members on "best ideas" and "liking." Those receiving the highest total ranking in each group were considered to be top ranked on these two dimensions. Slater was interested in whether those top ranked on "best ideas" in a group were also top ranked on "liking."

Table 3.3 shows the percentage of sessions where the top-ranked man on "best ideas" was also top ranked on "liking." In about half the groups the top-ranked men on the two dimensions coincided during the first sessions. After this, the number of occurrences was very low. While there are some fluctuations from sessions 2 to 4, these are small and probably not important. Thus, for most groups the lack of correspondence between these two dimensions was found in the later sessions.

In order to gain more insight into why this was occurring, Slater examined the interaction profiles of forty-four subjects who were top ranked on "best ideas" but not on "liking" and those forty-four subjects who were top ranked on "liking" but not on "best ideas." In this case, Slater was not concerned about

Table 3.3

Percentage of Cases in Which the Same Man Holds Top Position on Like Ranking and Idea Ranking at the Same Time, by Sessions. (Slater, 1955, p. 303)

Sessions			
1	2	3	4
56.5%	12.0%	20.0%	8.5%

differences in sessions, so the top-ranked men of each type were grouped together regardless of the session number. He then added together the number of unit acts initiated by all best-idea men and all the best-liked men in each of the twelve categories. This enabled him to compute and compare an interaction profile based on all the best-idea men with another based on all the best-liked. The most important difference that he found between the two types was that the men top ranked on best ideas initiated more interaction in the "attempted answers" categories and that the best-liked men initiated higher rates of interaction in the "positive social-emotional" categories. The best-idea men also tended to disagree more and show slightly more antagonism than the best-liked men.

What we see from this is that not only are those recognized as making the greatest contributions to the instrumental problems excluded from high liking but those who are given the highest ranks on "liking" receive them because of their contributions to the social-emotional problems in the group. According to Bales, in many of the groups, two specialists emerge: one type, the instrumental leader, takes charge of moving the group toward the solution of the instrumental problems; the other, the social-emotional leader, takes care of group solidarity problems. To refer to these types as "leaders" is somewhat misleading, since they are in the groups for relatively short periods of time, and there is no reason to believe that the members see them as leaders or that they think of themselves as leaders in the way the term is usually used. The point is, however, that those valued by group members as having the best ideas and being best liked do tend to engage in activities which are oriented toward the group task on the one hand and toward establishing group solidarity on the other. It should be pointed out however, that this does not mean that the best-idea man contributes no positive social-emotional interaction or that the best-liked initiates no task-oriented interaction.

We should caution against the idea that this separation of activities will occur in all groups. In many discussion groups, as shown by Borgatta, Couch, and Bales (1954), a single person may contribute to both the instrumental and social-emotional problems of the group. However, as Slater's study suggests, this kind of person seems to be rare. According to Bales, the opposing demands of instrumental and social-emotional problems make it difficult for any one person to meet both. To successfully move the group toward the completion of the task requires behavior that allows little time for contributions to group solidarity and that will likely raise some hostility among other members. On the other hand, one who contributes to group solidarity needs to avoid the extreme behavior of the task specialist. According to Bales, the emergence of "specialists," even though the members are not aware of their existence, is one way a group responds to the opposing systems problems facing them. This interpretation of the data gathered on discussion groups is made all the more compelling by parallels found in other types of social systems. For example, the status of the husband and father in the U.S. family, (and in most other countries) involves activities which are oriented toward the instrumental problems of the family. Likewise, the role of the wife and mother is directed more toward the social-emotional problems of the family system Parsons (1955), and his colleagues at Harvard have also shown that other social systems develop specialized roles in these two areas, and therefore it seems that Bales's scheme successfully explains much of the operation of laboratory discussion groups as well as other types of systems. This is perhaps what has made Bales's work so attractive to social scientists.

Bales's interpretation that specialization contributes to group solidarity is consistent with his theory. However, if some thought is given to the matter there is some question as to whether specialization really does increase group solidarity. In our discussion of cohesion as a dimension of solidarity, we mentioned that members had to be attractive to one another for most informal groups to be high in solidarity. The interaction patterns and sociometric choices that Bales and his associates call specialization involve the consistent rejection of one member. More important, this rejected member is not an ordinary member: he is recognized by other members as being the major contributor to task solutions.

Is a group that rejects the member who makes the greatest contribution to its instrumental problems really high in solidarity? We are left with an uncomfortable feeling that Bales's interpretation may not be entirely correct. However this is not the place to modify Bales's theory, and we shall return to this issue in Chapter 9.

HOMANS'S SYSTEM THEORY

In his book *The Human Group* (1950), Homans develops a sociological theory in the form of a series of hypotheses that can be tested in groups of all types. These hypotheses are based upon his reanalysis of studies that had previously been carried out by other investigators. In this section, we shall examine Homans's analysis of the men in the bank wiring room, the Norton street gang, and the changes that occurred in a small town.

The Development of an Informal Group

In developing his theory, Homans states that he wants to begin with concepts that are based upon observable events. He therefore isolates three terms or elements that he feels are necessary to discuss the processes that occur in groups of all types. These are *activities, interaction,* and *sentiments.* The first of these elementary concepts is fairly obvious; it refers to the things that people do either alone or with others. Homans's use of the concept interaction is similar to the way it has been used previously in this book. The thing which distinguishes interaction from activities is that interaction refers not only to behavior directed toward other people but also their reactions and reciprocal behavior. Sentiments refer to drives, emotions, feelings, and attitudes. Unlike the other two elements, sentiments are not directly observable and are usually inferred from the activities and interaction of people. However, most social scientists talk about them and in many cases attempt to measure them (e.g., sociometry). Because of this and because he bases his theory on the interrelationship between the three elements, Homans feels sentiments is a necessary concept, even though it is not directly observable.

Homans's theory consists mainly of showing the various ways in which the three elements are interdependent—i.e., how changes in one element lead to changes in others and vice versa. These interrelationships are illustrated in Figure 3.7. All other concepts that Homans introduces are related to these three elements. Homans develops his theory by first looking at the factors which brought the men in the bank wiring room together. He starts with sentiments such as the desire for money which originally brought men looking for work to the Hawthorn plant. Those men who, for whatever reasons, were chosen to work in the bank wiring room were given a series of activities such as soldering or inspecting in exchange for a salary. Thus, Homans demonstrates the first link between two elements—in this case he shows how *sentiments* lead to certain *activities.* Because each man worked on a different aspect of the equipment manufactured in that room, his efforts had to be coordinated with those of others and this required interaction. A wireman completing his activities acted as a signal to a solderman to begin working on the piece of equipment just finished; and a solderman's activity in turn required interaction with an inspector. Problems arising during the work day required interaction with the supervisor. Thus, interaction was linked to the activities of the men; and Homans suggests that if the activities of the group had been different, the pattern of interaction in the room would have been different as well.

Thus far we have seen the following sequence: *sentiments→activities→ interaction.* We earlier stated that these elements were interdependent, and this suggests that the arrows ought to flow from each element to every other element. We shall see in a moment that this is in fact the case, but it is necessary to stop with what we have for a moment. The sentiments which brought the

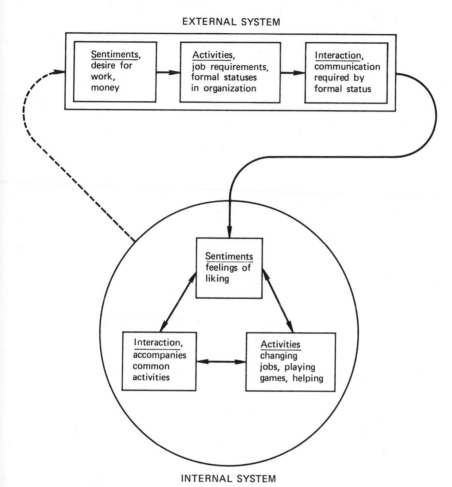

Figure 3.7. Relations between elements in the external and internal systems.

men to the Hawthorn plant, the activities to which they were assigned, and the interaction which was required by these activities are referred to by Homans as the *external system* of the group. The external system really involves everything which went on in the bank wiring room that was required by the larger formal organization (the Hawthorn plant). If the men had been assigned to separate rooms and equipment passed from one to the other by conveyor belt, this would have constituted the external system, and there would have been little more of interest to study. But, as we know, something more did happen in the room above and beyond what was planned and required by the larger organization. Homans calls this something more the *internal system;* and to account for this aspect of the bank wiring room group, Homans continues looking at the interrelationship between elements.

To show how the internal system developed out of the external system, Homans describes how interaction, the last element in the external system, leads to sentiments among the men over and above the desire for money. Homans states this idea in the following hypothesis: "persons who interact frequently with one another tend to like one another" (1959, p. 111). This hypothesis as it stands is likely to cause much disagreement because almost everyone can think of instances where he or she has interacted frequently with some person and has grown to dislike rather than like that person. However, judging from his comments, Homans did not mean that men in a situation like the bank wiring room will become close friends, but rather that on the whole they should become more friendly with one another than with others with whom they interact less frequently (i.e., in other departments). To be sure, some of the men in the Bank Wiring Room were rather unfriendly toward one another, but according to Homans they were probably more friendly toward each other than with outsiders.

As seen in Figure 3.7, Homans's next link is between sentiments and activity. To deal with the interdependence between sentiments and activity in the internal system, he formulates the following hypothesis: "persons who feel sentiments of liking for one another will express those sentiments in activities over and above the activities of the external system, and these activities may further strengthen the sentiments of liking " (p. 118). For example, the workers who liked each other tended to help one another and the fact that they helped one another gave them the opportunity to develop stronger ties of affection. Finally, Homans states that activities in the internal system and interaction are also interdependent. Activities like helping necessitated interaction among the men which, again, was not required by the external system.

With this relationship, the cycle, as diagrammed in Figure 3.7 is complete. The whole process is referred to as *elaboration* by Homans. The internal system emerges and becomes a part of the external system, even influencing or changing the external system. What Homans refers to as the internal system is the same as what we have called the informal group. Homans's external system constitutes what we will call the environment. Translating Homans's theory somewhat, we can say that informal groups represent the elaboration of activities, sentiments, and interaction above and beyond those originally required of members by the environment.

Standardization and Differentiation

The mutual interdependence between the three elements (in so far as they are elaborations upon the external system) represents the internal system. Along with the elaboration process in the bank wiring room, Homans says that there is evidence for a process called *standardization:* "The more frequently persons interact with one another, the more alike in some respects both their activities and their sentiments tend to become" (p. 120). This hypothesis states that as the internal system develops, members begin to behave more and more alike. This process is often seen in the literature as involving "pressures toward uniformity". The result is the emergence of norms requiring members to behave in a similar manner. For instance, standardization in the bank wiring room led members to produce at similar levels, to play games together and to eat the same types of candy.

According to Homans, as the internal system develops, *differentiation* also occurs; not only do members become similar but they also become dissimilar in various ways. Many of Homans' hypotheses are devoted to describing this process. Because Homans wanted to use only the most basic concepts, he did not use the term "status" in his theory. Instead he sees what we have called a status structure as consisting of differences in sentiments, interaction and activity. According to Homans, as differentiation occurs, the workers in the bank wiring room became dissimilar in their activities and patterns of interaction (e.g. level of participation, types of contributions, and so on). Based on these differences, the members developed different sentiments toward one another. Thus, ranking (or status differences) in a group is seen by Homans as a sentiment that results from comparisons made between the activities and interactions of members and certain standards; the closer a person comes to behaving in ways that approximate those standards, the higher will be his rank. Let us look at the data from the bank wiring room which Homans uses to support this hypothesis. It may be helpful for the reader to refer back to Figures 1.1, 1.2, and 1.3 (p. 3, 4) while considering this evidence.

It will be recalled that the activities (and consequently the interaction) of the men in the two cliques were different because of the different requirements made by the officials in the larger organization. Working on the connector equipment involved more prestige, being placed in the front of the room and, in most cases, receiving higher wages. All of these things, Homans points out, are highly valued in our society. Thus, the connector wiremen felt superior to the selector wiremen; and evidently this was acknowledged, if not totally accepted, by the selector wiremen. In other words, the differences in activities between the men led to differences in sentiments or ranking.

The existence of a norm necessitates common activities among members of a group, and so Homans hypothesized that: "the higher the rank of a person within a group, the more nearly his activities conform to the norms of the group" (p. 141). The reader will recall that clique *A* consisted mainly of connector wiremen whose output was closer to the group norm than that of clique *B*. According to Homans, the high rank of those in clique *A* was due, in part, to their conformity. Likewise it was the nonconformity in clique *B* which led to their rejection. Homans also states that Doc's rank in the Norton street gang was due to the fact that he conformed most closely to the group norms. For instance, Doc was the most willing member of the group to lend money to anyone who needed it.

In attempting to establish a link between ranking (i.e. sentiments) and interaction, Homans suggested the following hypothesis: "the higher a person's social rank, the wider will be the range of his interactions" (p. 145). Evidence for this comes from the fact that the high ranking connector wiremen in the bank wiring room traded jobs with workers outside their own clique while selector wiremen did not. Further, the most popular man in the room W_3 (Homans calls him Taylor) interacted more widely with *all* workers than did anyone else. Like Taylor, Doc was sought after by the members of the Nortons to give advice and settle disputes. However, as the lines of influence on Whyte's chart suggest (Figure 1.4), those ranking immediately below Doc (Mike, Angelo, or Danny) would often be contacted by members of lower ranks to pass on relevant suggestions or information to Doc. Likewise, if Doc had an idea or suggestion that concerned the whole group, he would have it originate with some person of intermediate rank who would, in turn, pass it to the lower-ranking members. This evidence shows that most of the communication in informal groups flows toward and away from the high ranking members, although in more complex groups this may occur indirectly.

A related hypothesis was: "the higher a man's social rank, the more frequently he interacts with persons outside his own group" (p. 186). Homans argues that Taylor's rank was partly dependent upon his influence outside the group, as witnessed by his ability to get high quality wire for the workers when others had failed. Similarly, Doc interacted most widely throughout Cornerville, especially with important people in the community such as the racketeers, politicians, and other gang leaders. Homans doesn't make much of this, but as the leader, Doc was allowed and even expected to be involved in these relationships outside of the group, even though such actions reinforced the low rank of most of the other members. There is a cyclical aspect to this in that Doc used his outside contacts to benefit the gang as a whole and this helped maintain the positive sentiments that were the basis of Doc's high rank in the group. In other words, because of his high rank Doc was allowed to engage in outside relationships, and these outside relationships helped him maintain that high rank.

Homans's analysis shows that standardization and differentiation are integral parts in the emergence of informal groups. The processes Homans describes can also be seen as the development of solidarity. Homans's theory does not include the six dimensions of solidarity, but one of his elements, interaction, is one of the dimensions and what Homans calls standardization is really the formation of *norms,* while differentiation is really the formation of a *status structure.* Most of the hypotheses formulated by Homans involve the relationship between interaction, norms, and status structure as group solidarity develops.

Anomie in Informal Groups

To formulate his ideas on anomie, Homans reanalyzes a study of Hilltown (Hatch, 1948). When it was established in 1767, Hilltown had a population of 150; and although it was surrounded by poor land it became an agricultural town. All of the townspeople were acquainted with one another, participated in town hall meetings and the affairs of the single church and helped each other in building farms and in plowing. The population of Hilltown grew rapidly until the middle part of the 1800s; then it declined some and leveled off at a little over 1,000 people in the early 1900s. Around the middle of the 1800s, railroads opened up a pathway to more fertile land to the west and caused a decline in Hilltown's population. During this period, agriculture began to decline, and home- and factory-based industries became the major factors in the economy. During the early 1900s the church split into two groups whose disdain for each other ran very deep. In addition to town hall and the church activities, many other social activities proliferated, such as visiting, parties, and spelling bees at the school.

Much of the industry that supported Hilltown throughout the nineteenth century had gone by the twentieth. Whatever farming took place was oriented to and controlled by markets outside of Hilltown. With the introduction of the automobile, Hilltown declined as a retail center and became the suburb of a neighboring industrial city. Thus, most people living in Hilltown in the 1940s were oriented toward job markets, stores, and other activities located outside of Hilltown itself. These changes led to gradual changes in the social life of Hilltown. Social clubs died out, few people attended church, and there was little visiting among neighbors. The number of divorces and forced marriages increased, and premarital sex was no longer overtly frowned upon. Hilltowners became so apathetic that when a public official stole $8,000 of public funds, there was little concern or reaction. While in earlier times the social standing of any family was known and established, by 1945 there was little consensus about where class lines should be drawn.

In his analysis of Hilltown, Homans begins with the external system—the sentiments, activities, and interaction that developed as the original settlers reacted to their environment. In the beginning, neighbors were drawn together (sentiments) out of a need for accomplishing common activities, which, of course required some level of interaction among them. This gave rise to the internal system—all the sentiments, activities, and interaction not required by the environment—i.e., the "social life" of Hilltown. However, as we mentioned above, this social life dwindled over time. According to Homans:

> When the land had been cleared, and the barns and houses raised, the need for neighbors to work together became much less than it had been. As transportation improved, local industry declined, and mill towns grew up round about, the interests of Hilltowners led them to take part in organizations, such as markets and factories, outside the town rather than inside it (p. 359).

In other words, "the number and strength of the sentiments that led members of the group to collaborate with other members had declined" (p. 359). Of course, this led to fewer collaborative activities, which in turn meant that they interacted less frequently. In the bank wiring room, had the men lost their desire to work, had they been fired, or had the required activities been changed, the internal system would have dissolved or changed radically. This is what Homans saw happening in Hilltown. Since the environment no longer required the sentiments, activities, and interaction that comprised the external system, the internal system also declined. As common activities and interaction over and above those required by collaboration declines, so do the mutual sentiments of liking within the community. This process is just the reverse of the process of elaboration by which the bank wiring room group presumably developed.

If elaboration is reversible, then standardization and differentiation should also be reversible; and there should be examples of this in the Hilltown study. As for a reverse in the standardization process, Homans hypothesizes: "a decrease in the frequency of interaction between the members of a group and in the number of activities they participate in together entails a decline in the extent to which norms are common and clear" (p. 362). This was manifested in Hilltown by the lack of concern about divorce, premarital sexual activities, and the behavior of public officials. Not only was there a lack of consensus about what was proper in these and other areas, but there was little evidence of negative social sanctions administered by those who considered a particular person a deviant. In other words, the old norms disappeared. To account for a reversal in the process of differentiation, Homans offers the following two hypotheses: (1) "as the number of activities carried out by the members of a group declines, the social ranking based on leadership in these activities will become less definite; (2) as the norms of a group decline in the degree to which they are clear to, and held in common by, all members of the group, so the ranking of members of the group will become less definite (pp. 364–65). If members rarely engage in common activities and interact with one another, they have little basis for evaluating and ranking one another's qualities. Furthermore, the reader will remember that Homans earlier hypothesized that high rank results from conformity to group norms. It is difficult for ranking to occur when the criteria upon which ranking is based are highly ambiguous. Of course, ranking in Hilltown was carried out within the social class system but the class system, which once was an important source of differentiation, was largely meaningless by the end of the study.

We saw in our treatment of Durkheim in Chapter 1 that anomie is a condition where members of a society become detached from one another and societal norms are no longer clear. This is exactly what happened in Hilltown over a period of time, and Homans uses the term "anomie" to describe the results of the decline in sentiments, activities, interaction, and norms that made up the internal system of Hilltown. Although Homans does not attempt to do so in his book, it does seem that the concept of anomie also describes certain changes in the Norton Street gang. While the data available are not as clear-cut as those for Hilltown, they are worth looking at, because we plan to say more about anomie in informal groups in later chapters.

The disintegration of the Norton gang as described in Chapter 1, would seem to be an example of a drift toward anomie. It will be recalled that with the worsening of the Depression, Doc and several other high-ranking members were particularly hard up for money. The change in the environment necessitated changes in their behavior that took them from the group; this, in Homans' words, led to a decline in interaction, common activities, and sentiments. The old system of obligations was often broken, and other norms concerning appropriate activities no longer applied. Furthermore, in line with Homans's hypothesis concerning the effect of decline on the internal system, the old ranking system, as reflected in the bowling scores, deteriorated. What makes this case an even more convincing example of anomie was the emergence of Doc's and Long John's psychological difficulties during this time. It is generally accepted by sociologists that a certain proportion of members in anomic societies or groups will manifest symptoms of stress. It seems safe, then, to conclude that Durkheim's concept of anomie can be applied to small groups of the type covered in this book as well as to whole societies.

Social Control

The term "social control" refers to the forces that keep members of a social system conforming to the norms and status expectations of that system. In most societies and in some smaller groups, there may be persons or groups who maintain control (e.g., policemen, judges, and so on). However, according to Homans, in most small groups no such specialists are required because social control is inherent in the group processes which he considers in his theory. If a person fails to behave in ways that are expected of all members of a group or of a person of his rank, the other members will react in subtle but strong ways to keep his behavior in line with their expectations. For example those who deviated from the norms in the bank wiring room or the Norton gang were not liked (sentiments), were excluded from activities, or were excluded from interaction by others in the group. To translate, we can say that social control is present whenever a group exists. The greater the solidarity of that group the greater the social control.

While it is true that reactions of the group members bring deviant behavior back into line, Homans recognized that there is more to social control than that. A person in a group can anticipate what would happen if he were to behave in ways considered inappropriate. Thus, each member, when he behaves in conforming ways, contributes to the social control in the group because he helps set a standard against which deviant behavior can be defined. This does not mean that change does not occur in groups where control is high. But, where it does occur, the leader, or perhaps other members as well, consciously specify the new normative and status expectations of each member, insuring that conformity to the new expectations is rewarded while conformity to the old is not.

SOME CONCLUDING COMMENTS

One of the difficulties in the social sciences is that individual theorist and researchers use concepts without regard for how they have been used by others. Many times two or more scholars will attach different labels to essentially the same phenomenon. The diagram in Figure 3.8 shows that this is the case with several of the concepts which we have introduced. In the last chapter, the six dimensions of solidarity were introduced to illustrate how interdependence among group members manifests itself in informal groups and to provide procedures for measuring the degree of interdependence. To say that interdependence is great in an informal group is just another way of saying that the group has attained a high level of solidarity. Thus, in figure 3.8 "high interdependence" has been equated with solidarity and "low interdependence" with anomie. According to Homans, the development of the internal system (i.e. informal group) through elaboration, standardization and differentiation entails the building up of greater social control. To say that a group is relatively high in social control implies high solidarity. Thus "high social control" has been placed at the solidarity end of the continuum in Figure 3.8. In a relatively anomic group, the interrelationship between sentiments, activities and interaction are not highly developed. Thus, the behavior of one person is not closely linked with that of others and vice versa; each will behave more less independently of one another or in conflict with one another. So, as seen in Figure 3.8, "low social control" has been placed under anomie.

Finally, we want to emphasize the fact that Homan's theory is consistent with the perspective being developed in this book. Accordingly, we have shown in Figure 3.8 that to speak of a highly developed internal system (close relationship between sentiments, interaction and activities) means the same things as high group solidarity. Likewise, an underdeveloped internal system is anomic.

Another point of possible confusion should be mentioned. In Chapter 2, we spoke of interdependence as a condition which occurs between group members. Furthermore, we suggested at the beginning of this chapter that groups could be considered as systems because of this interdependence—each member being a system part. However, Homans uses the term interdependence to refer to the relationship between the elements of his theory. It should be pointed out that the two uses of this term are not inconsistent. As interdependence develops between members the behavior of one closely affects others and *vice*

Anomie ├————————————————┤ High Solidarity
Low Interdependence   High Interdependence
Low Social Control   High Social Control
No Equilibrium   Complete Equilibrium
Low Development of   High Development of
Internal System   Internal System

Figure 3.8. The solidarity-anomie continuum and related concepts.

versa. This is manifested in interdependence between their sentiments, activities and interaction.

Before concluding, we should mention two ideas postulated by both theorists that provide jumping-off points for subsequent chapters. First, both Bales and Homans see groups as displaying tendencies toward greater solidarity on one hand and toward anomie (lowered solidarity) on the other. This is clearest in Bales's theory where pressures to confront instrumental problems lead to low solidarity, while solutions to social-emotional problems contribute to high solidarity. For Homans, these opposing forces would be elaboration and disintegration, or anomie. Homans comments on these opposing tendencies in his discussion of elaboration:

> Interaction between persons leads to sentiments of liking, which express themselves in new activities, and these in turn mean further interaction. The circle is closed, and by the very nature of the pair relations the whole system builds itself up. How far it can build itself up we do not know, and, of course, it can build itself down. If for any reason interaction in the internal system decreased, then activity would decay and sentiments of friendliness weaken. The same relationships that cement the group may dissolve it, providing the process once gets going in the wrong direction. *In most groups there is a precarious balance between the two tendencies* (p. 119, author's italics).

Thus, both Bales and Homans would agree with the scheme presented in the last chapter which presents group solidarity is something that varies along a solidarity-anomie continuum. In the next three chapters we shall review a number of studies that show in detail how the tendencies toward solidarity and anomie are manifested in groups and how they combine to give each group its unique level of solidarity. We have chosen to examine the emergence of norms and status structures because researchers have been most interested in these phenomenon.

Second, both theorists mention the importance of the relationship between the group and its environment. For Bales, the social-emotional problems facing a group involve the development of solidarity, which means keeping the individuals together as a system with some degree of interdependence. Bales implies that the pressures toward anomie are inevitable whenever a collection of individuals confronts an instrumental problem present in the environment. The nature of the instrumental problem and its degree of difficulty are environmental factors that affect how much time and energy a group can devote to solving social-emotional problems; the instrumental problem, therefore, affects the degree of solidarity attained by the group. Thus, in Bales's theory, the degree of solidarity is determined to a large extent by the nature of the environment. Homans makes a similar point in his theory. What he calls the external system of a group is that aspect of the members' behavior that is more or less directly determined by environmental conditions. For example, the nature of the internal system of the bank wiring room—that is, the degree of solidarity—reflected the characteristics of the setting within which it developed. Likewise, changes in the external system of Hilltown led to changes in the internal system, as was reflected by the increasing anomie. In later chapters we will elaborate upon these ideas to show, in more detail, the ways in which informal groups are influenced by their environments.

SUMMARY

The essence of Bales's theory is that all social systems, including informal groups, must simultaneously solve instrumental and social-emotional problems. Instrumental problems for informal groups are those requirements and demands imposed upon the group members from the environment. Social-emotional problems within informal groups are those concerning the interpersonal relationships among members. How successfully a group solves these two sets of problems affects its overall solidarity.

Using a method called *interaction process analysis,* Bales and his associates provided evidence for his theory in their observations of groups in experimental laboratories. For instance, he found that most groups show some balance in their solution of the two problems: task-oriented interaction is generally high, more answers are given than questions asked, more positive than negative social-emotional interaction is expressed. Furthermore, members of a group successfully solving both problems were more satisfied than those in a group not doing so. Group members also showed the need to reestablish solidarity at the end of problem-solving sessions after a great deal of attention had been devoted to the solution of instrumental problems. Also, groups in which status consensus was highly developed were more successful in solving instrumental problems than groups with low status consensus. Status struggles and conflict, indications of low solidarity, were also observed in the low status consensus groups.

Bales and his associates found that many groups showed evidence of *specialization.* Specialization occurs in a group when the member ranked highest in terms of "best ideas" initiates relatively high rates of task-oriented interaction and is ranked relatively low on "liking." In the same group, the person ranked highest on "liking" tends to initiate relatively high rates of positive social-emotional interaction.

Homans illustrates, by examples from the bank wiring room and the Norton Street gang studies, how sentiments, interaction, and activities become interlinked. The interrelation between these elements constitutes the development of the internal system, or in our terms, the informal group. In his view, members build up sentiments, interaction, and common activities amongst themselves above and beyond that required by the environment. This process he calls *elaboration.* Accompanying elaboration are two other processes: *standardization,* which essentially involves the development of group norms, and *differen-*

tiation, which involves the development of a status structure. In Homans's terms, standardization occurs as members become alike in activities and sentiments through an increased level of interaction among themselves. Differentiation occurs as members evaluate one another according to their different activities and patterns of interaction in the group. While Homans specifically refers only to three dimensions of solidarity—interaction, norms, and status structure—it is clear that his description of the emergence of internal systems involves the development of solidarity as it has been defined in this book.

While most of Homans's analysis involves hypotheses describing the development of solidarity, he also recognizes that the reverse movement toward anomie is also possible. Most of the examples of this process are taken from a study of the disintegration of a whole town. However, it was shown that the Norton gang, at one point, moved toward greater anomie.

Another theoretical contribution made by Homans is found in his discussion of *social control.* Here he demonstrates that the mere existence of a group implies the existence of some degree of control. Since we have conceived of groups as varying in interdependence or solidarity, it is appropriate to say that they vary in the extent to which they exert control over members. To say that the interdependence or solidarity in a group is high is to say that the social control within the group is high.

four

Standardization within Informal Groups

INTRODUCTION

The process which Homans has called standardization has been the object of interest by social scientists working within the internal tradition. As we shall see, much of the research on the formation of norms has involved observing individuals as they develop similar opinions about some matter. It may appear, at first, that these studies have little to do with group norms, for the existence of a norm means that all members of a group are *behaving* uniformly. But several things should be kept in mind. The first is that the expression of an opinion is a behavior. In most cases, groups exert pressures on members to say the right thing as well as to do the right thing. Furthermore, whether we are talking about an opinion or some overt behavior like producing so much or smoking marijuana, the processes by which uniformity is reached in a group are the same. Many experimenters have set up situations where subjects can become similar by changing their opinions because this takes less time than changing other types of behavior. While somewhat artificial, we can learn something about the emergence of norms from these studies.

Forces Toward Solidarity and Anomie

At the conclusion of the last chapter, we mentioned that both Bales and Homans view group members as being exposed to two contradictory forces—those moving them toward greater interdependence or solidarity and those moving them in the opposite direction. Both theorists also see the relative strength of these forces as being determined by the nature of a group's environment. Later in the book we shall show how the various dimensions of solidarity and thus, the overall solidarity of a group, are determined by environmental factors. In this chapter, we will ignore the source of these forces and will assume that, for whatever reason, some groups face relatively strong forces toward solidarity while others are faced with relatively strong forces toward anomie. We shall then examine how standardization occurs under these two circumstances. Before doing this, however, it is best to provide the reader with a clear description of these two forces. As Thibaut and Kelley (1959) demonstrated in their theory of interaction, individuals constantly weigh the advantages of continuing in one social relationship with the advantages of various alternative relationships. To the extent that a person satisfies his needs through his relations with a particular group, he will behave in ways that will strengthen his interdependence with the other members. If however, he decides that his needs can be better met independently of that group, his behavior will detract from the solidarity of the group. When the behavior of a person contributes to his interdependence with others, we can say he adopts an *interdependent orientation* toward them. When his behavior detracts from interdependent relationships, either by merely maintaining his independence or engaging in conflict or competition with them (see Deutsch, 1960), he adopts an *individualistic orientation.* Over a period of time, a person may alternate between the two orientations, and in a particular group various members may simultaneously display both orientations.

When we speak of orientations we refer to specific actions or behaviors which members exhibit. A "disagreement" in Bales discussion groups, taken to be negative social-emotional interaction, is an example of an individualistic orientation. Likewise, an "agreement" is an instance of a member's interdependent orientation toward the group. A refusal to attend a group affair is an individualistic orientation while asking someone to dinner is an interdependent orientation. As we have said, which of these orientations is adopted most often depends on the nature of the situation facing a member. For example, if he is incompatible with others in the group he may find it easy to disagree with them or engage in some other individualistic response. If he has nothing else he would rather do he will find it rewarding to attend a group's affair. When group members are faced with circumstances which make the adoption of interdependent orientation rewarding, we can say the forces toward solidarity are strong. When individualistic orientations are encouraged, the forces toward anomie are strong (see Figure 4.1).

A person can be said to adopt an individualistic orientation only if there is also an opportunity for his adopting an interdependent orientation. For example, the decision of a factory worker to eat lunch by himself is not an individualistic orientation if there is no one else to eat with. Likewise it is meaningless to speak of forces toward anomie unless forces toward solidarity also exist. What allows us to say that the competitive situation in Deutsch's experiment (1949) set in motion forces toward anomie is that the subjects worked in one another's presence where there was always a possibility for them to develop

Amonie |————————————————————————| High Solidarity
Prevalence of   Prevalence of
Individualistic   Interdependence
Orientations   Orientations
among Individuals   among Individuals

Figure 4.1. Individualistic orientations, interdependent orientations, and the solidarity-anomie continuum.

cooperative harmonious (i.e., solidary) relationships. Thus, it is necessary to see any group or potential group as being simultaneously exposed to forces toward solidarity and anomie where every member has the opportunity to choose between interdependent and individualistic orientations. While this is so, the relative strength of these two forces can vary.

NORMS EMERGING FROM FORCES TOWARD SOLIDARITY

Interpersonal Attraction and Pressures Toward Uniformity

The studies discussed here consider norms to be the result of pressures toward solidarity that confront groups—i.e., they examine how groups move toward greater solidarity by developing norms. In Chapter 3, we briefly mentioned the study of housing projects at MIT carried out by Festinger, Schachter, and Back (1950). In this section we shall discuss this study in more detail and then go on to review several laboratory experiments that were designed to answer some questions raised by it.

The housing projects studied by Festinger and his associates contained housing for married students attending MIT. The oldest project, Westgate, consisted of 100 prefabricated single-story apartments that were arranged in U-shaped courts. Most of these courts consisted of thirteen houses, but some had less. Figure 4.2 is a diagram showing two of the larger courts. Each letter designates a separate house. All of the houses except those on the end (e.g., apartments *a* and *m*) face inward onto a central courtyard. The second project, Westgate West, consisted of more modern two-story apartments such as the one shown in Figure 4.3.

All of the residents were interviewed and one of the many questions they were asked was: "What three people in Westgate or Westgate West do you see most of socially?" This was considered by the investigators to be a sociometric-type question. The answer to this question may be a measure of who likes whom in the projects (or it may be a measure of who interacts with whom). The wording of the question leaves unclear exactly what is being measured. But, if

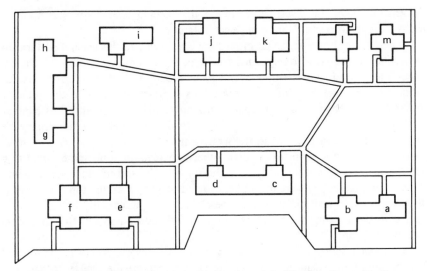

Figure 4.2. Schematic diagram of the arrangement of the Westgate Court. (Festinger, Schachter, and Back, 1950, p. 42.)

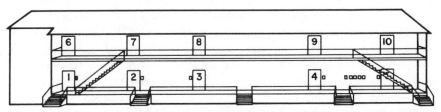

Figure 4.3. Schematic diagram of Westgate west building. (Festinger, Schachter, and Back, 1950, p. 36.)

Homans is correct, in most cases we will find that liking and interaction overlap so the ambiguity is no great problem.

One relationship the investigators examined was that between the responses to the sociometric questionnaire and physical distance between houses. For instance, the investigators found that most of the residents tended to interact socially with those in their own courts (Westgate) or their own buildings (Westgate West). In Westgate, the people living in adjacent courts were the next most likely to be chosen, while in Westgate West it was people in adjacent buildings. In each project the fewest number of choices were directed toward members of the other projects. Looking at choices made within each court of Westgate, the investigators found that most tenants chose their closest neighbors, the second most frequent choices were directed toward those living two doors away, and the third most frequent toward those three doors away, and so on. In Westgate West, people saw the most socially of those who lived in the closest apartments.

In general, then, the investigators found that people tended to "see more socially" those closest to them in physical distance.

There were, however, some interesting exceptions to this general pattern. In Westgate the people who happened to live in the end houses, which faced away from the central courts (units *a* and *m* in Figure 4.2), were chosen very infrequently by members of that court. This suggests that due to the peculiar physical arrangements of their apartments, these people came into less contact with others and were therefore less likely to develop social relationships with others in their court. In Westgate West, while people tended to choose their next-door neighbor more often than others, there were again some interesting exceptions. Those people living near the steps to the second floor (apartments 1 and 5 in Figure 4.3) were most likely to choose people on the top floor. Again because of their position, people in these apartments apparently had more contact with those living on the second floor and therefore had a better chance to become acquainted.

Of most interest in this discussion is how the investigators used the information about the social ties to measure cohesiveness of the courts of Westgate and the buildings of Westgate West. For Festinger and his colleagues, the cohesiveness of a group is the resultant of the various forces that attract members to the group. Since the people living in courts or buildings of these projects were not together for the purpose of collectively attaining a goal, the main source of attraction would be the satisfactions derived from interaction with one another socially. That is, social interdependence, not instrumental interdependence would be the bases of cohesion in the courts. The investigators reasoned that having most of one's friends in the same unit would make that unit more attractive than if one had only a few friends there. A court or building in which a large proportion of the members chose one another was said to be a highly cohesive unit.

If a court in Westgate had thirteen families and each family had three choices, there would be a total of thirty-nine choices being made in that court. The investigators determined what percentage of those choices was directed to persons inside the same court and what percentage was directed towards persons living in other courts or in Westgate West. The same method was used for each building in Westgate West. In Table 4.1 the column labeled *choices in-court/total choices* shows this measure for Westgate. Table 4.2 shows the same measure for Westgate West. Notice that Main court in Westgate has the highest proportion of in-court choices and is thus highest in cohesion, while Richards is lowest. Building 351–60 is highest in cohesion in Westgate West, while 331–40 is the lowest.

At some point in their investigation, Festinger and his associates realized that there was a problem with this simple measure of cohesion. The problem was that if a court or building was divided into several cliques whose members chose only one another, there would be a high number of in-court or in-building choices

Table 4.1

Cohesiveness of Court and Strength of Group Standard (Westgate)

(Festinger, Schachter, and Back, 1950, p. 92.)

Court and N of residents		% Deviates	Choices in court Total choice	Choices in court −½ Pairs Total choice
Tolman	13	23	.62	.529
Howe	13	23	.63	.500
Rotch	8	25	.55	.523
Richards	7	29	.47	.433
Main	7	29	.67	.527
Freeman	13	38	.48	.419
Williams	13	46	.53	.447
Miller	13	46	.56	.485
Carson	13	54	.48	.403
R.O. correlation with % deviates			−.53	−.74
t°			1.65	2.92
p			.15	.02

*Testing significance of rank order correlation as suggested by Kendall, M. C., *The Advanced Theory of Statistics*. London: Charles Griffin and Co., Limited, Vol. I, p. 401, 1943.

made, but the overall cohesion of the unit would not really be high. In this case, each clique (mutual choices) would be cohesive, but because the cliques were separate, the overall cohesion of the court or building would be low. While some reciprocal choices would be expected in these units, the investigators wanted to improve upon their measure of cohesion by correcting for an excessive number of mutual choices. To do this, they subtracted from the number of in-court or in-building choices one-half the mutual choices. The number one-half was chosen arbitrarily. The final column in Tables 4.1 and 4.2 represents the corrected cohesion score that the investigators used.

Before we continue, we must look at another piece of information the investigators solicited during the interviews. Not long before the study, a fire had broken out in a building that was being built in Westgate West; the fire came very close to spreading to some apartments in Westgate. Soon afterwards, petitions were circulated requesting MIT to provide a fire alarm and funds for a community fire hose. A short time after this, some students planned to form a tenant organization and distributed leaflets announcing a meeting. The first several meetings involved ineffective discussions which became bogged down by parliamentary procedure. In addition, several students took control of the meetings in ways that offended many of the other students who attended. Once the organization got on its feet, the members made ambitious plans, but very few were ever carried out. As a result of all of this, the residents had mixed feelings

Table 4.2
Cohesiveness of Building and Strength of Group Standard (Westgate West)
(Festinger, Schachter, and Back, 1950, p. 93)

Building	% Deviates	Choices in building Total choices	Choices in building–½ pairs Total choices
211–20	10	.58	.50
221–30	10	.66	.59
201–10	11	.60	.54
231–40	20	.80	.64
241–50	20	.70	.61
251–60	20	.74	.63
281–90	20	.80	.68
311–20	20	.66	.53
261–70	25	.57	.46
271–80	30	.47	.38
341–50	30	.62	.50
351–60	30	.83	.76
321–30	33	.62	.52
361–70	40	.67	.56
291–300	50	.59	.50
301–10	50	.72	.64
331–40	70	.42	.35
R. O. correlation with % deviates		−.20	−.27
t		.79	1.09
p		not significant	

about the utility of the tenant organization. Therefore, the organization provided the investigators with an issue, and each family was asked about its orientation toward the organization.

The respondents were classified as being favorable, unfavorable or neutral toward the organization and as to whether they were active or not active in the organization. The investigators looked at each court or building to determine the orientations that were held by a majority of the members. Based on this procedure each court was labeled as falling into one of the following patterns: (1) Favorable-active, (2) Favorable-inactive, or (3) Unfavorable-inactive. After determining the majority orientation of each unit, they determined how large that majority was, and this provided the basis for their operationalization of the variable they called "degree of homogeneity." The measure of homogeneity used by the investigators was the percentage of members in each unit who deviated from the majority orientation. Of course, the *larger* the percentage of deviants in a unit, the smaller the majority and the *less* homogeneous the unit. This information is listed for each court under the column headed *Percentage Deviants* (those not classified in the majority) in Tables 4.1 and 4.2.

As the reader has probably guessed by now, the intention of the investigators was to determine whether there was any relationship between the cohesion of the courts or buildings and the degree of homogeneity in orientation toward the tenant organization. They tested this by using both the original and the corrected measures of cohesion, but we shall comment only on the results where the corrected measure was used. An examination of Table 4.1 shows that in Westgate there was indeed a relationship between these two variables. Notice that Tolman court had the highest score on the *corrected* cohesiveness score (.529) and was also one of those with the fewest number of deviants. On the other hand, Carson court was the lowest in cohesiveness (.403) and had the highest number of deviants. These are the extreme cases but in general the pattern is the same; the highly cohesive courts had few deviants and courts low in cohesion had a larger percentage of deviants. The figures at the bottom of Table 4.1 show that there is a rank-order correlation of .74 between the corrected cohesion score and homogeneity. This is large enough to be statistically significant.

Referring to Table 4.2, however, it can be seen that there is no strong relationship between cohesion and homogeneity in Westgate West. Most of the residents of Westgate West had lived there only a matter of months when the study was carried out. Thus, they had moved in after the organizational crisis and had had contact with the organization for only about a month. Seventy-nine percent of the tenants in Westgate West were in favor of the organization and most were active. It appears, then, that most of the Westgate residents independently formed opinions of the organization, and most were favorable. Norms for each building did not really have time to develop as they did in Westgate courts, and therefore the cohesion of the buildings was unrelated to the degree of homogeneity within buildings.

To better understand why there was a correlation between cohesiveness and homogeneity in Westgate, the investigators looked more closely at some of the characteristics of those who deviated from the standards (majority orientations) of their court. In examining what these people said during their interview, Festinger and his colleagues discovered three types of deviants. The first type were those who were not sufficiently attracted to the members of the court to be influenced by the group's norms. The following case is an example of this type.

> *Mr. and Mrs. K. in Tolman court:* We think the organization is sort of silly. It isn't necessary for a group like this. We've gone to meetings because our court likes it and is very active. Our friends now are spread all over pretty much. We used to have a nice group here but several moved away. We see a lot of the people in our court now but we aren't too friendly except with one or two (p. 103).

The second type of deviant consisted of those people who for some reason were cut off from communication with others in the court and thus escaped the influence of the group. The following two cases are instances of this type.

Mr. and Mrs. S. in Freeman court: The organization is a good idea but the trouble with people like us is that we don't have time. That's why we haven't had anything to do with it. I think it's the consensus of opinion that people here don't have the time [actually the majority of the people in the court were active] (p. 103).

Mr. and Mrs. Z. in Miller court: We don't have much time for things like the tenants' organization and haven't had anything to do with it. Some are active and others aren't. There aren't any particular people we are particularly friendly with. Everyone is in the same boat though and people are generally friendly. It's been very nice living here and the people are nice too. We live on the corner though, and seem to get left out of a lot of things because of that (p. 103).

Festinger and associates found that of the sixty-eight people living in the houses that opened into the courtyards, 34 percent were deviants, while of the ten people living in the corner house facing away from the court, seventy (70 percent) were deviants. Clearly, the fact that residents in these end houses were cut off from the social life of their courts contributed to their becoming deviants in whatever group life emerged among the other residents.

The third type was comprised of those whose friends lived in other courts and who therefore conformed to the standards of those other courts.

Mr. and Mrs. M. in Carson court: We think the organization is fine and Mrs. M. is the chairman of the social committee which is holding its first big event tomorrow night. I don't see much of the others in this court. My real friends are in the next court over there, in Tolman court. There are only two people living in this court that do anything for the organization, myself and one other person. It's generally understood that the others have different interests. The people in Tolman court are more active. Carson people aren't as sociable as people in Tolman court.

On the basis of these interviews the investigators predicted that the deviants would be different from the conformers in the ways others reacted to them. Table 4.3 shows how frequently the deviants and conformers chose others in the same courts and the number of times the deviants and conformers were chosen by others in the same court. It can be seen that the deviants chose fewer people in the same court and were chosen less frequently. That the deviants

Table 4.3
Average Number of "In-Court" Choice of Deviates and Conformers in Westgate (Festinger, Schachter, and Back, 1950, p. 105)

	N	*Choices given*	*Choices received*
Deviates	36	1.25	1.11
Conformers	64	1.53	1.61

were infrequently chosen made sense because, as we saw, they were not attracted to their courts, were cut off from communication, or had friends in other courts.

Despite the wealth of information uncovered, this study does have the drawback that the data were gathered only at one point of time. Although we know that there is a fairly strong correlation between cohesiveness and homogeneity in Westgate, it is not immediately clear which leads to which. Although the study did not trace through the historical development of social relationships in each court as would have been desirable, the investigators did make some educated guesses about how this occurred, as well as some general theoretical statements about social processes in such groups.

Social reality and uniformity. According to Festinger and his colleagues, much of what we think and believe is based upon what they refer to as *physical reality*, which can be tested empirically. Whether the ice is thick enough for skating or whether a given food is tasty can be affirmed by certain definite procedures. On the other hand, there are many beliefs or opinions whose validity cannot be directly tested. Whether God exists or whether abortion should be legalized are examples of this type of issue. The correctness of a person's opinion on such issues can only be validated if he perceives that there are others who hold the same opinion. In these cases, rather than relying on physical reality, people rely upon *social reality*, which stems from being in agreement with others. Of course, in a complex society such as ours, people rarely find their own opinions coinciding with those of everyone else. For this reason, people seek out and interact with others whose opinions are similar to their own. Also, on such issues, we would expect that persons who do not have clearly formulated opinions would be influenced by the opinions of others around them. This idea is consistent with Sherif's work on norms (p. 30), where he found that subjects in the autokinetic experiment relied on the information conveyed to them by others because the stimulus was so ambiguous that the correctness of their own responses could not be assessed through physical reality testing.

We can imagine that right after the founding of the tenants' organization that many people in the same court would have different opinions about its existence and that some might not have any at all. It was Festinger and his associates' argument that in the high cohesion groups, where there would be more interaction, there would also be greater opportunity for members to be influenced by one another's opinions and arguments about these opinions. Furthermore, members who are highly attracted to one another, either because they like each other or because they depend upon each other to attain some goal, will feel compelled to have similar opinions on certain issues relevant to the group. In low cohesion courts, there was less interaction among the members and thus fewer opportunities for members to influence one another, as well as less concern about doing so.

Cohesiveness Experiments

Since this study did not provide enough information to allow the investigators to conclusively test their theoretical ideas, it was followed by a series of laboratory experiments designed to test these ideas under controlled conditions. The first laboratory study we will review was carried out by Back (1951), who worked with Festinger on the MIT study. Back was interested in testing the idea in the earlier study that members of high cohesion groups experienced pressures toward uniformity. To accomplish this Back asked students from college classes to volunteer to participate in a group experiment. The sign-up sheet included some questions which ostensibly were to be used by the experimenter in making up the groups. The subjects were asked to describe themselves and also the type of people they would and would not like to work with in the experiment. The procedure was very much like that used by computer dating organizations. When a subject showed up at his assigned time, he found himself with one other subject. Each dyad was randomly assigned to either a high or low cohesion condition. Depending upon the condition to which they had been assigned, they heard one or the other of the following instructions:

> *Low cohesion:* You remember the questions you answered when you signed up in class? We tried to find a partner with whom you could work best. Of course, we couldn't find anybody who would fit the description exactly but we found a fellow who corresponded to the main points, and you probably will like him. You should get along all right.

> *High cohesion:* You remember the questions you answered in class about the people you would like to work with? Of course, we usually cannot match people the way they want, but for you we have found almost exactly the person you described. As a matter of fact, the matching was as close as we had expected to happen once or twice in the study, if at all. You'll like him a lot. What's even more, he described a person very much like you. It's quite a lucky coincidence to find two people who are so congenial, and you should get along extremely well. (1951, p. 12)

In this case, the experimenter manipulated high and low cohesion by telling subjects they would or would not be personally attracted to one another. Since Back figured that there could be other causes of cohesion, some dyads were told either (1) they would (high cohesion) or would not (low cohesion) get a prize for good work; or that (2) they were in groups that should (high cohesion) or should not (low cohesion) work well together. For comparison's sake, Back also included a number of groups in a *negative treatment* condition, where subjects were told that the questionnaire results showed that they would not get along with each other.

Each member of a particular dyad was shown a series of pictures and was asked to write a story about what was occurring in the series. The subjects did not know it, but each member of the dyad was shown slightly different pictures. After each had finished his story, the two were brought together to discuss how to improve his story. They were told, however, that they did not have to end up with common stories. After the discussion they were again separated and told to write what they thought to be the best story.

During the discussion, an observer recorded the frequency of certain kinds of communication such as "attempts to influence" and "reactions to influence attempts." The experimenter also examined the stories to determine the number of changes that were made after the discussion. The various observations made of the group discussions showed that the members of the highly cohesive dyads (regardless of the source of cohesion) made more of an effort to discuss the stories and to influence one another. Generally, one member of the high cohesion dyads changed his story a great deal, while neither member in the low cohesion groups made many changes. Back's study, then, gives some support to Festinger's contention that members of highly cohesive groups are under pressure to influence one another through interaction and that this leads to high levels of homogeneity.

In a study by Festinger, Gerard, Hymovitch, Kelly, and Raven (1952), groups of six to nine members were placed in high and low cohesion conditions that were manipulated in the same fashion as the studies mentioned above. Other experimental conditions were imposed, but we won't consider these since we are interested only in differences in the cohesion conditions. The subjects in each group discussed a case and then privately indicated their opinions on a questionnaire. The subjects were later given fictitious information about their position relative to others. How this was accomplished can be seen in Table 4.4. All subjects were led to believe that they were represented by the letter D. The investigators told some subjects that they were conformers by placing the letter D along with a number of other letters. For example, the person who received the sheet pictured in Table 4.4 had checked, after the first discussion, an opinion which was numbered 4. If that subject was to be designated as a conformer, he would receive the information shown on the left, which placed him with the majority of members. If the experimenter wanted the subject to see himself as a deviant, he would be given the information on the right. Of course,

Table 4.4
Apparent Distribution of Opinion (Festinger *et al*, 1952, p. 333)

Opinion	Given to conformer	Given to deviate
1		
2		
3		
4	DCBFG	D
5	A	
6		A
7	E	CBEFG

the information received by a subject depended upon the number of the opinion he originally chose.

The subjects in this experiment were led to believe that they could communicate with each other by sending notes to whomever they pleased. This enabled the experimenter to intercept the notes and to substitute prewritten messages, and it also allowed him to keep track of who sent messages to whom. After the note-passing period was ended, a second measure of each subject's opinion was taken.

As one would expect, subjects who found themselves in deviant positions tended to change their opinions more often than conformers. Of more importance is the fact that more changes were made by deviants in cohesive groups. Again, there is evidence of greater pressure toward conformity in high cohesion groups. In addition it was found that conformers tended to communicate more to those holding extreme opinions than to those with opinions similar to their own, but this tendency was found in both high and low cohesion groups.

Control of the deviant. The study by Back (1952) showed that members of high cohesion groups attempted to influence each other more than members of low cohesion groups. The study by Festinger, Gerard, Hymovitch, Kelly, and Raven found that subjects who were led to believe they were conformers sent more notes to those they thought were extreme deviants than they did to less extreme deviants and other conformers, which suggests that they were attempting to influence these extreme deviants. It seems reasonable, from everything that has been said so far, that conformers, in high as opposed to low cohesion groups, would be most concerned with influencing extreme deviants. This was one of the hypotheses that Schachter (1951) attempted to test in a classic but highly complicated experiment. Because of its complexity and because many questions have been raised about some of its results, we shall report here only that aspect of Schachter's experiment which provided clear results and is relevant to this discussion.

Subjects in the experiment were college students who indicated in classes their desire to belong to one of four clubs: a radio club, a movie club, an editorial club, or a case study club. When members showed up for the first meeting, they found out that they had been assigned either to a club in which they had previously expressed great interest or to one in which they had very little interest at all. Subjects in the first case were considered to be in high cohesion groups, the others in low cohesion groups. Subsequent checks on the manipulations showed that members assigned to high cohesion groups were indeed more attracted to their group than those in the low cohesion groups.

One activity common to all of the clubs turned out to be a group discussion of the same case study. The problem in the case was selected so that there could be a wide range of possible solutions. Unknown to the subjects was the fact that in each club were three confederates paid by the experimenter to behave in predetermined ways during the group discussion. One confederate, "the mode," argued for a solution to the problem in the case study which the experimenter knew from experience would be most popular among the subjects. Another confederate, "the deviant," took an extreme position known in advance to be one no subjects were likely to assume. A third confederate called "the slider," began to take this extreme position but allowed his opinions to be changed over time until he ended up holding the same position as the mode.

During the discussion, observations were made concerning the flow of communication toward various members, including the three confederates. The results showed the following: (1) that the mode received relatively little communication throughout the study; (2) the slider received moderate communication but this decreased as the discussion progressed; and (3) the deviant received the most communication, and in most cases, this increased throughout the discussion. Schachter interpreted this as showing that members were attempting to influence the deviant. A study by Sampson and Brandon (1964) substantiates this interpretation. They found that subjects directed greater overall communication, less "communication expressing solidarity," more "communication expressing hostility," and more "information-seeking" to confederates representing deviant opinions than to other subjects. This study, however, did not attempt to manipulate cohesion, and Schachter's study found no difference in the amount of interaction directed toward the deviant in his high and low cohesion groups. So while it would be consistent with Festinger, Schachter, and Back's evidence to expect that cohesiveness leads to the influencing of deviant members, no experimental studies document that this is actually the case.

One other finding from Schachter's study is relevant here. After the group discussion the members were informed that since it might be necessary to break up the clubs and assign some members to other clubs, it would be helpful to know who wanted to remain together. The subjects were asked to rank each other according to who they would prefer to remain with them in the group. The subjects' rankings constitute the main dependent variable of interest here. The average rank assigned to the "modes" and the "sliders" in the various groups turned out to be the same. However, the average rank assigned to the deviants were significantly lower than that assigned to the mode and sliders. Furthermore, the average rank assigned to the deviants in the high cohesion groups was significantly lower than that assigned to the deviant in the low cohesion groups. That is, in all groups the deviants tended to be rejected, but this rejection was especially intense in the high cohesion groups. Emerson (1953) replicated Schachter's study and found the same pattern.

While extreme deviants in cohesive groups are more apt to change their position and are rejected if they do not, these studies provide no evidence that members of cohesive groups are any more concerned about influencing the extreme deviant than those in low cohesive groups. The lack of support for this is a puzzle and requires more research. It is likely that this observation is limited only to experimental groups where subjects, regardless of the cohesiveness of the group, are forced to interact with one another while knowing that the experimenter is interested in having them express their opinions. The fact is that attempts to influence deviants is a common technique of social control in informal groups. Evidence for this can be seen in the bank wiring room where those producing too high or low were often the targets of persuasive communications from others.

While in the studies reviewed, "rejection" is said to occur when a member is assigned a low sociometric rank, in naturally occurring groups this is accomplished by ignoring, insulting or embarrassing the deviant. In extreme cases, it may mean that the deviant is excluded from the group's activities altogether. In friendship groups and in groups like the Norton Street gang, where members come together voluntarily, a member can be rather easily dropped if he does not conform to group expectations. However, this is not so easily done in groups where members are restrained to some extent in their interaction with one another (as in the bank wiring room). In such cases, persuasion and rejection may occur simultaneously. For example the men in the bank wiring room who deviated from the restricted productivity norms were certainly devalued by the conformers in the group, but this was shown in low-ranking statuses in the group instead of by all-out exclusion. Observations of daily conversations in the room revealed that the deviants were constantly bombarded with pressures to conform. If the conformers had had their way, they probably would have thrown the deviants out of the room, but this was not possible. The result was that the deviants became targets of both hostility and attempts to persuade.

Does Cohesion Always Lead to Uniformity?

Groups, even highly cohesive groups, do not formulate norms which restrict the behavior of members in all respects. The range of activities over which the group imposes normative expectations will vary from group to group. For instance, it may not matter much to a group of men who play poker together once a week that they have different political opinions, but it does matter that they agree on and follow the rules of the game. It is not likely that members of a political action group would seek uniformity on religious beliefs, but they would concerning political beliefs. Group members exert pressure towards uniformity when this uniformity is seen as important or relevant to the group (see Schachter, 1951). That is, uniformity will be sought after if it is important for the maintenance of interdependence in a group. In the case of instrumental interdependence, we can expect that whatever activities facilitate performing the task, reaching the group's goal, or satisfying the needs of the members, will come under the control of the group. In either case, members must be aware of what the group considers important. This is probably the reason that the results of some studies are not consistent with Festinger, Schachter, and Back's theory. For example, some studies do not show the predicted tendency for greater conformity in high cohesion groups (Bovard, 1953; Downing, 1962; Rotter, 1967).

Rotter manipulated cohesion by giving subjects information which led them to believe that the other members of the experimental group either did or did not like them. He found that the subjects who thought they were liked by others in turn said they liked the others and so were considered to be in the high cohesion condition. Those who were told that they were not liked by the other members in turn rated the others low in terms of "liking" and were thus assigned to the low cohesion condition. The subjects in both conditions were placed in a modified version of the conformity situation used by Asch. Rotter found that the amount of conformity (i.e., the amount of yielding to the erroneous answers of confederates) among subjects was the same in the two experimental situations. Unlike Back's study, subjects in Rotter's experiment were not the objects of influence attempts; that is, they did not receive verbal statements from other members indicating that these others wanted them to change answers.

In Back's study, the subjects who eventually conformed had been influenced and so were aware of the fact that they were expected to change. On the other hand, there is no reason that the subjects in the high cohesion conditions of Rotter's experiment should have perceived that their being in a cohesive group meant that they were expected to conform. Often members of cohesive groups outside the experimental laboratory are attracted to a group because they know few expectations will be placed upon them. Only when members perceive that their attractiveness to others may be lowered if they do not conform to certain specified norms will conformity result from cohesiveness.

This point is shown very clearly in two experiments carried out by Walker and Heyns (1962). In both experiments, subjects who were placed alone in a room read a case study and indicated their solutions on a questionnaire, as in many of the studies mentioned so far. They then heard over earphones what they thought to be the voices of three other subjects in other rooms justifying opinions that were uniformly different from those of the subjects. In reality the voices had been previously recorded with the purpose of seeing how many subjects would change their initial opinion-positions after hearing the opinions and justifications of the "other subjects."

Cohesion was also manipulated in the same manner in both experiments. When subjects arrived for the experiment, they were assigned to either group *A* or group *B*. Cohesion was manipulated by what they were told about the two groups. In Walker's and Heyns's words:

> They were told that the members of Group A had been selected from persons whose past record indicated that they would be particularly competent and should be able to do well at this type of task. They were also told that the two groups would be given slightly different tasks to

work on in view of the different competence of the two groups. They were also told that some persons from Group A might be moved down to Group B and some persons from Group B might be promoted to Group A (p. 33).

In this way, those assigned to group *A* found themselves in a highly attractive group (high cohesion condition) while those assigned to group *B* found themselves in a less desirable group (low cohesion condition).

In the first experiment, subjects were assigned either to group *A* or group *B* and given the instructions described above. The investigators found in comparing the two conditions that there was no difference in the number of subjects who conformed to the "group" opinion. In the second experiment some additional instructions were added. The subjects were told that it was common knowledge that persons liked one another better and got along better when they agreed about common problems. To emphasize the point more, the investigators had each subject rate his liking for each of the "other subjects" (i.e., the voices) and rate how well he thought the others liked him. In this case more subjects in the high cohesion groups conformed than those in the low cohesion groups. The investigators concluded: "If conformity is seen as being instrumental to being liked, then the expectations that the more attractive a group the more cohesive the group, and the more cohesive the group the more pressures toward uniformity or conformity, tend to be fulfilled (p. 40)."

Conformity in highly cohesive groups then is not automatic. It comes about when members are aware of other members' expectations that they conform. The theory and research reviewed in this section show that such expectations are likely to arise in cohesive groups, but these must be expressed before conformity on some issues will actually occur.

Cohesion Based on Instrumental Interdependence

So far in this chapter, we have emphasized the relationship between the emergence of norms and cohesiveness where the latter variable has involved the measurement of interpersonal attractiveness in groups or its manipulation (in experimental groups). However, as we showed in Chapter 2, interpersonal attraction or social interdependence is only one source of cohesiveness in groups. Members may be attracted to a group to attain goals other than the rewards of merely interacting with other members. When groups become cohesive for these reasons, we say that they are based upon instrumental interdependence. Fortunately, Festinger, Schachter and Back's theory can also be applied to groups where members become interdependent to achieve some external group goals (instrumental interdependence). More specifically, if uniformity of behavior or opinions is necessary for members of a group to attain a group goal, we can predict that members would be more willing to conform. That this is the case is shown in a study by Deutsch and Gerard (1955). They told some of their subjects in an Asch-type situation that their group (the subject plus the confederates) was competing with other groups and that the members of the best group would receive tickets to a Broadway play (group condition). The idea behind these instructions was to make the subjects feel as if they were a part of a group and interdependent upon others to reach the goal. Other subjects (a control condition) were given no special instructions. The investigators found that conformity was higher in the group condition, even with no pressure to conform being exerted.

In comparison with Rotter's experiment, the subjects in Deutsch and Gerard's experiment were more likely to be aware that conforming behavior was expected by other members. Berkowitz (1957) has shown that subjects given instructions similar to those given in the group condition of Deutsch and Gerard's study performed a task more efficiently than those not given these instructions. According to Berkowitz, members of the highly interdependent groups were motivated to conform to whatever expectation was necessary to perform the task and win the reward. Likewise, in the Deutsch and Gerard experiment, subjects in the group condition must have been motivated to help them reach the goal. When confronted with overwhelming evidence that their own answers were at odds with those of the other group members, the subjects most likely saw that giving the majority answer (i.e., conforming) would be the best way to help the group reach its goal. A study by Berkowitz and Howard (1959) also provides evidence that instrumental interdependence exerts the same pressures toward uniformity as social interdependence.

Similarity Also Leads to Attraction

So far the evidence shows that pressures toward uniformity and the formation of norms result from group cohesiveness. But what conditions facilitate the development of cohesion? A study by Newcomb, *The Acquaintance Process* (1960), provides some answers to this question. To carry out his study, Newcomb arranged to have a number of students who were transferring to the University of Michigan live together in a cooperative housing unit. By living in the cooperative, the students could save a good deal of money in exchange for being subjects in a year-long study of social relationships. Transfer students were used to ensure that the subjects were not acquainted with one another before their arrival at the house. The study was carried out for two years with two different groups of subjects each year.

Before the subjects arrived on campus, they were asked to fill out questionnaires that measured a wide range of attitudes and values. At the end of the first week and at various times throughout the academic year, subjects were asked to provide information concerning their attraction to others in the house. The analysis of the data gathered over the two years is complex, but we can summarize the most relevant findings. During the early weeks of the study, Newcomb found that the subjects were attracted to those living near them in the house (e.g., roommates). However, as the study progressed, Newcomb found evidence that pairs of subjects came to be attracted to one another on the basis of similarity. Not only were those who gave similar answers on the earlier tests attracted to one another, but dyads of subjects who agreed on their attraction to other subjects were also highly attracted to one another. While one study (Curry and Emerson, 1970) that used dorm students failed to replicate Newcomb's results, Griffitt and Veitch (1974) were able to replicate it, using subjects living in a fall-out shelter.

Newcomb's study suggests that similarity on several dimensions provides a basis for the development of interpersonal attraction. A series of experiments by Byrne (1971) has consistently demonstrated that this can occur. A typical experiment involved exposing subjects to information about a hypothetical person who they were told would work with them on a task. Some of the subjects received information that made the hypothetical partner seem very similar to them on certain issues. Other subjects received information that indicated dissimilarity with the mythical partner. On a variety of attraction scales, the "similar persons" were rated by the subjects as more attractive than the "dissimilar persons."

Festinger and his associates (1950) did not determine why some courts in Westgate were more cohesive than others. But, based upon Newcomb's and Byrne's studies, we can predict that the residents assigned to courts that eventually became cohesive were in some way more similar than those which did not. For example, the members of a highly cohesive court may have all liked outdoor barbeques, which led to the institution of Sunday cook-outs in the central courtyard, which in turn led to interaction among members and high cohesion.

This process could go even further, because the formation of norms entails similarity among members. The existence of group norms could lead to the development of even greater cohesiveness. For example, the emergence of similar orientations toward the tenant organization could have contributed to the cohesiveness of the already highly cohesive courts and perhaps to greater solidarity on other dimensions as well. How far this could go depends upon the strength of anomic forces. But one can imagine that a court whose members were uniformly for or against the tenant organization might meet to make plans to carry out political action of some sort. The formation of goals could increase the feelings of belonging to a court and perhaps to the formation of highly defined statuses (i.e., president, secretary, treasurer) to help coordinate the group's actions. All of this would contribute to group solidarity.

To conclude, a diagram of the processes discussed in this chapter, along with Homans's conception of standardization is provided in Figure 4.4. Cohesion is seen as leading to interaction. During interaction, group members may attempt to influence one another, some eventually conform, and a group norm emerges. The existence of this norm means that members are similar in behavior or

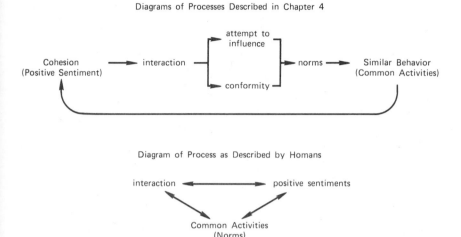

Figure 4.4. Two conceptions of standardization.

opinions, which contributes to cohesion. Homans discussed standardization in terms of his three elements; but if we substitute "cohesion" for sentiments, and "norm" (or "similarity") for activities (i.e., common activities), the two diagrams become very similar. Homans saw interaction and positive sentiment as being interlinked, and therefore an increase in either leads to common activities. Since all relationships between the elements are mutual, the development of common activities contributes to the further development of interaction and sentiments (i.e., cohesion).

NORMS AS A REACTION AGAINST THE FORCES TOWARD ANOMIE

Thibaut and Kelley's Theory

To develop the argument behind this approach to norms, we shall return to Thibaut and Kelley's (1959) theory. It will be remembered that they viewed interaction as involving maneuvers between two participants who were dependent upon one another in order that each could increase his own payoffs. When participants settle on a pattern of interaction where both can maximize their payoffs, a stable relationship will result. However, even in fairly stable relationships both participants will not always be able to simultaneously maximize their payoffs. Conflicts will enter the relationship whenever the most attractive behavioral alternative of one is not consistent with that of the other. How this is prevented is an essential element of Thibaut and Kelley's theory. To discuss this problem, they introduce the example of a husband and wife who cannot agree on the evening's activity. The husband wants to go to the movies while the wife wants to go dancing; the outcomes that yield high rewards for these two persons are in conflict. The matrix for this situation is shown on the left hand side in Figure 4.5. According to this matrix the wife can receive full satisfaction from dancing only when her husband accompanies her, and the husband receives full satisfaction only when he is accompanied by his wife to the movies. Each is dependent upon the other and each has control over the other's rewards. One can imagine that this would lead to a great deal of bickering and fighting every time a weekend draws near, and the couple could conceivably spend many nights at home if each was reluctant to give into the other.

Situations where favored outcomes are in conflict and participants spend much time engaged in unpleasant interaction foster the development of social norms. Thibaut and Kelley define a norm as a "behavioral rule that is accepted, at least to some degree, by both members of the dyad" (p. 129). According to them, a norm substitutes for (and cuts down the costs of) maneuvering, for attempts to influence, and for bargaining between the interaction participants. If a norm were to emerge in the situation depicted in the matrix under consideration, it would be manifested in several ways. First, we would expect to find a regular pattern of behavior that would allow both participants to receive high outcomes. For instance, the couple may compromise so that one weekend they go dancing and the next they go to the cinema. Second, neither person should try to influence the events that are to occur on any given weekend. Third, if a norm is in existence, neither would refer to their agreement while things were running smoothly. However, if one of the partners refused to adhere to the norm, the other would probably mention "our agreement" and the fact that the other was not comforming. Finally, the guilty party would behave in ways that indicated his recognition of the norm. This might be manifested either in showing guilt or conflict or by succumbing to the other's plea for continued conformity to the norm.

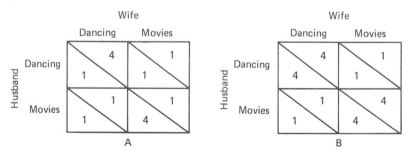

Figure 4.5. Matrix showing conditions of norm formation. (Adapted from Thibaut and Kelley, 1959, p. 127, 137.)

It should not be implied from this that the members of a dyad would sit down together and consciously work out the details of the various norms which pertain to their relationship. Rather, according to Thibaut and Kelley, norms develop through a process of trial-and-error learning:

> This process could be described in reinforcement learning terms: the pair are reinforced when they adhere to a given rule because it cuts cost, increases dependability of rewards, or in general makes the situation more predictable and comfortable. Thus, they learn to follow it consistently (p. 141).

If the married couple in the example begin to realize that their outcomes are in conflict and attempt to influence each other to engage in compatible behavior, the outcomes themselves will change. For instance, the husband may not find going to the movies as desirable if he must struggle to get his wife to go along. In other words, the *costs* of these activities begin to counteract the rewards. If some sort of agreement in the form of a norm begins to emerge, then engaging in activities that are consistent with the norm becomes more rewarding. Thus, we find that the outcomes would change from that pictured in the matrix on the left to that shown on the right (Figure 4.5).

It probably is not by chance that Thibaut and Kelley picked a married couple to illustrate the formation of norms as a substitute for influence. Although they do not mention this, it does seem that nonvoluntary dyads are most likely to develop norms of this type. This is the case for married couples. If the husband decides to seek high rewards by accompanying another woman to the movies, he may not find his wife at home when he returns. No matter how much he likes going to the movies, he may not be willing to pay the cost, and he will thus be more willing to adhere to a compromising norm. On the other hand, in dyads where the participants are more free to seek rewards elsewhere, a conflict such as that faced by the married couple would probably terminate interaction between them. However, even among voluntary dyads there will be situations where the outcomes of the two are not congruent and where for the various reasons they cannot or do not wish to find alternative rewards elsewhere. In these cases, norms will emerge in the fashion outlined by this theory.

Thibaut and Kelley conceive of individuals in interaction as being confronted with mixed motives. In the terms which we have been using we can say that participants in interaction can adopt both interdependent and individualistic orientations. To the extent that members can maximize their payoffs by interacting with one another, the stronger will be the interdependent orientations. However, all participants in social relationships will reach points where payoffs may be greater elsewhere and individualistic orientations may prevail. In the example of the married couple, each participant's highest payoff was to be gained through activities that were potentially disruptive to the solidarity of the existing relationship. In other words, the emergence of the norm stating "when we will go dancing and when we will go to the movies" was a means of preventing the mutual adoption of individualistic orientations and the threat of conflict and disruption.

Some Empirical Evidence

The development of norms under these conditions can be seen in an experiment by Bonacich (1973). In his experiment, Bonacich assembled five-person groups to play a series of five games. The subjects were told that during each game they would have the opportunity to give the other players a certain amount of money and that this money would be worth more to the recipients than to the giver. Thus, in each game the subjects were faced with the alternative of *giving* or *keeping*. *Giving* in the game was the equivalent of assuming an interdependent orientation and *keeping* entailed adopting an individualistic orientation. All players began with a certain amount of money.

In order to explain the game, we will look at the rules: although these rules changed from game to game, depending upon the experimental condition, the groups in both conditions started with the same rules. The members of each group could *give* 1¢ to each person. Since there were four others, if a member chose to *give*, he would lose 4¢. If he chose to *keep* he would save 4¢. However, as in social relationships, a subject's final gain depended on the behavior of the other members. If they all chose to *give*, he would receive 1¢ from each. But according to the rules, 25¢ was added to every 1¢ he received. Therefore, if all of the others *gave*, a subject would receive 4 (1¢ + 25¢) or $1.04. If all *gave*, except the subject in question, he would earn $1.08 because he would *keep* his 4¢. If he *gave* along with all of the others, he would earn $1.00 since his original 4¢ would be subtracted from what he received. Of course the larger the number of other subjects who chose to *keep*, the smaller the subject's gain, regardless of whether he chose to *keep* or *give*.

Thus, the game was set up so that subjects maximized their gain when others *gave* but they also enjoyed a slight advantage when they themselves chose to *keep*. The best situation for any subject would be if all others chose to *give* while he *kept*. But numerous studies utilizing similar situations have shown that once one person adopts an individualistic orientation (like *keeping* in this game), all others will adopt the same response. What generally happens is that subjects learn that it is to their advantage to settle on a interdependent-oriented strategy. In this way all members gain in the long run even if the gains are moderate in comparison with what a single member might attain through assuming an individualistic orientation. Generally, research of this type utilizes dyads in a formal bargaining situation (Thibaut and Faucheux, 1965). Bonacich, however, wanted to see whether the same results would occur in larger groups and in groups where members had the chance to engage in informal interaction with one another.

As the subjects moved from Game 1 to Game 5, Bonacich increased the gains if subjects elected to keep and not give. In the low dilemma condition, these increases were slight. In the high dilemma condition, the increases were large; by the fifth and final game, a subject could earn up to $17.00 by keeping, depending on what the other subjects chose to do. Obviously, the temptation to keep was very high in this latter condition.

After a while, however, the members developed among themselves certain practices such as sharing nonsales tasks and taking turns waiting on customers. These practices effectively solved the social-emotional problems that had arisen because of the need to compete for high commissions. While these practices, and the expectations that they be adhered to by group members, evolved informally in the group, they later were accepted by management and became formal policy.

Because of the temptation not to adopt interdependent orientations, the members of the high dilemma groups, when interacting with each other, were faced with difficult social-emotional problems. Bonacich hypothesized that the members of these groups would spend more time discussing the game and would show more interest in the experiment than the low dilemma groups. The results confirmed this hypothesis. There was no way in which individualistic responses could be sanctioned, because the members did not know who had or had not chosen to keep. However, if members spoke negatively of "keepers" in the discussion, this would be an indication that they were attempting to establish norms to restrict "keeping." The results showed that such negative terms were used more often in the discussions held by the high dilemma groups. Subjects in the high dilemma condition were also more apt to use words like "fink," "liar," and "selfish" to describe "keepers" on questionnaires administered at the end of the study than were subjects in the low dilemma condition. Finally, Bonacich reasoned that when members of a group, like those in the high dilemma situation, resist the temptation to seek high rewards at the expense of others, there should be feelings of friendliness and solidarity. Since the temptations were greater in the high dilemma conditions, he predicted that friendliness would be higher in these groups. The results show that the members of these groups rated their groups as being more friendly than did those in the low dilemma groups.

Bonacich's groups did not stay together long and therefore norms were not fully developed. However, the evidence shows that the expectations concerning appropriate behavior (i.e., giving) were developing in those groups where forces toward anomie was greatest. Furthermore there was evidence that these groups were beginning to develop along some of the other dimensions of solidarity. In order to understand these results, the total situation must be understood. If these subjects had been assigned to separate rooms and never allowed to see one another, there is every reason to believe that the "keep" strategy would have prevailed. But because the members were brought together and told to discuss whatever they wanted, the temptations of the high rewards to be gained through "keeping" became a social-emotional problem for the group. It is not easy to be selfish and compete against others when you must face them in group discussions. Thus, the temptation to "keep" became an anomic force because there were also some forces toward solidarity as well. In other words, the anomic orientations become social-emotional problems to be dealt with by the group members. The emergence of norms, then, may be seen as a device by which the subjects solved their social-emotional problems which stemmed from the forces toward anomie set up by the experimenter.

A study by Babchuck and Goode (1951) provides a final example of norms that arose in reaction to an increase in forces toward anomie caused by changes in the environment. This study reports on a group of salesmen in a department store. Because the men were experienced and management did not want to lose them to higher paying defense jobs, the salesmen were offered a new wage system that enabled them to increase their salaries. Under the old system, each salesman was given a base wage plus a 1 percent commission on his sales. Under the new system each man could continue under the old plan or work for a straight 6 percent commission. Given the choice, all the salesmen felt they had to choose the straight commission because this offered them the opportunity to make the most money. However, soon after the switch, existing informal relationships became disrupted by such competitive practices as "sales grabbing," where the salesmen would actively compete for customers, and "high-pressure selling." The interpersonal relationships among the salesmen became strained and often erupted in antagonism. Although the salesmen reported to the investigators that they were unhappy with this system, they all felt that they had to continue competing.

After a while, however, the members developed among themselves certain practices such as sharing nonsales tasks and taking turns waiting on customers. These practices effectively solved the social-emotional problems that had arisen because of the need to compete for high commissions. While these practices, and the expectations that they be adhered to by group members, evolved informally in the group, they later were accepted by management and became formal policy.

SOME CONCLUDING COMMENTS

In reading the studies reviewed in the first segment of this chapter, one gets the impression that norms arise more or less naturally whenever two or more individuals interact with one another. In the second segment, however, the emergence of norms is portrayed as something that must be worked at by group members. It must be kept in mind then, that the two sets of literature are dealing with norms which emerge under different circumstances.

Where norms emerge out of the forces toward solidarity, members conform because of their attraction to the group and their desire for interdependent relations with the other members. Norms emerging as reactions to anomic forces are more or less consciously established to inhibit individualistic orientations. Because members remain tempted not to conform, norms of this type must constantly be restated through attempts to influence and negative sanctioning.

In the case of norms that stem from forces toward anomie, the behavioral alternatives facing the individual are clear-cut; one either restricts productivity or one does not, one either "keeps" or "gives," one either competes for customers or one does not. It is easy to understand from the group's environment why a particular norm emerged. For the other type of norms this is not so. The clique members in the bank wiring room who customarily ate expensive candy together could have easily agreed upon some type of candy, some other food, or even some other activity altogether. Similarly in the MIT study, there was nothing about the situations confronting the different Westgate courts that enabled the investigators to explain why certain courts developed the particular standards which they did. The "content" of such norms cannot be understood as a direct reaction to a particular situation, but only through tracing the history of interaction in the group.

Although we have spoken of two types of norms, the differences seem to be more of degree than kind. Any group is faced with both forces toward solidarity and forces toward anomie, and any particular norm is not in reality the result of one or the other of these forces alone. The conflict facing the couple in Thibaut and Kelley's example was problematic only because they both had to consider how anomic responses would affect the solidarity of their marriage. Bonacich's subjects were put in a situation where they had to interact face-to-face with people whom they were tempted to deprive of rewards by adopting a "keep" strategy. The salesmen in Babchuck and Goode's study had already developed satisfying social relationships with one another which were threatened by changes in the method of payment. In all cases, the members were also confronted with forces toward solidarity, which is why they were under pressure to solve the social-emotional problems caused by the forces toward anomie.

The norms that result primarily from forces toward solidarity are also responses to existing (or potential) anomic forces. For instance, if the interdependence in a group is based upon members' attractions to each other, and holding a particular opinion (or eating a particular type of candy) is considered by most to be a part of that attractiveness, there will be pressures toward the formation of a norm of this nature. In such cases, there is no immediate threat to the group, but still the norm structures the members' behavior so as to avoid the social-emotional difficulties which Bales says is inherent in any group situation.

Finally, it should be mentioned that the processes observed by Festinger and his colleagues and the subsequent experimenters are also at work when norms are primarily reactions to anomic forces. What Thibaut and Kelley call the "development of norms through bargaining" involves the "attempts to influence" and "conforming" described by Festinger *et al.* The processes are similar, but when forces toward anomie are prevalent they involve more conscious effort and more conflict than when forces toward solidarity prevail.

SUMMARY

This chapter reviews studies that conceive of norms as developing from two different sources. The first are norms that stem from forces toward solidarity; they are a natural result of interaction among members who have assumed interdependence orientations toward one another. Conformity to such norms is an expression of the member's attraction to the group. Norms of the second kind have their primary source in reactions to forces toward anomie. These norms are the result of implicit bargaining processes in which members agree not to adopt individualistic orientation toward one another. When a member conforms in such situations, he does so in exchange for the assurance that his interests are not threatened.

In our discussion of norms having their source in forces toward solidarity, we provided evidence that groups whose members are attracted to one another manifest strong pressures toward uniformity. That is, in highly cohesive groups, homogeneity is sought either through processes of mutual persuasion and influence, by negatively sanctioning deviants, or by rejecting them from the group. These studies show that norms are most likely to emerge in groups whose members are already interdependent upon one another. This interdependence may be either social or instrumental. We also showed that homogeneity on certain important dimensions can also lead to cohesiveness, which can contribute to further uniformity.

Those studies which treat norms as reactions to forces toward anomie deal primarily with situations where group members are strongly tempted to seek rewards in a manner that causes social-emotional difficulties. Thibaut and Kelley said that members must bargain with one another in order to establish some procedure where all parties gain more than they lose. The results of Bonacich's research also show that subjects are inclined to form norms in this manner.

five

Differentiation within Informal Groups

As was the case with standardization, researchers interested in differentiation have taken two different approaches. Some view status structures emerging naturally as a result of forces toward solidarity. Others view status structures as being established so that group members can neutralize what we have called forces toward anomie. Thus, we shall treat each approach separately, as we did with norms in the previous chapter.

Differentiation is the process whereby individual members or subgroups of members of informal groups come to behave differently from one another. Differentiation does not give rise to random differences in behavior but to differences that persist through time and are interconnected to some extent in an organized way. In other words, differentiation is the development of a status structure, and since most social scientists conceive of statuses as being the basic elements of social organization, we shall examine the emergence of statuses in informal groups.

In Chapter Three we said that statuses consisted of common expectations about the behavior of each member. Although this is a typical way of thinking about statuses, expectations are not observable or directly measurable. There are two main ways an observer might learn about the status structure of informal groups. The first is to notice consistent differences in the behavior of the various members. If these differences persist, it can be assumed that the other members are aware of, expect, or condone them. The second method consists of asking members about their expectations. In most cases, however, social scientists have not directly asked such questions as, "How do you expect person A to act?";

or "How will you behave in the group tomorrow?" Generally, the method used is similar to Bales's, where members are asked to rank or rate each other on a series of behavioral characteristics. When a member is ranked high for furnishing good ideas or providing guidance, it is assumed that he will most likely do this in the future as well; and therefore the behavior described is a part of his status in the group. However, observers will find more consistency in the behavior of members in some groups than in others, and the members of some groups will agree more about their ratings of individuals than will the members of other groups. That is, the status structure of groups will vary depending on how clearly it is defined.

Despite the fact that much research has been done with various aspects of differentiation, the literature remains confusing. In part, this has to do with the fact that studies have been carried out in different settings and are therefore difficult to compare. Another reason for the confusion is that various researchers study groups at different phases of development. The social structure of a newly formed group will certainly be different from one that has existed for a relatively long period. Our discussion of differentiation will trace how a stable social structure forms in most groups. We have selected those studies which provide the most information about groups *in general*—that is, those that best illustrate how differentiation occurs in all groups regardless of the type of group or the environment within which it has formed. Since differentiation involves the formation of statuses, and statuses are comprised of expectations, we will focus on the development of expectations.

STATUS STRUCTURE AS A RESULT OF FORCES TOWARD SOLIDARITY

As with the emergence of norms, some studies on emergent status structures consider them to be the result of the members' search for consensus and of a common definition of the situation. In these cases, the expectations that emerge to form a status structure seem to flow naturally from the interaction whenever individuals form interdependent relationships. These status expectations are primarily the result of forces toward solidarity working within the group.

External Status Characteristics

We can begin by looking at a study by Fisek and Ofshe (1970), who observed three-man discussion groups working in a situation like that used by Bales. We know from Bales's work that individuals who theoretically are equals at the beginning of an experimental session do not end up as equals. By the end of the session members are differentiated according to their participation rank, which in turn is related to how they are ranked in terms of "best ideas" and "liking." But Fisek and Ofshe found that in about half of the groups they observed, stable differences in participation were determined in the first minutes of the discussion. That is, in these initially differentiated groups one could predict who would have the first, second, and third highest contributions to the discussion at the end of the session by looking at the rank order in the first minutes. This early rank order was also related to rank order on "best ideas," "guidance," and "ability" at the end of the session. In the remaining groups (initially undifferentiated), participation during the first minutes of the session was almost identical for all three members. Although differentiation in participation levels evolved over time, it was never as great as that found in the initially differentiated groups. At various times throughout the session the person who ended up with the highest overall participation level ranked below those who ended up with lower overall rates of participation, and vice versa. Fisek and Ofshe also showed that the relationship between participation and the various status rankings found for the initially differentiated group was not found in the undifferentiated groups. The initially undifferentiated groups are, in some ways, similar to the low status consensus groups in Heinecke and Bales's study (see p. 70). It will be recalled that the low status consensus groups in their study were scenes of status struggles and that from the beginning members could not agree on status evaluations. The initially undifferentiated groups in Fisek and Ofshe's study also showed evidence of status struggles, and the fact that participation was uncorrelated with the status evaluations indicates that there was a lack of status consensus in these groups.

All of this suggests that whether or not discussion groups have social-emotional difficulties depends, in part, upon the characteristics of the individuals in the groups. If, for whatever reason, they initially come to some understanding (perhaps not consciously) about the status order in the group, the members are spared certain social-emotional difficulties. The initial status hierarchy provides the members with a structure with which to go about the business of solving the problems presented by the task. If this structure does not jell immediately, the group must constantly deal with the various social-emotional and instrumental problems at hand. Groups of this sort would be faced from the start with the various forces toward anomie discussed in the last chapter. This study suggests that the individual members bring to the group certain characteristics that enable members to assess and evaluate one another, and these characteristics determine their behavior toward one another. If the right combination of individual characteristics is present in a group, differentiation occurs from the start. If the proper combination is missing, differentiation will develop with difficulty.

Think for a moment of what occurs in those awkward moments when you are compelled by circumstances to speak to a person you have never met before. We can imagine such an interchange, for instance, as occurring between two strangers who have signed up for the same six-week tour of Europe. More than likely the conversation would begin with the strangers asking each other a series of questions. One of the first questions to be asked in such situations, especially among men, is: "What do you do?" If the two found out that they were both doctors, it can be predicted that they would be pretty likely to form a stable relationship for the remainder of the tour. On the other hand, if it were determined that one was a doctor and the other a janitor, we would predict that the conversation would be rather strained and that the two would not be likely to seek each other out for continued interaction. If they did, or if they were compelled to continue interacting, we can bet that the nature of their relationship would differ from that between two doctors or between two janitors. Other differences such as those of social class and ethnic background, as well as the obvious status differences of age and sex, would also affect the nature of such relationships.

Although our example used only two persons, they do point out the importance of what social scientists call *external status characteristics* as they influence newly forming relationships such as those which occur in informal groups. By external status characteristics we refer to the cues that one carries with one concerning one's statuses in social systems other than the group under consideration. Factors such as sex, age, occupation, and ethnic background can have some bearing on how members of informal groups behave once they get together and are often responsible for the initial structuring of statuses when groups are beginning to form. In the absence of experience, members rely heavily upon cues such as external status characteristics to help them coordinate their interaction with one another. When there is no other basis for forming expectations about others, external status characteristics of members help to provide this information.

The importance of external status characteristics is clearly shown in a series of studies reported by and carried out under the supervision of Berger, Cohen, and Zelditch (1974). In one such study by Moore (1968), two subjects who were placed so they could not see each other were shown a series of rectangles made up of smaller black and white rectangles. They were to decide whether there were more black or white rectangles: a difficult task since the numbers were approximately equal. First the subjects answered by pressing buttons in front of them. Subjects then "communicated" their answer to one another through a system of buttons and lights and then gave a final answer. They were told that getting advice from others was necessary and legitimate and that the goal was to make their final choice the correct one. The communication between subjects was, in fact, manipulated by the experimenter so that the subjects thought that the other person disagreed with them on a given number of problems. This enabled the experimenter to determine whether subjects changed their initial answers after seeing that their partners disagreed with them.

In this experiment the subjects were all junior college students. Some of them were told that the subject working with them was from a nearby high school. In this condition subjects thought they held the highest external status. The rest of the subjects were led to believe that the other participants were from Stanford University and therefore they felt that they were lowest in external status characteristics. In addition, half the subjects who thought their partners were high school students were specifically told that junior college students generally performed better than high school students. The other half was told nothing in this regard. Likewise, half of those who thought they had a Stanford student for a partner were told that Stanford students traditionally did better on the task. The rest of the subjects in this condition did not hear these instructions. Moore found that the subjects who were led to believe that their partner was of higher external status (i.e., a Stanford student) changed their answer more often than those who thought that they were the ones with the highest external status. This was true whether or not the subjects were led to believe that Stanford students consistently performed better.

Differences in status rank involves differences in power, which are manifested in informal groups whenever one person is observed to consistently influence the behavior of another. The fact that subjects in one experimental condition of Moore's experiment allowed themselves to be influenced more often, suggests that these subjects would, if interacting within a real group, be relegated to a low-ranking status over time. The only difference between those who did and did not allow themselves to be influenced was the nature of the information they received about their educational status relative to that of their partners. As Berger, Cohen, and Zelditch (1974) explain it, the knowledge about the external status characteristics sets up, for the subjects, expectations (anticipations) about their own performance and that of their partners on the experimental task. Even when the subjects were given no specific information by the experimenter that would lead them to expect educational position to be related to performance, these expectations were clearly at work.

An interesting study by Strodtbeck, Jones, and Hawkins (1957) provides more information that is consistent with this interpretation. Choosing subjects from jury pools, the investigators set up mock juries by having the subjects listen to the tape recording of an actual trial and then deliberate as if they were a real jury. This allowed the investigator to observe the group's social processes, something which could not be done with real juries. The major variables of interest were participation rates of members, the degree to which members were influential in the discussion or were influenced by the discussion, and how members evaluated one another. The major aim of the study was to determine how these factors differed depending upon the sex of the subject and his occupational position—proprietor, clerical worker, skilled worker, or laborer.

One of the first events that occurs when juries meet is electing a foreman. The fact that subjects classified as proprietors were most likely to be chosen foremen is indicative of the results of this study; so too is the fact that women were clearly underrepresented as foremen. For instance, Strodtbeck and his associates found that the higher the occupational status of a member (male or female) the greater the likelihood that he would participate highly throughout the deliberation. When they compared men and women having the same occupational status, they found that men always had the highest rate of participation.

The investigators had each subject indicate how he or she would decide the case before the group actually met. This enabled them to determine who shifted their answers after getting involved in the group discussion. It was found that the least active participators, who also tended to be those with lowest external status characteristics, were most likely to be influenced. Those subjects in the highest-ranking occupations had the most agreement between their predeliberated choices and the groups' final recommendations. This suggests, as did Moore's study, that those who have relatively low external status in groups look to the high status members for advice on relevant issues.

Another approach to examining the effects of external status on differentiation was taken by the investigators when they asked members to indicate at the end of the session who contributed most to helping the group reach its decisions. This question was designed to measure pretty much the same thing as Bales's "best ideas" questions, but was worded to determine who the members perceived as having the most influence in the group. As in the case of "best ideas" in Bales's research, subjects in this study who were high participators were most likely to be named as "helping." Furthermore, the data clearly show that the average number of votes received was lowest for laborers and consistently increased for each occupational group, with proprietors receiving the highest number of votes. As with the differences in participation rates and votes for foreman, men were designated as being "helpful" more often than women. Commenting on the findings the investigators state:

> . . . We assume that the business discipline and related experience of higher status occupations involve both substantive knowledge and interactional skills that may be used during the deliberations. Hence, in the competition for available deliberation time, higher status males may rise to prominence because their comments are perceived to have greater value. On the other hand, since the cues of status—dress, speech, and casual references to experiences—are easily read, the differentiation may in part be explained by these expectations instead of actual performance (p. 718).

Clearly external status characteristics determine group processes. But some further evidence provided by Strodtbeck suggests that this effect may wear off as the group meets over time. The responses to one other question given at the end of the session is of interest. The subjects were asked to choose "four of your fellow jurors whom you would best like to have serve on a jury if you were on trial." While there was still a tendency for those of high occupational status to be chosen, it was not as clear-cut as in previous cases. It appears that on the basis of actual experience together members began to respond to the characteristics each person actually possessed rather than to stereotyped expectations associated with their external statuses. That is to say, while the expectations that are based upon external status characteristics may be important in structuring group inter-action during the formative stages, they may dwindle over time as members learn more about one another.

Some additional evidence that this is so comes from an experiment by Freese and Cohen (1973). They used an experimental setup similar to that used by Moore (1968), described above. As in Moore's study, the subjects received infor-mation about whether they were higher or lower than their partners on an ex-ternal status characteristic. But they were also given information about how they and their partners had scored on a paper and pencil test that supposedly mea-sured the subjects' abilities. Some subjects were led to believe that they were high or low on the external status characteristic relative to their partners. Other subjects were led to believe that they scored relatively high or low on the ability test. Still other subjects were given information about their standing on both the external status and the ability test. The idea was to determine which of these factors most affected the subject's tendency to yield when they were in disagree-ment with their partners.

Freese and Cohen found, in support of Moore's study, that subjects who be-lieved that they were low on the external status characteristic yielded more frequently than those who were told they were high. The investigators also found that the subjects who were told that they scored low on the ability test yielded more frequently than the high scorers. Of importance here is the finding that among those subjects given information about both external status charac-teristics and past performances, yielding was influenced more by whether the subject had a relatively high or low test score than by his standing on the ex-ternal status characteristic. That is, if a subject had information about his own and his partner's past performance, knowledge about their external status characteristics made little difference. These results reinforce what we have said before: external status characteristics are most important when members have little information about one another's competence or skill in various areas. Generally this would be during the early stages of group development.

In the Freese and Cohen study the subjects were not told that there was any necessary connection between performances on the ability test and the experi-mental task. In most groups, however, when members reach the stage where they begin to assess each other, they gain information about those abilities considered to be important in the group. Therefore, we would expect that external status characteristics become even less relevant as determinants of differentiation when members are directly evaluating one another's performances on abilities which the members consider to be important. This situation is certainly found in dis-cussion groups where members can constantly evaluate the importance and usefulness of everything that everyone says. If a member who has participated little begins to make useful contributions to the task, other members will antic-ipate that he will do the same in the future. They may be more willing to listen to him and therefore will give him more of an opportunity to make contributions in the future. If his contributions continue, it may even reach the point where members expect him to speak and provide good ideas.

Evidence that something like the above can occur is nicely demonstrated in a study by Bavelas *et al* (1965). In their study, four-man groups were observed in a situation similar to that used by Bales. The only difference was that in front of each subject was a piece of equipment with a red and a green light. The box was designed so that only the subject who sat in front of the box could see the lights. The subjects were given a case study to discuss for a ten-minute period. After this discussion they were asked to rank each other in terms of: (1) amount of participation; (2) quality of ideas; (3) guidance and leadership. Before a second discussion, half of the groups (the experimental groups) were told that the observers would flash green lights to subjects when their contributions were helpful to the discussion and red when they hindered the discussion. The remaining groups (control groups) were told that they would not receive any feedback *via* the lights. Unbeknownst to the subjects in the experimental groups, the investigators selected the third or fourth ranked participator in the first discussion as a target person. During the second discussion the target person was shown green lights whenever he spoke while all others were shown red lights when they spoke. After this second session the subjects again filled out a sociometric type questionnaire. The results showed that both the rate of participation and the rankings received from others on the various sociometric questions increased significantly for the target person from the first to the second discussion. Subjects in the control groups were ranked at the end of the second session in about the same order that they were ranked at the end of the first session.

This experiment clearly shows how a member's performance in the group influences the status structure of that group. In this case reward and punishment came from outside the group; however, in most groups, members, through their reactions to one another, encourage or discourage participation of certain kinds and even participation in general. This, of course, may take time, but certainly the same techniques of reinforcement, in more subtle forms, are at work in affecting the process of differentiation in groups.

So far we have shown that when individuals begin to interact with one another they behave differently and form expectations accordingly. In some cases these expectations may be associated with external status characteristics. To the extent that these expectations guide the behavior of all individuals present, there will be a minimum of social-emotional problems such as "who should do what," "who can tell who what to do," and so on. If external status characteristics become less important over time or if they are not clearly defined, the members will have to resolve such problems through their interaction experiences such as competition, conflict, and status struggles. Whether this occurs or not, newly developed expectations will be based upon the actual observed behavior of the members instead of upon deductions derived from external status characteristics, and these expectations will form the basis of the emergent status structure.

Status Consensus and Status Congruence

Statuses consist of expectations for behavior which are evaluated differently by group members. The members' agreement on evaluations such as "who has the best ideas" indicates that they hold certain common expectations about one another's behavior in the group. These expectations may vary from anticipations to ought expectations, depending upon the type of group and the degree of development, but the fact that there is some agreement should mean that social-emotional problems will be held to a minimum. Recall that Heinecke and Bales (1953) found satisfaction and efficiency to be higher in groups with relatively high status consensus (p. 122). Also, Shelly (1960) found that members of girls' clubs that had high agreement on first choice for leaders were more satisfied with their clubs than those with low agreement on leadership choice.

Even though social scientists refer to an agreement among group members on rankings on some dimension as status consensus, a person's rank does not constitute his status as we have defined the term. A person's status is comprised of expectations, and his rank on some dimension ("best ideas," for example) only indicates that other members have a common idea as to the quality of his ideas and how he will or should behave in the future. There may well be other expectations not associated with the contribution of ideas that also contribute to the definition of a member's status in the group. To determine these expectations, a researcher might ask group members to rank order each other on several dimensions, as did Bales and his associates when they asked for ranks on "guidance," "best ideas," and "best liked." Dimensions such as these may be called *internal status characteristics,* since a member's rank depends upon the other members' perception of his behavior in the group, rather than upon his status in an outside group.

A number of researchers have obtained information on both internal and external status characteristics. In general, these investigators have been interested in determining the extent to which members' positions on various dimensions are consistent or congruent. When members are consistent across all dimensions (consistently high, low, or medium), the group is said to be high on *status congruence.* However, there is a problem of definition: the term "status congruence" as used in the literature implies that there is consistency among various statuses in the group. But members have only one status in a particular group. What status congruence means, then, is that there is consistency across several objective dimensions that provide information about certain aspects of the member's status. Another way of putting it is to say that status congruence occurs when members hold consistent positions on several external and internal status characteristics. There are several studies which examine the effects of status congruence in informal groups.

Adams (1953) studied fifty-two bomber crews. He ranked men on a series of dimensions, some of which were external status characteristics (military rank, assigned position, length of service, age, education), while others were internal

127

status characteristics (group's assessment of ability, popularity). He then computed a congruence score for each member that indicated the degree to which their ranks across the various dimensions were consistent or inconsistent. He also gave members of each crew a questionnaire that measured: (1) how much confidence members had in one another; and (2) the degrees of friendship they felt for one another. Using the congruence scores for each member, Adams then computed an average score of status congruence for each crew. What he found was that, in general, those crews which had the highest levels of status congruence also had the most confidence and the greatest friendship for one another.

Exline and Ziller (1959) examined the effects of status congruence and incongruence in a laboratory experiment where three-person groups worked on problems in one of four experimental conditions. The subjects in the same groups were told that they differed in abilities as indicated by scores from a test taken earlier. They were also assigned a different number of votes in the group's decisions. Some groups were composed so that the ability and number of votes of the various members were consistent with one another, while other groups contained discrepancies between these two dimensions. For example, in congruent groups, members who supposedly possessed high problem-solving ability had the highest number of votes while those with low ability had fewest votes. In the incongruent groups ability and number of votes were not consistent. The investigators found less conflict and better decision-making in the congruent groups.

Sampson (1963) presents an interpretation of the results of status congruence studies such as Adams's and Exline and Ziller's. According to him, each status characteristic has certain expectations associated with it that are shared by group members. Some examples of what Sampson had in mind are as follows: An older group member may be expected to have the best ideas in the group; a woman member may be expected to be generally passive; a person seen as having had good ideas in the past may be expected to be the "best idea man" again. According to Sampson, when a person has several status characteristics where expectations conflict or contradict each other, the result is psychologically discomforting for the person and for others in the group. This may happen, for instance, if the older member produces poor ideas or if the woman is especially dominant in the group. Speaking of a person whose status characteristics involve incongruent expectations, Sampson states:

> He finds himself in a situation which is doubly unpleasant. In the first place, multiple, incongruent expectations may make it difficult for him to maintain a consistent picture of himself; and in the second place multiple incongruent expectations may make it difficult to interact with him and to coordinate their behavior with his (p. 229).

Sampson's theory is important because it predicts social-emotional difficulties only when incongruent status characteristics lead to inconsistent expectations among the members. Thus, what may appear to be status incongruence in a group to an outside observer may have no importance for group functioning, because the expectations associated with the apparently incongruent status characteristics are not inconsistent in the eyes of the members. An experiment by Brandon (1965) especially designed to test Sampson's ideas showed this to be the case.

In concluding this section, let us reemphasize the fact that differentiation occurs (i.e., status structure develops) in groups as members come to agree on the expectations about one another's behavior. Status consensus, as manifested by members ranking one another similarly on some dimension, contributes to group solidarity because members share the same expectations about who should do what in the group. Any differences in behavior between members is expected and accepted, allowing for smooth interaction in the group. Status congruence, consistency between several external or internal status characteristics, is also indicative of solidarity since members are in agreement about the expectations associated with each member's status characteristics.

STATUS STRUCTURES AS REACTIONS TO FORCES TOWARD ANOMIE

We shall now examine how anomic forces contribute to the development of status structures. In these cases, status structures are seen as necessary means to solving various social-emotional problems that inevitably arise in informal groups.

The Comparison of Abilities

Whenever individuals come together in interaction, the possibility for individualistic orientations exists. One of the sources of this is competition among members. Deutsch's study (1949) clearly showed that when members of the same group are presented with the opportunity to compete for objects or rewards outside of the group, individualistic orientations are likely to prevail. In discussion groups, members compete for talking time and for devising the best solutions to problems. In work groups, members may compete to be the most, or the least, productive. In gangs, members may compete for leadership or to be considered the best fighter. In social groups, members may compete to be judged the most witty or popular by their peers. Members of all groups constantly observe and evaluate one another along the dimensions that are considered important in that particular group.

The aspect of Festinger's (1954) social comparison theory that deals with the comparison of abilities provides some insight into this phenomenon as it occurs in informal groups. Festinger's theory of social comparison really consists of two parts—one dealing with the comparison of opinions, the other dealing with the comparison of abilities. While there are similarities in both types of comparisons, there are some important differences. When individuals compare opinions they tend to become similar to one another through the various standardization processes discussed in the previous chapter. The comparison of abilities (i.e., How good am I in comparison to you?) is likely to lead to other results. When members seek to compare their abilities with others who have similar abilities, they are also always under pressure to improve their performance and to surpass those around them. Festinger describes the two types of comparisons as follows:

> When and if uniformity of opinion is achieved, there is a state of social quiescence. In the case of abilities, however, the action to reduce discrepancies interacts with the unidirectional push to do better and better. The resolution of these two pressures, which act simultaneously, is a state of affairs where all the members are relatively close together with respect to some specific ability, but not completely uniform. The pressures cease acting on a person if he is just slightly better than the others. It is obvious that not everyone in the group can be slightly better than everyone else. The implication is that with respect to the evaluation of abilities, a state of social quiescence is never reached (p. 155).

Thus, Festinger's theory portrays informal groups as involving constant struggles and competition among members to out-perform one another on abilities of all sorts. Deutsch (1949) and Fouriezos, Hutt, and Guetzkow (1950) have shown that such competitive processes disrupt solidarity. However, competition and the comparison of abilities are often central to the process of differentiation in groups. This raises the critical question of how differentiation and solidarity can develop together in informal groups.

A study by Benner and Wilson provides some answers to this question (Wilson and Benner, 1971). The investigators asked students in a series of classes to take what they led the students to believe was a paper-and-pencil test of leadership abilities. In a later class session a false leadership score was returned to each subject supposedly reflecting their performance on the earlier test. Since they were given only a number, the leadership score could not really be interpreted without additional information. Supposedly toward that end, the experimenter also provided the subjects with information as to how they ranked in relation to four other students of the same sex in their class. All subjects were led to believe that they ranked third out of five and were also told that they would be meeting with the four other students (ranks 1, 2, 4 and 5), at a third class session.

The ostensible purpose of this third session was to enable the experimenters to establish how well the scores from the paper and pencil leadership test predicted actual leadership performances. To do this the experimenters had supposedly devised a leadership exercise in which the subjects would take sides on certain issues and defend their viewpoints extemporaneously in front of the other four members of the group. According to what they were told, the other members would then rate each participant on leadership so that the experimenters could compare these ratings with the scores on the test.

Each subject knew his own score, his rank, and the fact the two people in the group scored higher and two lower. The investigators were interested in whom the subjects would compare themselves to in trying to determine how much leadership ability they possessed. Earlier studies of this nature (Wheeler, 1966; Thornton and Arrowood, 1966) suggested that the subjects want to learn more about the performance of the person or persons they compare themselves with. For that reason, the Wilson and Benner study was designed to allow the subjects to learn more about the group member of their choice. Since the only information they had about the fictitious other members were their ranks, the subjects were given the opportunity to indicate the rank of the member they wanted to learn more about. This was done in two ways.

Half of the subjects were told that they would be participating against one other subject in the leadership exercise. Each participant would argue for one side of the assigned issue while being rated by the other group members. This was called the public comparison condition. The other half of the subjects were told that because of a lack of time they would most likely be only observing (and rating) several members in their group rather than performing. Supposedly to help the experimenters arrange the next session, subjects in the public comparison conditions were asked to indicate the rank (based on the fictitious leadership scores) of the group member they would most like to participate against. For the same reasons, subjects in the private conditions were asked to indicate the rank of the person they preferred to observe. All subjects were also administered a self-esteem test, which may be viewed as a measure of the subject's self-confidence.

Wilson and Benner suspected that female and male subjects might react differently. They found, in fact, that females tended to choose the top ranked person less than males in all conditions but especially in the public conditions. Other experiments have shown that females tend to be less competitive in such situations, and the females in our study were the same. For this reason, the investigators tested each of their predictions separately for males and females. Earlier tests of Festinger's theory, which utilized a private comparison situation, found that subjects felt that they could get the most information for evaluating themselves by obtaining information about the highest-ranking person. (Wheeler, 1966; Thornton and Arrowood, 1966). Therefore, Benner and Wilson predicted that the subjects making private comparisons would choose the highest-ranking person, since this would enable them to learn the most about where they stood. The investigators predicted that in public comparisons, subjects would be highly concerned about how they compared with others, and so would be likely to choose someone closer to themselves in rank. They reasoned that these subjects would not want to look bad in the eyes of the other members and so would be more cautious in their choices. The results showed that most of the subjects, whether male or female, chose the top rank in the private comparison condition, while those in the public comparison condition chose lower ranks (usually ranks

2 or 4). Since Benner and Wilson thought that subjects would be more concerned about their images in the public condition, they predicted that self-esteem would be most important in determining choices in the public, as opposed to the private, condition. They found this to be true for males but not for females. Those males with high self-esteem chose high ranks more often in both the private and public conditions. But those with low self-esteem tended to choose high ranks in the private condition and low ranks in the public condition. In other words, these subjects were the most concerned about avoiding a comparison which would make them look bad in the eyes of the group. Self-esteem for females made a difference in the private condition but not the public condition.

We shall discuss the results for males first since most of the earlier groups, such as those in the bank wiring room study and the Norton Street gang, consisted exclusively of males. Let us assume we have a newly formed group and that members have interacted with one another enough to have formed some vague impression of where they rank relative to others in leadership skills. According to Festinger's theory and the pattern of choices in the private condition, most members would be interested in determining how they compare with those seen, as being at the top on various dimensions. This would lead to the competition and status struggles observed in most newly formed groups (see Heinecke and Bales). But because everything is open for public scrutiny in groups, the situation quickly comes to resemble the public comparison condition. While in the beginning everyone will set his sights on being highest in the group on leadership and other skills, this is not likely to continue indefinitely. Several things will probably happen that are understandable in terms of the experiment. Since comparisons are public, it is likely that self-esteem or related characteristics of the members will begin to have an effect. Self-esteem can be taken as the degree of confidence which one has about oneself as one moves into new situations. It is based upon one's memory of how well one has performed in various situations in the past, and if one has a high self-esteem this would mean that one likely expects not to fail in future endeavors. This means that in the ambiguous situation at the early part of group formation, those with low self-esteem will tend to avoid public comparison while those of high self-esteem will continue striving to be highest in the group. As this process continues, only a few members may choose to remain in the spotlight, while the majority, although comparing privately with those seen as being highest in leadership skills (or any skill relevant to the group), avoid public comparison. This, then, allows some degree of quiesence, or equilibrium, which Festinger felt could not be attained in groups because of the need of members to strive for higher rank.

It is probably the case that most members are constantly comparing themselves with others in the group, especially those ranking low, wishing they could be on top. But few are willing to risk the humiliation or embarrassment in trying to achieve this and failing. As the group structure develops, it becomes less and less probable that any challenge to high ranks will take place. Not only will the members currently holding high statuses become more confident about their abilities while the lower ranks grow less confident, but as we saw in the Norton Street gang, the members not involved in such a challenge will do everything possible to build up the confidence of the leader and tear down the confidence of the challenger.

Before finishing with this topic, we must say something about females in groups. In our experiment the female subjects thought that they were assigned to groups with other females. In this situation most females, regardless of self-esteem, tended to avoid public comparison. One might conclude from this that competition and status struggles in all female groups will be minimized relative to male groups. Unfortunately, there are no other studies that can help us to assess the validity of this conjecture. What we can say with more confidence is that in groups of both sexes, females are more likely to act like the low self-esteem males in our study and will tend not to enter public comparison with males. Certainly this is not true of all females, and this will change as the female role in our society changes, but all we can do is say what is most likely to happen given all the information we have. It is interesting that social psychologists have recently been charged with formulating their theories about human behavior based upon their knowledge of males as if they were the only members of the human race. In retrospect, it occurs that we may have been guilty of this type of thinking as we formulated our hypotheses for this experiment.

Blau's Theory of Integration

A description of the early stages of group formation which is consistent with that given above is provided by Peter Blau. Blau's theory is based on the idea that exchange underlies all social relationships. We will look briefly at his description of what he calls "the paradox of integration." It should be pointed out before we proceed that what Blau means by "integration" is the same as what we have previously called "solidarity."

According to Blau, potential members come to join a group because they are attracted to the group. Even if the primary source of his attraction is to reach some other goal, he must be attracted to the other members to some degree if the group is to become an important source of satisfaction. However, if he is to become a part of the group he must also be accepted or found attractive by the other potential members. Therefore, according to Blau, each potential member of a newly forming group must attempt to impress every other member with his attractiveness. The attempt on the part of potential members to impress one another, says Blau, leads to competition in the early phases of the group's development and sets the stage for the differentiation of statuses later on. Some notion of the complexity of this process can be seen in the following statement by Blau:

The more successful A is in impressing B and earning B's high regard, the more displeasure he causes to C whose relative standing in the eyes of B has suffered. All group members simultaneously play the role of A, B, and C in this scheme, which greatly complicates the competitive process. Every member has an interest in witholding evidence of having been greatly impressed by the qualities of others, since his manifestation of high regard for their qualities would give them a competitive advantage over him by contributing to their standing in the group. The fact that impressive members are simultaneously attractive to others constitutes the "paradox of integration." (pp. 44–45).

If all members continued to deny their attraction to any other members, no group would form. At some point, those members who most require acceptance, even if it means acknowledging the impressiveness and superiority of another, will give up the competitive strategies initially employed. Often this is accomplished by the opposite strategy of self-deprecation. According to Blau:

By calling attention to his weakness, a person gives public notice that he withdraws from the competition for superior standing in the group and that he considers acceptance as a peer sufficient reward for his attractive qualities and for whatever contributions they enable him to make (p. 48).

Interestingly, Blau claims that the highly impressive and attractive members of the group are likely to go through the same process. Whatever makes a member impressive in the eyes of others can also make him unattractive, because for members to admit his attractiveness is to admit their own inferiority. Thus the strategy of such a person is to be impressive but not so much that he will not be accepted at all. We saw in Bales's groups that those who talked the most and gained high rank on "best ideas" were not particularly liked by the other members. According to Blau's theory, if such a person is going to remain impressive in long-term groups he must adjust his behavior so that he will be more acceptable (better liked) by those not having the same skills (in this case having good ideas). Jones and his associates (1963) tested this aspect of Blau's theory and found that high-ranking members in experimental groups tended to understate their unimportant qualities but not those which were important to their being accepted as high-ranking members. The self-deprecation of unimportant qualities would tend to make the high-ranking members more "approachable"— i.e., more like one's equal—without undermining their claims to high-ranking statuses.

The competition among members to make satisfactory first impressions does not continue indefinitely. Those who appear to be impressive must back this up with action. According to Blau, in order to remain impressive and eventually gain a high-ranking status in the group, a member must go on to provide rewards for the other members in order to command their approval and respect. However, the fact that several members give some of their fellow members approval, does not mean that a status structure has emerged. This, according to

Blau, occurs only when there is a consensus, a public recognition of the fact that their companions deserve especially high levels of approval or respect. By being dependent upon the superior members for rewards, the members place themselves in their power and introduce the potential for conflict between the powerful and powerless. This raises the question as to why the members who lack superior qualities would accept being controlled by the superior members. Let us look at what Homans has to say on this issue.

Power and Status Differentiation: Exchange Theory

After *The Human Group* (1950), Homans published a second book entitled *Social Behavior: Its Elementary Forms* (1974), where he developed an approach to informal groups known as *exchange theory*. In this book Homans formulates a series of basic propositions which he feels can be used to explain all elementary behavior including animal and human behavior. Fortunately, Homans's ideas about the nature of social relationships are similar enough to those developed by Thibaut and Kelley (1959) that we need not discuss each of his basic assumptions. Essentially, Homans sees elementary social behavior as involving exchanges between individuals where each is motivated to increase his rewards and decrease costs.

According to Homans, differences in power result when one individual can supply a second with rewards that make the second dependent upon him. Homans uses, as an example, two office workers, Person and Other. Person, a newcomer to the office asks Other, a veteran, for help with his work. Doing this involves certain costs, for Person has to take time from his work and must suffer the embarrassment of asking for advice and giving approval (appreciation, recognition and so on). However the rewards which Person receives in the form of advice outweigh the costs. Likewise, for Other, giving advice and receiving approval yield sufficient rewards to overcome the cost of having to leave his own work. Because they reward each other, Person and Other form a social relationship.

But according to Homans, Other, in this example, has more power than Person because Person is more dependent on Other than *vice versa*. To illustrate this, Homans introduces into his example another worker. Third Man. Third Man also asks Other for help which results in competition between Third Man and Person. This competition for Other's help makes it both scarce and valuable to the two workers and puts Other in a position where he can either refuse to help Person or demand that Person provide him with even greater approval than before in exchange for his advice. Other has power over Person because he is capable of making Person change his behavior in a manner that is rewarding to him.

To summarize, the emergence of powerful members in a group can create competition among the less powerful members contributing to anomie and power differences can become so large in an informal group that many members, feeling that they had no control at all, would choose to leave the group. Because of this, some newly formed groups never really become established and existing groups dissolve. However, many groups, facing such problems, do not disintegrate, and Homans's theory provides some clues as to how this is accomplished.

According to Homans, status structures emerge through subtle negotiations between various members. Those who can provide the most valuable rewards to the other members can demand approval and high rank in return. Because they can get the other members to change their behavior they are said to have power. The less powerful members are willing to change their behavior in ways demanded by those with power because they are dependent upon them for scarce and valuable rewards. However, if the low-ranking members refuse to provide approval or leave the group, the basis of the high-ranking members' power would vanish. As a result, the high-ranking members are also dependent upon the low-ranking members. It is this interdependence which is responsible for what Homans calls the "equalization of power". Powerful members can press their advantages only so far without losing their positions. In exchange for wielding their power in a reasonable fashion, other members come to an agreement that the powerful members should be given high degrees of approval or esteem. When the low-ranking members reach consensus about the statuses of the high-ranking members this status consensus is the basis of a stable status structure, In other words, by curbing their power, which is potentially disruptive of solidarity, the powerful members are provided a high-ranking status in the group.

An example of the type of bargaining which overcomes anomic forces and gives rise to status structures can be seen in the results of an experiment by Burnstein and Wolosin (1968) which involved subjects working in dyads on a cooperative task. The subjects were told that success at the group task would lead to monetary rewards and that they were free to decide among themselves whose answer had the most weight in determining the group's outcomes. Initially each subject was given an equal number of points but these could be reallocated through agreements among the subjects so that when the subject with the most points performed the best, the group would get the highest reward. By providing false feedback, one subject in each dyad was made to perform consistently better than the other. This meant that to obtain the highest rewards for the group the subjects would have to agree that the superior performer should be given all of the points.

The details are too complex to mention here, but some groups were exposed to conditions where the inferior performers faced great costs (both monetary and lowered self-esteem) if they agreed to give points to the superior performer. So, as in the Bonacich experiment (1972) discussed in the previous chapter, some groups were exposed to conditions which would tempt (individualistic orientation) the inferior performer from giving his points to the superior member (interdependent orientation). While Bonacich's experiment dealt with the conditions which gave rise to acceptance of norms as responses to anomic forces, this study dealt with the acceptance of status distinctions under similar conditions.

The investigators found that all groups eventually came to an agreement that the superior performer should have all the points but that this occurred more slowly in those groups facing the anomic forces. Of interest is the fact that the superior performers in these groups were less insistent that they be given the full number of points than were the inferior members. It appears that although at first reluctant, the inferior performers once having made up their minds, decided to throw all the points to the superior subject, thus accepting their inferior positions. While admitting their inferiority on the group task, they may have been making claims at competence on another dimension. Burnstein and Wolosin state:

> There is, however, another area of activity—the decision to distribute responsibility—which is equally important in determining the value of the group outcome. If the inferior performer appears to understand what is required before his more successful partner does, he may be able to recoup respect and compensate himself for the humiliation of being devested of task responsibility (p. 428).

Furthermore, by allowing the decision to be made by the poor performer, the superior performer avoided many of the social–emotional difficulties which could arise if he were to usurp power on his own (see Michener and Tausig, 1971). Thus, we see in this case an instance of exchange where the high-ranking member receives responsibility (and the power that goes with it) while the low-ranking member is spared the humiliation that could be associated with accepting an inferior position. In the groups not facing anomic forces, the acceptance of status differences (i.e., the establishment of a status structure) occurred quickly and naturally, as described in the first part of the chapter.

We said in Chapter 2 that status expectations may be broken down into status rights and obligations. The status obligations of the high-ranking or powerful members involve the expectation that they continue providing scarce and valuable rewards. These members, in turn, have the right to receive expressions of approval and compliance to commands, suggestions, and influence attempts. The status obligations of the low-ranking members involve giving approval and complying, while they have the right to receive rewards and be protected from unjust power. It is the inequity of these expectations that causes members to evaluate one another differently. The expectations that comprise the statuses of various members reflect their outcomes or gains in the implicit bargaining which social exchange theorists see as being responsible for the development of status structures.

Coalitions

An observer can locate a coalition in an informal group by looking for a cluster of members who show signs of greater interdependence amongst themselves than with the remaining members. Usually coalitions are the focus of conflict with other members, and we often refer to them as cliques or subgroups.

Most of the research on coalitions comes from laboratory studies in which a subject is given the opportunity to choose between several other subjects to form a coalition. In most cases, the purpose of these experimentally created coalitions is to gain points or to get someone elected in a mock political convention. The aim of such research has generally been to determine the conditions under which subjects choose to form a coalition. Although coalitions within informal groups rarely form to reach explicit instrumental goals, the results of these experimental studies can be helpful in understanding informal coalitions.

According to Lawler and Young (1975), research has established three conditions that lead to coalition formation. First, each member must perceive that he has something to gain by cooperating with other potential members. A convention delegate, for example, may decide that he will join a coalition to nominate a candidate after he has been assured that, if elected, the candidate will work to benefit his home state. Second, the potential member must perceive the coalition as being successful. Our delegate wants to be certain that the other coalition members have the political power to make the candidate a winner. Third, members share a certain degree of similarity along important dimensions. Members of the same age group or sex are more likely to form a coalition than those not sharing these characteristics. Members who have similar attitudes and value are more likely to form a coalition than those with opposing attitudes and values. The importance of similarity seems to be, as Newcomb (1961) has shown, that it provides the basis for pleasant unconflicting relationships.

Within most informal groups, the issues that precipitate coalition formation revolve around subtle social-emotional problems of the group. For example, we can return to the office situation described by Homans. Recall that Other gained rank and power because both Person and Third Man were dependent upon him for advice. If Other's demands for displays of social approval become too costly for Person and Third Man, they could get together and attempt to help each other. This would amount to the formation of a coalition since each, by forming an interdependent relationship, could lessen Other's power over him. In the previous section we said that members may leave the group if others become too powerful. However, an alternative to this is that such "revolutionary coalitions" (Caplow, 1968) may form among the powerless members. In other words, the actual or potential formation of a revolutionary coalition contributes to the equalization of power that Homans sees as being necessary for the development of a status structure. An experiment by Michener and Lawler (1971) has shown that such coalitions are most successful in undermining the power of a high-status member when he or she has been ineffective in moving the group toward those goals which are rewarding to the members. Once a status structure has developed, it can be maintained through the emergence of what Caplow (1968) calls a "conservative coalition." This is where a high-ranking, powerful member of a group forms an alliance with lower-ranking members. By providing the lower-ranking members with certain rewards (e.g., allowing them to make some leadership decisions or giving them the privilege of associating with the leader) the high-ranking member can be assured of their efforts to preserve the current structure. An example of this can be seen in the study of the Norton Street gang. Danny and Mike, Doc's lieutenants, were both instrumental in thwarting Alec's attempts to upset the status hierarchy. Thus, the existence of a conservative coalition in an informal group contributes to the exchange process between high- and low-ranking members that ultimately leads to a stable status structure.

In conclusion, coalitions within informal groups can upset as well as maintain current status structures. But coalitions in most informal groups become a part of the structure because they balance the power among members and help reach some consensus about relative ranks. Little research has been carried out on informal coalitions probably because of their subtle nature. As compared to political coalitions, for instance, they tend to be less stable and have less clearly defined goals. More attention should be paid by future researchers to how coalitions form within informal groups and to their consequences once formed.

SOME CONCLUDING COMMENTS

The two "routes" to the development of status structures are not as distinct as our treatment of them might suggest. Unfortunately, none of the studies reviewed here involves direct observations on the processes by which groups develop status structures. Therefore, we can only piece together the rather indirect evidence available to us in attempting to describe this process. Groups, depending upon the environment within which they formed and the characteristics of the members, will vary in the extent to which solidarity and anomic forces prevail. The studies we have reviewed suggest that in some groups, consensus about the expectations that form the basis of a status structure develops quite easily. In such groups, the forces toward solidarity outweigh those toward anomie, thus enabling members to arrive at consensus naturally as they interact with one another. In other groups, forces toward anomie are relatively strong and a status structure emerges only through the resolution of the resulting competition and power struggles. Of course, if the forces toward anomie become too strong a group may dissolve; this is especially likely in the formative stages when there is little "reserve" of solidarity to help the members through the social-emotional problems they face. In conclusion, a group's status structure may evolve through some combination of both "routes," the importance of either "route" being dependent upon the relative strength of the forces toward solidarity and anomie within the group.

SUMMARY

As with the emergence of norms, status structures are responses to either forces toward solidarity or forces toward anomie. The literature reviewed in the early part of this section contains no hint that statuses emerge in groups to reduce the threat of anomie. Rather, in this view, status expectations develop to insure solidarity. As members recognize legitimate differences in abilities and skills, they organize themselves in the most efficient way.

Where information about these differences is not available, members base their expectations on external status characteristics such as age, sex, and occupation. Members ranking high on relevant external status characteristics are likely to be high participators, to be highly influential, and are given esteem by other members. However, as a group meets over time, members have a chance to assess one another so that a person's actual behavior in the group becomes a more important criterion in the formation of status expectations. If members are asked by an investigator to rank one another along dimensions such as "best ideas," a person's resulting rank is his internal status characteristic.

The development of solidarity in a group involves the emergence of both status consensus and status congruence. Status consensus is high when members agree upon one another's position on some internal status characteristic. Status congruence is high when the expectations associated with each of several internal or external status characteristics do not conflict with one another in the eyes of the group members. Measures that indicate high status consensus and status congruence tell an investigator that members share a common definition of their rights and obligations, that there are likely to be few status struggles, and that solidarity is relatively high.

Status structures also form to minimize what we have called forces toward anomie. Whenever individuals begin to interact, the possibilities for anomic responses and thus social-emotional problems are apparent. In the early stages, members compete for superiority and recognition. In order to avoid disintegration and to insure the development of solidarity, certain members must abstain from competitiveness. The Wilson and Benner experiment, and Blau's theory show that members with little confidence in their abilities or superiority drop out from overt competition, thus contributing to the solidarity of the group. But, this also allows for differences in power which can be a potential threat to solidarity. However, in most groups, there is a limit to the degree of power a member can attain. Low-ranking members are dependent upon those of high rank for rewards which they cannot attain elsewhere. But, these high-ranking members are, in turn, dependent on the lower ranks for approval and recognition that provides the basis of their power. As a result, the powerful members cannot press their advantages too far. Homans's theory suggests that the development of an agreement among low-ranking members that a powerful person should be given social approval, legitimates the power differences. If a powerful member exploits the low-ranking members he can lose this legitimacy and his position in the group. Thus, the development of status consensus equalizes power, stabilizes conflict, and contributes to group solidarity.

Status structures which arise in response to anomic forces are the results of subtle bargaining processes among members. Members who cease to compete for power gain acceptance. Members who legitimize the power of another receive certain benefits, while the powerful member receives the group's recognition in the form of high rank. Often these bargaining processes include coalitions which consist of subgroups of members seeking the same goal. Two types of coalitions were identified as being most likely to emerge in informal groups; those comprised of low-ranking members seeking to neutralize the power of the high-ranking members, and "conservative coalitions" consisting of high- and lower-ranking members seeking to preserve the current status hierarchy.

six

Leadership in Informal Groups

INTRODUCTION

One of the things that make informal groups interesting is the fact that the expectations which the members hold for one member, thus defining his status, are different from the expectations they hold for another. Thus far in our discussion of the emergence of status structures, we have not been much concerned about the content of status expectations. In this chapter we shall examine the characteristics of those members who, because of their unique statuses in groups, are called leaders.

Despite the large amount of research devoted to the study of leadership, there is little agreement about what it is. Many leadership studies have dealt with authorities or supervisors in formal organizations. Although there may be some similarities between informal and formal leaders, they are not the same thing, and these studies are of little interest to us. Another approach to leadership is for investigators to rather arbitrarily set up criteria for distinguishing leadership and designate those observed to meet these criteria as leaders. For instance, Bales and Slater (1955) referred to those subjects scoring highest on "best ideas" and "liking" as "task" and "social-emotional" leaders respectively. It is doubtful whether other researchers or even the subjects in that study would think of these members as leaders.

Since there is no convention in this regard, we are free to view leadership the way we feel is most practical. We reserve the term to refer to those members of informal groups who, because of their high-ranking statuses, are likely to be recognized and referred to as leaders. What this means is that much of what we have already said about high-ranking statuses is also true of leadership statuses.

This perspective is consistent with contemporary thinking on the subject of leadership (see Hollander and Julian, 1969).

As a status structure develops, through the processes discussed in the previous chapter, a status hierarchy also develops—that is, there are fewer members whose statuses are said to rank high than there are members with low-ranking statuses. However, the nature of status structures can vary widely, and in some cases it is meaningful to speak of the emergence of a leadership status. The following hypothetical example is helpful in illustrating when it is or is not appropriate to speak of a leadership status, according to our point of view.

Let us assume that we are observing a series of groups with the aim of understanding the status structure of each. Based on past research of this type, we would probably collect the following types of information: (1) differences in influence; (2) differences in interaction; and (3) differences in sociometric rankings. In the first case, would would look for instances where it is clear that one member systematically influences the behavior of others. There are several ways this can be done. We can see whose suggestions or orders are followed most and by whom, and we can see who asks whom for suggestions or advice. Related to this would be the flow of interaction. We would expect, following Homans's hypothesis in the *Human Group,* that members giving commands and suggestions would initiate and receive high rates of interaction. Finally, the members should be able to recognize those they consider as having the most influence and differentiate them from others on sociometric dimensions. All three types of information would reveal differences in the ranks of the status of various members. We would probably examine each type of information separately; but for sake of illustration, we will combine them in our consideration of three hypothetical groups (Figure 6.1).

We shall assume, for the sake of argument, that members are ranked consistently on these three dimensions—that is, a person high on influence will also

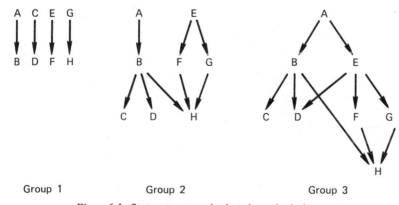

Group 1   Group 2   Group 3

Figure 6.1. Status structures in three hypothetical groups.

be high on interaction rate and sociometric ranking. There is plenty of evidence that these three variables are usually correlated, but it is not likely that one would find perfect consistency in most real life groups. In Figure 6.1, the persons at the top of each diagram are considered to exert more influence, initiate and receive more interaction, and are ranked higher on a sociometric dimension than those immediately below (connected by arrows). For instance in group 2 of Figure 6.1, we see that person *A* was observed to exert more influence over *B, C,* and *D,* and was ranked highest by *B, C,* and *D.*

The three diagrams in Figure 6.1 (groups 1, 2, and 3) represent findings from three different hypothetical groups that show the range of different patterns that status structures can take. The number of possible patterns that could have been included is enormous. The three that were chosen represent varying degrees of group unity or solidarity. The structure of group 1 is probably found only in newly formed groups or groups extremely low in solidarity. In this case it is possible to isolate status differences only in particular pairs. The diagram indicates that *A* exerts influence over *B,* that he initiates interaction for him, and that *B* recognizes *A*'s superiority. We can conclude that *A* has provided scarce and valuable rewards for *B,* and that he has power over *B.* But we know nothing about how *A* or *B* stand in relation to any of the other members. It is possible that the members of group 1 have had little interaction with one another because they do not wish to. In any case, there could be very little status consensus in group 1 because all the individuals are separated into smaller cliques. It is really questionable whether the individuals in group 1 could be said to constitute a "group" in the true sense of the word because the solidarity among them is extremely low.

In group 1 we say that *A, C, E,* and *G* have high-ranking statuses, but of course, they have a relationship with only one other member. In group 2 we can say that persons *A* and *E* have high-ranking status. In fact, we are more justified in speaking of their *statuses* or of them ranking high in the *group* than we are in group 1, since there is evidence that some degree of consensus exists among members about the statuses of *A* and *E.* This is suggested by the fact that several members relate to *A* and *E* in similar ways indicating that they have arrived at some common definition of their statuses. However, there is not likely to be any clear consensus about this, especially if the cliques or subgroups which appear in that group are antagonistic, or if the ranks of members within each clique are unclear or disputed. If this were the case, it would be best to diagram the status structure as consisting of two separate groups instead of as a total unit. At any rate, the diagram of group 2 suggests that it is a group of higher solidarity than group 1.

The status structure in group 3 resembles in many ways that of the Norton Street gang. Like the Norton gang, there are two cliques, each with its own hierarchy, joined together by a single high-ranking member. In this case, there is obviously more consensus in the definition of the high-ranking member's status, and the group has greater solidarity since the acceptance of *A* (Doc in the case of the Norton gang) unifies the two separate cliques. It is person *A* in group 3 whom, as occupant of a high-ranking status, we choose to call a leader. Some investigators might call persons *A* and *E* in group 2 leaders, saying that groups can have more than one leader. However, it does seem to be conventional to speak of a group as having a single leader, and when there is one person who members agree ranks highest, that person is usually considered by the members and by himself to be the group leader.

In all three groups diagrammed in Figure 6.1, it was possible to pick the members with high-ranking statuses. But only in group 3 was the high-ranking member the center of the group. In a sense, everything we have said about the relationship of high-ranking members to other members is true of leaders except that for leaders it applies to their relationship to all or almost all members. For instance, Homans's exchange theory states that members of high rank will provide scarce and valuable rewards for, and have power over, their subordinates with whom they have established a relationship. This would be manifested in differences in influence, interaction, and status ranking. However, in the case of groups with distinct leaders, the person considered leader would provide scarce and valuable rewards for the group as a whole. With respect to power, which we have said is manifested in differences in influence, interaction, and sociometric ranking, leaders would have influence over the whole group, would be the center of interaction in the group, and would receive uniformly high sociometric ranking from the other members.

We think that most readers who have followed the argument of the previous chapters would agree that group 3 of Figure 6.1 would appear from the diagram to have reached a higher level of solidarity. Group 3 has this appearance because more of the members are interlocked by lines than in the other groups. This suggests, then, that groups whose status structure includes a distinct leader are higher in solidarity. This raises the question of what it is about the existence of a leader that contributes to the solidarity of a group.

While examining leadership and group solidarity, we also hope to demonstrate that the processes of standardization and differentiation, although treated separately in the last two chapters, occur together in reality. That this is the case can be seen in the results of Back's study (1951) on the effects of cohesion. Recall that he found highly cohesive dyads becoming more uniform on their stories than the low cohesion dyads. That is, standardization was more highly developed in the highly cohesive groups. But we also know that this happened because one member influenced the other to conform to his ideas. Back was not really interested in *who* changed his opinion, only in the fact that one subject in the highly cohesive groups changed. One person influencing another to change his opinion constitutes the beginnings of a status structure; therefore, standardization and differentiation are part of the same overall process and go hand-in-hand, as we shall see.

LEADERSHIP AND GROUP SOLIDARITY

Legitimation

If a leader, by the fact of his or her power, poses a potential threat to the less powerful members, how can a leader contribute to group solidarity? In his discussion of leadership, Homans (1974) says that leaders have authority in addition to power. Traditionally, sociologists speak of power that is accepted by subordinates as *legitimate power,* or *authority.* Homans makes some interesting comments about power and authority in informal groups within the context of exchange theory. According to Homans, both power and authority refer to the process by which one person changes the behavior of another. However, when a person has power over another, he controls rewards and punishments which are directly exchanged with the other person. For instance, if *B* does not behave in the manner which *A* desires, *A* will punish or fail to reward *B* by an *internal* process of control. In the case of authority, the control is external to the exchange: whatever rewards a person gains by following the commands or suggestions of an authority come from a source other than the authority itself. If you consult a horse-racing authority for a tip on the next race, you may be rewarded by following his advice, but he is not the source of the rewards. A person comes to have authority in a group if the other members profit from that person's suggestions or commands.

Homans points out that although the concepts of power and authority are analytically distinct, they are usually found together. A person may need power first to get others to start following his commands or suggestions and find them rewarding. On the other hand, an authority who has provided rewarding commands or suggestions in the past can gain power because he may, if he chooses, withdraw his rewarding suggestions in order to secure compliance from others. Generally, when a person is considered to be the leader of the group, that person has authority. That is, members are willing to carry out that person's commands or suggestions because these have led to rewards in the past. Leaders' authority, in a sense, complements their power, making whatever threat is associated with them more acceptable to the members.

For this reason, the leader may be seen as successfully contributing to both the instrumental and social-emotional problems of the group. Slater (1955), whose study was discussed in Chapter 3, provides evidence of this. While he asked group members to rank each other on "best ideas" and the other dimensions at the end of each session, he also had them rank each other on "leadership" at the end of the fourth and final session. He wanted to determine how the person ranking highest on leadership would rank on the other dimensions. The following results show the percentage of times the person top ranked on "leadership" was also ranked highest on the other dimensions: "guidance" (80 percent), interaction received (65 percent), "best ideas" (59 percent), interaction initiated (55 percent), and "liking" (25 percent). While not highly related to "liking", "leadership" was highly related to "guidance" and receiving interaction. These two factors were, in turn, most highly related to "liking," suggesting that they are indicators of the social approval given to an individual by the other group members. According to Slater:

> This fact seems less strange if we consider the generalized character of leadership. Subjects choosing a leader must take into account a wider range of abilities and virtues than in deciding who has the best ideas and whom they like the best. The chosen leader of a group is perhaps the man who has the highest hypothetical *combined* rating on all possible characteristics related to the group's purposes and needs. The man so chosen is not likely to be *disliked,* nor to have unacceptable ideas, nor be unable or unwilling to participate in the discussion. Hence those measures which are themselves more general, that is, related to a wider range of abilities, will correlate more highly with leadership (p. 617).

It is not likely that the members of these temporary groups would have called anyone a leader if the idea had not been put in their heads by Slater's questionnaire. In other words, it is not clear that this study really deals with "leadership" as we have defined the term. What it does suggest, however, is that those subjects to whom members felt the label "leader" best applied were those who provided a wide range of solutions to their group's problems, both instrumental and social-emotional.

Groups that have a member able to meet both instrumental and social-emotional demands should attain a high level of solidarity. Recall from Chapter 2, both camping groups studied by the Sherifs (1966) had leaders who exerted power and influence over the other members. However, Crane, leader of the blue group, received more friendship choices on a sociometric test than did Shaw of the red group. Crane was accepted as leader by the members of the red group while Shaw gained power through coercion. In other words, Crane's leadership status was seen as legitimate, and this contributed to the overall solidarity of his group.

Further evidence along this line comes from a study of laboratory discussion groups carried out by Borgatta and his colleagues (1954). Unlike earlier multi-session studies, the groups in this study contained different members at each new meeting. During the first session, the investigators isolated eleven subjects whom they labeled *great men.* These were subjects who received the highest scores on several factors related to abilities in solving instrumental problems (leadership ratings, IQ scores, and participation rates) and in solving social-emotional problems (sociometric popularity). These men were followed through as they met with new groups, and were consistently chosen highest on leadership and popularity and were consistently observed to have the highest rates of interaction. Compared to groups with no great man, those with a great man had higher rates of interaction, which we categorized in Bales's scheme as "suggestions and orientation," had fewer arguments and more positive social-emotional interaction. The authors suggest that groups containing great men were better able to handle instrumental and social-emotional problems and thus had higher levels of solidarity.

However, it should not be concluded from Borgatta's study that some men are born leaders, and that they will be leaders in whatever group they find themselves. A large amount of research has been devoted to proving that this is not true (see Gibb, 1969). A person who may have the skills and qualities to get himself accepted as leader of a gang, for instance, will not necessarily become the leader of the philosophical society. But in groups such as those used by Borgatta, the skills required were the same in all the groups, making it likely that a person capable of solving the instrumental and social-emotional problems of one group could do the same in others.

The leader, then, becomes a leader because of his ability to help the group solve both instrumental and social-emotional problems. But the emergent leader does not solve the task problem alone. If this were true there would be no need for a group. He or she may contribute more to the solution of the specific problems facing the group, but in most cases he or she is also the one who best coordinates the group to reach the instrumental goal.

In groups like the Norton Street gang, which have no specific task, the leader is the one who suggests goals and helps the members attain them as a unit. Whatever the nature of the instrumental problems facing the group, because the members of the group are interdependent, the leader can reward the group as a whole by being largely responsible for moving the group toward its goal. This helps him maintain his leadership position and also contributes to the solidarity of the group. When there is a fairly high level of interdependence and solidarity, the leader will maintain and strengthen them by helping to solve social-emotional problems. For instance, Doc's status in the Norton gang involved expectations that he solve internal disputes and insure compliance among members of lower rank to the group's norms and status expectations. Further evidence of this comes from the fact that the two cliques in the Norton gang (see also group 3 Figure 6.1) were unified because they both accepted Doc as a leader, and the fact that the Norton gang, as it was originally constituted, disintegrated when Doc was no longer on the street corner. The leader, because he is at the center of the group, becomes a "keystone" of solidarity. His behavior, more than any other single individual's, can determine the level of solidarity attained by a group.

Leadership and Group Norms

Differentiation contains the seeds of anomie. The behavior of members with high-ranking statuses must be rewarding to the other members in order for their power to be accepted as legitimate. No member who consistently deviates from group norms can gain or maintain a high-ranking status in the group. Through the process of differentiation, members who come to have a high rank conform closely to norms as they develop.

Leader-established norms. In chapter 4, Homans suggested that Taylor's high rank in the bank wiring room probably stemmed from the fact that he conformed to important norms; however an alternative explanation is that Taylor, because of his status in the group, had a good deal of influence in establishing those norms. Although it was not possible in that study to establish which process was more important, there is evidence that both processes develop in informal groups. Let us look at some evidence concerning the idea that high-ranking members are responsible, to a large degree, in establishing group norms.

It should be clear from the previous section that a leader cannot impose norms on others. The Norton gang's experience with the Aphrodite Club shows that Doc's influence was limited, and Whyte implies that it was Doc's recognition of this that helped him maintain his leadership in the group. A high-ranking person, then, must be sensitive to the feelings and opinions of his subordinates. A study by Chowdry and Newcomb (1952) provides evidence that this is the case. Their study was based upon information gathered from a religious group, a political group, a medical fraternity, and a medical sorority. The members of each of these groups filled out questionnaires that measured their opinions on a number of issues. Some of the issues were relevant to each type of group and some were irrelevant. For example, the relevant issues for the religious group concerned religion, for the political group, politics, and so on. The answers of each member were converted to numerical scores, and an average score for each item was computed for each of the four groups. The members of each group were also asked how they felt the members of their group, as a whole, would answer each item. Then, through a rather complicated procedure, the investigators determined how much these estimates deviated from the members' actual answers.

In addition to this, the members of each group were asked to evaluate one another on four sociometric questions. On the basis of these responses, the investigators categorized the members of each group as "leaders," "nonleaders," and "isolates." The leaders, as designated by the investigators were those who received the greatest number of sociometric choices. The investigators found that on relevant opinions, the leaders gave more accurate estimates of the groups' answers than did the nonleaders and isolates. In a similar study, Trapp (1955) found that leaders of a sorority were better able than nonleaders to guess how other members would reach to a series of hypothetical social situations.

The high-ranking members in these studies were most sensitive to the behavior and opinions of the other group members, especially when they were important or relevant to the group. However, there are two feasible explanations for this. The first is that leaders, because they are at the center of interaction, are in a better position to gain information about others. The second is that those who are most sensitive to the feelings and opinions of others are better able to behave in ways that yield them a high rank in the group. Probably both interpretations are correct, but Chowdry and Newcomb point out that having contact with others is of no use if the person does not have the sensitivity to process whatever information he or she may gain. Thus, in the early stages of a group's formation, those who have this sensitivity are most likely to become leaders because they can move others in directions they are willing to be moved. By helping to establish such norms, a leader can reward the members, who then would respond by giving him or her the approval and thus further establish the leader's high-ranking status in the group. After their high rank is secured, leaders are in an even better position to sense what norms will or will not be accepted by the members and get these norms accepted through their influence.

Leadership and nonconformity. In *The Human Group* Homans hypothesized that a member's conformity to group norms leads to high rank. We now want to examine the feasibility of that hypothesis. Let us begin by looking at what Homans says about the same hypothesis in his more recent book, *Social Behavior: Its Elementary Forms* (1974). Homans states:

> In my book, *The Human Group* [Homans, 1950, pp. 180–181], I put foward the proposition that a member of high status would conform to a high degree to all the norms of his group. What I had in mind was a man like Taylor in the Bank Wiring Room of the Western Electric Company, a piece of research reviewed in that book. Besides being held in high esteem for other reasons, Taylor also conformed, indeed conformed more closely than any other member, to the highly valued output norms of that industrial group. I still hold that a member of high status will conform to the more highly valued norms of his group. His conformity in this respect may only be one aspect of the behavior that wins him high status: his capacity to provide the others with rare and valued rewards. He may, indeed, as a leader have done more than any other member to get the norms accepted, and may even himself set a higher value on conforming to them than do any of the others. But I no longer believe that a member of high status conforms fully to *all* the norms of his group. Instead, his high status may itself allow him some freedom in lesser matters (p. 331).

Let us look at some of the evidence that seems to have changed Homans's mind. Bartos (1958) carried out a study on six YMCA clubs. He grouped the members of the clubs into four categories: leaders, elected officers, appointed officers, and followers. Each member was placed in a conformity situation resembling that used by Asch. While a subject was carrying out the task of matching lines, he "overheard" voices giving him hints, which he was led to believe were the other members of the group waiting in an adjoining room. In reality the voices were recorded and the hints were incorrect. The purpose of the experiment was to determine which members were more likely to conform to what they thought was the standard of their group. Bartos found that those subjects who were leaders of the group were less likely to be swayed by the influence of the group, providing some evidence that high-ranking members may not be the ones who conform the most.

Work done by Hollander (1964) provides some further information as to why this may be true. In one experiment, Hollander had groups working on a series of fifteen problem-solving tasks which, when done properly, could have earned money for the group members. Before each trial, the group had time to discuss the procedures to be used, such as: (a) the order of reporting; (b) how to arrive at a group solution; and (c) how to divide up the money at the end. One member of each group was a paid confederate of the experimenter; the confederates, because they possessed certain information, were always the most competent persons in the group. They also deviated from the agreed upon procedures on certain trials depending upon the experimental conditions. In some groups they violated these rules in early trials, while in others in middle and later trials. The dependent variable in each case was a measure of how much group members were influenced by the suggestion of the confederate. Hollander found that the confederates who deviated in later trials exerted more influence over the members than those deviating in the early trials.

In agreement with Homans's exchange theory, Hollander says that a highly competent member of a group will reward the other members through his behavior, and he in turn is rewarded by being accorded a high-ranking status in the group. Built into the expectations that define the status of a high-ranking member is what Hollander calls "idiosyncrasy credit," which specifies the degree to which the member may deviate from the general norms of the group before negative sanctions are applied. According to Hollander, the higher a member's rank the more "credits" he has and the more he may deviate from group norms. As a member gains rank in a group, his credits build up, and as he deviates they are expanded. The extent to which the confederate in the experiment influenced the group is an indication of his acceptance. We know from earlier discussions that deviants are likely to be rejected by conforming members of a group. However, the groups' acceptance of the confederate's deviance in Hollander's experiment indicates that they were not concerned with sanctioning him. The fact that those members who conform at first, thus building up credits, were most influential towards the end of the experiment supports Hollander's theory.

It is now clear that the relationship between rank and conformity is more complicated than Homans stated in *The Human Group*. While leaders and members with high-ranking statuses are expected to conform to group norms, they may deviate under some circumstnces with impunity. In a sense, leaders or high-ranking members must strike a balance between conformity and deviance. Although such members are not required to conform strictly to all group norms, they are not really allowed to deviate in the usual sense. They are allowed to stray from group norms only if their actions lead, or are seen as being likely to lead, to valuable rewards for the group members. The idiosyncrasy credits associated with high-ranking status allow the occupant to *innovate* rather than deviate, for a leader is expected to move the group in new directions and this would not be possible if strict conformity were demanded. Doc's attempt to set up contacts with the Aphrodite Club, something that was previously considered inappropriate for the Norton gang, is an example of such innovative behavior. In that case, his attempt was unsuccessful, but apparently Doc had enough idiosyncracy credits to engage in such behavior without having his status rank threatened. Had this endeavor been successful—that is, had all members found bowling with the girls rewarding—it would have contributed to Doc's surplus of "idiosyncracy credits" and made his leadership status even more secure.

Pressures Toward the Maintenance of the Status Structure

As we have pictured it, the status structure of an informal group develops as members share expectations (have the same ideas about rights and obligations) concerning the behavior of various members. Because a group's status structure involves expectations, it operates in very much the same way as a norm. A norm involves expectations that require similar behavior from all members, while a status involves expectations that require different but interrelated behavior from all members. It has been previously illustrated that once there is a relatively high degree of consensus about some specific norm, the probability is fairly great that it will remain unchanged. Any person who deviates from the norm will be negatively sanctioned, and of course, this increases with the solidarity of the group. The same may be said of the status structure. Once it is set, it becomes difficult to change. An existing social structure might change if a member of high status deviates from the norms and loses his supply of idiosyncracy credits, or when a low-ranking member begins to perform better on some relevant dimension than a high-ranking member. Events such as these may be found in newly forming groups and those low in solidarity, but are rare in groups where solidarity is high.

Why are statuses difficult to change when expectations concerning the status structure become set? A study by Harvey (1953) and another by Sherif and his associates (1955) provide some insight into this question. Harvey gathered information about boys of various status rank who were chosen from naturally occurring cliques. Based on the observations of adults familiar with the cliques and sociometric questions, the members of each clique were assigned ranks in the group. Three individuals—the leader, the lowest-ranking member, and a boy of intermediate rank—were chosen from each clique to participate together on an experimental task. The subjects were shown a dart board consisting of concentric circles with score values for each circle. The task for the subjects was to throw darts at a board that was the same size but did not have the circular markings. Just before a subject threw a dart, he predicted how well he thought he would actually score. Afterwards, each subject recorded how well he thought he actually did score. The other two subjects also recorded their predictions of the subject's future performance and their evaluation of his actual performance.

Harvey was interested in the extent to which predictions of future performances deviated from scores assigned after each dart was thrown. For each subject he computed a discrepancy score based on the difference between the other members' expectations for a subject's future performance and the assessment of his actual performance. Harvey found that the higher the status rank of a subject in his clique, the more he overestimated his own expectations about his future performances. Likewise, the others in the group also tended to overestimate his future performances. In other words, high-ranking members were expected to perform better even if their actual performance did not warrant that expectation. The problem with his study was that there was no objective measure of how subjects actually performed on the task. It is likely, as we will see in the next study, that the subjects also overestimated the actual performances of the high-ranking members.

Some of the cliques in Harvey's study consisted of boys from high-income families, while others were made up of boys from low-income families. Harvey felt that the boys from low-income families would be the most dependent on the clique for social satisfaction because they would find it more difficult to find acceptance in other groups and because of the pressures to join groups for protection in low-income areas. This being the case, he expected the groups from low socioeconomic backgrounds to be higher in solidarity. As evidence of this, he found that the correlation between status rank and overestimated performance expectations was higher for these groups. According to Harvey: "Our findings seem to point to the conclusion that the expectations an occupant of a given status in a well-defined informal group holds of himself are largely determined by the expectations which have become defined by the group as appropriate to that status" (p. 366).

A second study, carried out by Sherif, White, and Harvey (1955), was designed to investigate another aspect of the expectations that members of informal groups have about persons of various ranks. In this study, the investigators divided a larger group of boys at a camp into two smaller groups that were kept separate throughout the summer. One of the groups developed what the investigators judged to be a relatively high level of solidarity, and several observers ranked the members of each group according to their statuses in the group.

The members of the two groups were tested in an experimental setup similar to the one used by Harvey, except that in this case, the subjects threw handballs at a target. The target was covered with a cloth to obscure the markings to the subjects, but the experimenter was able to record the actual scores made by each subject. The subjects were asked to estimate the performance of every other subject. The dependent variable then was the discrepancy between the members' estimates about a subject's performance and the scores actually attained by that subject. The investigator found that, although actual task performances were not related to status rank, the degree of discrepancy between group members' estimates and actual performances were related. In both groups the members tended to overestimate the actual performances of the higher-ranking members. This suggests that the members' expectations that high-ranking individuals will perform better, which were found in Harvey's experiment, are carried over into the members' perceptions of actual performance. At least this is the case when there are no clear-cut criteria for evaluating performances. As was the case in Harvey's study, this experiment also found that these expectations were most highly correlated with status rank in groups judged to be high on solidarity.

Both studies show that the greater the level of solidarity in a group, the more defined the status structure, which makes competition and status struggles unlikely. The fact that high-ranking members in the high solidarity groups were clearly expected to perform the task better than the others and were actually judged to perform better, illustrates this. The high-ranking members of such groups would have to perform very badly before their performances would begin to have any effect on their ranks.

The fact that Sherif and his colleagues did not find a correlation between status rank and actual performance does not mean that performance is irrelevant in informal groups. Most leaders cannot maintain their high ranks unless they periodically prove their superiority in various areas to the other members. In the studies by Harvey and Sherif, the task was new to all the groups. Whatever status structures had developed were based upon members' performances in areas other than the one used by the experimenters. But groups may face new activities and members may get a chance to evaluate each other's performance anew. These studies indicate that when this occurs, the high-ranking members are at a distinct advantage. To begin with, the high-ranking members are *expected* to perform well, and this can instill the confidence needed to turn out a good performance. This is especially important in those areas where, like bowling, for the Norton gang, self-confidence is necessary for an adequate performance. Also the high-ranking members were seen as performing better than lower-ranking members even when there was little or no difference in the performances. Again, where there are no clear-cut criteria, the high-ranking members, especially leaders, have an advantage in maintaining their high rank.

For a leader to drop in rank and another to gain, a high-solidarity group would have to drastically revise its expectations. We have seen in our discussion of status congruence (Chapter 4) that these expectations, once set, serve both the psychological needs of members for consistency and predictability and also provide one possible solution to the group's social-emotional problems. Thus, once expectations are formed and members attain and perceive a degree of consensus about these expectations, they are difficult to change. The Norton gang's reactions to Alec's attempt to out-bowl the high-ranking members and to challenge Doc's superiority in romantic endeavors is a good example of how the pressures toward *status quo* are manifested in such groups. There are several other factors that maintain an existing status structure. The first is the fact that leaders, because of their "idiosyncracy credits," are allowed to violate certain normative expectations as long as they conform to those thought to be most important by the group members. Thus, if a member continues to perform adequately in those areas most relevant to the group, he can afford not to be the best in less important areas. This leads to the second factor. As we have seen, high-ranking members exert more influence over the group and therefore can steer it toward or away from certain activities. This being the case, it is not surprising that high-status members will move the group toward those activities in which they personally excel and where they can continue to reward others through their performances. If a high-ranking member can do this successfully, he will be judged competent on several dimensions, thus contributing to the level of status congruence in the group and assuring him a secure position in the group. Once high-ranking statuses are formed, their occupants are in a good position to maintain the structure and insure the present level of group solidarity.

Leadership, Norms, and Solidarity

One final comment can be made about the link between standardization and differentiation and how these processes relate to group solidarity. In the introductory section of this chapter it was mentioned that the existence of a leader in a group is a reflection of and a contribution to the solidarity of the group. Another way of thinking about this is to say that the leader's authority has the same function in a group as the existence of norms, which, as we have shown, contribute to the solidarity of a group. The leader's authority means that his orders (whether in the form of commands or suggestions) will be carried out by the other group members. Commenting on this, Homans states:

> In this sense an order belongs to the same class of things as a norm. The differences between them are matters of degree not of kind. An order may govern behavior only within a relatively brief span of time: a norm is generally supposed to remain in force without limit of time; it is, as we say, a "standing order." Again an order emanates from a single person or office, whereas we usually find a norm being stated by a number of members of a group, though even so it turns out that leaders have more of a say in establishing norms than followers do. In any particular case we might find it difficult to decide whether something was properly labeled an order or a norm (1974, p. 277–78).

While the leader may be the source of an order, his authority, the fact that he is accepted by the members, gives it the same moral force as a norm which members agree upon and accept. Both orders and norms provide guidelines for the behavior of members which help to coordinate their interaction with one another and to reduce social-emotional problems. In other words, both norms and leaders contribute to group solidarity.

SOME CONCLUDING COMMENTS

One dilemma facing the social scientist is that isolating certain features or processes of groups for detailed examination leads to an oversimplified view of groups. Studies that take an internal approach to small groups usually examine certain aspects (i.e., conformity, influence, leadership) and ignore how they are related to others. Among other things, this chapter was intended to demonstrate the interconnectedness of informal groups. Thus, what we took apart for the sake of analysis in the previous chapters, we tried to put back together in this one. Although it is done all the time, it is a distortion of reality to discuss the emergence of norms and how they affect members, for example, without also discussing the differentiation of statuses.

A second dilemma facing social scientists is that groups are simultaneously static and dynamic. Concepts such as norm and status are useful because they call attention to the fact that some of the behavior of members in a group follows stable patterns over time. Unfortunately, these concepts often carry with them the image of complete and unchanging regularity. We have tried to avoid this image in several ways. By calling attention to the fact that groups vary in solidarity, we hope to convey the idea that in many groups, even though there may be enough regularity to speak of norms and statuses, these will be vague and ill-defined. Second, by concentrating on the emergence of norms and statuses we hope to sensitize the reader to the fact that norms and statuses are manifested in interaction among members. For instance, we know that a norm exists in a group if one member is the target of influence attempts or of hostility from others, or that statuses exist if one person consistently influences the behavior of another. Norms and status refer to processes and these processes never cease. They may lead to further elaboration and differentiation and thus solidarity, or they may lead in the opposite direction. Norms and statuses change as the circumstances facing the group change. Furthermore, no expectations placed upon a group member, even in high-solidarity groups, will specify exactly how he should behave in all situations. As new situations arise, the members react anew and their behavior is constantly shaping the normative and status expectations in the group.

Finally, the existence of norms and statuses in a group are often taken as indications of harmony and consensus. We have argued that norms and statuses contribute to group solidarity, but we also pointed out that this may emerge as a rather tenuous resolution of social-emotional problems stemming from forces towards anomie. Although norms and status structures pose a solution to these problems by restricting "overt competition" and conflict, the forces toward anomie remain. As we will point out in the remaining chapters, groups whose environment imposes strong anomic forces are limited in their development of solidarity, yet norms and status structures do develop in these groups. Thus, in some groups, the existence of norms and statuses may be indicative of underlying conflict, competition, and dissension.

SUMMARY

In this chapter leaders were defined as members of informal groups who, because of their high-ranking statuses, are recognized and referred to as leaders by other group members. While all groups will have high- and low-ranking statuses, only in some is it appropriate to say that a leadership status exists. Leadership, then, does not refer to a type of person but to certain types of relationships in a group. Generally, this occurs when one member is the center of *influence, interaction,* and *sociometric* choices in the group.

The leader, as does any high-ranking member, poses a threat to solidarity because of his power over other members. In order to maintain the leadership position, a member must provide scarce and valuable rewards to the members. This insures that members remain in the group and that they accept his status as legitimate. Research evidence suggests that the leader contributes to the solution of both instrumental and social-emotional problems facing the group. Although any member may hold power over others, it is the high sociometric rating that separates the leader from other high-ranking members. The fact that almost all members like the person who exerts power and influence over them indicates that that person is accepted as a legitimate leader.

The presence of a leader contributes to group solidarity by helping to establish norms. Because leaders are, by definition, at the center of interaction in the group, they are in a position to determine what group members want or what they would accept in the way of group action. Furthermore, there is evidence that those members who emerge as leaders are more sensitive to the needs of the other members than are nonleaders. A leader, in a sense, must also be a follower.

One unique aspect of the leadership status is that a leader is required to conform to some norms but is "allowed" to deviate from others. According to Hollander (1964), by conforming to central norms in the group, the leader builds up "idiosyncracy credits," which can be expended by deviating from other norms. This license to violate certain norms can be seen as one of the leader's status rights. However, the leader's deviance cannot go unchecked. If he deviates without building up more credits through conformity, his right to deviate will be withdrawn by the other members. In general, deviation involves innovation on the part of the leader and results in new goals and activities for the group. If successful, the leader's innovation contributes to group solidarity and the stability of his own position.

Once the status structure in a group is set, there are pressures at work that tend to preserve the *status quo.* This is especially true when the structure includes a legitimate leader. When such a leader is present, members generally expect him to be the most adequate performer in group activities. For one thing, this expectation bolsters the leader's self-confidence so that he actually can perform more adequately than other members. Also, in activities where there are no clear-cut criteria for judging the adequacy of members' performances, the leader is given the benefit of a doubt by the lower-ranking members. The persistence of the status structure contributes to the solidarity of the group.

Finally, it was pointed out that the commands or orders given by a leader take on the authority of a norm. The very existence of a leadership status, then, provides members with guidelines for behavior that coordinate their activities, diminish social-emotional difficulties, and contribute to overall group solidarity.

seven

Informal Groups and Their Environments: The Case of Gangs

INTRODUCTION

In previous chapters we have, from time to time, used the concept "environment" without really specifying why it is important in the analysis of informal groups. The last four chapters will be devoted to this matter. An informal group's environment consists of those external factors that affect certain characteristics of the group, and are affected by these characteristics. We shall first discuss some of these factors and then analyze adolescent gangs and their relationships to their environments.

ENVIRONMENTS OF INFORMAL GROUPS

Identifying relevant environmental factors for informal groups is especially difficult first of all because there are so many of them. It is helpful, therefore, to distinguish between three classes of environmental factors: physical, cultural, and structural. All three types are interrelated, but we shall place greater emphasis upon structural environmental factors in the remaining chapters.

Physical Factors

Included in this category are aspects of architecture and the arrangement of physical objects that impinge in some way upon the informal group. Communication network studies (Bavelas, 1951; Leavitt, 1951; Shaw, 1954) clearly show how physical restraints on communication can influence certain group

159

characteristics. In these studies five subjects had to solve certain problems by passing messages to one another. Each subject started out with a piece of information essential to the solution of the task. The subjects were physically separated from one another by barriers and had to pass the messages through network of slots.

The different types of networks that have been used in these studies are illustrated in Figure 7.1. Each circle represents a subject's position; the numbers represent the "centrality" of each position. The higher the number, the more central the position in the network. These studies have shown that messages generally flow to the central positions, and the subjects in these positions typically end up coordinating the incoming messages to solve the problem. As we might expect, other variables are related to this flow of communication to the central positions. Subjects assigned by the experimenter to the central positions have been found to be more satisfied with their positions than those in less centralized positions. The centralized subjects were also more likely to be chosen as leaders at the end of the experiments. Subjects in circular networks, where there was no single central position, were likely to make many

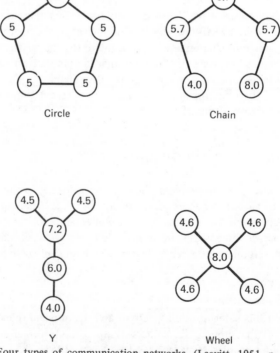

Figure 7.1. Four types of communication networks. (Leavitt, 1951, p. 47. Copyright © 1951 by the American Psychological Association. Reprinted by permission.)

-more errors in problem-solving than those in networks with clearly defined central positions.

Most informal groups are theoretically free to form their own structures based upon the skills and traits brought by the various members. Network studies show, however, that group characteristics are influenced by physical characteristics of the environment. We have seen some examples of this in earlier chapters. The reader will recall that Festinger and his associates (1950), found that physical proximity was a determinate of interaction within the housing projects studied. Newcomb (1961) showed the importance of the physical arrangement of his boarding house in the emergence of friendships. In the bank wiring room, the layout of the room influenced the formation of cliques in the group. In addition, Sommer (1969) has presented evidence that various seating arrangements at tables are consistent with different types of relationships (e.g., conversation, cooperation, competition).

One should not conclude from these studies that all aspects of a group's physical surroundings should be considered a part of its environment. For instance, the arrangement of windows in the bank wiring room had no implications for the group. The placement of tables and work places for the various workers did, however, because workers with high status rank were located at the front of the room. Thus, the existence of objects or their arrangement in space are important to the group process only when they have social implications which place constraints upon group members and thus determine certain characteristics of the group. Physical features affect informal groups mainly by serving as boundaries that tend to throw a set of individuals into social relationships with one another or keep them from interacting with others.

Cultural Factors

Group interactions do not occur in a vacuum. Most groups consist of members of the same society, which means that they share a common culture. That is, they hold certain beliefs, customs, habits, and values in common. When they interact with one another, even for the first time, they carry with them normative expectations about what is appropriate behavior for themselves and others in particular situations—i.e., the first date, the interview, the laboratory discussion group, and so on. Even when a group develops its own unique set of norms and status expectations, the expectations of the larger culture that is shared by the members still provide guidelines for much of the interaction. This is one of the facts that make it difficult to distinguish clearly between social systems and their environments.

Most of the general cultural expectations that members carry with them from group to group are so subtle and "taken for granted" that members are not even aware of their existence. Goffman (1959) has identified the existence and importance of numerous rituals that apply to all social contacts among members of the same society. Proper greetings and good-byes are only one example of these rituals. One friend is expected to pay proper respect to the other in his greeting by asking about his wife and family without going too far by demanding information inappropriate to the friendship. Such subtle rituals demand that participants in any enduring relationship be sensitive and respectful to each other's "self."

Gouldner (1960) has pointed to another specific norm which, although apparently existing in all societies, remains largely implicit. This is the "norm of reciprocity," and it specifies the moral obligation of persons who have received some good or benefit from another to reciprocate in an appropriate fashion. This obligation pervades all social relationships and applies to such diverse situations as the exchange of Christmas cards to the exchange of "hellos." According to Gouldner, the norm of reciprocity acts as a "starting mechanism" which "helps to initiate social interaction and is functional in the early phases of certain groups before they have developed a differentiated and customary set of status duties" (p. 176). Thus, group solidarity may develop out of the relationships formed as individuals conform to the norm of reciprocity. A person may offer a cherry pie to a new neighbor who later responds by inviting the first to lunch. It is not automatic, but further elaboration of this reciprocity could lead to the development of a full-fledged friendship between the two neighbors. Many groups that form within a society do so according to the expectations specified by the norm of reciprocity.

We have little information about how these general norms vary from culture to culture, but what evidence does exist points to some fascinating differences. Hall (1969) has shown that the expected physical distance and amount of physical contact between interacting individuals varies between cultures. Two Arabs, for instance, stand much closer together when talking than do two Americans. They also stare into each other's eyes and breathe in each other's face, practices that make Americans uncomfortable because they violate the American social habit of bodily privacy. More evidence of cultural differences that influence informal relationships comes from Milgram's (1961) cross-cultural study of conformity. Using a modified Asch situation, he found that Norwegian students conformed more to erroneous judgments of confederates thought to be peers than did French students. Differences like these are probably associated with a greater involvement in informal groups in some societies relative to others.

The importance of these unstated cultural expectations for small groups in American society has been demonstrated in an important article by Cloyd entitled "Small Groups as Social Institutions" (1965). An institution is defined as a widely followed normative pattern within a society; the complex of norms governing family, educational, political, and economic activities are most commonly referred to as institutions by sociologists and laymen. However, this term can be extended to refer to any regularly followed norm shared by most members of a society. According to Cloyd, many such norms are so widely accepted that they are not even recognized as institutions, and many of them provide guidelines for behavior when individuals are engaged in face-to-face interaction in small groups. According to Cloyd:

> American culture contains an ideology of the small group. This ideology is expressed in day-to-day conversation about social relationships, in advice columns in newspapers, and in inspirational literature of human relations. For more systematic expressions of this ideology one can look to the "practical" small group books designed to aid participants in committees, boards and so on (p. 376).

Central to this ideology is the value placed on the small group. Business decisions are made in "teams"; creativity is spawned in "brainstorming sessions"; the decisions of a jury are considered to be infallible. Democracy, group consensus, high productivity, and high morale are goals to be attained in groups. Books are written on how to "win friends and influence people," and children in school are rated on such traits as "gets along well with others," "ability to lead," and the "ability to follow." All of this suggests that Americans share a common set of expectations about group behavior; these expectations are the result of a life-long socialization process that allows them to enter any informal group or to participate in the formation of an informal group with a common definition of what the desired outcome should be. These expectations are flexible enough so that what is considered appropriate behavior will depend upon such factors as the number of people present and the goals of the group. Thus, the norms of the society place certain restraints on the behavior manifested by members and determine, to some extent, certain characteristics of the group. However, cultural factors are common to all groups whose members share the same culture; and since we intend to show how variations in the environment cause groups to differ, we shall say relatively little about cultural factors.

Structural Factors

The structural aspects of a group's environment are those characteristics of individuals, groups, and organizations that are outside the group in question but influence the behavior of the group members.

All informal groups are parts, or subsystems, of larger social units. The structural features of a group's environment depend upon the type of group being examined. Many groups, like the bank wiring room group, arise within larger formal organizations. The behavior of the members as they interact with one another is determined to a large extent by the formalized rules and regulations of the organization. In groups such as these, the structure of the formal organization helps shape the characteristics unique to the informal group in question. Other groups are less directly influenced by structural factors in the environment. Homans (1950) referred to such groups as "autonomous groups," using the Norton Street gang as an example of this type. It is appropriate to conceive of groups as varying along an *autonomy continuum,* but even those groups considered to be highly independent of environmental influences are not completely autonomous. The characteristics of gangs, like the Norton Street gang, are determined by such structural features as the number of jobs available in the neighborhood, the existence of rival gangs, and so on.

One way in which structural factors affect groups is through the external status characteristics which members bring to the group. Differences in external status characteristics may stem from members occupying statuses in the same or different outside groups. In Chapter 4, we considered external status characteristics that resulted from members having different statuses in the same society— i.e., age, sex, occupation. Differences in external status characteristics can also result when members have different positions within another group or organization outside the informal group in question. For example, members of the bank wiring room all held statuses in the formal structure of the organization. Those with the highest-ranking statuses in the formal organization (the connector wiremen) had the highest rank within the informal group. Differences in external status characteristics may also occur because members differ in the extent to which they hold positions in separate outside groups. For instance, Doc was involved in a wide range of social systems in the Norton gang's environment and this contributed to his prestige in the gang.

There are other ways that structural factors can influence informal groups. For instance, the existence of rival groups in a group's environment will create competitive pressures and limit the range of behavior exhibited by group members. Furthermore, the threat of a rival group can lead to solidarity or toward anomie, depending upon the circumstances. The presence or absence of alternative groups that provide members with greater satisfaction can affect the nature of groups, especially friendship groups. For example, a group whose members have joined it because there was really no other alternative will differ from one whose members have picked each other in spite of available alternatives. Also another system within a group's environment may have the power to control the members under certain circumstances. For instance, the behavior of a group of students may well be determined by the fact that the dean of students has been keeping an eye on them.

AUTONOMY AND CONSTRAINT IN THE ENVIRONMENT

Before analyzing gangs and their environments, it is necessary to introduce several key concepts that will recur in this and the remaining chapters. It is impossible to describe every physical, cultural, and structural feature of a group's environment and to determine how the presence of each influences the group. We must therefore isolate the *major* way in which all environments determine the characteristics of informal groups that form within them. One way we shall do this is to concentrate upon how the unique combination of physical, cultural, and structural features of an environment exerts *constraints* upon group members and how it gives them *autonomy*. When we speak of environmental constraints, we refer to ways in which the features of an environment control the behavior of group members and limit their alternatives. Autonomy is the absence of these constraints.

The physical arrangement of a factory (a physical environmental factor) may make it difficult for some workers to talk with one another and may thus limit the alternatives for interaction. The norm of reciprocity (a cultural factor) may require a person to pay back another who gave him a gift, even though he doesn't really want to. A foreman who will not allow workers to trade jobs with one another (a structural factor) limits the extent to which workers can interact. These constraints (or their absence) affect the behavior of the individuals and therefore influence the characteristics of existing or potential groups. As we shall see in the remaining chapters, the environment of a group consists of a unique pattern of autonomy and constraint. This pattern sets up the forces toward solidarity and forces toward anomie which impinge upon the group, determining its level of solidarity as well as other group characteristics. The patterns of constraint and autonomy are different for each type of group, and so each requires a separate analysis. However, it is possible to show in a general way how environmental constraints and autonomy contribute to forces toward solidarity and anomie.

Informal groups form when individuals, who are unable to reach certain personal goals alone or in alternative groups, develop interdependent relationships to mutually reach these goals. Some examples of this are: (1) persons working in the same room on a boring job who devise games to play among themselves to alleviate the tedium; (2) boys in a neighborhood with no recreational facilities who hang out together on a street corner, (3) students excluded from high prestige cliques at school who form their own group. In these cases, the environment sets up certain constraints on the behavior of the individuals and makes it advantageous for members to adopt interdependent orientations. These constraints, which must be present for any group to form, contribute to the forces to solidarity. On the other hand, the environment must also provide some measure of autonomy for informal groups if they are to continue to exist. The bored workers could not become a group if their games were outlawed by their immediate supervisor. Members of the street corner gang would not enjoy their solidarity if they were harassed by the police every time they came together. If constraints within a group environment restrict activities which contribute to interdependence among members, they constitute forces toward anomie.

The effects of autonomy and constraints can be illustrated by introducing another key concept, "group product." Biologists view organisms as entering into a direct exchange with their environments (i.e., the exchange of carbon dioxide for oxygen). Some groups are involved in similar exchanges with their environments, such as when a factory exchanges money for raw materials and finished products for money. Although for most informal groups the relationship with the environment is not so clear, the existence of the informal group and the activities of its members does have an influence on the environment in the form of group products. By "group products" we mean any activities in which members engage as a group that are visible to persons and groups in its environment. Where these activities are a primary reason for interdependence among members, the group product may be a goal of the group. The importance of group products is that they provide outsiders with a basis for evaluating and reacting toward the group in question. Depending upon the nature of the evaluation and response, a group may be faced either with forces toward solidarity or forces toward anomie.

Take as an example a hypothetical clique of mental patients on a large hospital ward who have voluntarily formed a group. The members did not come together to collectively attain some specific goal or product; the goal of the group is largely social, not instrumental. However, one consequence of the fact that these individuals have become a group is that they often refuse to eat in order to get better treatment and special privileges from the staff. This action constitutes a group product in the eyes of the staff who, recognizing that unpopular action on their part toward members of the clique could lead to resistance or persistent complaining, are likely not to cause problems for them. In so doing, the staff, an important element of the group's environment, continues to provide the autonomy necessary for the patients to continue as an informal group. It is important to recognize that this is not automatic; staff members do have the power to separate group members and enforce rules that would make group solidarity impossible. They could, for instance, revoke privileges to group members and counteract any group pressures by punishing the individual members. Such actions would, of course, constitute anomic forces for the group.

It is not necessary for all individual members to participate in the output of a group product, but the group product must be something more than the independent behavior of individual members. In some cases, outsiders may consider the behavior of an individual to be a group product because of his association with a group. This is an example of an erroneous reaction from the environment. The existence of a genuine group product, however, indicates that members have formed interdependent relationships to carry out the particular activity. The greater the number of group products, the greater the internal social control and solidarity of the group.

When the products of a group are seen as harmless, outsiders in the environment will not interfere or react toward the group in any fashion. In other words, members will be given autonomy to engage in those particular activities. If individuals, groups, or organizations in the environment judge a group product to be useful, they may actively help the group in carrying out the desired activities. If, however, they judge the group product to be harmful or problematic, they will react by trying to eliminate the activity or the group producing it. Needless to say, this process is not always fully carried out. Groups are capable of anticipating what activities will bring negative reactions and will either stop producing them temporarily or will attempt to keep them secret.

In our hypothetical clique of mental patients, "group pressure" was considered to be the group product. However, a group product may be many other things. For instance, the same group may also play cards together. Playing cards and similar activities would probably be of little interest to the staff and consequently to social scientists because it has no relevance for the group's relationship to the environment. However, what is important is the fact that this activity is allowed by the environment. This means that the inmates involved are given the autonomy to define card-playing as a group activity, which in turn contributes to interdependence and solidarity. If the card-playing involved gambling, a violation of ward rules, this activity would become salient in the eyes of the staff, who might decide to restrict this basis of the group's solidarity.

What products associated with a group become the focus of interest for social scientists depends, in part, upon the type of group and the interest of the investigator. But this is usually determined by his understanding of the activities to which outsiders react. In the case of a group of teen-age boys, social scientists will be more interested in the fact that they throw stones at passing cars than the fact that they collect pop bottles for deposit money. The original investigators of the bank wiring room attached much less significance to the fact that the men consistently bought and ate candy than the fact that they restricted productivity. In both cases, the products of interest were those that had the greatest importance for the environment. Stone-throwing by the teen-age group can lead to arrest, attempts to break up the group, or attempts to get members involved in legitimate activities. Lower productivity in a work group could lead to members being fired, lower wages, or some form of discipline that would limit the group's activities.

To summarize, autonomy gives members the opportunity to engage in common activities, which, in turn, help develop solidarity. Where group activities are restricted, solidarity will also be restricted. Therefore, while most informal groups do not enter into a direct exchange of group products for something tangible, an exchange of sorts does take place. Useful (or at least nonoffensive) group products are exchanged for autonomy, which allows the group to maintain or increase its solidarity. In environments where constraint is high, certain products may not be allowed to develop or they must develop covertly. Just how this works will be shown in the next section where we shall look at adolescent gangs and their environments and how physical, cultural, and especially structural factors in the environment combine to influence the characteristics of gangs. To be more specific, we will be interested in how the patterns of autonomy and constraint in the environment effect group solidarity and the nature of the group product in such groups.

ADOLESCENT GANGS

By "adolescent gangs" we refer to informal groups that emerge among adolescents who, for whatever reason, come into contact with one another. Usually such groups form among persons who attend the same school or live in the same neighborhood. The term "gang" is problematic because it is often used to refer to groups of adolescents who have engaged in delinquent activities (Sherif and Sherif, 1967). It might be appropriate to say that gangs are groups of friends, except the term "friendship" suggests a level of intimacy among members that does not seem to be present in all gangs. The term "peer group" could be substituted, except that this term seems to refer to all peers with whom one is associated (i.e., schoolmates) without allowing for the fact that some associations with peers involve more solidarity than do others. We shall use the term "adolescent gang" with the understanding that such groups are not necessarily involved in delinquent activities.

The fact that so much attention has been paid to ganging among adolescents is a cue that there is something special about the status of adolescents that may contribute to the widespread formation of gangs. Adolescence is that period during the life cycle when a person moves out of the status of childhood and into the status of an adult. It is generally considered to be a time of "storm and stress," but the extent to which adolescence is considered to be problematic varies from society to society. For example, Margaret Mead (1950) found that Samoan adolescents faced few of the problems of their counterparts in industrialized societies. This difference can be attributed to the fact that the transition from childhood to adulthood is less abrupt in Samoa. In that society, members take on the expected duties for adults of the same sex as they become physically capable of doing so. A boy begins to follow his father around and help him with his chores and a little girl does the same with her mother, eventually taking on the responsibility of caring for younger siblings. The children, because they grow up under the direction of older siblings, do not experience the sharp break from parental authority that faces children in modern society. Also, children in Samoa are not discouraged from sexual play and experimentation, and adolescents begin to engage in sexual activities as soon as they become physically mature.

In contrast, within highly industrialized societies, adulthood responsibilities (i.e., earning a living, being a parent, and so on) are suddenly thrust upon the individual, who has had little time for preparation and practice. This change also usually involves a drastic break from one's parents as one matures. Further, unlike adolescents in the Samoan society, those in industrialized societies are discouraged from engaging in sexual activities until they are adults. This means that many are unequipped to handle the expectations of adulthood. Much of this is due to the fact that the required formal education process is prolonged way beyond the point where adolescents are physically capable of fulfilling adulthood status requirements. Further problems arise from the fact that the age at which adolescence ends is never clearly specified. That is, the ages at which a person is allowed to join the army, vote, drive, or drink alcoholic beverages—all activities associated with adulthood—are different.

In nonindustrialized societies, the adoption of adult responsibilities occurs gradually, but the formal transition from childhood is rapid. Usually this takes place by participation in a special ceremony such as a puberty rite. Once a child reaches the proper age and has passed through this ceremony, he is formally recognized as an adult and he assumes the appropriate rights and obligations. Eisenstadt (1956) and Block and Niederhoffer (1958) have argued that puberty rites ease adolescents into adulthood, helping them meet the problems associated with any status transition. According to the latter where formal procedures are lacking in a society, "adolescents tend to develop informal substitute systems of their own" (p. 127). The substitute system that they see emerging in such societies is the ganging process where adolescents of similar age and the same sex band together to form groups separate from the remainder of society. Block and Niederhoffer offer evidence that in primitive societies where, for one reason or another, the old puberty rites no longer serve the function of helping adolescents through their period of transition, there is a high incidence of ganging. They argue that because industrialized societies totally lack these formal institutions they have such a great number of adolescent gangs.

Associated with the lack of clearly defined status expectations for the adolescent in industrialized societies is conflict with older generations (Sherif and Sherif, 1967). It is the adults in a society, the parents, teachers, and judges, who are responsible for imposing, on a day-to-day basis, the conflicting expectations associated with the period of adolescence. For example, adults encourage adolescents to break their dependence upon adult figures but simultaneously place limits on their independence. According to Sherif and Sherif:

> Like any human being caught in a dilemma and striving to re-establish more or less stable ties with social life, the adolescent looks around him. He discovers that he is not alone in his feelings nor in his plight: his agemates face the same problem. Hence they gravitate toward one another, to exchange notes and gripes, to seek ways in concert to assert and satisfy their desires (p. 50).

The gang, then, provides adolescents with acceptance by someone other than the problematic adults in their lives and a way to attain a clearly defined status that requires behavior typically associated with being an adult.

In more general terms, the structure of modern society (as an environment) places constraints on the behavior of adolescents by limiting the ways in which they can attain certain personal goals. While blocking various avenues to personal goals, society provides the autonomy for the formation of gangs. Thus, adolescents often join gangs to reach those goals which cannot be met through alternative means.

Three Types of Gangs

How are different types of gangs shaped by their immediate environments? In his classic study, *The Gang* (1927), Thrasher identified various categories of gangs such as the *diffuse type,* the *solidified type,* the *conventionalized type,* and the *criminal type.* The first two types indicate that Thrasher observed gangs that varied in solidarity; the last two types reveal that other gangs varied in goals or group products. The conventionalized gang is one whose group product is fully condoned by outsiders, while the criminal gang is one whose activities are defined as illegal. This section deals with the ways in which solidarity and the nature of group products in gangs is determined by environmental factors— namely, the members' social class position and neighborhood type.

As an aid in assessing results of gang studies, it may be helpful to sensitize the reader to the theoretical assumptions that have guided this research. By and large, social scientists have been most interested in lower class gangs that engage in delinquent activities. Several researchers have shown that criminal acts by adolescents are rarely carried out alone. Social scientists have directed their attention to the relationship between delinquents and their peers and this has led to an interest in gangs. Furthermore, in attempting to explain delinquency, theorists have tended to see delinquency as a lower class phenomenon. Thus, most theory and research has dealt with lower class gang members. This interest in lower class gangs has probably been bolstered by the fact that the activities of such gangs most frequently reach the newspaper headlines. The typical image of a gang is that of a group with a fierce-sounding name (e.g., "Gladiators") and militarylike structure, whose members are sworn to loyalty, illegal activities, and warfare with neighboring gangs. While some gangs at times approximate this image, we are beginning to realize that most do not. Not all gangs are lower class and not all gangs are organized for the pursuit of criminal activities. Furthermore, most gangs do not attain the high level of solidarity suggested in the above description.

Unfortunately, the typical image of gangs has been slow to change, and subsequently much sociological work has been based on it. Thus, more information is available about delinquent than nondelinquent gangs. Similarly, we know more about lower class than middle class gangs. Typical of most sociological approaches is the theory of Cloward and Ohlin (1960), who see gangs as forming among lower class adolescents because they are barred from the conventional routes to achieving success in our society. Having in common the fact that they are denied legitimate opportunities to attain these goals, they join together to create alternative structures for this purpose. Again, we see in this theory the assumption that gangs are a lower class phenomenon.

Although information is not as complete as we would like, we have chosen three types of gangs that are referred to frequently in the literature in order to analyze their relationships to the environment.

The criminal gang. One of the major types of gangs covered in Cloward and Ohlin's theory is the *criminal gang*. This type of gang engages mainly in illegal activities that bring economic gain to the members. According to the theory, criminal gangs form in stable, lower class neighborhoods where illegal activities are socially organized, politically protected, and accepted by most local residents. A neighborhood such as this provides the proper environment for groups whose major group product involves illegal activities. Criminal gangs serve as an initial step for adolescents moving toward criminal careers, more especially, as a training ground for those moving into organized crime at the adult level.

Block and Niederhoffer (1958) give a rather detailed description of a criminal gang called the Pirates:

> The Lords of _____ Street were the Pirates, a lower-class delinquent gang of adolescents in their late teens. At any time of the day from eleven in the morning until one o'clock the next day, some member could be found on the favorite stoop observing the territory, ready to carry messages, give information to other members, warn them of danger, etc., etc. Although rarely did more than ten members congregate there at one time, there was reason to believe that they could mobilize seventy-five on short notice, especially since they could count on the support of Corner Boys, an auxiliary group of younger boys located one block west (p. 197).

Being a sophisticated group, the Pirates did not adhere much to ritual and ceremony. Their only move in this direction involved the wearing of dark brown lumber jackets with the word Pirates written across the back. The Corner Boys, however, went all out and wore "zoot" suits and ducktail hair styles. The Corner Boys were educated and tested by the Pirates, and if they showed signs of promise, were allowed to accompany the Pirates on their exploits.

No one Pirate was in control. There existed instead a "collective leadership" among four members, each having particular skills and functions in the group. Paulie had connections with professional gangsters, fences, and bookies who provided him with information concerning likely "jobs," with an outlet for stolen goods, and with connections to "fix" cases against arrested members. Lulu took care of planning the burglaries. He had great skill in working with tools and electrical devices and so was of great value to the gang. Solly's prestige in the gang was due to his ability to handle the frequent contacts with the police:

> Solly played the part of the decent fellow commiserating with the police over the bad habits of the other Pirates. He gave the impression that he

was on the side of the law and eager to contribute any information that would be of value to the police in their search for burglars and other criminals. But all that he actually volunteered was heresay reports of past activities about which nothing could be done (p. 203).

The last leader was Blacky; although often the butt of the members' joking, he maintained prestige as the gang's social director. Blacky was more sophisticated sexually and was responsible for setting up sexual encounters for the other members.

Although the Pirates were responsible for numerous criminal activities, which made them a problem for the police, they dressed up every Sunday and attended the local Catholic church. This fact is indicative of the atmosphere in a stable lower class neighborhood where various social institutions, legitimate and illegitimate, are interwoven. Furthermore, the gang's integration into legitimate institutions was to their advantage. According to Block and Niederhoffer:

> Priests in such neighborhoods did exercise strong practical influence in everyday affairs. Sometimes, when called upon for help by a member of their parish, they might intercede with the police to gain another chance for some miscreant of "tender" years (p. 212).

This accommodation to legitimate institutions extended even to the police. At one point when they were being harassed daily by the patrolman assigned to their territory, leaders approached him in a conciliatory fashion. As a result, an unspoken, covert, and informal agreement was formed whereby burglaries in the area declined as did police harassment. This tended to raise the prestige of the patrolman in his department and provided some autonomy for the Pirates.

Short and Strodbeck (1965) in a fairly comprehensive study of gangs in Chicago could find none that fits the description of the criminal gang—although they did find cliques of gangs whose primary basis of solidarity involved criminal activities. This suggests that criminal gangs as described by Cloward and Ohlin may be rare. Kobrin and his associates (1967) predicted from Cloward and Ohlin's theory that although other types of gangs may exist in a relatively stable lower class neighborhood, criminal gangs should have the highest status ranking by members of the local community. They found that a criminal gang which they classified as the "sophisticated delinquents" engaged in infrequent but lucrative theft and was consistently ranked by outsiders as being the most prestigious group. According to Kobrin:

> Informants pictured them as the commonly recognized elite group of the local street world. They come from well-connected families, had "plenty of clout," commanded good jobs through politics and the rackets when they worked, were well supplied with money, and were the first in their age group to own new automobiles. They were described as "just as tough as anybody else" but not inclined to go out of their way to prove it (p. 103).

So integrated was this gang into the neighborhood that a local storeowner robbed by them would not report it because of the gang members' family and political connections. Finally, Spergel (1964) compared several different types of neighborhoods and found that gangs in the stable, lower class neighborhood served to socialize adolescents into organized crime at the adult level.

It appears that, although they are found infrequently, criminal gangs do tend to develop in stable and organized environments where their criminal activities are accepted and protected. Furthermore, because these groups have an instrumental goal which, when reached, brings money and prestige to members, they appear to be fairly high in solidarity.

Conflict gangs. According to Cloward and Ohlin's theory, *conflict gangs* form in unstable slums that are characterized by rapid changes in land use and population, by conflict among ethnic groups, and by massive housing projects consisting of people who are strangers to one another. There may be high rates of crime and deviance in this type of neighborhood but the crimes and deviance tend to be individualistic rather than organized as in the stable lower class neighborhoods. According to the theory, adolescents in unstable lower class neighborhoods are cut off both from legitimate and illegitimate opportunities to gain symbols of success. As a substitute, aggression and conflict become the only means to gain prestige, and therefore gangs in these areas resort to conflict.

Probably most lower class gangs are best categorized as conflict gangs not so much because their members engage in constant warfare, but because the reputations of these gangs are based primarily on past incidents of violence. It is this type of gang that most frequently makes the front pages of newspapers, and most of what has been written about them tends to support the typical image of gangs described earlier. However, the results of recent research tend to question the validity of this image.

We shall begin with the research of Yablonsky (1959), who spent four years observing conflict gangs in New York City. Yablonsky views collectivities as being arrayed along a continuum of "organizational development," which closely resembles the solidarity dimension presented in Chapter 2. At one pole of the continuum are "true groups" where social organization is high. At the other end are "mobs," individuals loosely formed into short-lived collectivities. Midway between these two poles are what Yablonsky calls "near-groups," which he feels best describes most conflict gangs. According to Yablonsky, the normal structures of such gangs contain the following elements: (1) unclear status definition; (2) limited cohesion; (3) impermanence; (4) minimal consensus of norms; (5) shifting membership; (6) disturbed leadership; (7) limited definitions of members' expectations. The similarity between most of the items on this list and the six dimensions of solidarity should be obvious (see Table 2.1). What Yablonsky is saying, then, is that the conflict groups he observed were low in solidarity.

According to Yablonsky, the reported size of such gangs depends upon who one talks to and when. While a central core of members can be identified, the majority are peripheral members who occasionally join gang activities. The following examples of why certain members were involved in a gang fight illustrate the marginal nature of their membership:

> I didn't have anything to do that night and wanted to see what was going to happen.

> I always like a fight; it keeps up my rep.

> My father threw me out of the house; I wanted to get someone and heard about the fight.

According to Yablonsky, conflict between gangs is rarely planned and usually involves many peripheral members who fight because they have nothing better to do. The leadership positions in these groups were ill-defined and unstable. Yablonsky feels that gangs, or near-groups, serve as an outlet for the aggressive needs of the boys, and for this reason, the members tend to rally around emotionally disturbed boys who are prone to violence. However, the conclusion that gang leaders are disturbed in a clinical sense does not necessarily follow. It is more likely that their behavior reflects the fact that they are integral parts of an anomic social situation and so are affected in the same way that Doc's behavior was affected when anomie was high in the Norton gang (see also Gordon, 1967, p. 58). Yablonsky's characterization of conflict gangs as "near-groups" is not consistent with the idea that such groups are high in solidarity.

Klein and Crawford (1967), having observed numerous gangs in Los Angeles, also question that conflict gangs are high in solidarity. To discuss this issue, they differentiate between what they call the "internal" and "external" sources of cohesion. By "sources of internal cohesion," they mean the interpersonal attraction, or "mutual liking," which is a basic part of solidarity in a group that has no explicit instrumental goals. "Sources of external cohesion" refers to pressures arising in the environment that "push" members into association with one another. Some examples of these external sources are the lack of legitimate or illegitimate opportunities for success, the existence of rival gangs, and the lack of acceptance by police and other authorities. Klein and Crawford believe that the external sources of cohesion outweigh those generated internally in gangs, and that eliminating these external sources would lead to the disintegration of most gangs.

In their explanations of why internal cohesion is weak in most gangs, Klein and Crawford deal with five aspects of groups that closely parallel our dimensions of solidarity. The first is *goals*, which they maintain are not clearly developed in gangs. The most commonly expressed goal of the gang members they studied was "protection from rival gangs." This, the authors argue, indicates an external, rather than internal, pressure toward cohesiveness. They report that gang members who associate with a gang worker (social worker) may learn to verbalize goals for the group but this usually involves nothing more than mere verbalization.

The second aspect mentioned was *membership stability,* which was reported to be low for the gangs observed in Los Angeles. Membership turnover was high, with many members joining with gangs for only short periods of time. According to investigators, suspicion and distrust among members weaken ties to the gang.

Group norms in the gang are described as being relatively nonexistent except those that hold for all members of the lower class in general, and for certain myths. Myths include the belief that members do not inform upon each other or that they aid one another in time of attack—norms that are evidently more often verbalized than acted upon.

The next aspect of gangs, *role differentiation,* refers to the development of what we have called a *status structure.* Concerning this, the investigators say that while there may be positions with official-sounding names such as "president" or "war counselor," the influence of those occupying such positions is questionable. There is usually little agreement among members about what is expected of incumbents of various statuses. Furthermore, they report that leadership positions tend to shift from person to person rather frequently.

The last aspect mentioned is *group names.* Gangs with names such as Gladiators, Egyptian Kings, and so on, are usually assumed to be the locus of great in-group loyalty. Klein and Crawford state that gang names often change and are strong sources of identification only during conflict when cohesion is heightened by external threat. Also, according to Klein and Crawford, many names are taken from streets or neighborhoods, which again shows the reliance on external factors as a basis for identification.

Since the five factors discussed by Klein and Crawford are closely related to the dimensions of solidarity, it does not seem out of place to conjecture that they, as did Yablonsky, would conceive of conflict gangs as being rather low in solidarity. The results of one other gang study, this time in Chicago, are consistent with this view (Short and Strodtbeck, 1965; Gordon, 1967).

Using a series of measures, Short and Strodtbeck determined that the Chicago gangs which they studied were low in what Klein and Crawford called "internal cohesion." Despite the great deal of time spent together, the level of satisfaction attained by individual members was disproportionately low. This is true, according to the investigators, because most gangs have no goal or purpose and are not integrated into an "external system" (as Homans used the term) such as the larger community (Gordon, 1967). Thus, like Klein and Crawford, the Chicago researchers see gangs as existing mainly because the boys are thrown together by a series of external forces. The primary external factor which they isolate for detailed discussion is "social disability." This refers to the lack of social assurance and interpersonal competence that characterizes the gang members' social relationship with persons outside of the gang. The social disability of gang members probably results from a complex, vicious cycle. Put very simply, being born into disadvantaged families, they do not develop the appropriate social skills to succeed in outside social situations, and being thus excluded, they never have the chance to gain these at any later point. Whyte (1965) recognized the importance of this factor for the Norton gang, as evidenced in the following statement made by Doc:

> Fellows around here don't know what to do except within a radius of about three hundred yards. That's the truth, Bill. They come home from work, hang on the corner, go up to eat, back on the corner, up to a show, and they come back to hang on the corner. . . . (p. 256).

Short and Strodtbeck suggest, however, that social disability is even greater among the gangs they observed, especially among the boys in more disadvantaged neighborhoods. Gang workers assigned to particular gangs spend much of their time trying to get boys to engage in activities other than merely "hanging out" on the street corner. Usually these efforts are strongly resisted by the members with high-ranking statuses because they are afraid that their lack of skill in some new activity would undermine their positions in the group (see Mattick and Caplan, 1967).

The concept of "social disability" enables us to see how the exclusion of lower class adolescents from the legitimate opportunity structure is manifested at the interpersonal level. It also shows that the lower class adolescent plays an active role in this exclusion by clinging to familiar territory and faces, no matter how unsatisfactory the results, rather than risking failure on the outside. It is not surprising then, that groups which form as a result of such a process cannot attain high levels of solidarity.

The modified image of gangs that has emerged from the studies reviewed above suggests that most lower class gangs are incapable of sustaining any viable norms and goals, including organized conflict or violence. Yet, these groups usually become known throughout the larger community for their violence, and violent conflict is often a source of identification for gang members. What role, then, does conflict play in the lower class gang? In order to address this question, it is necessary to look at the gang over a period of time. No gang engages in conflict constantly; therefore we have to ask which situations precipitate conflict and what effect conflict has upon the gang.

To begin, we shall look at an excellent and detailed study of a single gang over time. Jansyn (1966) computed several indices that reflect the solidarity of the gang at various times. The first of these, which he called the *index of solidarity,* involved a count of the number of hours spent together by members of the gang. This index, then, is really a measure of the frequency of interaction among members. A chart of this index over a year's time showed that the gang went through cycles of high and low solidarity. Based on notes gathered when meeting with the gang as a gang worker, Jansyn also identified periods of organization and disorganization. According to his definition, group organization was high when the status structure was clearly defined and recognizable. A comparison of these two measures revealed that when attendance was high so was the level of organization. In other words, he found that the frequency of interaction and the development of the status structure were correlated, which helps to confirm our position in Chapter 2 that the dimensions of solidarity are usually interrelated.

Jansyn also examined changes in a variable he called "group activity." This was broken down into three types: (1) actions of the entire group; (2) delinquency of the entire group; (3) delinquency of individuals and cliques. The first two of these variables really involved the extent to which the members pursued group goals. Jansyn then compared these variables with his index of solidarity (attendance). His analysis showed that the number of group activities, especially group delinquency, increases during times of low solidarity. This is interpreted as showing that group-oriented delinquent activities were an important means by which the solidarity of the group was regained after periods of anomie. Jansyn does not say what proportion of the group delinquencies involved conflict, but it can be inferred from his examples that the majority of them did. While gangs that are not "criminal gangs" may engage in a criminal caper *as a group,* it appears from the literature that this is uncommon. Conflict is the major means by which such groups increase solidarity.

Short and Strodtbeck (1965) offer a similar explanation for the tendency for lower class gangs to engage in conflict. According to their observations, conflict often results when a leader or high-ranking member needs to reestablish his influence (or "rep") in the gang. For instance, they observed several cases where past leaders returning from jail found it necessary to instigate fights in order to regain their old statuses. Other "threats" to leadership—such as being "put down" by a gang worker, having one's gang defeated in an athletic event, or not having money to take part in group activities—were observed to lead to similar results. The last case, lack of money, is of interest because it resembles Doc's problems with the Norton gang at one point in his leadership. Doc, however, did not initiate violence or other forms of delinquency as a response. Unlike Doc, leaders in the gangs observed by Short and Strodtbeck had relatively few resources at their disposal to use as rewards and punishment and few activities available for proving their worth to the gang. Doc's leadership was bolstered by his many relationships with individuals and groups outside the Norton gang. These relationships provided him with ways of rewarding group members. Where a leader's rank in a gang is based upon fighting skill alone, he may be known outside of his group but will not necessarily have the kinds of connections that will help sustain his leadership within the gang. Thus, when his influence begins to wane, more conflict is the only solution.

Conflict between gangs rarely involves planned and organized confrontations of a military nature (Gannon, 1967). Usually, fights are spontaneous eruptions in response to situations which gang members happen to confront during their activities together. A gang need not be thoroughly and decidedly beaten for members of the opposing gang to experience the satisfaction of victory. Any confrontation, no matter what the outcome, provides a gang member with the opportunity to establish his skill and daring in the eyes of fellow members. By encouraging or allowing sporadic violence, high-ranking members can not only reestablish their positions but allow other members to renew their "reps" as well. In fact, the same aim can be accomplished if the leader or group as a whole can contrive a situation where they all display their willingness to fight but do not actually fight. Since establishing one's "rep" is one of the few satisfactions to be gained from gang life, conflict increases the cohesiveness of the group. This, together with the more clearly defined status hierarchy that may result, contributes, at least temporarily, to the overall solidarity of the gang.

Conflict as a group product is more difficult to understand sociologically than is a highly organized effort to commit some illegal act. Whether or not a fight occurs depends upon so many accidental factors like the weather, the availability of others to fight with, and so on. It is true that conflict gangs become known throughout the environment because of their past conflicts. But perhaps it is best to conceive of such gangs as having the potential to engage in conflict should the situation arise. While it is impossible to make any general predictions about when or how often this type of gang will fight, we can say something about the environmental conditions that make fighting likely.

Conflict gangs have few opportunities to engage in activities that provide the basis for norms and a well-defined status structure. Therefore conflict becomes an attractive means by which individual members can meet their needs and maintain some semblance of solidarity. However, the environment must also provide the autonomy for a conflict gang to carry out their most notable group product. By comparison, middle class gangs have relatively little autonomy to engage in illegal acts of any type, and an organized criminal gang would not want to take the risk of calling attention to itself by engaging in extensive conflict (see Whyte, 1965). For conflict gangs, the situation is different. According to Short and Strodtbeck's estimate, not more than one in five instances of violence in Chicago led to serious consequences (i.e., serious injury or death). Furthermore, they say:

> When serious consequences arise, these are discovered by the authorities in only approximately one-fifth of the cases, and this figure is less than one in ten when the injury is inflicted in individual and group fighting. For average Negro gang boys the probability of arrest for involvement in instances of potential violence is probably no greater than .04 and for the very skillful this figure might fall to .02 (1965, p. 258).

According to Short and Strodtbeck, violence is not so much a result of the boys' disordered personalities, as Yablonsky suggested, but a result of rational choices that "make sense," given the alternatives. With little chance of being caught or punished and with every chance of gaining prestige within the group, the probability of a gang member being involved in violence is high. This is especially true for the leader who would have much to lose if he failed to fight when it was expected of him. Short and Strodtbeck give an example of a gang leader who was handed a gun while observing a fist fight between several members of his gang and nonmembers. Although nothing was said, there was a heavy expectation that the leader should do something. He did, and several people were wounded as a result.

The available information on conflict gangs points to some of the difficulties in determining group solidarity. Many conflict gangs have all the trappings of high solidarity groups (names, official titles, oaths of allegiance, uniforms), yet seem to be very low in cohesion. How can we account for this discrepancy? It was shown in Chapter 4 that when groups confront forces toward anomie, members create norms to maintain or boost solidarity (Bonacich, 1972). The satisfaction of belonging to a conflict gang is minimal; therefore, members, or potential members (i.e., those in the neighborhood), adopt an individualistic orientation. Names, uniforms, and titles provide the group with a degree of unity not otherwise attainable. Just as high status members are likely to seize the opportunity for conflict to increase solidarity, they are usually the ones most responsible for imposing the trapping of solidarity on the group.

In summary, the unstable lower class neighborhood is the source of strong forces toward anomie. Thus, any gangs forming in such an environment are restricted in solidarity. Conflict and violence are the primary means by which such gangs attempt to maintain some minimal level of solidarity.

Middle class gangs. Cloward and Ohlin's theory is typical of most research on gangs in that it ignores middle class gangs altogether. This would lead one to believe either that middle class adolescents do not form gangs or that there is little difference in gangs by social class. Sherif and Sherif tend toward this latter view with some qualifications. They state:

> The concern for "rep" so frequently reported in studies of "gangs" is not unique to the lower-class. Strivings to be recognized by other groups, to best them, to be on friendly terms with some and to avoid or eliminate others as competitors are also found among upper- and middle-class groups. What does differ among class settings is the regulation of such intergroup contacts by authority and, notably, the enormous differences between facilities and space in advantaged and disadvantaged neighborhoods. Advantaged neighborhoods have homes, clubs, and a variety of public locations in which to pursue their course toward recognition; thus, in these areas "territoriality" is seldom the issue that it becomes in a crowded inner city (p. 52).

What the Sherifs are saying is that while middle class adolescents form groups that meet their status needs (as in lower class groups), for a variety of reasons the members of these groups are not as likely to engage in delinquent acts or conflict. This is not to say that no middle class groups resemble Cloward and Ohlin's *criminal gang*. For instance, Greeley and Casey (1963) observed an upper middle class gang of boys involved in minor but systematic theft and vandalism. However, the authors suggest that this group was unique because such behavior is usually detected and prevented by family members or school authorities.

Meyerhoff and Meyerhoff (1964) found that the major activities carried out by the middle class gang observed by them revolved around cars. Most of the gang members were also members of separate formalized car clubs. The investigators also learned that many members had engaged in various white-collar crimes such as stealing from employees. However, these activities were not frequent and were carried out by individuals and not by the gang or a whole. Occasionally, some boys would do something that would be called to the attention of the police. However, these activities were generally viewed as pranks and not taken seriously.

The pressures to engage in economically related criminal acts that Cloward and Ohlin assume to be important in the formation of lower class gangs are not present for middle class adolescents. On the whole, middle class youths are well integrated into schools and various organizations or clubs that provide them with certain symbols of success and esteem. Coupled with the fact that middle class adolescents do not require alternative routes to economic goals or symbols of success is the fact that they are under close scrutiny by conventional authority figures. Middle class youths spend more time with their families than lower class youths; and because of their involvement in various middle class legitimate institutions, they have less time to spend in autonomous interaction with peers. Furthermore, as Sherif and Sherif (1967) pointed out, while middle class gangs may engage in intergroup competition, these processes are not exaggerated by the need to establish territory or "turf." All these factors tend to make middle class gangs less visible, almost to the point that many people feel that they do not exist. This is where the semantic difficulties connected with the term gang come in. Many social scientists are willing to call a group a gang only when members are involved in delinquency or violence and come into noticeable conflict with other groups, individuals, authorities, or agencies in their environment. This, of course, is less likely to occur in the groups that form among middle class adolescents.

Delinquent group products then are rare in middle class gangs. Being free of environmental pressures to enter into interdependent relationships outside of middle class legitimate institutions, middle class youths appear to join gangs primarily to meet social needs. While middle class adolescents may have less free time for interaction with peers than their lower-class counterparts, the pursuit of these social needs seem to be encouraged by most middle-class adults who value "belonging" and "social success" (Riesman, 1964). Such gangs, then, are based on friendship; members join voluntarily and are excluded if, for whatever reason, they are not liked.

Dunphy's (1960) study of middle class adolescents in Sidney, Australia, provides some insight into the dynamics of middle class gangs. He identified two overlapping social groupings in his study—the clique and the crowd. According to Dunphy, a clique is "a small group of intimate friends which provides a basic security for the individual and a center for the exchange of ideas, particularly concerning the relations of the sexes" (p. 59). The crowd "is the centre of larger and more organized social activities, such as parties and dances, which provide for interaction between sexes" (p. 59). What Dunphy calls a "clique" is what we are calling a "gang."

The most important factor in an individual's acceptance in a clique is his or her willingness to conform to the expectations of the group. They must be able to talk the language of the group, and they must be able to keep up with the level of social development of the other group members.

Younger adolescents tend to be members of same-sex cliques in which members espouse negative orientations to members of the opposite sex. However, at some point, the higher-ranking members of these cliques begin to date and to lead the remaining members toward heterosexual crowds. Later mixed-sex cliques begin to form; these usually consist of couples who are dating on a steady basis. Thus, the composition of cliques and crowds is never static. As a person becomes sexually and socially mature, he or she may drop out of the old group and join one involved in activities better suited to his or her needs. Likewise, individuals who fail to change fast enough and "keep up" with the development of other group members may be slowly excluded from group activities.

While members of the cliques denied having leaders when asked directly, they tended to name the same person when asked: "Who do people usually ring up (call by phone) when they want to know what is going on?" or "Who usually has the best ideas about what to do?" The clique leaders tended to be those who were advanced socially and usually had a steady relationship with a member of the opposite sex. As in other groups, the clique leaders were better known and had wider contacts outside the clique itself. The larger crowds formed when members from several cliques were brought together by their leaders, who were friends with one another. Clique leaders were, therefore, the most informed members of the clique, and this contributed to their high rank in their groups. Also, as clique leaders, they were accepted as representatives of their particular clique by members of the crowd. This pattern is similar to Doc's position in the Norton gang and his relationship to the larger community of which the Norton gang was a part.

In summary, then, the middle class gang revolves around those needs not met through other conventional channels—namely, friendship and heterosexual relationships. Each group may have its own standards for language, dress, and attitudes, and these criteria are used in determining who will become a member. By and large, an individual becomes a member of a specific group because he or she is attracted to the others and is accepted by them. Thus, cohesiveness in such groups is based upon interpersonal atrraction, as is usually the case in voluntary, informal groups. Because the environments in which middle-class adolescents find themselves provide them with the autonomy to pursue these social goals in groups of this type, the solidarity of most middle class gangs is high.

SOME CONCLUDING COMMENTS

We have discussed gangs in terms of type, corresponding social class, and neighborhood because this is the way most sociological thinking about gangs is organized. This approach utilizes a theoretical device called "ideal types," where hypothetical individuals or groups are constructed for purposes of comparison. Tönnies' concepts, Gemeinschaft and Gesellschaft, are "ideal" types because no real society fits all the characteristics of one or the other. With respect to gangs, most will not conform exactly to the three types described. Thus, it is possible that criminal gangs may become involved in conflict; conflict gangs may emerge in stable lower class neighborhoods; middle class gangs may engage in criminal activities; or conflict gangs may hold dances.

There are two ways in which deviations from the ideal types can be understood. One is that in classifying a gang one must consider the characteristics—levels of solidarity or group products—that occur most frequently. For instance, a criminal gang may engage in conflict because it was attacked by members of a rival gang. However, if observations made over time suggest that the members do not actively seek conflict and that conflict is not central to the solidarity of the group, it would not make sense to classify it as a conflict gang. Members of a conflict-oriented gang may, because of the prompting and financing of their gang worker, sponsor dances. But if this type of activity is short-lived and does not replace violence as a source of solidarity, the gang is best classified as a "conflict gang" (see Jansyn, 1966).

Gangs may also deviate from the ideal types because their characteristics are not congruent with the class and neighborhood settings which, according to Cloward and Ohlin's theory, are supposed to produce them. This happens primarily because Cloward and Ohlin's theory is oversimplified. Thus, conflict gangs may form in stable, lower class neighborhoods, criminal gangs may form in middle class neighborhoods, and gangs with middle class characteristics may emerge among lower class adolescents. However, in these specific cases, we would expect to find the environmental conditions said to be associated with the various types. For example, Kobrin and his colleagues (1967) found a conflict gang in an area characterized as a stable, lower class neighborhood. However, this gang was less prestigious in the eyes of the local community than the criminal group (the "sophisticated delinquents"). Furthermore, there was a decline in the old power structure within the neighborhood, which, according to the investigators, contributed to conditions that encourage the emergence of conflict gangs. Gannon (1967) found that lower class gangs whose members were able and interested in getting jobs and in going to school measured status along these dimensions, so that conflict and "rep" were less important.

Greeley and Casey's (1963) study of a middle class gang that regularly engaged in criminal activities also provides evidence as to why this group deviated from the ideal type. The members of this group were, for a variety of reasons, alienated from their families, school, and church. Structurally, then, the environment facing the members of this gang was similar to that of criminal gangs. They were cut off from conventional society and had enough autonomy to seek alternative avenues to success. As we reported earlier, the authors state that such a group is of interest because it does deviate from the usual middle class group. However, any deviations should be understandable in terms of the patterns of constraint and autonomy that confront the particular group under analysis.

Autonomous Groups

This chapter has focused on gangs because research and theory in this area are more abundant than for any other type of autonomous informal group. Yet, what we have said about the relationship between gangs and their environments should hold for any autonomous group. We can now make more general statements for all autonomous informal groups. First, the more acceptable or useful the group product is to some segment of the environment, the greater the autonomy given an informal group. If the informal group provides some product or service, like a formal organization it will receive money or some reward in return that it can use to support itself and satisfy its members. In cases where group products are not necessarily useful but are not offensive to segments of the environment, the group will be allowed to exist with no interference. Most autonomous groups are friendship groups made up of individuals whose main source of satisfaction is derived from interacting with one another and whose group products, while not necessarily useful to outsiders, are not offensive. Of course, where group products are negatively evaluated, bringing forth environmental constraint, the group must either disintegrate or carry out its activities in secrecy. Such groups can exist if there is sufficient need for the group product or sufficient autonomy to allow the group to operate underground. In these cases, the need for secrecy may contribute to the solidarity of the group.

Groups whose primary activities involve meeting the social goals of the members usually are given enough autonomy to carry out their activities. However, the solidarity of such groups, in part, depends on the extent to which members are constrained to interact with one another. We saw that lower class adolescents are, for a variety of reasons, limited to interacting with others in their immediate neighborhood. The result was low solidarity groups. Friendship groups that form among members in the same work organization would, in general, be lower in solidarity than those comprised of members who have chosen each other from a wider variety of potential members (see Lipset *et al.,* 1956). To the extent that members are compelled by environmental constraints to form interdependent relationships with one another, the satisfaction they gain from their membership will be minimal and solidarity will be low.

SUMMARY

The environment of an informal group consists of those external factors that influence certain characteristics of the group and are affected by them. Three kinds of environmental factors can be identified: physical, cultural, and structural. In trying to explain why a particular group has certain characteristics, it is necessary to look for the patterns of autonomy and constraint as determined by the structural factors in the environment. The pattern of constraint and autonomy facing a particular group sets up forces toward solidarity and anomie that affect the group, including the nature of its group products and overall solidarity. The term "group products" refers to group activities that are visible to persons and groups in its environment. To illustrate this point, we examined adolescent groups to show how structural variations such as social class and neighborhood organization lead to different types of gangs.

The criminal gang is the only type that has an instrumental goal. Most gangs of this type derive some solidarity from the interpersonal attraction among members, but the instrumental goal—i.e., the illegal group product—is the primary basis of solidarity. Criminal gangs form in neighborhoods where their group product is accepted, desired, and allowed by important individuals and organizations. The stresses and strains experienced by all adolescents help such groups to develop, but they are reinforced in neighborhoods where adolescents are barred from easy access to conventional routes to success. The threat of detection and arrest requires criminal gangs to operate in secret, a factor that further increases solidarity. Except for the nature of the goal and the need for secrecy, criminal gangs are not much different from various conventional groups such as those that sponsor social events or improve neighborhoods. To exist, both must have supportive environments.

Gangs which approximate Cloward and Ohlin's "conflict type" exist in an environment which lacks the forces toward solidarity found in the first. Like the criminal gang, the members of conflict gangs are deprived of conventional means of achieving success goals, and this acts as a force toward solidarity that is common to both types. But, unlike the criminal gang, the conflict gang does not exist in an environment which supports the development of illegitimate instrumental goals. With no common instrumental goals, the solidarity of conflict gangs, as for middle class gangs, depends upon interpersonal attraction.

However, for a variety of reasons, this does not seem to be enough. For one thing, the social movement of lower class adolescents is restricted; they do not have the range of choices for social relationships that middle class adolescents have. This difficulty is compounded by the emphasis placed upon territory, or "turf," in overcrowded slums. In other words, unlike middle class gangs, lower class gangs form along geographical lines, thus restricting membership to those who happen to live together (Gannon *et al.*, 1967). Because the lower classes place value on aggressiveness, in-gang fighting is a constant threat to solidarity. Other anomic forces can be attributed to the lack of protection against police and the lack of adult support for gangs in the unstable lower class slum. Whatever solidarity develops in conflict gangs comes, as Klein and Crawford (1967) suggest, from external pressures and not instrumental or social goals that fit into and are encouraged by the gang's environment.

While members of conflict gangs spend most of their time standing around and talking, their most notable group product is occasional violence. This provides an opportunity for members to establish their "reps" and to develop some degree of solidarity as a group. Because of the unstable lower class neighborhood, the possibilities of arrest and punishment for being involved in conflict are outweighed by the minimal positive advantages. In other words, conflict groups exist in environments that give them sufficient autonomy even though they engage in illegal behavior.

Middle class adolescents have neither the need to pursue illegal group products nor the opportunity. Most middle class adolescents find it relatively easy to attain success through conventional institutions and so are not compelled to seek illegal alternatives. Because they spend a relatively great deal of time in contact with conventional authority figures, including parents, they do not have the autonomy to develop illegal instrumental goals as a part of the ganging process. This does not mean that middle class gang members do not engage in deviant acts. But, just as relevant authorities and social scientists overlook the nondeviant activities of lower class gangs, they also overlook the illegal behavior of middle class gangs. However, unlike criminal gangs, most middle class gang members do not consider deviant group products to be the goals of their groups.

The major activities of the middle class gang appear to be social events—parties, dances, and other informal gatherings. The needs for security and sense of identity are met in middle class gangs, but these are not the group goals. While middle class adults constrain the development of illegal group products, they seem to tolerate and even encourage the development of middle class gangs because they value "belonging" and "social success." Middle class gangs do not form along neighborhood lines; and since their members have chosen one another from a larger population, such groups tend to be relatively cohesive.

While this chapter dealt with the analysis of gangs, there were several general conclusions made which can be extended to all relatively autonomous informal groups. One is that the more acceptable or useful the group products to some segment of the environment, the greater the autonomy provided the group. When group products are negatively evaluated by persons in the environment so that constraint results, the group will tend to disintegrate or carry out activities in secret. Finally, solidarity will be low to the extent that members form interdependent relationships with one another because the nature of their environment makes it impossible for them to relate with others outside of the group.

eight

Formal Organizations as Environments

INTRODUCTION

The environments to be considered in this chapter are formal organizations, and the informal groups of interest consist of individuals who have been placed together as a subsystem (a department, unit, shop, or ward) of the larger formal organization. These subsystems consist of individuals who, because of their common status in the organization and their physical proximity, are in a position to develop some degree of solidarity among themselves. We shall call these units *informal subsystems*.

Members of informal subsystems are placed together; they do not come together voluntarily, as members of more autonomous groups do. In most cases, the larger formal organization's control over a particular subsystem has its source in what can be called an *external authority*. An external authority is a person (or group of persons) who, because of his position in the formal organization, exerts some degree of control over the behavior of a number of subordinates in the organization. This control is legitimized by the external authority's status in the organization. Some examples of external authorities are prison guards, factory supervisors, work foremen, and hospital attendants.

The fact that the members of subsystems are *placed* together is one indication that they are under control of the external authority. However, the external control also includes regulating the subordinates' activities or behavior in the formal organization. For example, members of the bank wiring room were told by the external authority (the immediate supervisor) what activities to carry out and when. However, the members also specified appropriate behavior for themselves in the form of normative and status expectations. Thus, each worker was

187

exposed to social control from the informal groups as well as from the external authority. The fact that the members of the group were constrained by two sources of authority—the external authority and the emergent group itself—qualifies it as a subsystem.

Informal subsystems vary along a continuum where external authority exerts a high degree of control at one extreme and a low degree at the other. In this chapter we will examine informal groups located at various points along this continuum. As we did with gangs, we shall focus on how the patterns of constraint and autonomy in the environment influence the characteristics of four kinds of subsystems. Three kinds are found in autocratic total institutions and the fourth is found in work organizations. We shall look first at the general characteristics of autocratic total institutions.

AUTOCRATIC TOTAL INSTITUTIONS

Concentration camps, traditional prisons, and custodial mental hospitals, while having different goals, are all "total institutions" (Goffman, 1961). According to Goffman, most members of modern society sleep, play, and work in different places, with different people, under different authorities; most people have no organized schedule for these various activities. In total institutions, these three spheres of life are not physically separated. First, all life activities are carried out in the same place under the same single authority. Second, each phase of the members' daily routine is performed in the immediate company of a large number of others, all of whom are treated alike and are required to do the same things together. Third, daily activities are tightly scheduled. One activity leads, at a prearranged time into the next, the whole sequence being imposed from above by a body of officials through a system of explicit formal rules (Goffman, 1961, p. 6).

Total institutions include a wide range of organizations such as monasteries, boarding schools, and merchant marine ships. But the three organizations considered here are autocratic because power lies almost exclusively in the hands of the officials who coerce their subordinates into compliance. Despite the lofty-sounding stated goals of many of these organizations (i.e., therapy, rehabilitation), total institutions are organized to maximize the efficiency of handling large numbers of inmates. Thus, the formal structure of such organizations is designed for surveillance and regimentation. In short, the inmates participate in these organizations because they are forced to; total authoritarian power gives these organizations their unique atmosphere and shapes the social relationships that form among the inmates.

Goffman sees much of inmate life in total institutions as involving a process of adjustment. According to Goffman:

In total institutions there will also be a system of what might be called secondary adjustments, namely, practices that do not directly challenge staff but allow inmates to obtain forbidden satisfactions or to obtain permitted ones by forbidden means. These practices are variously referred to as "the angles," "knowing the ropes," "conniving," "gimmicks," "deals," or "ins." Secondary adjustments provide the inmate with important evidence that he is still his own man, with some control of his environment (1961, pp. 54–55).

To the extent that adjustments require cooperation among inmates, informal relationships develop. There is a considerable amount of literature examining the nature of these informal relationships among inmates; however, the attention played to these phenomena—often referred to as "inmate societies" or "inmate cultures"—has reinforced the idea that these informal relationships are inevitably high in solidarity. Commenting on this, Goffman says:

> Although there are solidarizing tendencies such as fraternalization and clique formation, they are limited. Constraints which place inmates in a position to sympathize and communicate with each other do not necessarily lead to high group morale and solidarity (p. 60).

We shall examine three autocratic total institutions and illustrate how the characteristics of each influence the nature of the informal subsystems that arise among the inmates.

Nazi Concentration Camps

Soon after Hitler's rise to power in Germany, Hermann Göring, Prussian chief of police and cabinet minister, established concentration camps as a means of controlling Communists. However, the system of concentration camps in Germany grew in size as larger segments of the German population were labeled "undesirable" or "enemies of the state." The largest number and most persecuted of these, of course, were Jews. According to Bettelheim (1943), the camps served the following interrelated functions:

> *To break the prisoners as individuals* and to change them into docile masses from which no individual or group act of resistance could arise; *to spread terror among the rest of the population* by using the prisoners as hostages for good behavior and by demonstrating what happens to those who oppose the Nazi rules; *to provide the Gestapo members with a training ground* in which they are so educated as to lose all human emotions and attitudes and learn the most effective ways of breaking resistance in a defenseless civilian population; *to provide the Gestapo with an experimental laboratory* in which to study the effective means for breaking civilians' resistance, the minimum food, hygienic, and medical requirements needed to keep prisoners alive and able to perform hard labor when the threat of punishment takes the place of all other normal incentives, and the influence on performance if no time is allowed for anything but hard labor and if the prisoners are separated from their families (p. 418).

As World War II progressed, these camps were also used to exterminate Jews brought in from countries occupied by Germany and to provide labor for the war effort.

There were several kinds of camps in the system. Some were dedicated exclusively to exterminating inmates, while others used those who managed to stay alive for labor. It is this latter type which is of interest here. The organization of such camps involved a rather complex division of labor. The management of these camps was in the hands of an elite branch of the S.S. called the "Deathhead regiments." Members of these regiments had to spend three months in training as guards in order to become used to murder and brutality. A trainee who failed to perform "adequately" would be sent back to nonelite regiments of the S.S. Also in authority at the camps were members of the "political department" of the Gestapo, the Nazi secret police. They controlled such processes as the release, examination, and trials of prisoners and decided who should be sent to the gas chambers (Cohen, 1953).

Depending upon the particular camp, the inmate population consisted of a variety of German criminals, Communists, gypsies, religious groups unsympathetic to Naziism, homosexuals, Jews, and many others considered undesirable by the state. The different types of inmates were identified by patches worn on their clothing. All prisoners were tatooed with identification numbers, given the same inadequate uniforms, and had their heads shaved. However, some prisoners were given better treatment and more privileges than others. Often these "elites" were composed of criminals (as opposed to political prisoners) and those who possessed specialized skills required by the authorities.

There are probably few cases in history where human beings have been so systematically stripped of their identity and autonomy as those in the German concentration camps. Inmates were constantly under surveillance by the authorities and were rarely given the opportunity to determine their own behavior. Guards were given free reign to use any method whatever to ensure the compliance of the inmates. Imprisonment usually began with an "initiation" in which new prisoners were systematically beaten and tortured for not less than twelve hours. This served to exhaust the inmates and allowed the authorities to flaunt their power. An inmate who violated any of the numerous rules could be tortured or even killed. Many rules were explicitly designed to prevent stable social relationships from developing among the prisoners. Inmates were often moved from labor group to labor group and from barracks to barracks to discourage friendships. According to Bettelheim (1943), inmates were prohibited from talking to one another during most of the day. Furthermore, anyone suspected of protecting another inmate or even tending to another's wounds was punished. To make life even more difficult, authorities enforced these numerous rules arbitrarily and invented new ones on the spot.

Informal relationships among inmates. Most of the research on concentration camps has been concerned with the prisoners' psychological adjustment to these extreme conditions. However, there is enough information to allow some conclusions about the formation of social relationships among inmates. Because of the close surveillance, inmate relationships were confined to those assigned to the same labor group or barracks. It is amazing that any social life could exist at all under such oppressive circumstances, and the available evidence suggests that solidarity among inmates was indeed limited. Luchterhand (1967) reports that only in a few prisons and only during the last months of the war did underground organizations emerge among prisoners. Based on interviews with ex-political prisoners, most friendships among inmates involved pairs or small groups. Seventeen of the forty-seven respondents described their relationships with others as "exploitive" rather than "friendly." Many described their pair relationships as incompatible. Most of the pair relationships involved the reciprocal sharing of food or any other scarce resources. Seven of those interviewed by Luchterhand admitted to stealing from other inmates, while five said that they had considered stealing at some time.

Bondy (1943) also reports that small groups or cliques were the most stable form of relationship among political prisoners. According to Bondy, inmates lacked a sense of responsibility, and quarrels and conflict were normal. Contrary to Luchterhand, he states that social organizations involving trade among inmates and the means for establishing contact with the outside existed in all camps, but adds that these organizations were not well developed. He also suggests that those inmates who gained some degree of control over others adopted the values of the jailors and tended to exploit their fellow inmates. Cohen (1953), who relies on information based on her own experiences as well as those of others, says that comradeship existed in all camps, but only when it involved few sacrifices. Finally, Block (1947) also reports that the high death rate and the pressure for survival prevented social organization among inmates from developing to any extent.

Forces toward solidarity and anomie. The social relationships that did form among inmates served primarily to provide scarce resources such as food and the will to continue living. Several of the authors writing about concentration camps indicated that those inmates who entered no social relationships were the first to perish. However, the available data clearly suggest that solidarity among inmates was underdeveloped.

Aside from the concentration camp, probably no other environment has been structured to so effectively reduce subsystem solidarity. The amount of power in the hands of the external authorities in the camps made the inmates almost completely dependent upon them for survival. So strong was the dependency which developed that many inmates could not face the prospect of being free at the war's end. Had the camp authorities been able to attain their goals, the prisoners would very likely have been totally separate from one another, each relating only to the guards. If that ideal had been reached, it would be meaningless to even speak of the inmates as constituting a subsystem.

However, the costs of maintaining complete control over every inmate and completely obliterating solidarity would have been too high. Therefore, the inmates found some autonomy in which to carve out for themselves a limited social life. In the barracks after work and during meals the inmates would talk among themselves and form friendships. According to Bettelheim (1943), inmates used to have conversations before dawn and after dusk while on the job even though talking was prohibited. Contributing to their willingness to engage in such forbidden behavior was the fact that the guards' reactions were so arbitrary that they could not predict what behavior would be punished. In their minds, it was worth the risk to talk since punishment was inevitable anyway.

The extreme dependency on the external authorities that prevented the interdependence necessary for solidarity among inmates can be seen in the following illustrations. Bettelheim reports that the older prisoners accused those who refused to develop a childlike dependency on the guards of threatening the security of the group. This was not far from the truth, for the Gestapo would often punish the group for the misbehavior of individual members. Abel (1951) reports that inmates who "fought back against the terror imposed by the authorities were neglected and despised by fellow inmates." Bettelheim, Abel, and Cohen report that some prisoners identified with the formal authorities by imitating their speech, manner, and dress. Some of these prisoners would even enforce Gestapo rules by the very same methods used by their captors.

In summary, because of the degree of dependency upon authorities, most inmates, most of the time, adopted individualistic rather than interdependent orientations, which made solidarity in barracks and labor groups very low.

Traditional Prisons

Compared with the sparse information on informal relationships in concentration camps, the literature on prisons is abundant. In order to understand the way prisons in America are organized, it is necessary to look at the goals the larger society expects prison administrators to attain. According to Cressey (1960), the first is *retribution.* Most members of our society feel that criminals deserve to be punished and deprived of civil liberties. The second goal, *deterrence,* is based on the widespread assumption that the threat of being sent to prison discourages criminal behavior. The third goal is *protection* and is based upon the idea that criminals should be isolated from the larger society, thereby insuring the safety of decent citizens. Although not usually voiced by common citizens, a related goal of prisons is protecting prisoners from one another. Finally, there is the expectation that prisons should *rehabilitate* prisoners.

The first three goals—retribution, deterrence, and protection—are generally consistent with each other. Restraining prisoners within prison walls fulfills the need for protection. The extreme control based on physical coercion and the monotony of regimented prison life fulfill the other two. In early American prisons this type of organization embodied the prevailing ideas about the kinds of treatment which lead to rehabilitation. According to Cressey (1960), "In prisons of the traditional type the mechanism assumed to be the most effective for reform was likely to be the same used in performing other functions: almost complete totalitarian control over inmates, with corporal punishment and extreme isolation imposed for violation of rules" (p. 83). However, conceptions of what is necessary to reform or rehabilitate have changed since then, and prison organization has had to be altered.

By and large, rehabilitation has come to mean "treatment" in much the same way that this term is used in psychiatry. However, as we shall see in the next chapter, attempts to include "treatment" in the formal structure of prisons have led to many conflicts and problems, and, as a result, actual organizational changes have been minor. Some penal institutions have managed to offer real treatment or rehabilitation, but most exist primarily to maintain custody of prisoners; they are referred to as custodial, or traditional, prisons.

Informal relationships among inmates. Informal relationships among prison inmates have been observed by many researchers who have referred to them variously as "inmate social systems," "inmate cultures," or "prisoner communities." Informal systems in traditional prisons are usually revealed through the existence of *inmate codes* and *argot roles.* Inmate codes consist of norms or rules that are allegedly accepted by all inmates as guides for their behavior in prison. Sykes and Messinger (1960) have divided these codes into five categories. The first category prohibits any behavior that prevents an inmate from making the easiest possible adjustment to prison life. The most important rule is: "Never rat or squeal on a con," which prohibits telling the authorities about the illegal behavior of another inmate. So strong is the feeling against passing on information to authorities that any communication at all with the guards or other authorities is suspect (i.e., "Don't talk to a screw [guard]"). The second category of rules prohibits quarrels or conflicts with fellow prisoners. These rules are often phrased in such terms as "Don't lose your head," "Play it cool," and "Do your own time." The third category is composed of rules which advise prisoners against taking advantage of one another: "Don't exploit inmates," "Don't break your word," "Don't steal from cons." The fourth area covered by the inmate codes has to do with what Sykes and Messinger refer to as "maintenance of self." Positive value is placed upon the ability to withstand frustration and punishment without complaining or completely submitting to the external authorities. As stated by inmates these rules are: "Don't whine," "Don't copout," "Don't suck around," "Be tough," and "Be a man." The final category consists of maxims that forbid any positive orientations to the officials of the prison: "Don't be a sucker," "Never trust a screw."

"Argot" is the specialized vocabulary used habitually by a particular group of individuals. One well known use of argot is to attach distinctive names to people who habitually behave in a particular manner. "Argot roles" are usually used when the behavior of those labeled is of importance to the group. We have already seen that the terms "chisler," "rate buster," and "squealer" were used in the bank wiring room to refer to a member who failed to conform to the norms of the group. Among prison inmates such labels are attached to those who either conform to or deviate from the inmate code.

The inmate who violates or is suspected of violating the norm forbidding the betrayal of another inmate is referred to as a *rat* or *squealer*. *Centermen* are those inmates who openly take the perspective of the authorities. Highly aggressive inmates who fight with other inmates are called *toughs*. The *tough* may gain the respect of the other inmates but it is respect based on coercion, and *toughs* are not usually considered to be leaders. A *ball buster* is a man who is openly defiant of authority. Other inmates may respect a *ball buster* if his rebelliousness is for a worthy cause. Usually however, ball busters are regarded as troublemakers because they are likely to bring "heat" (increased surveillance or retaliation from the authorities).

The term *gorilla* refers to those who use force to gain their ends. *Merchants* or *peddlers* are those who sell or trade scarce goods which, according to the code, ought to be shared or exchanged. A *politician* is an inmate whose power is based on his ability to transmit information between officials and inmates. He gains access to information by making informal deals with authorities or by getting himself employed where information can be obtained. He has power over other inmates because he can reward or punish them by giving or withholding information, a scarce resource in the prison system. The *wolf, fag,* or *punk* are argot roles that arise from the lack of heterosexual opportunities in prisons; wolves are aggressive, masculine inmates who initiate, often through force, homosexual relationships with others; fags are inmates who were homosexuals before they entered prison; punks are those inmates who have submitted to wolves.

Most of the argot roles described so far involve behavior that helps an individual adjust to the deprivations and rigors of prison life, but at the expense of other inmates. The rare inmate who lives up to the values of the inmate social system is referred to as a "real man," or "right guy." Sykes and Messinger (1960) described this type as follows:

> A *right guy* is always loyal to his fellow prisoners. He never lets you down no matter how rough things get. He keeps his promises: he's dependable and trustworthy. He isn't nosey about your business and does not shoot off his mouth about his own. He doesn't act stuck-up, but he doesn't fall all over himself to make friends either—he has a certain dignity. The *right guy* never interferes with other inmates who are conniving against the officials. He doesn't go around looking for a fight, but he never runs away from one when he is right. Anybody who starts a fight with a *right guy* has to be ready to go all the way. What he's got or can get off the extras in the prison—like cigarettes, food stolen from the mess hall, and so on—he

shares with his friends. He doesn't take advantage of those who don't have much. He does not strong-arm other inmates into punking or fagging for him; instead he acts like a man. In his dealings with the prison officials, the *right guy* is unmistakably against them, but he doesn't act foolishly. When he talks about the officials with other inmates, he's sure to say that even the hacks with the best intentions are stupid, incompetent, and not to be trusted; that the worst thing a con can do is give the hacks information— they'll use it against you when the chips are down. A *right guy* sticks up for his rights, but he doesn't ask for pity: he can take all the lousy screws can hand out and more. He doesn't suck around the officials, and the privileges that he's got are his because he deserves them. Even if the *right guy* doesn't look for trouble with officials, he'll go to the limit if they push him too far (pp. 10–11).

As might be expected from this idealistic description, "right guys" are rare among prisoners.

The highly developed, often verbalized inmate codes and argot roles clearly indicate that inmates within the same cellblock do form an informal subsystem within the formal organization of the traditional prison. The basis of this solidarity is the common antagonism toward the prison authorities.

Forces toward solidarity and anomie. The similarities between the authority structures of concentration camps and the traditional prison are almost too obvious to mention (see McCleery, 1960; Etzioni, 1961). Yet, as we have seen, inmate solidarity in the concentration camps was almost nonexistent but is relatively well developed in traditional prisons. The reason for this is that inmates in traditional prisons have greater autonomy. Once source of this autonomy is the protection society gives inmates because of the value it places on humane treatment. Such values were nonexistent in Nazi Germany; external authorities could torture or even kill inmates. Therefore, because prison guards have less control over the rewards and punishments that coerce inmates into compliance, inmates have greater autonomy.

There is another important source of autonomy for inmates in traditional prisons. Despite the guards' high degree of control because of their formal statuses in the prison structure, various pressures make it unlikely that they will always utilize the total amount of control available. This failure to exert full control is called the "corruption of authority." According to Sykes (1958):

Guards frequently fail to report infractions of the regulations; guards transmit forbidden information to inmates, neglect elementary security requirements, and join inmates in outspoken criticism of higher officials. This "corruption" of the guard's authority is apparently seldom to be attributed to bribery—bribery is usually unnecessary, for far more subtle influences are at work which tend to destroy authority of the cellblock guard (p. 258).

Sykes maintains that corruption of authority can occur through several processes. One of the more important of these is *corruption through friendship*. Although the guard is a prison official, he is at the bottom of the authority hierarchy and spends more time on the job with inmates than with other authorities. Thus, both guards and inmates are in inferior positions and may have many common complaints which they can share because of their close physical contact. Furthermore, because of this contact, guards often find their jobs easier if they act in a friendly manner and do not antagonize an already hostile group of men. Last, Sykes suggests that guards whose income and prestige is rather low may even envy a successful criminal and gain some psychological reward through associating with him.

Another aspect of the corruption of authority is the process which Sykes calls *corruption through reciprocity.* This stems from the fact that the guard depends on inmates for receiving positive evaluations from his superiors. Much of what occurs in the cellblock is not observable by the guard's superiors (high authorities in the prison system) and they must rely upon whatever information is available to assess the effectiveness of a guard. A guard whose cellblock comes to the attention of his superiors because of fights, escapes, and other illegal activities will be perceived as being unable to handle the prisoners, which, in a traditional prison, is a major criterion of success.

Although the guard is in a position of power, the direct application of force is not a feasible way to ensure order. First, the guard cannot watch all prisoners in his charge simultaneously. Second, even though he has force on his side, he would be helpless if all the prisoners went after him at once. If he called for additional help, he would only draw the superior's attention to his problem. Third, the withdrawal of privileges and solitary confinement are not all that effective in inducing conformity from men who are already extremely deprived. The constant disciplining of prisoners by a guard causes administrative work for higher authorities and again calls their attention to his incompetence. The guard, then, is under pressure to run his cellblock smoothly by providing certain informal positive inducements in exchange for compliance. Therefore, he is likely to overlook minor offenses and "not see" violations of rules that could never be detected by the higher authorities. The guard can also reward prisoners by assigning them to easy jobs or jobs that are desirable because they enable a prisoner to obtain food, information, or other scarce commodities.

Once a guard's authority has been corrupted, it is difficult for him to regain it. If he broke his informal agreements, the inmates could behave disruptively or send anonymous letters to the higher authorities describing the guard's past violations of prison rules. Also important in maintaining the informal exchange is the guard's realization that he might well become a hostage in the event of a riot or break. In such situations he would certainly not want to have the reputation for reneging on informal agreements.

All of these factors provide inmates a certain degree of autonomy that allows them to deviate from prison rules. This autonomy contributes to the development of the inmate system.

The *inmate system* helps individuals make the unpleasant experience of being in prison as bearable as possible. According to Cloward (1960), the inmate system provides a means to seek material goods, power, and prestige, all of which are scarce commodities in a prison. We have seen in earlier chapters that those who supply scarce rewards for other group members gravitate toward high status or leadership positions. Those inmates who gain access to scarce goods or information do so only with the help of external authorities. Those who become merchants must be put in positions where they have access to illegal goods. Those who become politicians must be placed in situations where they can gain information not usually available to inmates. Similarly, the right guy's prestige comes, in part, because he is respected by prison authorities. The authorities do not, for a variety of reasons, treat all inmates as equals, and this is responsible for much of the differentiation within the inmate system. Inmates given special privileges by the guards are usually those who, for whatever reason, are capable of controlling the nonelites. Because of the strong suspicion of anyone dealing with guards, only some inmates can engage in informal exchanges with the authorities with impunity. Those who are allowed to violate the dictate "Don't talk to screws" have been able to convince the others that their dealings with the guard are to the advantage of the whole group—that is, whatever is to be gained (whether material goods or information) will be distributed among the others. An inmate's ability to provide such resources for the other inmates gives him even more "idiosyncrasy credits" (see p. 151) to engage in further informal agreements with the authorities.

By allowing these elites to emerge and have access to scarce resources, the guards gain a measure of control over the inmates that they normally would not have. The guards hold the key to scarce goods and thus the key to the power which the high-ranking inmates have over the others. In exchange for the advantages which come from dealing with the guard, the high ranking inmates must exert control over the other inmates. This keeps the inmates orderly, which, in turn, keeps the guards out of trouble with their superiors. The interests of the guards and inmates, who both benefit from the informal agreements, become the same: preservation of the system. Inmates who behave in ways that would come to the attention of higher authorities are a threat to the guard, the high ranking inmates, and the inmates who benefit from the informal agreement between the two. Thus, a guard can rely upon those inmates with power to maintain control in areas his own power cannot reach.

So far we have considered how autonomy that is introduced through the corruption of authority allows interdependent relationships among inmates to be established. Autonomy from the control of external authority produces environmental forces toward solidarity, but the nature of the prison environment also produces strong forces toward anomie as well. Although inmates are given autonomy, it is limited. Despite the corruption of authority, the inmates' power never approximates that of the guards, who control access to scarce commodities and can withdraw privileges.

In spite of the constant verbal emphasis on the inmate code, there is reason to believe that it is constantly violated. The large number of argot rules with negative connotations attached is one indication of the extent to which inmates deviate from the inmate code. Often those who most loudly espouse the inmate code are the ones who most frequently violate it. Much of the conformity to the various norms is the result of terror tactics and not of genuine acceptance by the inmates. Although a guard's power is not complete, his control over rewards makes inmates more dependent upon him than upon each other. The inmate leaders must constantly discourage competitors from negotiating with the guards for special privileges. This is accomplished either by labeling them as rats or through the use of force. As stated earlier, the terms "merchant" and "politicians" are used with a mixture of respect and hostility. Thus, those high-ranking inmates who appear to be gaining too much for themselves at the expense of others are likely to be labeled as such and eventually deprived of power. Even leaders and "right guys" whose behavior is above reproach find it difficult to maintain their high status in the atmosphere of distrust which permeates the traditional prison.

A study of a traditional prison by Clemmer (1958) supplies some information about the nature of informal relationships that form among prisoners. Inmates interviewed were classified as either belonging to a primary group, a semiprimary group, or as being ungrouped. The difference between the first two categories pertained to the degree of intimacy and "we-feeling shared by the inmate with fellow group members." Clemmers found that only 17.4 percent of those interviewed belonged to a primary group. Forty percent belonged to semiprimary groups, and 41.9 percent were ungrouped. It is interesting to look at what the inmates had to say about the informal social relationships in prisons. The following results were obtained when inmates were asked to answer a series of true-and-false questions (Clemmer, 1965, p. 123).

1. Seventy-two percent of the subjects stated that friendships in prison are of short duration.
2. Seventy-seven percent stated that familiarity in prison breeds contempt.
3. Seventy percent of the subjects concluded that the friendships in prison result from the mutual help which man can give man rather than because of some admired trait.
4. Ninety-five percent of the subjects were of the opinion that most prisoners are more interested in themselves than any other prisoner.

The results of Clemmer's study do not lead one to the conclusion that the inmate system is characterized by extremely high solidarity.

In summary, interdependent relationships seem to be formed mainly for reaching instrumental goals that are not continued when there is nothing to be gained. The power of the prison authorities fosters dependence upon them to the point that prisoners are greatly tempted to adopt individualistic orientations, even if they have to risk violating the inmate code. Cohesion based on interpersonal attraction, which usually develops when people are in close proximity, also seems to be limited by competition and distrust among inmates. Perhaps the following quote from Sykes and Messinger (1960) best describes the results of the forces toward solidarity and anomie set up by the environment in traditional prisons.

> The population of prison, then, does not exhibit perfect solidarity in practice in spite of inmates' vehement assertions of group cohesion as a value; but neither is the population a warring aggregate. Rather the inmate social system typically appears to be balanced in an uneasy compromise somewhere between these two extremes (p. 17).

The Traditional Mental Hospital

Researchers have pointed to parallels between the organization of traditional mental hospitals and prisons. Inmates and mental patients are usually confined involuntarily, and solidarity is limited by numerous formal rules and regulations.

Early mental hospitals, like early prisons, emphasized physical punishment, a "treatment" consistent with the prevailing ideas about mental illness. Progressive conflict between the goals of custody and rehabilitation has always existed in mental hospitals and prisons. However, much more so than prisons, traditional mental hospitals have included professionals such as doctors, psychiatrists, and nurses, whose official functions involve promoting rehabilitation. Along with rehabilitation has come an increasing acceptance of the idea that mental patients are sick persons who are not responsible for their behavior. Despite these changes, most wards in traditional mental hospitals are still organized for custody and not rehabilitation. "Therapeutic communities" are exceptions and will be discussed in the following chapter.

Because the goals of custody are still primary, techniques of coercion in traditional hospitals are often disguised as rehabilitative functions. There are several obvious examples. One is the administration of drugs. Ostensibly drugs are supposed to help patients come to terms with reality by arresting hallucinations and violent psychotic outbreaks. Drugs, however, also have the latent function of making patients more manageable. The authorities determine who receives drugs and how much and therefore have a great deal of control over the patients. Another technique of control that supposedly has therapeutic value is electroshock therapy. There is evidence that the threat of receiving this extremely painful procedure strengthens the control of the authorities over the patients.

Compliance is also gained by the authorities' control over the patients' ward assignments. In most traditional hospitals there exists a hierarchy of wards. The front, or "hopeful," wards house patients whose prognosis for discharge from the hospital is good; "back wards," "chronic wards," or "agitated wards" are usually located in out-of-the-way places and supposedly house patients whose illnesses are so severe that they have little hope for release. The authorities in charge of front wards allow patients more privileges and freedom of movement than do those in charge of back wards. However, psychiatric considerations are not the only ones which affect the assignment of patients to the various wards (Goffman, 1961). Patients who violate rules or who are considered difficult to manage may be sent to back wards. All patients know that in order to get out of the hospital they must work their way from back to front wards, and that this requires "good" behavior.

While doctors who work in mental hospitals are primarily oriented toward rehabilitation and less concerned with coercion, their influence is not strong enough to mitigate the extreme control placed over mental patients. According to Dunham and Weinberg (1960), the custodial traditions in a particular hospital counter any attempts at innovation. Doctors' diagnoses and recommendations are made with the overall goal of maintaining order. In other words, doctors' behavior reinforces the emphasis on custody. Any disapproved behavior is regarded as abnormal, and measures to counteract such behavior are legitimized as part of the patient's treatment. Furthermore, the doctors' contact with back ward patients is limited in traditional hospitals.

The persons who have most contact with patients are the nurses, aides, and attendants. It is their job to meet the needs of the patients, enforce the hospital's rules, and keep order. Nurses who have a higher-ranking status are usually in charge of dispensing drugs and taking care of administrative duties. According to Stanton and Schwartz (1954), the attendant, by preventing escapes, enforcing rules, and acting as both disciplinarian and supporter of patients, plays the role of policeman. Usually those recruited for the position of attendant are not highly educated and are generally insensitive to the rehabilitation goals of the hospital. Like the prison guard, attendants are the main instruments of control over the patients. Because they are generally unsupervised, they often resort to physical coercion to ensure order. Although not officially condoned, violence is more justifiable in mental hospitals than in prison. Since attendants must deal face to face with persons who are recognized as "disturbed" and thus "potentially violent," they can rationalize any physical coercion as a necessary response to violent attack.

One other difference between prisons and mental hospitals should be mentioned. This concerns the difference in the psychological characteristics of the patient population. Passivity, dependency, and disorientation are frequently mentioned characteristics of mental patients. These can result, in part, from the patients' adjustment to the regimentation of the hospital. However, they are also characteristics that those diagnosed as mentally ill bring with them to the hospital (Rosenberg, 1970). Whatever the reason, patients seem to require a highly structured situation with many rules and close supervision. In fact, much of the behavior of mental patients toward the staff and toward one another can be understood in terms of their general dependency upon hospital authorities.

Informal relationships among patients. The unit for the analysis of informal relationships among mental patients is the hospital ward. Most of the patients' time is spent in the ward and they have little opportunity for interaction with patients other than those assigned to the same ward. Characterizing the nature of the informal subsystems in hospital wards involves a difficulty not encountered in the analysis of prison inmate systems: Patients assigned to various wards differ in their diagnosis and in their prognosis for cure. The staff's evaluation of the severity of a patient's illness is closely related to the patient's capabilities of engaging in social relationships. Thus, social activity of any type is severely limited in chronic or disturbed wards, while it is higher in the front wards where "better adjusted" patients are assigned. Therefore, any discussion of the patient subsystem must make constant reference to type of ward being described.

While nothing as highly verbalized as an inmate code seems to exist in mental hospitals, there is evidence that patients in the same ward behave consistently in ways that suggest the existence of norms. In wards where the probability of discharge is high, patients may support the therapeutic aims of the hospital by talking about personal problems, giving support to each other, and espousing norms demanding cooperation with the staff (Smith and Thrasher, 1963; 1964; Caudill *et al.,* 1952). In less hopeful wards, patients may agree that illness should be denied and not discussed. Most patients in all wards seem to accept the norm to "get along"—that is, patients should adjust to the idiosyncracies of others and should not bother one another (Dunham and Weinburg, 1960).

Argot roles are also not so highly developed among patients as among prisoners; however, patients do usually share some jargon such as "bad ward," "going-home ward," "mental talk," and various terms like "buggy," to describe the more disturbed patients.

The interaction among mental patients is relatively low, but this, of course, varies with the severity of illness. In general, a large proportion of the interaction on a ward transpires between staff and patients (LeBarr, 1964; Henry, 1964). The more socially active patients on a ward tend to ask much of nurses and attendants, and the staff in turn initiates more interaction with patients who are capable of responding. Likewise, the less-impaired patients interact more with one another than with other patients, which leaves the disturbed patients isolated from both staff and patients.

Patients in mental hospitals are usually not as deprived of material goods as their counterparts in prison. Yet, systems of exchange and barter do exist and usually involve such legally attainable goods as cigarettes, reading material, food, and money (Goffman, 1961). These exchanges rarely involve more than a friendship pair or a small clique differing from the elaborate system found in prison. The better adjusted and more socially active patients are often given freedom and privileges not available to other patients, and these advantages are often shared with friends. However the failure to distribute such scarce goods equally throughout the patient system apparently does not have the disturbing effects it has in prisons.

Most observers of informal relationships in traditional wards convey the idea that buddies and cliques are the dominant type of social grouping. Cliques are usually formed among the more communicative patients, and much of the solidarity of such cliques is based upon antagonism toward the more severely ill patients (LeBarr, 1964; Henry, 1964; Goffman, 1961). The members of such cliques deny their own illness while ridiculing and often punishing those whose behavior they consider bizarre. This stratification among patients is often (although perhaps unintentionally) encouraged by the attendants, who interact more with the communicative patients and share their disdain for the "crazy" patients. As in prisons, rank in cliques and on the ward as a whole depends upon a patient's being able to take care of himself and relate successfully to the authorities. However, once a status structure has emerged, competition and status struggles appear to be rare.

Forces toward solidarity and anomie. The development of patient solidarity is not officially discouraged in mental hospitals to the extent that it is in traditional prisons, yet patient subsystems seem to remain relatively undeveloped. The reason for this is that patients remain dependent on the authorities; this is due not only to the power of the authorities over rewards but also to the personal characteristics of mental patients.

The patient subsystem provides the opportunity for conversation, gossip, and mutual aid to annoy the staff until they grant special privileges. However, rather than banding together to reach some instrumental goal, most patients rely upon the staff to provide for their needs. Negative reactions are expressed through complaints and covert verbal hostility directed to close friends. Despite the autonomy to do so, patients rarely engage in any collective reaction against the authorities; patients therefore have little internal social control. Patients generally accept the authorities' use of force as necessary and legitimate. Dominant patients may even negatively sanction patients who act "crazy," but this sanctioning occurs because such behavior violates general societal norms, and not any emergent norms peculiar to the patient subsystem.

Based on his observation of patients in mental hospitals, Goffman (1961) states:

> . . . instead of clinging together to uphold their patient status against the traditional world, they sought in cliques and dyads to define themselves as normal and to define many of the other patients present as crazy. Very few patients, in short, were or came to be proud of being patients. Reactive solidarity was further weakened by the fact that it was difficult to define all staff as being restrictive and harsh, even though conditions of life on the ward might be consistently so (p. 302).

Thus the extreme dependency upon the authorities for rewards, together with the lack of meaningful instrumental goals, hinders the development of solidarity in the patient subsystem.

WORK ORGANIZATIONS

The organizations dealt with in the earlier sections existed to "handle" or "process" people. Here we are concerned with organizations designed to produce objects or provide services in order to make a profit. In these cases, the members of informal subsystems have been placed together to accomplish some particular task required by the formal organization.

Informal Relationships among Workers

Although there are wide variations within work organizations it seems safe to say that, in general, workers are given greater autonomy than inmates in autocratic total institutions. According to Katz (1968), it is *indirectly delegated autonomy* that is responsible for the emergency of informal groups in work organizations. Workers are free to form interdependent relationships and to carry out certain joint activities on their own because the authorities have not specified rules that would prevent these activities. Katz conceived of this type of autonomy as being a part of the barter arrangement between workers and the managerial authorities who hire and pay them. Workers exchange a certain amount of compliance to the formalized expectations of management for a limited degree of on-the-job autonomy. Katz essentially argues that this autonomy allows workers to engage in informal relationships in order to gain rewards not furnished through their relationship to the formal organization. Thus the rewards gained through informal relationships, whether they be prestige, social satisfaction, or alleviation of boredom, function as payoffs for compliance to formal rules and regulations above and beyond the economic incentives provided by the formal organization.

It is inaccurate to assume that all workers in all work organizations form highly solidary informal groups (see Etzioni, 1961, pp. 165-166). Informal relationships are neither formally required nor restricted, thus allowing the nature of the formal structure to influence the extent to which solidarity develops among members of the same subsystem. For example, Faunce (1958) found that the introduction of assembly-line procedures in an automobile factory restricted interaction among workers and the formation of friendships on the job. Informal relationships were not officially discouraged in the new automated plant, but the fact that workers were placed farther apart and had less control over their work, along with some other factors, led to lowered solidarity.

No matter how restricting the formal rules and work requirements, the autonomy "built in" to formal statuses allows for the development of informal relationships to some degree. Even if the relationships among workers have no other discoverable purpose than to alleviate boredom, the interaction among them will have a definite structure. This is illustrated in a study by Roy (1960), who observed workers assigned to the same work unit while he held a job operating a punch press.

> What I saw at first, before I began to observe, was occasional flurries of horseplay so simple and unvarying in pattern and so childish in quality that they made no strong bid for attention. For example, Ike would regularly switch off the power at Sammy's machine whenever Sammy made a trip to the lavatory or the drinking fountain. Correlatively, Sammy invariably fell victim to the plot by making an attempt to operate his clicking hammer after returning to the shop. And, as the simple pattern went, this blind stumbling into the trap was always followed by indignation and reproach from Sammy, smirking satisfaction from Ike, and mild paternal scolding from George. My interest in this procedure was at first confined to wondering when Ike would weary of his joke or when Sammy would learn to check his power switch before trying the hammer. . . .
>
> But, as I began to pay closer attention, as I began to develop familiarity with the communication system, the disconnected became connected, the nonsense made sense, the obscure became clear, and the silly actually funny. And as the content of the interaction took on more and more meaning, the interaction began to reveal structure (p. 161).

The fact that the work required much of the men's time and the fact that the men felt no antagonism toward the authorities seems to account for the observation that they did not collaborate to work against the managerial goals of the company. Rather, the group interaction provided a means by which the men could structure the twelve-hour work day and thereby make it somewhat more tolerable.

Productivity in informal groups. Most studies of informal subsystems have concentrated upon groups like the bank wiring room, whose norms required behavior contrary to that desired by the large formal organization. In fact, social scientists seem to have the same fascination for such groups as they do for inmate social systems because of the apparent paradox that such groups are allowed to exist by the formal organization (the inmate system was actually encouraged by the prison authorities). A similar explanation accounts for the informal subsystems within work organizations that espouse norms contrary to the organization.

The supervisor, usually a foreman assigned to a formally designated group of workers, is often in a position resembling that of a prison guard. He is dependent upon the cooperation of his subordinates to work at a level sufficiently high to satisfy the demands of his own superiors. Although the foreman's position gives him considerable power, the workers can make life miserable for him, especially if the relationships among them are solitary. This can be accomplished through various means. For example, workers may passively resist the foreman's demand for high productivity by "forgetting" where to find lost tools or failing to prevent the breakdown of a machine. Another way is for workers to adhere to shop rules to the letter and not produce any more than formally required, even though the foreman is behind the production schedule.

Like the prison guard, the foreman is given considerable autonomy from higher authorities in the day-to-day running of his work unit. He is therefore able to enter into informal relationships with his subordinates and exchange a certain amount of autonomy for necessary cooperation. In some cases this may simply involve the supervisor's "not seeing" violations of minor rules (Blau, 1971). A supervisor's failure to demand compliance to all the formal rules that he could legitimately enforce makes him appear less "formal" and the kind of person with whom workers are willing to cooperate by producing at an acceptable level.

In some cases the supervisor will even allow workers to commit major violations. For instance, a foreman may allow workers to restrict productivity when his own superiors are satisfied with the unit's output. A good illustration of this comes from the bank wiring room (Roethlisberger and Dickson, 1947). The men in the room frequently filed "daywork allowances" with the group chief, their immediate supervisor. Daywork allowances were justification for a worker's slack in productivity. For example, a worker might claim that he was delayed because of defective materials or because of the slowness of one of the inspectors. The supervisor knew that not all daywork claims were justified but could not prove it. Although as a representative of management he felt obligated to minimize these claims, he was under pressure from his workers to accept them as justified. Similarly, the workers were not to trade jobs unless a worker's fingers became sore. Like the daywork claims, the legitimacy of a worker's claim of sore fingers was difficult to establish.

The immediate supervisor of the workers in the bank wiring room had enough autonomy from higher authorities that his acceptance of daywork claims and job-trading was never challenged. Roethlisberger and Dickson state:

> In the face of such problems as these the group chief could either let the employees do as they wished and say nothing about it, or he could report their conduct to the foreman and attempt to force them to do his bidding, or he could steer a middle course. In practice he did choose a middle course. He tried his best to make the men obey his orders, sometimes successfully, but he never on any occasion "told the old man on them." Then, again, not all of his orders were disputed. . . . The investigators felt that he countenanced disobedience to some rules largely because he himself thought them unimportant; yet his position demanded that he give lip service to them. His chief interest was in seeing that the men turned out an acceptable day's work, and this they unquestionably did. If they liked to talk and "cut up" a bit while doing it, he did not strenuously object (p. 451).

The autonomy which allowed the group members to engage in various "illegal" activities was granted by the group chief, who because of the status rights of his position *could* have eliminated these activities. However, it is equally true to say that because the men engaged in these activities *as a group,* the immediate supervisor was under pressure to give them autonomy. As in the "corruption" of the prison guard's authority, much of the autonomy given workers by their supervisors or foremen may be the result of informal negotiations with the workers.

Although work groups that have restriction-of-productivity norms are common, not all members of these groups automatically conform to them. Those who produce at higher levels than the norm (rate busters) are, for a variety of reasons, usually not dependent upon rewards available through forming interdependent relationships with the other workers. Usually such members are "isolates," but it is not always clear whether their isolation is the cause or the result of being rate busters. According to one study (see Whyte, 1955), rate busters are usually workers who for various reasons do not have much chance of being accepted as members of their subsystem. The rate busters explained their behavior by saying that they were oriented toward management and interested in making money while the conformers stated that loyalty to the group was more important than having more money. Rate busters, then, do not rely upon the group for whatever rewards they get from their jobs, while conformers gain important rewards through their relationships with one another. In other words, the rate busters have adopted individualistic instead of interdependent orientations.

Members of work groups that have informal norms calling for behavior not allowed by formal rules will be very concerned with concealing their activities. Thus, any member who, for any reason, is seen as a threat to the continuance of the group's activities (and solidarity) is likely to be labeled a deviant. A part of the reaction against rate busters can be seen in this light. If, as in the case of the bank wiring room, a rate of productivity below the capabilities of the workers is accepted by management as "the best they can do," any worker who consistently produces above the norm calls this assumption into question. Calling the authorities' attention to the group could lead to an investigation of the workers' activities on the job and to the possible disruption of established group routines. Even a sympathetic supervisor could do little to help maintain the group's autonomy if his own supervisor decided to restrict it. As in the case of the prison inmate subsystem, members of work groups restricting productivity are suspicious of anyone who communicates too much with authorities; the prohibition against squealing is a major norm of such groups.

Productivity and solidarity. Many studies of work groups have focused on group productivity. In many subsystems within work organizations, members' jobs are defined so that the work-related activities of all members are coordinated to make them interdependent. In other cases, subsystem members may be working independently of one another, each being responsible for his own output. Those variations in the formal work structure do, as we saw with the assembly line, affect the nature of the emergent relations among subsystem members. However, regardless of the technical arrangement of work, productivity-level norms emerge in most subsystems.

How, then, is productivity related to subsystem solidarity? In most cases, researchers have operationalized solidarity by using some measure of cohesiveness. Some studies have started out hypothesizing that highly cohesive work groups are more productive, while others have hypothesized just the opposite. Sensible arguments for either can be formulated, and the reader may want to pause for a moment to choose. For instance, it may be argued that highly cohesive groups are better able to "get together" and produce at high levels. On the other hand, it may be argued that cohesive groups spend a great deal of time interacting and socializing, thus neglecting their work. With some thought, the reader may be able to come up with several other reasons for selecting one or the other hypothesis. Let us see what research on this topic has yielded.

Interestingly enough, support has been found for both hypotheses (see Etzioni, 1961; Stodgill, 1972), which suggests that the relationship between cohesiveness and productivity is not a simple one. A study by Stanley Seashore (1954) is the one study that has been most helpful in making this relationship clear. In the large-factory studied, Seashore gathered data on 228 formally defined work units (i.e., subsystems). Based on responses to scales on a questionnaire, Seashore derived a numerical measure of each worker's attraction to his particular work group. In addition, he obtained a measure of each worker's average productivity. With this information, Seashore constructed a cohesiveness score for each subsystem (the average of the members' attraction) and a group productivity score (the average of the members' productivity scores). He then compared groups with relatively high and low cohesion scores to determine whether they differed in productivity. He found no difference, suggesting, as we have already stated, that there is no simple relationship between cohesiveness and productivity. Seashore then decided to look at the distribution of productivity scores within the high and low cohesion groups. He found that in each of the high cohesion groups the individual productivity scores of the members tended to be similar, while in each of the low cohesion groups they were relatively dissimilar. This is consistent with everything that we know about cohesion in groups—namely, that members of highly cohesive groups tend to behave similarly on important dimensions. Certainly in work groups, the level of productivity is an important dimension. Thus the dissimilarity of productivity scores in low cohesion groups indicates that pressure toward similarity was not at work and that each individual, more or less, set his own standard.

In summary, Seashore found that there were high, medium, and low productivity scores among both the high and low cohesion groups. Any comparison between the high and low cohesion groups showed no difference in productivity. However, in high cohesion groups, members were *uniformly* high, medium, or low, which indicated the existence of a norm in each group for appropriate productivity levels for each member. Consistent with this are the results of an experiment by Schachter *et al.* (1951) who found that subjects in highly cohesive groups could be induced to change productivity levels while those in low cohesion groups could not.

These studies indicate that where solidarity is high, norms may develop supporting either high or low productivity; therefore, it is impossible to predict the productivity level of a group when all we know is the group's solidarity level.

The next questions to be raised, then, are: What other information is necessary? What environmental conditions affect the tendency of high solidarity groups to support norms of high or low productivity? Although some research has been devoted to answering these questions, the results are not clear. There is some evidence (see Likert, 1961) to suggest that workers relatively free from supervisory constraint (i.e., those with high autonomy) are likely to be high producers. However these studies do not show that cohesive *groups* with high autonomy develop norms supporting high levels of productivity. It is possible that in some cases group members, grateful for the freedom provided by their superior respond by developing norms supporting a high level of productivity. But, workers with a lenient supervisor could also restrict productivity because they are dissatisfied with other aspects of the job (i.e., their wages or chances for promotion). On the other hand, group members dissatisfied with their superiors' close control could express their dissatisfaction by restricting productivity. But, the close supervision that engenders dissatisfaction is also likely to prevent these workers from restricting productivity (see White and Lippitt, 1960; Day and Hamblin, 1964).

The best we can say at this point is that whether a group of workers accept norms which favor high, medium, or low productivity depends upon the workers' perceptions of the relative advantages of each. This consideration is certainly influenced by the degree of constraint and autonomy in their relationships with the external authority, but there are numerous other environmental factors which may be at work.

Forces Toward Solidarity and Anomie

The fact that workers within work organizations have a certain degree of autonomy "built into" their formal statuses acts as a force toward the development of solidarity of informal subsystems. While the degree of autonomy varies from subsystem to subsystem, the fact that authorities in such organizations generally do not restrict informal relationships accounts for many of the differences between subsystems in work organizations and those in total institutions. The freedom for workers to develop informal relationships, together with the restraining influence of their being assigned to the same shop or work unit, makes it likely that *some* degree of solidarity will emerge within these subsystems. A further source of autonomy stems from the authorities' practice of allowing subsystem members to behave in ways that violate formal status requirements and rules of the larger organization. Thus, autonomy may act as a further force toward solidarity because it gives workers the opportunity to control among themselves certain activities that otherwise would be out of their hands.

In comparison with informal subsystems within total institutions, the solidarity of those within work organizations is inhibited by the fact that members spend less time together. Although not as great as in total institutions, the constraints that the external authority imposes in work organizations act as a force toward anomie. By enforcing formal rules and regulations, the external authority limits the activities that could be controlled by the subsystem members themselves. By controlling rewards and punishments, a supervisor increases his subordinates' dependency upon him, thus fostering individualistic behavior such as competitiveness and rate busting.

That the mere existence of external authority can create a force toward anomie in a subsystem is nicely illustrated in a study by Gross (1961). He identified the informal groups that emerged among the approximately ninety persons in an office by observing which workers ate lunch together, helped one another, and so on. The office consisted of several separate work units, each with its own supervisor. The workers in each of these departments could be considered as subsystems in our terms. This study, however, did not focus upon the informal relationships that emerged among members of each subsystem. Instead, Gross studied autonomous informal groups which drew their members from various departments or subsystems around the office.

Eleven informal groups, ranging in size from two to six members, were identified. He found that no members of the same group had the same job or the same supervisor. In other words, no group had members who belonged to the same department. The reason for this, according to Gross, was that workers who had the same job or supervisor were in competition with each other because authorities compared these workers to one another when considering promotions and salary raises. Gross argued that members who are competitors because of their formal statuses in the organization are likely to be ill-at-ease in each other's presence. This made noncompetitors more attractive for the formation of informal relationships.

While Gross did not examine the various subsystems within the office, we can conjecture that whatever informal relationships emerged among members of the same subsystem would not involve high interdependence. The mere existence of an external authority who evaluates and compares members of the same subsystem tends to set up forces toward anomie. Of course, the extent to which this occurs varies depending on, among other things, the nature of the formal position and the personality of the external authority. As we shall see in the next section, variation in the degree of control exerted by the external authority affects the solidarity of the subsystem under him.

AUTONOMY AND SOLIDARITY

A general proposition which can be derived from the early sections of this chapter is that the greater the autonomy provided by an external authority, the higher the solidarity of the informal subsystems. In order to understand why this is the case, we must see how control and autonomy are translated into forces toward anomie or solidarity and how they affect interdependent and individualistic orientations among members.

A General Explanation

As was stated before, the *dependence* of subsystem members is related to the degree of control exerted by external authorities. Another factor related to external control is "alienation," which refers to the feelings of dissatisfaction and antagonism that subsystem members experience as a result of being controlled by an external authority. Alienation is defined in terms of *feelings* of dissatisfaction, because whether or not these feelings are expressed depends upon the situation. It must be kept in mind that when we speak of subsystem members as being alienated, we are referring to their negative orientations toward the larger formal organization and the external authority, not toward one another. In general, both dependence and alienation of subsystem members increase as the control of the external authority increases.

The level of solidarity of an informal subsystem within a formal organization is a result of the interplay between *alienation* and *dependence,* which in turn are a product of the relationship between the subsystem and external authority. In general, the alienation produced by the constraints applied by the external authority acts as a force toward solidarity and thus tends to encourage interdependent orientations. This occurs because the external authority is seen as a common threat or problem to the subsystem members. Unlike members of autonomous groups who may voluntarily withdraw if highly dissatisfied, members of subsystems are constrained, to some degree, to remain together in the same location. Any attempt to lessen alienation through rebellion, passive resistance, or by attaining alternative rewards through covert activities requires the establishment of interdependent relationships among members, thereby increasing solidarity.

However, dependence as a result of control by the external authority tends to act as a force toward anomie, thus fostering individualistic orientations among subsystem members. The greater the dependence of the subsystem members, the more likely they are to comply with the formal expectations enforced by the external authority and the more expectations, the fewer activities members can control themselves. For instance, if the supervisor of a work group specifies that all members should produce at a set rate or suffer the consequences, there is little possibility that the group members will develop a norm amongst themselves specifying the appropriate level of productivity. It does not matter that the workers think the imposed productivity level is too high or that they hate the supervisor, they will comply with his demands because they are dependent upon him to reward (or not punish) them. Compliance with the expectations of the external authority necessitates an individualistic orientation among subsystem members simply because these expectations do not allow for the development of interdependent orientations. In the above example there would be no autonomy for the emergence of a norm that would provide the basis for interdependent orientations, internal control over activities, and thus solidarity.

In addition, the external authority's control over rewards and punishments may foster individualistic orientations in subsystem members by encouraging competition among them. An example is Deutsch's (1949) experiment where members of a group competed with one another for the high grade (reward) which was dispersed by the experimenter (external authority). This was a very simple social situation, but in most formal organizations authorities reward or punish individuals depending upon their willingness to comply with formal expectations. Therefore, the results are similar. This especially is the case in organizations where the external authority maintains strict control over subordinates (Street, 1965). In fact, as we shall show in the next chapter, the mere presence of an evaluating authority can drive subordinates to attempt to make themselves "look good" in comparison to their peers, or, alternatively, make others "look bad" in the eyes of the authority. Individualistic orientations are likely to show up in overt competition and conflict behavior when rewards are scarce or when rewards and punishment are largely under the control of the external authority. In cases of extreme control, the tendency toward interdependence (and solidarity) caused by the members' alienation are outweighed by the forces toward individualistic orientations caused by their dependence upon the external authority. In subsystems given greater autonomy by the external authority, the relationship between members and the external authority is more symmetrical and interdependent, allowing more activities and issues to be determined by the subsystem members themselves, not by the external authority. This provides the basis for greater interdependence among members.

When autonomy is relatively high, subsystem members are free from requirements imposed by the external authority. But, the fact that a certain activity or level of performance is not required (or prohibited) by the external authority does not mean that the subsystem members will automatically formulate their own requirements or prohibitions concerning that activity. It is likely that this will occur in most cases, however. Since members of subsystems are confined to the same location, anyone adopting an individualistic orientation becomes a source of irritation and conflict and is likely to be pressured into complying with emerging group norms. For example, if the members of a work group are given the autonomy to determine and control their own level of productivity, it is likely that they will. If each individual worker set his own level of productivity, some might produce so low or so high as to attract the attention of higher authorities and thus endanger whatever autonomy the group has. As shown by Thibaut and Kelley (1959) and Bonacich (1972) (see Chapter 5), it is in such situations that group members are likely to experience pressure to form norms restricting such individualistic responses.

Since members of relatively autonomous subsystems depend less on external authority, they are under less pressure to comply with the demands of an external authority that generally encourages an individualistic orientation. Alienation in such groups is also likely to be lower, but except for extreme cases, not absent altogether. This leads to the interesting situation found in the traditional prison, as well as in other organizations, in which interdependent orientations based on common feelings of alienation are "allowed" to develop to some degree because of the external authority's failure to exert complete control.

A Comparison of Subsystems in Similar Environments

The evidence reviewed in the previous sections confirms the idea that subsystem solidarity is higher where autonomy is greater; but comparisons of subsystems in different organizational environments are difficult to make, since many factors other than the degree of control and autonomy may account for variations in subsystem solidarity. It is more meaningful to compare subsystems within environments that are similar except for the amount of constraint or control exerted by the external authorities.

The studies to be reviewed in this section were not carried out explicitly to demonstrate the relationship between control-autonomy and subsystem solidarity. However, they all provide enough information to enable us to use them for that purpose. In all cases, two similar subsystems were compared; and in each study, there is sufficient information to compare them along at least one of the six dimensions of solidarity (see Table 2.1) and to determine the relative degree of control exercised over their members by external authorities. Variations on one or more factors listed below indicate differences in the degree of external control applied to the subsystems being studied. Subsystem members whose relationship to the external authority is relatively high in one or more of the following factors can be considered to be high in control or low in autonomy: (1) a large number of formal rules and norms enforced; (2) highly specified formal status in the larger organization; (3) surveillance techniques used by the external authority to ensure compliance; (4) reward and punishment largely under the control of the external authority; (5) a high degree of compliance on the part of subsystem members to formal rules and status (see Gouldner, 1954; Etzioni, 1961; Day and Hamblin, 1964; Rushing, 1966; Scott, 1967; Rosengren, 1967; Katz, 1968).

A comparison of subsystems within prisons. Polansky (1942) asked prisoners who had spent time in more than one traditional prison to compare them along a series of dimensions on a questionnaire. He then examined the questionnaires to determine which dimensions were or were not related to one another. The first finding of relevance in Polansky's study was that when respondents indicated that they were generally contented with a particular prison, they also tended to rate that prison high on a dimension measuring "liking for the administration." This indicates the extent to which prisoners depend upon prison authorities for their well-being and happiness. In addition, he found that when a subject rated a prison as being relatively high in "strictness of discipline," the prison was also rated high in "internal squabbling among inmates" and "resentment toward inmate politicians." These dimensions measure the extent to which interdependent or individualistic orientations prevail, and the results suggest that the forces toward individualistic orientations or anomie are strongest in prisons with a high degree of external control. According to Polansky:

> In determining whether the other inmates shall be liked, the relationship to the administration is as important as interrelationships among the inmates. . . . By its very nature, the prison group, run according to strict authoritarian lines, will show more member-to-administrative dependence than member-to-member dependence (p. 22).

Polansky's study indicates that the dependence upon authorities is high where control is great and that this leads to individualistic rather than interdependent orientation among inmates.

This finding is reinforced in McCleery's (1962) comparison of the inmate social structure under normal circumstances in a traditional prison with that of "incorrigible units," where restrictions on the inmates' autonomy are extreme. Like the relationships in the traditional prison, those in the incorrigible units were characterized by "hostility," "suspiciousness," and "scapegoating," only more so. In this unit the pressure against talking to guards was taken to extremes, and suspected violators were totally rejected from the inmate in-group. Because of the general suspiciousness, the leadership position was even more unstable than among the inmates in the incorrigible units, showing the same tenuous balance between individualistic and interdependent orientations, with the former being somewhat stronger.

As can be seen in a comparison of Soviet labor camps with American prisons (Cressy and Krassowski, 1957), the plight of political prisoners in Soviet labor camps resembles in many ways that of inmates in German concentration camps.

In the Soviet Union, the acts of imprisoned *criminals* were blamed on vestigial capitalistic counter-revolutionary tendencies, and criminals were given preferential treatment compared to *political prisoners*. In the case of the latter, authorities restricted autonomy and deliberately minimized inmate solidarity. The lack of inmate organization and deep apathy noted in the Nazi camps was also found among the Soviet political prisoners. Many political prisoners identified with officials and resisted any involvement in inmate activities that camp officials could interpret as disloyal. Among the criminals, leaders were given administrative jobs and were officially encouraged to control the political prisoners. Since the relationship between criminals and authorities in the Soviet labor camps resembles that between inmates and authorities in American prisons, it is of interest that the authors describe the inmate organization among Soviet criminals as being similar to that of American prisoners. Autonomy and solidarity for Soviet political prisoners were both low, as in German concentration camps, while for criminals both were somewhat higher, as in American prisons today.

Berk (1966) compared three prisons which ranged along a continuum from a strong treatment orientation that gave prisoners a great deal of autonomy to a strong custodial orientation that gave them little. In comparisons between the two extremes, it was found that the inmates in the treatment-oriented prison were more positive toward the staff and institution than those in the custodial prison. Leaders and inmates highly involved in the inmate organization of the treatment institution were the most positive in attitude, while their counterparts at the custodial prison were the most negative. The informal leadership structure was limited to a few dominant men in the custodial prison, but was more dispersed in the treatment-oriented prison. Also, leadership positions in the custodial prison were occupied by more authoritarian inmates who were less liked and more unapproachable than leaders in the treatment prison. The situation in the custodial prisons studied by Berk is like most other traditional prisons where inmates who are capable of working the system ascend to positions of leadership and impose their wills on fellow inmates, often through techniques more brutal than any used by the guards. In the treatment institution there was evidence that inmate solidarity was based on their voluntary participation in the organization.

Street (1965), who compared juvenile correctional institutions with custodial and treatment orientations, provides even more evidence that inmate solidarity is higher in treatment institutions. Like Berk, he found inmates in treatment institutions to be more positive toward the institution than those in custodial institutions. Using a variety of indices, Street found that inmates in treatment institutions had more highly developed primary relationships and stronger orientations of solidarity than inmates in the custodial settings. Studies by T. P. Wilson (1968) and by Studt, Messinger, and Wilson (1968) support the findings of Berk and Street where, in general, autonomy is associated with indices of inmate solidarity.

A comparison of subsystems within mental hospitals. Descriptions of traditional or custodially oriented wards characterized by locked doors, a high degree of regimentation, and close supervision of patients suggest that both autonomy and solidarity among patients is low (Smith and Thrasher, 1963; Caudill *et al.*, 1952; LeBar, 1964; Sommer and Osmond, 1968; and Goffman, 1961). In comparison, the literature suggests that solidarity among patients in open wards, therapeutic communities, or wards emphasizing milieu therapy is relatively high (Rioch and Stanton, 1953; Bloom *et al.*, 1962; Kaplan *et al.*, 1964). However, because patients judged to be more independent of staff direction and capable of fairly high social participation are usually those chosen for more autonomous wards, it is difficult to assess the relationship between autonomy and solidarity among mental patients on the basis of this literature alone.

There are, however, several studies that do provide more direct evidence on the relationship between autonomy and solidarity while controlling for patient types. Murry and Cohen (1959) compared the number of reciprocal sociometric choices on three wards: (1) a milieu therapy ward for schizophrenics; (2) a locked somatic ward for schizophrenics; and (3) a nonpsychiatric control ward. They found that the proportion of reciprocal sociometric choices on the control ward was 75 percent, while the proportions for the milieu therapy ward and the locked ward were 78 percent and 27 percent, respectively. Similar results were obtained when the study was replicated after a complete turnover of patients. The authors also ruled out the possibility that the use of electric shock and drug treatment on the locked ward was responsible for the low number of choices, since those patients most involved in the sociometric network on this ward were also those receiving the most intensive treatment.

Gressler (1964) reports the differences in the number and intensity of interpersonal choices between patients randomly assigned to a traditional ward or to an experimental treatment ward that gave patients greater autonomy and emphasized group decision-making. He found that patients on the experimental ward made a greater number of sociometric choices and showed greater overall ward cohesiveness than patients on the traditional ward. Studies by Wing and Brown (1961) and by Jungman and Bucker (1967) also provide evidence that levels of interaction among patients are greater on more autonomous wards as compared to more controlled wards.

A comparison of subsystems within work organizations. There are several studies of groups in industrial settings that allow for the comparison of group solidarity under conditions of low and high autonomy. Blau (1955) has described two sections of an employment agency in which supervisors evaluated individual productivity with statistical measures of the various activities of the workers. After this system was instituted in one section, the individual workers actively competed to make the highest number of job placements, because this was the number that entered the statistics. Competition led to trickery, deceit, and conflict. In the other section, workers developed cooperative norms that combated competitive tendencies. It was found that the supervisor of the latter section publicly put less emphasis on the results of the statistics in evaluating the workers. A more indirect means of evaluation deemphasized the importance of job placements and allowed each worker more personal autonomy in carrying out his job. Blau also found that workers in the section that exhibited a higher degree of solidarity were, for several reasons, more secure in their jobs. This would mean that they were less dependent upon the external authority and therefore more autonomous. Thus, the Blau study is consistent with the idea that solidarity is inhibited when an external authority's control over members of a subsystem is high.

A study of industrial work groups by Sayles (1958) also offers some support for the idea that autonomy and solidarity are associated in industrial settings. Sayles relied on managers of various factories to isolate and describe the different types of groups that formed to deal with grievances. Groups which he labeled *strategic groups* were described as being higher in organizational effectiveness and internal unity than the other types identified. He found that members of strategic groups in comparison with members of the other two types of groups had jobs that were: (1) of higher status; (2) more important (to management); (3) less constrained by technological procedures; and (4) less constrained by time-and-motion standards. In other words, members of strategic groups, because of their positions, were more independent of control by the formal authorities than members of the other groups and had developed higher solidarity as well.

Finally, one aspect of a study by Gouldner of a gypsum company (1954) is relevant. He found that miners who had been given a high degree of autonomy by officials on the surface, also showed various characteristics indicating high "informal group solidarity." In comparison, men working on the surface experienced relatively low degrees of autonomy and group solidarity. Although Gouldner pointed to several factors that could account for the differences between the surface workers and miners, the fact that relatively high autonomy and solidarity occurred together accords with the other studies reviewed thus far.

Obviously the environmental factors surrounding the various subsystems are quite different. However these studies indicate that regardless of the type of subsystem—that is, regardless of the kind of the formal organization within which it is located—the nature of the members' relationship with the external authority affects subsystem solidarity. While other environmental factors can influence the characteristics of such groups, this factor appears to be an important one.

SUMMARY

This chapter deals with the ways in which environmental factors influence the characteristics of informal subsystems. Informal subsystems are units of formal organizations in which individuals, because of their common statuses in the organization and physical proximity, can develop some degree of solidarity amongst themselves. The organization's control over members of an informal subsystem has its source in the external authority directly responsible for the subsystem members.

Studies examining informal relationships within four different formal organizations were reviewed. Evidence shows that in Nazi concentration camps autonomy was so low and prisoners so concerned with survival that there was little opportunity for interdependent relationships to form. Many subsystem norms supported the external authorities' power. In American traditional prisons, many subsystem norms encouraged deviance from official policies. Group solidarity was higher in prisons than in concentration camps, and this was due to the fact that guards provided autonomy through a process called the "corruption of authority." This process consisted of an exchange in which the inmates received certain favors or rewards from the guards in return for help in maintaining order. The autonomy allowed the inmates to develop solidarity and internal social control and keep deviant behavior that would embarrass the guard in check.

Although the structure of traditional mental hospitals resembles that of prisons, solidarity among patients generally seems to be lower than among prison inmates. This is partly due to the fact that most patients have fewer social skills than prisoners. Small cliques usually consisting of the more communicative patients are the dominant type of organization on hospital wards.

Autonomy to develop solidarity in industrial organizations is provided as a part of the barter arrangement between management and workers, as well as through practices resembling "corruption of authority." Subsystem solidarity can be influenced by such factors as the arrangement and scheduling of work procedures. The most common norms in work groups are those specifying appropriate work behavior such as levels of productivity. Generally, uniformity among members concerning productivity occurs in groups where solidarity is highly developed. Whether the members' activities support or contradict the goals of the large organization depends upon whether or not members are satisfied with various aspects of their jobs and upon their perception of the advantages and disadvantages of the alternatives.

The studies reviewed suggest that the greater the autonomy given an informal subsystem, the higher its solidarity. It was argued that high levels of control foster both alienation and dependence among subsystem members. While alienation sets up forces toward solidarity, these are counterbalanced by dependence, which encourages individualistic orientations. Where autonomy is high, subsystem members are given the opportunity to act upon their common feelings of alienation and form interdependent relationships. Furthermore, greater autonomy gives members a wider range of activities to control, which contributes to solidarity. The level of solidarity attained by any particular subsystem depends upon the amount of alienation and dependence fostered by the external authority, which in turn determines the relative strength of forces toward solidarity and anomie.

Studies comparing subsystems in environments which were similar, except for the degree of control (or autonomy) provided by the external authority, were reviewed. Based on observations of subsystems in a variety of formal organizations, these studies support the proposition that relatively autonomous subsystems develop higher solidarity than those under high control by external authorities.

nine

Problem-Solving Groups and Solidarity

INTRODUCTION

In industrialized societies, many groups form or are formed solely for solving problems. We are not referring here to the occasional gathering of friends for conversation but to groups which meet to arrive at a decision or solve a problem of some sort. In most cases, problem-solving groups are subsystems that operate under the control of an external authority; but like the subsystems discussed in Chapter 8, members of problem-solving groups generally have enough autonomy to influence the nature of the discussion and other aspects of group life. This fact allows us to consider them as informal groups.

Many experimenters have brought strangers together in the laboratory for the purpose of discussing a topic or problem. In most cases, these experimenters have not been interested in discussion groups *per se* but have used them to learn about the dynamics of groups in general. Since we are interested in environmental factors, we shall begin by examining how such groups are influenced by the nature of the experimental situation. Having done this, we will turn to non-experimental groups like committees and conference groups—discussion groups with particular decision-making goals that exist within formal organizations.

THE EXPERIMENTER AS AN EXTERNAL AUTHORITY

Until recently, most researchers have assumed that subjects in experimental situations, much like rats in a psychologist's maze, were unaware of and un-effected by anything in the experiment except the experimenter's manipulations. However, the experimental situation can be considered an environment that affects behavior. It includes a particular physical arrangement and certain structural configuration (i.e., the experimenter is an authority in the setting), and subjects enter the situation with expectations about what behavior is appropriate. An understanding of how this environment affects the behavior of subjects, particularly when subjects interact with one another, is important because social scientists rely so much upon laboratory experiments to learn about informal groups.

A majority of laboratory experiments are carried out on college campuses with students serving as subjects and professors as experimenters. Many of the expectations that define student-professor relationships are carried into the experimental setting. Chief among these is the expectation that the experimenter is the authority and will tell the subject what to do.

A study by Milgram (1963) shows how complete this acceptance of the experimenter's authority can be. Milgram directed subjects to administer what they thought were electric shocks to a subject (really an actor-accomplice) in an adjoining room. He found that almost all subjects continued to increase the voltage when so directed by the experimenter, even after hearing screams of pain from the other room. While most experimenters do not require such extreme behavior, students do, by agreeing to take part in an experiment, tacitly agree to submit to the control of the experimenter.

A related expectation subjects bring into the experiment is that they will be observed and evaluated by the experimenter. This arouses *evaluation apprehension* (Rosenberg, 1965) in the subjects, who become motivated to behave in ways they believe will make them look good in the eyes of the experimenter. Whether in school or on the job, a person who is being evaluated by an authority figure wants to behave in ways that will assure him a positive evaluation. As a result, he will seek cues as to what the authority expects or considers to be "good" behavior. This seems to be a predominant motivation for experimental subjects. Orne (1962) argues that subjects closely observe the behavior and words of the experimenter for *demand characteristics*. These are cues that tell subjects what behavior is appropriate (i.e., what will please the experimenter by substantiating his hypothesis). Although some subjects may have just the opposite motivations, most want to cooperate to the fullest extent with the experimenter after having volunteered to be subjects. For instance, Schulman (1967) found that subjects placed in a setting like that used by Asch were more likely to conform to a confederate's erroneous answer if they believed that the experimenter would not be informed of their answers. This suggests that the subjects in Asch's study were as much influenced by the experimenter's instructions and his presence as the behavior of the confederates. Had Asch not been present during his experiment, more subjects would have conformed to the erroneous answers.

Although the experimenter is not necessarily a part of a larger formal organization, his relationship to his subjects resembles that between the external authority and subsystem members within formal organizations. The experimenter assigns a task and is in fact responsible for defining the conditions under which the subjects perform. Speaking of the importance of the experimenter in small-group experiments, Mills (1967) states:

> . . . The experimental group is almost wholly dependent upon him for its substance, form, and direction. Now, it is *he* who admits and excludes, *he* who assembles and dismisses, *he* who announces the purpose, sets the agenda, prescribes the rules, shifts directions, shields against outside influence, and so on—all in order properly to achieve comparable groups, standard procedures, and a reduction in experimental error. . . . Oddly, with one hand the experimenter creates the potential for a group but with the other takes away its means for becoming one. Quite precisely, in forming the group he gives it form; he creates the character of his experimental subject.

> By bringing people, together, the experimenter *creates* a group. Although it is young, indistinct, and illusive, it is nonetheless a new unit with a potential for development. If this point be granted, then we may suggest that the *manner* in which persons are brought together, the way the group is conceived, if you will—makes a difference in what it can and cannot become (pp. 51–52).

The characteristics of experimental discussion groups are determined, to a large extent, by the environmental conditions constructed by the experimenter. We shall explore two types of influences the experimenter has on discussion groups. First, the mere presence of the experimenter in the situation causes subjects to be concerned about behaving appropriately to please the observing experimenter. Second, when the experimenter sets the goals for the group, subjects are usually not motivated to accept these goals as their own.

The Effect of the Observer

The first type of influence is illustrated by an experiment carried out by the present author (Wilson, 1969). The design of the experiment was simple. Ten groups of five persons each were given a discussion problem while working in the presence of the experimenter who made notes on what was transpiring. Another ten groups were given identical problems but were unaware that they were being observed through a curtain-covered, one-way mirror. The interaction among subjects in the two sets of groups was recorded and classified into categories similar to Bales's (1950). Table 9.1 shows the interaction profiles for groups in the two conditions. It is seen that the observed groups initiated higher percentages of task-oriented interaction than the not-observed groups. This interaction would have been also classified as task-oriented in Bales's category system. "Task-irrelevant" interaction involved discussion having nothing to do with the experimental task. As can be seen, this was significantly higher in the

Table 9-1
Interaction Category Rates by Experimental Conditions (Modified from Table 1,
Wilson, 1969, p. 227)

Interaction Categories	Observed			Not-Observed			t Values
	$\overline{X}$	S.D.	N	$\overline{X}$	S.D.	N	
Task-Oriented	59.71	8.33	10	45.61	12.69	10	2.92	P<.01
Task-Irrelevant	4.77	4.25	10	24.13	16.70	10	4.33	P<.01
Positive Social-Emotional	21.91	8.14	10	16.98	6.64	10	1.45	N.S.
Negative Social-Emotional	11.72	6.95	10	6.38	2.88	10	2.33	P<.05
Positive Task Morale	1.40	0.53	10	0.89	0.87	10	1.93	N.S.
Negative Task Morale	0.47	0.59	10	6.03	5.83	10	4.24	P<.01

not-observed condition. There was also a higher rate of negative social-emotional interaction initiated in the observed group. The only other significant difference in interaction involved that categorized as *negative task morale.* Negative comments about the task, the situation, or the experimenter (e.g., "I think the whole idea of this experiment is stupid") were placed in this category. As can be seen, such comments were made more often when the experimenter was "not present."

If the experimenter's presence is viewed as a constraining force, these differences make sense. The subjects were being paid to work on a task and, as evidenced by the high rate of task-oriented interaction, felt more constrained to do so when the experimenter was present. The high rate of negative social-emotional interaction in the observed condition can be explained by the fact that this type of interaction is usually correlated with task-oriented interaction (Bales, 1950). While there was more task-oriented interaction in the observed groups, this did not really indicate greater productivity. The solutions of the groups were rated for quality by two judges who found no difference between the two experimental conditions. The task orientation of the subjects in the observed condition, then, was primarily a reaction to the fact that they were being observed. This would also explain why fewer negative task morale comments were made in the observed conditions. It was also found that specialization, as measured by Bales, was higher in the not-observed groups. The reason for this seems to be that the task-oriented best idea man was more annoying to the members of these groups because they were generally not task-oriented. Their failure to rank the best-idea man as "best liked" resulted in specialization.

Both observers in this study received the impression that the observed subjects were playing roles that they thought would please the experimenter—i.e., being concerned about the task and earnestly arguing with one another. It is of interest that the highest participators in the observed condition were those sub-jects who scored high on self-orientation on the Bass (1962) orientation inven-tory (Wilson, 1971). This personality type has been described as "one who likes to assert himself, to compete, to stand out, and be visible" (Bass, 1965, p. 12). The presence of the observer seemed to provide the appropriate arena for meeting such needs, and the self-oriented individuals took advantage of it by initiating high rates of interaction. The high participators in the observed condi-tion also tended to initiate unusually high rates of interaction classified as *positive task morale*—i.e., positive comments about the task, situation, and experimenter. This can only be interpreted as their having made ingratiating comments, again, for the sake of the observer.

All subjects who are recruited for discussion-group experiments are likely to display signs of "evaluation anxiety." However, this is certainly heightened when the experimenter directly observes their performance—standard procedure in discussion group experiments.

Low Task Interest and Specialization

One of the most frequently cited aspects of Bales's research is his finding that subjects frequently tend to specialize in their contributions to instrumental and social-emotional problems. It will be remembered that Bales viewed the specialization of statuses as being inherent in all social systems. This implies that informal groups in which specialization has emerged are more fully developed—and thus higher in solidarity—than those with nonspecialized structures. In line with this, Slater (1955) interpreted his finding that specialization occurred more frequently in later sessions as indicating that the groups became more "orga-nized" or "structured."

In Chapter 3 we mentioned that we had some serious doubts that specializa-tion in laboratory groups could be taken as a sign of high solidarity. We can now examine the reasons for these doubts in some detail. First, with respect to Slater's findings, we should remember that it is not necessarily the case that the same subjects were specializing as "best idea" men or as "best liked" session after session. Evidence that the same specialists were emerging in successive meetings would indicate that a group had achieved a stable structure. But Slater's data does not support this conclusion. Second, specialization is really the opposite of status congruence, which, as defined in Chapter 5, is associated with high solidar-ity. Groups that have members who make outstanding contributions to the in-strumental problem but who are not highly liked (i.e., high specialization or low status congruence) are low in solidarity. Based upon the evidence reviewed in Chapter 5, most groups evolve toward greater status congruence, not toward greater specialization.

All of this suggests that there may be something about the experimental situation that makes specialization prevalent in experimental groups. As shown in Chapter 8, subsystem members often did not accept as their own the goals which the external authority set for them. In laboratory discussion groups, members may follow instructions and do what the experimenter expects by solving the problem, but their orientation is not the same as members of a group that sets and pursues its own goals. Over a period of time the author has given subjects in forty-two different laboratory discussion groups the opportunity to indicate, on a numerical scale, the extent of their interest in the experimental task. The responses indicate that while there is variation, most subjects are "neutral" or "indifferent" towards the task. The data also show that the overwhelming majority of the subjects participated only because they were being paid to do so. Thus, like the members of the informal subsystems discussed in the previous chapter, experimental subjects remain together for reasons other than any inherent satisfaction from interaction together or acceptance of the task as a group goal.

What is the connection between low task interest and specialization? According to Verba (1961), subjects in experimental groups may be able to recognize the members who contribute the most to the solution of the task by ranking them high on best ideas, but subjects will not necessarily care enough about the task to like these members for their contribution. In other words, specialization occurs when the members do not receive enough satisfaction or reward from the successful completion of the task to be especially attracted to persons most responsible for this accomplishment. As Verba sees it, this is highly likely in experimental groups where task interest is low. Studies by Turk (1961) and Burke (1967, 1968) tend to support Verba's explanation.

In addition to low task interest, Verba identified a second related aspect of the experimental situation that could contribute to specialization in discussion groups. Even though the experimenter sets up a goal, the subjects are left on their own to develop a structure to reach it. Of course, it is the goal of the experimenter to observe this process. But, as a result, subjects are faced with a situation in which no one is expected to assume leadership or exert control over others. According to Verba, anyone who distinguishes himself by contributing outstandingly to the task and controlling others is not going to be liked. The result, of course, is specialization as defined by Bales.

Recent studies (Lewis, 1972; Bonacich and Lewis, 1973) have provided evidence that Bales' and Slater's procedures exaggerate the extent to which specialization occurs in laboratory discussion groups. This research is important because it reminds us that specialization is not inevitable in laboratory groups. However, the important issue here is why specialization occurs more frequently in laboratory discussion groups than in other groups.

Whether or not specialization exists in a naturally occurring group probably depends upon its level of development. Specialization is more likely to be found in a newly formed group. Such groups, if they are autonomous, may well disintegrate if they do not eventually attain status congruence. Naturally occurring *subsystems* may not disintegrate because of the external constraints holding them together, but those in which specialization exists should show other indications of low solidarity. In laboratory discussion groups, the distinction between high and low specialization (or congruence) would be less noticeable than in naturally occurring groups. This is because laboratory groups are together for only a short period of time and development is limited. So while laboratory groups may vary with respect to specialization or status congruence, it will have little to do with solidarity. When comparing laboratory groups with naturally occurring groups, we would expect to find lower solidarity in laboratory groups, unless we were observing the first few hours of the nonlaboratory group's existence. The frequent occurrence of specialization in laboratory groups, then, is merely one indication of their lack of solidarity.

Before concluding this section, let us look at specialization from a slightly different viewpoint. If we were to apply Bales's methods to subsystems within formal work organization, we might ask members to rate one another according to "who produces the most" and "liking." From the evidence covered in the previous chapter, it is certain that in most work groups, the person rated highest on "productivity" would not be, in most cases, rated highest on "liking." This is because in such subsystems, high productivity indicates contributions to the external authority's goals for the group and not the goals that emerge informally among the members. Imagine if we were to ask: "Who does the most to give the group relevant information?" or "Who does the most to keep group secrets from the supervisor?" or "Who produces most consistently at the group's accepted level of productivity?" In this case those members of the work group who were rated highest would also tend to be highly liked. Specialization on these factors would indicate lack of structure and low subsystem solidarity.

The meaning of specialization, then, depends upon how it is defined. Being rated high in terms of "best ideas" apparently has the same meaning for members of laboratory groups as being rated high on "who produces most" in work subsystems. Bales erroneously assumed that the experimental task was *the* instrumental goal for the subjects—that they accepted the task as important and relevant. A subsystem within a formal organization may develop informal goals of its own that may or may not include the goals imposed by the external authority. Members of laboratory discussion groups do not really have the time or the opportunity to engage in activities which would be defined as informal goals of the group. Thus, Bales and others could only ask members to rate one another in terms of contributions to the imposed task. Defined in this manner, specialization was certain to occur with some frequency in the laboratory environment.

THE PRODUCTS OF PROBLEM-SOLVING GROUPS

Research on discussion groups in the Balesian tradition has not been much concerned with group solutions. The task was only a device to provide a rationale for having individuals communicate and reveal the interaction process that produced the solution. Presumably, all of Bales's groups came up with solutions, but we know little from the research about their quality or how quality related to the interaction process.

Apart from Bales's research, there are a number of studies of factors that contribute to or detract from "good" solutions. In this line of research, the main issue was whether "better" discussions were made by groups or by individuals working alone (see Dashiell, 1935). The typical experiment involved having several groups (real groups) discuss and arrive at a group solution on standard problems. For the sake of comparison, a series of individuals would work on the same problems alone. The investigator generally used problems which allowed him to derive some numerical indication of success (i.e., number of errors). The individuals who worked alone were grouped together into *nominal groups* for the sake of comparison. For instance, if the real groups had five members, the scores of five individuals who had worked alone would be chosen. Using these five scores the investigators would compute an average score that would be considered the "success" score for that nominal group. To determine the relative superiority of groups and individuals, the investigator would then compare the success scores for the nominal and real groups.

These studies have provided conflicting results. As is often the case, the original question was worded too simply. The answer to whether the group or the individual is better at problem-solving is: "It depends." It depends upon the type of problem being solved, and it depends upon what is meant by "better." Consider, for instance, the problem of judging the temperature of a room or the number of beans in a jar. A real group would probably come to some solution by averaging the estimates of the various individuals. Thus, the real group's solution would probably come closer to the right answer than any single individual's estimate, although there should be little difference between the answers of real or nominal groups. However, real groups are generally superior on intellectual tasks that, unlike judging beans, require group discussion (Kelley and Thibaut, 1969). There are several reasons for this. A particularly bright or skillful member may be able to solve the problem correctly and quickly and, therefore, be able to convince others to adopt his solution. Obviously, bright individuals working alone would be equal to a group solving the same problem, but this would not be the case for other persons working alone. There is a greater chance that someone in a group will come upon the solution or an important part of it, and this may contribute to the superiority of real groups on such problems. Second, in many problems, "good" solutions emerge when members hear different viewpoints. One person's erroneous solution can be caught by others as he explains it to the group. Also, the sheer number of creative ideas—such as advertising slogans—produced in real groups might be greater than those produced by a single individual, but research has shown that real groups are inferior in this regard to nominal groups (Taylor *et al.*, 1958; Dunnette *et al.*, 1963).

What criteria should be used in judging the relative success of groups and individuals? If group success on some problems is due to the presence of a superior individual, should we expect a group to do better than their best individual alone or better than the average of all members working alone? If an employer wanted good solutions to problems, should he hire a single good problem-solver or a group of average problem-solvers? The answer to this, as we have seen, probably depends upon the kind of problem. But even if the problems were of the type that would, in most cases, benefit from group discussion, the employer would still have to consider whether it is worth the man hours to get the superior group solution (Vroom *et al.*, 1969).

While fascinating, this line of research is only of academic interest. The fact is that despite questions about their efficiency, decision-making groups are used in a variety of settings for the solution of a variety of problems. Generally, this type of discussion group is referred to as a committee or conference. Although they are common, relatively little research has been done on existing committees, and most of what we have learned about decision-making or problem-solving groups comes from laboratory studies. Despite the problems involved in generalizing from such studies, we will use some of this research in conjunction with studies of committees in natural settings to try to understand how environmental factors influence the group products of naturally occurring committees.

Environmental Pressures Toward Uniformity

As a starting point, let us examine a consistent finding of group problem-solving experiments. Typical is a study by Thomas and Fink (1961) in which subjects in groups were asked to discuss a problem. After this, each individual was asked to give his own solution in private and disregard, if he wished, the group discussion. Despite the instructions to disregard the discussion, 64 percent of the groups gave unanimous answers. Commenting on this and other experiments showing similar results, Hoffman (1965) states:

> The continued existence of the group itself is a subtle barrier against the free expression of ideas. In laboratory groups there is a strong tendency for the members to agree on a single solution to a problem, even when instructed to ignore the prior discussion in reporting their own conclusions. It is as if the members did not want the group to be divided at the end of the session. We have often had subjects who violently opposed the majority's solution announce their capitulation with "I thought we were all supposed to agree!" (p. 101).

There is also evidence that discussion groups in other contexts face the same pressures. Consider, for example, Whyte's (1956) description of committees in his highly critical book about formal work organizations:

> In a committee which must "produce" something, the members must feel a strong impulse toward consensus. But if that something is to be a map of

the unknown country, there can hardly be consensus on anything except the most obvious. Something really bold and imaginative is by its nature divisive, and the bigger the committee, the more people are likely to be offended.

At this vital moment, the moral responsibility one feels to his colleagues becomes a downright hindrance. A committee member might be inclined to support an idea, but he is also not inclined to put up the fight for it (p. 223).

There is the strong implication in Whyte's statement that the solutions or decisions made in committees leave something to be desired. There are perhaps two interrelated ways in which committee solutions fail in his view. One is that committees suppress bold, new, creative solutions. In other words, they are too cautious and conservative. The second is that committee solutions tend to be bad or wrong. Both of these result from what we have called pressures toward uniformity. We shall look at research pertaining to both of these charges by Whyte, and in so doing will demonstrate how environmental factors influence pressures toward uniformity and affect the products of committees.

Pressures Toward Uniformity and the Risky/Cautious Shift Phenomenon

A series of experiments by researchers at MIT (Stoner, 1961; Wallach, Kogan, and Bem, 1962) seemed to demonstrate that groups make more risky decisions than individuals working alone. Since this contradicts Whyte's observations about groups, these experiments aroused great interest. However, since these contradictory results were obtained in experimental groups, there is some question as to whether they really have any implications for naturally occurring committees. In order to assess this we must examine the environments of both types of groups. We will begin with a look at the conditions under which the risky shift was observed.

In the original studies, as well as replications, subjects were given the *choice dilemma questionnaire* (CDQ), which contained a series of problems. The subjects were to act as a counselor to the central person in each problem, advising him how to solve his problem by recommending one of several alternatives provided on the questionnaire. The following is a sample problem provided by Brown (1965).

> *1.* Mr. A, an electrical engineer who is married and has one child, has been working for a large electronics corporation since graduating from college five years ago. He is assured of a lifetime job with a modest, though adequate, salary, and liberal pension benefits upon retirement. On the other hand, it is very unlikely that his salary will increase much before he retires. While attending a convention, Mr. A. is offered a job with a small, newly founded company with a highly uncertain future. The new job would pay more to start and would offer the possibility of a share in

the ownership if the company survived the competition of the larger firms.

Imagine that you are advising Mr. A. Listed below are several probabilities or odds of the new company's proving financially sound. Please check the *lowest* probability that you would consider acceptable to make it worthwhile for Mr. A to take the new job.

——The chances are 1 in 10 that the company will prove financially sound.
—— "   "   " 3 in 10 " "   "   "   "   "   "
—— "   "   " 5 in 10 " "   "   "   "   "   "
—— "   "   " 7 in 10 " "   "   "   "   "   "
—— "   "   " 9 in 10 " "   "   "   "   "   "
——Place a check here if you think Mr. A should *not* take the new job, no matter what the probabilities (pp. 657–58).

As can be seen in the example, the *lower* the probability of success of the new company, the *greater* the risk. The other problems on the CDQ followed the same format. After the subjects made their individual decisions on the problems, some were placed in groups of six to discuss each problem. These subjects were instructed to reach consensus among themselves as to which alternatives should be chosen. After the group decisions, the same subjects were asked to again indicate their private, individual choices. The remaining subjects, the controls, did not meet in groups but made a second set of choices after studying the problem for awhile.

By assigning numerical values to each alternative, the investigators could measure the degree and direction of the changes the subjects made in their choices. It was found that the individuals deliberating in groups made, on the average, more risky recommendations than they had previously when answering alone. It was also found that these subjects tended to make more risky choices alone after the group discussion than at first. On the other hand, the control subjects made no significant shifts from their initial choices after studying the problem alone.

These results have been replicated numerous times under the same or similar experimental conditions and with various types of subjects. They have also been replicated in experiments where subjects discussed the items but no unanimous group decision was required. Furthermore, a risky shift has been produced, although not as strongly as with a discussion, by having members simply announce their initial choices to one another (Teger and Pruitt, 1967; Bell and Jamieson, 1970). One of the early explanations of this phenomenon was the "diffusion-of-responsibility" theory (Wallach, Kogan, and Bem 1964). This theory views the shift to risky decisions as being a result of the fact that individuals become relieved of responsibility for risky recommendations when they are involved in group decisions. According to this theory, any blame associated with a poor risky decision is shifted (diffused) to the whole group. This is similar to the idea behind the adage "there is safety in numbers."

This theory was widely accepted until it was discovered that not all shifts in groups were in the direction of greater risk. Nordhøy (1962) found that after discussing certain problems, subjects consistently moved toward greater caution. One such item is printed below:

> Mr. M is contemplating marriage to Miss T, a girl whom he has known for little more than a year. Recently, however, a number of arguments have occurred between them, suggesting some sharp difference of opinion in the way each views certain matters. Indeed, they decided to seek professional advice from a marriage counselor as to whether it would be wise for them to marry. On the basis of these meetings with a marriage counselor, they realized that a happy marriage, while possible, could not be assured. Imagine that you are advising Mr. M and Miss T. Listed below are several possibilities on odds that their marriage could prove to be a happy and successful one. Please check the lowest probability that you would consider acceptable for Mr. M and Miss T to get married. (Brown, 1965, p. 703).

The discovery of items that precipitated shifts away from risk necessitates a new type of theory, one that allows for shifts toward either extreme along a risk-caution continuum. The explanation of this phenomenon must really account for two things. The first is why individuals shift toward one extreme or the other on particular items. The second is why these shifts are facilitated by discussions or other experiences in which subjects learn about one another's positions.

Shifts as a result of pressures toward uniformity. We have seen that members in groups of all types experience pressures toward uniformity. Is it possible that the risky/cautious shift is a class of this phenomenon?

In thinking about this, we find it useful to compare the responses of typical risky/cautious shift subjects with the responses of subjects in some conditions of the Sherif experiment (p. 30). The two are similar in that the subjects initially respond not knowing how others have responded, but as a result of experimental procedure later gain this information. In the Sherif experiment, this information was made available to subjects when they heard other subjects call out their estimate of the light's "movement." In the risky/cautious shift experiment, this occurs during the group discussion or, in some experiments, when members announce their initial CDQ choice. To carry out this comparison, the reader is referred to Figures 9.1 and 9.2. Figure 9.1 illustrates the changes made by subjects in a typical risky/cautious shift experiment. In this case, the CDQ item was one which subjects consistently change in a risky direction after a discussion. The choices made by each subject alone (before being placed in a group) can be seen as the line to the left. (Subjects are identified by capital letters.) The farther up the line a subject is, the more risky his initial choice. The final choices are indicated on the line to the right. This diagram does not differentiate between a subject's recommendation to the group and his private choice after the discussion. Although subjects in some groups might give recommendations to the group that differ from their later private recommendation, in most

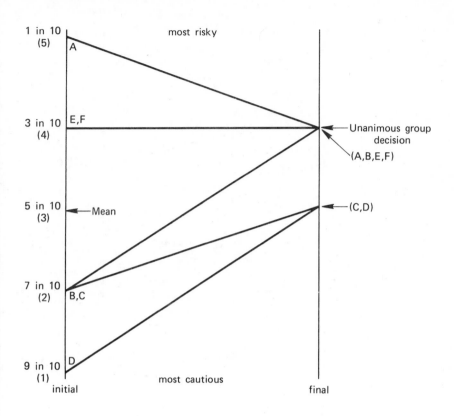

Figure 9.1. Risky shifts—Example #1. (Brown, 1965, p. 665.)

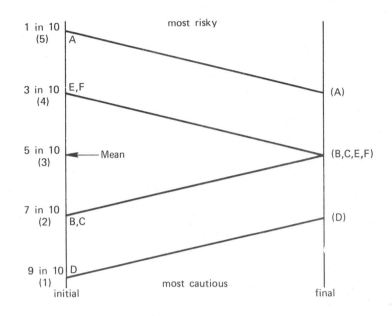

Initial Choice Mean

$$\frac{A + B + C + D + E + F}{6} = \text{Mean}$$

$$\frac{5 + 2 + 2 + 1 + 4 + 4}{6} = \frac{18}{6} = 3.0$$

Final Choice Mean

$$\frac{A + B + C + D + E + F}{6} = \text{Mean}$$

$$\frac{4 + 3 + 3 + 2 + 3 + 3}{6} = \frac{18}{6} = 3.00$$

Figure 9.2. Risky shifts—Example #2.

cases these two choices would be the same. As an example, we can see from Figure 9.1 that subject *A* initially gave the most risky choice (1 in 10) and that he changed to a more cautious choice (3 in 10) after the discussion. In this case, the group did not reach complete agreement, and so the alternative where the probability was 3 in 10 was the group recommendation, under majority rule.

The numbers in parentheses at the left in Figure 9.1 indicate the values arbitrarily assigned to each choice by the investigator. This allows him to compute the mean (average) for the initial and final choices. In this case, the more risky alternatives have higher numbers. The calculations of the means are at the bottom of Figure 9.1. As can be seen, the mean of the initial choices is 3, which corresponds to the 5 in 10 alternative. The mean for the final choices is 3.5, which, because it is larger than that for the initial choices, indicates a shift of choices in the direction of greater risk.

In Figure 9.2, which is to be read in the same manner as the previous figure, we tried to portray the kinds of changes which would be made if the risky shift phenomenon were exactly the same as that found by Sherif. Here we see that subjects initially are the same as those in Figure 9.1. However, after the discussion, the mean of the choices is exactly the same as the mean of initial choices. It can be seen from Figure 9.2 that although subjects changed their choices as a result of the discussion, they did not shift toward an extreme. Rather, they tended to converge on the mean. In the Sherif experiment, this pattern was interpreted as being the result of pressures toward uniformity.

Are pressures toward uniformity limited to the Sherif situation? A second look at Figure 9.1 reveals that the choice changes made in the typical risky/cautious shift experiment also converge toward the mean. With a few exceptions (Singleton, 1976; Cartwright, 1971), more attention has been paid to the fact that there is a shift in means in such groups than to the fact that choices converge after the discussion. The usual argument against taking the convergence seriously is that the patterns of choices during the typical risky/cautious shift experiment differ from those in the Sherif experiment (Brown, 1965). However, it is possible that the risky/cautious shift phenomenon may be a special kind of convergence resulting from the pressures toward uniformity found in all groups.

To assess this possibility, we must look more closely at the similarities and differences between the Sherif and risky/cautious shift experiment. The Sherif experiment was designed to give subjects the opportunity to develop group standards to use in reporting their estimates of the supposed light movement. These subjects were not certain what the appropriate or "correct" estimates were and so relied upon one another to arrive at some group definition of them. The subjects in risky/cautious shift experiments also faced uncertainty, but not to the same extent. They do not enter the experiment with ideas about what the "right" alternative would be. But, according to most researchers on this topic, they do have some vague ideas about whether relatively risky or cautious alternatives are more *desirable* on any given CDQ item. For example we have reported that some CDQ items elicit shifts toward greater risk while others elicit shifts toward greater caution. This suggests that in some CDQ situations, subjects value risk more highly while in others they find caution more attractive. According to Brown (1965, 1974), people value both risk and caution depending upon the circumstances. However, these values are rather vague and ambiguous since they do not specify just how risky or how cautious one should be in any particular situation. As an example let us use a value that does not involve risk or caution. People generally place a high value on honesty, but holding this value does not specify to a person how to behave in all situations that may arise. For instance, what does an honest man do when accused of cheating? when asked to inform on a friend? when his friend asks him to comment on his negative traits? when a relative with a terminal illness wants to know what is wrong with him? Values must be translated into specifications for behavior. According to Brown (1974), when individuals find themselves holding a common value but are unclear as to how to behave in a particular situation, they will turn to one another for cues.

The discussion, or its equivalent in various risky/cautious shift experiments, allows subjects to derive some idea as to how much risk or caution is appropriate for the particular situation. In the Sherif experiment, this was accomplished when subjects heard one another's estimates, and they used this information in making their own estimates. The reason that all subjects were influenced to shift toward the mean is that each estimate they heard was equally important. The only information available to Sherif's subjects was that contained in the estimates themselves, since subjects knew nothing about the characteristics of the person giving each estimate. In other words, there was no way in which one estimate heard by a subject would be any more influential than another. This, however, was not the case in the risky/cautious shift experiments. In most of these experiments, subjects discussed the CDQ items with one another, and therefore each obtained information about the others above and beyond their initial choice on each item.

Some theorists have suggested that those subjects who are initially most extreme in the risky/cautious shift experiments are likely to be more confident about their views and, therefore, more influential (Collins and Guetzkow, 1964; Marquis, 1962). This would account for the fact that there is a shift toward the most extreme subjects rather than a shift of both extremes toward the middle. While there is evidence that this may occur in experiments using group discussions (see Pruitt, 1971), it leaves unexplained why shifts toward the extremes occur in experiments where only initial choices are announced. These experiments resemble the Sherif experiment even more than those where discussions were used, since Sherif's subjects were not exposed to a discussion. But, there is an important difference. Subjects in risky/cautious shift experiments place value on one extreme or the other, depending upon the CDQ item. The subject or subjects who take relatively risky positions on items where risk is involved would then tend to have an unequal influence on others. Even if subjects do nothing more than state their positions, the less extreme subjects learn that there are others who have given more extreme responses in the valued direction. According to Pruitt (1971), the knowledge of others' choices "releases" the less extreme subjects and allows them to move in the direction of the alternatives they preferred in the first place.

In several studies (Levinger and Schneider, 1969; Pilkonis and Zanna, 1969), respondents have been asked to indicate on CDQ items their "best" or "ideal" alternatives as well as their personal choices. Generally, the respondents' personal choices were less risky than their ideals on CDQ items which typically showed risky shifts in other experiments. Likewise, on items showing cautious shifts, subjects made personal choices that were less cautious than their "ideal" choice. Furthermore, subjects have been found to perceive themselves as choosing more extreme alternatives in the valued direction than others (Hinds, 1962; Levinger and Schneider, 1969; Pruitt and Teger, 1969). Apparently, when subjects are faced with novel alternatives, they assume that their choices either conform to or go slightly beyond the valued direction of alternatives they think "most others" would choose. The discussion, or its equivalent, then informs members of the discrepancy between the imagined and the real distribution of choices. Since most subjects chose fairly moderate alternatives, the discovery that more extreme choices were made tends to compel them to move toward the valued extreme.

It is interesting to note that research shows that subjects initially making extreme choices in the valued direction do not usually shift to more extreme choices (Vidmar, 1970; Singleton, 1976). Rather, they either maintain the same position or, as in the hypothetical subject A in Figure 9.2, tend to shift slightly toward the middle. This means that most of the shifting is done by those who were less extreme. Whether this occurs because the more extreme subjects serve as positive models, because of the arguments offered in favor of such a shift, because of the influence of these extreme subjects, or some combination of these factors, the results are the same: The choices converge, with most subjects shifting in the valued direction.

Despite the hundreds of experiments dealing with shifts toward risk or caution, this dimension is probably only one of many that could be used to illustrate this point. For instance, Schroeder (1973) found that subjects in an experiment initially saw themselves as being more "altruistic" than others on items measuring altruism. It was also found that group discussion elicited shifts toward greater altruism. According to Brown:

> What *do* most people of your economic bracket give to the United Fund? I certainly don't know. . . . But suppose this were a situation in which just the same value, generosity, were predominantly activated in everyone, and the facts were confidential so that no one knew how to be generous, which is a relative thing after all. If we recorded our intentions in private and in ignorance, and then recorded them again after full disclosure of the intentions of whatever group we take as a point of reference, should there not be a shift to increased generosity, a "generosity shift?" (1974).

Brown is saying, then, that the importance of the risky/cautious shift research is not what it tells us about shifts toward risk or caution. Rather, these studies are important for what they show us about how individuals determine where they should be along some value dimension (risk, generosity, honesty, and so on) when in a novel situation. In some cases, they may want to determine what the majority is doing because they want to be a part of it; in others they may want to be slightly more risky, generous, or honest than the majority.

Implications for committees. The research evidence, then, does not suggest that group discussions must automatically lead to either risky or cautious results. The outcome seems to depend upon the issue being discussed and the values of the members. Thus, if committee meetings generally lead to cautious results it could be that the environment within which they form encourages cautious values among the participants. This idea is really a part of Whyte's observation about committees, but it is made much more forcefully by Merton (1957). According to Merton, if a bureaucracy is to operate efficiently, it must attain a large degree of reliability from its participants. In order to do this, all personnel work under the constraints of rules that dictate what they can and cannot do under given circumstances. So great is the emphasis on conformity to rules that participants become afraid to take actions not specified by rules or condoned by a higher official. In other words, conformity and caution become predominant values for bureaucrats.

Since most committees meet within such environments, we can see how cautious solutions to problems would be valued. Committee discussions occurring within such environments may well involve a process by which members determine how cautious they should be in adopting a particular solution. Contributing to this value placed on caution is the fact that, unlike subjects in the shift experiments, participants in committees must live with their decisions. For instance, a group of executives trying to decide whether their company should undertake a risky project know that a wrong decision could be disastrous not only for the organization but their careers. With these environmental factors at work, the pressures toward uniformity (that arise in all groups) would result in the cautious and conservative solutions observed by White.

Pressures Toward Uniformity and the Quality of Group Products

The second implication of Whyte's (1956) statement about committees was that they are notable for making bad or incorrect decisions. We have seen a great deal of evidence that pressures toward conformity are important in influencing the nature of discussion group products, and therefore we shall now examine the relationship between pressures toward uniformity and the *quality* of group decisions.

Groupthink. We have already pointed to some of the difficulties in making such evaluative statements about group solutions or decisions. However, there are groups which, we can agree at least in retrospect, have made bad decisions. For example, President Kennedy is supposed to have asked some time after the

Bay of Pigs invasion: "How could we have been so stupid?" The answer, according to Janis (1971), who spent two years studying such decisions, does not lie in the stupidity of those making the decision. After all, the men who participated in that decision—President Kennedy, Dean Rusk, Robert MacNamara, Douglas Dillon—were not lacking in intelligence. Rather, Janis sees such "stupid decisions" as being the result of *extreme* pressures toward uniformity, a condition he calls *groupthink*. According to Janis:

> The symptoms of groupthink arise when the members of decision-making groups become motivated to avoid being too harsh in their judgments of their leaders' or their colleagues' ideas. They adopt a soft line of criticism, even in their own thinking. At their meetings, all the members are amiable and seek complete concurrence on every important issue, with no bickering or conflict to spoil the cozy, "we-feeling" atmosphere (p. 43).

While groupthink does not occur in all groups, it is likely to be found "when members work closely together, share the same set of values, and, above all, face a crisis situation that puts everyone under intense stress" (p. 44). Furthermore, groupthink does not inevitably lead to bad decisions. But as Janis states, critical evaluation and rationality are secondary whenever groupthink prevails.

Where groupthink exists, members feel pressured not to express doubts or critical dissent. Janis cites the following example based on his study of the Bay of Pigs decision:

> President Kennedy probably was more active than any one else in raising skeptical questions during the Bay of Pigs meetings, and yet he seems to have encouraged the group's docile, uncritical acceptance of defective arguments in favor of the CIA's plan. At every meeting, he allowed the CIA representatives to dominate the discussion. He permitted them to give their immediate refutations in response to each tentative doubt that one of the others expressed, instead of asking whether anyone shared the doubt or wanted to pursue the implications of the new worrisome issue that had just been raised. And at the most critical meeting, when he was calling on each member to give his vote for or against the plan, he did not call on Arthur Schlesinger, the one man who was known by the president to have serious misgivings (1971, p. 74).

Another example of pressure stifling dissent was seen in groups meeting under President Johnson. Bill Moyers, who opposed the president's decision to escalate bombing in Vietnam, was referred to by Johnson as "Mr. Stop-the-Bombing."

Members of groups subject to groupthink need not always be exposed to overt pressure against dissent; they are also likely to feel a need to censor themselves. According to Janis:

> . . . Schlesinger was not at all hesitant about presenting his strong objections to the Bay of Pigs plan in a memorandum to the President and the Secretary of State. But he became keenly aware of his tendency to suppress objections at the White House meetings. "In the months after the Bay of Pigs I bitterly reproached myself for having kept so silent during

those crucial discussions in the cabinet room." Schlesinger writes in *A Thousand Days*, "I can only explain my failure to do more than raise a few timid questions by reporting that one's impulse to blow the whistle on this nonsense was simply undone by the circumstances of the discussion" (p. 74).

Group pressures toward uniformity and self-censoring lead to what Janis calls an *illusion of unanimity,* which is the false assumption that those members who remain silent are in total agreement with what others are saying.

"Our meetings took place in a curious atmosphere of assumed consensus," Schlesinger writes. His additional comments clearly show that, curiously, the consensus was an illusion—an illusion that could be maintained only because the major participants did not reveal their own reasoning or discuss their idiosyncratic assumptions and vague reservations. Evidence from several sources makes it clear that even the three principals—President Kennedy, Rusk and MacNamara—had widely differing assumptions about the invasion plan (p. 74).

Groupthink, then, seems to be primarily an attempt by members who work closely together and who must continue to do so to avoid conflict and keep relationships as pleasant as possible. This attempt will lead to the following group products which can affect the quality of solutions or decisions made by the group.

1. The group limits its discussions to a few alternative courses of action (often only two) without an initial survey of all the alternatives that might be worthy of consideration.
2. The group fails to reexamine the course of action initially preferred by the majority after they learn of risks and drawbacks they had not considered.
3. The members spent little or no time discussing whether there are non-obvious gains they may have overlooked or ways of reducing the seemingly prohibitive costs that made rejected alternatives appear undesirable to them.
4. Members make little or no attempt to obtain information from experts within their own organization who might be able to supply more precise estimates of potential losses and gains.
5. Members show positive interest in facts and opinions that support their preferred policy; they tend to ignore facts and opinions that do not.
6. Members spend little time deliberating about how the chosen policy might be hindered by bureaucratic inertia, sabotaged by political opponents, or temporarily derailed by common accidents. Consequently, they fail to work out contingency plans to cope with foreseeable setbacks that would endanger the overall success of their chosen course (p. 75).

Whatever final decision is recommended by a group having one or more of the above products is likely to be found wanting. One can imagine the difficulty of avoiding all of the listed pitfalls, and so it is not difficult to understand why Whyte and other social scientists have questioned the rationality of group decisions.

ENVIRONMENTAL FACTORS
THAT INFLUENCE COMMITTEES

The one theme which has run through much of this chapter is that the pressures toward uniformity obviously affect the value of group products. We shall now systematically discuss some environmental influences on committees that contribute to this pressure toward uniformity.

We can begin with a rare piece of research that examines why committees are formed and how they are used by executives. Kriesberg and Guetzkow (1950) asked executives in different organizations their reasons for calling conferences or committee meetings. Two kinds of answers they received were what we might expect: (1) to gain awareness of problems; and (2) to solve problems. But there appears to be a third reason which is often overlooked by social scientists. Many executives stated that committees are needed to help secure the acceptance of ideas and to implement these ideas. According to Kriesberg and Guetzkow:

> By including the individuals who would later execute the decisions, ability to implement the group's solution intelligently would be increased. . . . Executives use conferences to explain decisions, to ascertain lack of understanding, and to clarify aspects of the solution which are difficult to grasp. . . . But even more important than providing understanding, executives thought conferences help arouse sufficient motivation to insure execution of decisions (p. 95).

Three situations are seen as giving rise to the need for a committee meeting. The first occurs when an executive faces a problem that does not fully fall within his province. In such cases, if he were to make a decision on his own others who would be affected by it might object. In order to get his solution accepted by all those who might be affected, he calls a committee meeting. If there are some executives who object, a solution can be worked out that is agreeable to all concerned. Another situation giving rise to committee meetings is where the action of an executive must be approved by a superior. In this case, a meeting may be called as a means of gathering collective support for one's decision. Referring to the interviews, Kriesberg and Guetzkow state:

> . . . aside from the possibility that the group decision would be better than one arrived at by the executive alone, many said a decision reached in conference carried the impression of careful deliberation and broad consideration. . . .

> The anonymity of group decisions makes conferences useful as a covering device. The executive may call a meeting, not necessarily because he believes the group decision will be better than his own, but because the group will thereby have assumed the responsibility for whatever decision is made (p. 96).

The last situation occurs when an executive wants to assure that a decision he has made will be accepted by subordinates. Even if an executive has made up his own mind, he can present the problem anew to the gathered subordinates as if they were to collectively solve the problem and make a decision. During the discussion, he can attempt to influence the others to adopt his proposal or modify it in face of any strong opposition. This strategy helps the executive avoid looking like a dictator, since he has employed democratic group procedures. Furthermore, because the subordinates have worked on the problem and have become identified with it, they are more likely to comply with whatever decision is made by the group. Of course, the superior will have a chance to argue for his view, and it is unlikely that the group solution will be very different from his original proposal.

It appears from this study that committee meetings are not called solely because it is generally believed that groups produce the best decisions. In the three cases cited above, meetings were called with the expectation that consensus should and would be the final outcome. It is also likely that all participants enter such a meeting with the same expectations. This is consistent with Cloyd's (1965) contention that group meetings such as these follow institutionalized patterns that are shared by members of our culture (see page 162).

Unlike a laboratory group, a committee meeting does not involve strangers sitting together to solve a single isolated problem that has no later implications for the members. Rather, committees typically are formed of individuals who are members of the same organization and whose activities on the job require them to interact frequently. Committees can be thought of as temporary subsystems which form when the occasion arises. Like more permanent subsystems, the members are constrained by external forces to participate and so we would expect members to develop the means to make their interaction with one another as pleasant as possible. Whenever committee members face problems together, the possibility always arises for the expression of different opinions which can lead to conflict and lowered solidarity. However, as we stated in Chapter 5, when members of a group are exposed to forces toward anomie, members try to form norms and status structures to strengthen interdependence (Thibaut and Kelley, 1959; Bonacich, 1972). The symptoms of groupthink help avoid any forces growing out of the discussion that may threaten group solidarity. In fact, a study by Guetzkow and Gyr (1954) shows that members of groups facing extreme social-emotional problems may withdraw from the discussion and postpone controversial issues rather than risk further conflict. Rational decisions would be difficult to make under such conditions.

The Chairman as an External Authority

We have already pointed to some ways in which committees resemble other types of subsystems. In Chapter 8, the point was made that the external authority was important in setting up the conditions within which the subsystem operated. In laboratory discussion groups, the experimenter is the external authority. For committees, the committee chairman serves this function. Most committees have a chairman—whether elected by members or appointed by some other official in the larger, formal organization—whose leadership in the group has a legitimate basis. In some cases the chairman may have a position in the formal organization equal to that of the other committee members. But more frequently, the chairman has a higher-ranking formal status and therefore has authority over them. In such situations, the chairman is an external authority because he has some control over members and because he sets up and guides the committee meeting. Thus, in understanding how environmental factors influence committees, we should examine how the actions of the committee chairman can influence group processes.

We have seen that committee members enter meetings valuing unanimity and expecting that it will be attained. There are several ways in which the chairman contributes to this. First we saw from Kriesberg and Guetzkow's study that executives frequently call meetings (thereby becoming chairmen) when they require group agreement on some matter. Being chairmen, they are in a good position to see that consensus is attained. This is especially true when the chairman holds a higher status in the formal organization because when members are dependent upon the chairman for salary raises and promotions, they are unlikely to advance ideas that counter those favored by him. For instance, it is clear from Janis' (1971) analysis of governmental decision-making groups that Presidents Kennedy and Johnson each contributed greatly to the groupthink attitudes of their subordinates.

Guetzkow and Gyr (1954), in a study of actual business conferences, provide further evidence of the importance of the chairman in moving members toward consensus. In this study, they identified and measured two types of conflict which occur in committee meetings. The first, *affective conflict,* involves emotional clashes that arise during interpersonal struggles among members. The second is *substantive conflict,* which involves opposition among members about solutions to be adopted. Some degree of substantive conflict is inherent in problem-solving groups, since rarely will members be in complete agreement about solutions from the beginning. The danger of substantive conflict is that it can always turn into affective conflict where hostility and antagonism are openly expressed. The investigation found that a predominance of affective conflict in committees was resolved mainly through members withdrawing from the discussion (by not paying attention or doodling on note pads) and by postponing the agenda items leading to the conflict. On the other hand, groups with high levels of substantive conflict reached consensus through more positive means. Of particular importance is the fact that the chairmen of such committees were highly active in seeking information and facts from members. They also tended to propose many tentative solutions and, in general, were the centers of communication during the discussions. By actively participating in the discussion, the chairmen apparently made members aware of the issues that created the conflict and helped them think through or choose between alternatives. It does not directly show in Guetzkow and Gyr's data, but it is likely that the chairmen in the groups resolving substantive conflict proposed many suggestions and compromise solutions.

Berkowitz (1953), analyzing data from the same groups, provides further evidence of the influence of chairmen over group processes. Berkowitz broke committees down into two types according to how much urgency members gave to the solution of group problems. Groups giving great urgency to problems were thought to have higher interdependence among members than those that saw their problems as less urgent. In the nonurgent groups, he found that the members' ratings of satisfaction with the meeting were negatively related to *leadership-sharing.* Leadership-sharing occurred when the designated chairman did not play the role of leader, and the members talked more to one another than to the chairman. We have seen in previous chapters that group members tend to maintain status consistency and feel more comfortable when established status hierarchies are maintained. It appears that members enter committee meetings expecting the chairman to be in charge and guide the discussion. When this does not occur, competition and status struggles break out among members. These anomic forces are likely to spawn member dissatisfaction. Further support for this idea can be seen in research by Heyns (1948), Shelly (1960), and Burke (1966). The fact that leadership-sharing was not disruptive in groups with urgent problems was probably due to the members' greater interdependence. Emergent leaders are more acceptable in solidary groups because they are seen as making valuable contributions. Thus, members of groups with urgent problems would be more concerned with solving them and less concerned with who was most responsible for leading the group toward the solution.

The studies discussed thus far graphically illustrate the nature of the conflict between instrumental goals and social-emotional goals in committees. Undue emphasis on maintaining group solidarity can lead to groupthink. Too much disagreement caused by the members' desires to come up with the best solution can lead to disruptive social-emotional difficulties (affective conflict). Because the chairman has a high degree of influence within the committee, he is the one whom members see as being responsible for guiding them between these two extremes. There is not much question about whether this *can* be accomplished by a chairman. Little research exists on the topic, but certainly not all groups experience the extreme forms of pressures toward uniformity that Janis has called groupthink. Presumably, then, some chairmen help their committees avoid this.

Avoiding groupthink. It is impossible to make a general statement about the type of person who will be the most effective leader or supervisor. A leader's effectiveness not only depends upon his or her personal characteristics, but upon the nature of the task as well as the characteristics of the group members.

Fiedler (1967), for example, has demonstrated that different types of leaders or supervisors are effective in different settings. While we cannot generalize about what is the best type of chairman to guide a committee away from groupthink, we can indicate what a chairman would have to do. Having carried out a series of studies using leaderless discussion groups, Hall (1971) concluded that the most effective groups were those in which all members participated actively and in which points of disagreement and conflict were tolerated. On the other hand, ineffective groups used simple decision techniques like majority rule, averaging, and bargaining as quick methods to come to decisions. Based on these observations, Hall wrote some instructions that he felt could help groups attain high quality decisions. Subjects were given the *lost-on-the-moon* test. This test had subjects assume that they have crash-landed on the moon. They were given a list of survival items (e.g., matches, milk, a compass, and so on) and asked to rank them in order of importance to survival. The subjects' solutions were compared to the solution worked out by NASA officials in order to determine the quality of the answers. The subjects were then placed in groups to solve the problem. Half of the groups were given the problem after reading and discussing Hall's instructions. The remaining group met without exposure to the instructions. Here are Hall's written instructions that act as an antidote to the symptoms of groupthink.

Group-Decision Instructions

Consensus is a decision process for making full use of available resources and for resolving conflicts creatively. Consensus is difficult to reach, so not every ranking will meet with everyone's complete approval. Complete unanimity is not the goal—it is rarely achieved. But each individual should be able to accept the group rankings on the basis of logic and feasibility. When all group members feel this way, you have reached consensus as defined here, and the judgment may be entered as a group decision. This means, in effect, that a single person can block the group if he thinks it necessary: at the same time, he should use this option in the best sense of reciprocity. Here are some guidelines to use in achieving consensus:

1. Avoid arguing for your own rankings. Present your position as lucidly and logically as possible, but listen to the other members' reactions and consider them carefully before you press your point.

2. Do not assume that someone must win and someone must lose when discussion reaches a stalemate. Instead, look for the next-most-acceptable alternative for all parties.

3. Do not change your mind simply to avoid conflict and to reach agreement and harmony. When agreement seems to come too quickly and easily, be suspicious. Explore the reasons and be sure everyone accepts the solution for basically similar or complementary reasons. Yield only to positions that have objective and logically sound foundations.

4. Avoid conflict-reducing techniques such as majority vote, averages, coin-flips, and bargaining. When a dissenting member finally agrees, don't feel that he must be rewarded by having his own way on some later point.

5. Differences of opinion are natural and expected. Seek them out and try to involve everyone in the decision process. Disagreements can help the group's decision because with a wide range of information and opinions, there is a greater chance that the group will hit upon more adequate solutions (pp. 54, 86).

As individuals, the subjects in the two conditions had scored about the same. In both conditions, the average group scores tended to be higher than the average of the individual scores. But, as might be expected, the group working under Hall's instructions performed better than the one working without. What this study illustrates is that conditions can be set up by outsiders in which substantive conflict can be maximized without increasing affective conflict, and in which some balance between instrumental and social-emotional goals can be achieved. For these groups the conditions were contrived and artificial, having been created by written instructions from the experimenter. However, if Hall had imposed these conditions while sitting with the group, he would be operating much like a committee chairman. The point is that a chairman, with the proper combination of knowledge and skill, can be very instrumental in facilitating effective decision-making in his committee. As we mentioned before, this seems to depend upon whether the right person is chairing the right committee working on the right problem.

SOME CONCLUDING COMMENTS

In order to avoid repetition, we have not explicitly said much about environmental constraints or autonomy in this chapter. But the reader should be aware that the environments discussed can be seen as patterns of constraint and autonomy. For instance, the experimenter applies constraints upon laboratory groups by providing a task and by acting as an observer. Autonomy is provided when the experimenter fails to create a structure for the subjects (i.e., by not assigning a leader or other statuses). Experimental groups in risky/cautious shift experiments were given autonomy by the fact the members were not required to make decisions that would affect them personally as in committees. The decisions of committees are often limited by the values and expectations of the members. Committees are also constrained by time limitations, lack of adequate knowledge, and by the actions of the chairman.

SUMMARY

The experimenter can be viewed as an external authority who sets the conditions under which subjects interact with one another. The influence of his presence is seen in the Wilson (1969) study in which discussion groups met under observed and not-observed conditions. The results of this study indicate that the behavior of members in typical discussion group experiments is oriented toward meeting the perceived expectations of the experimenter.

Verba (1961) has argued that specialization is more likely to occur in laboratory discussion groups because of conditions inherent in the laboratory environment. For one thing, subjects in experiments are not likely to accept the given task as their own group goal. Thus, those subjects contributing the most to the solution of the task are not necessarily liked by the other members. Also, anyone who assumes the role of task specialist must violate expectations of equality and become the target of hostility from the other members. The trend toward greater specialization seems to be peculiar to experimental groups and not naturally occurring groups, where it is an indication of low solidarity.

In the second section, the discussion revolved around the two dimensions that have been used to evaluate the products of group decisions. The first of these was the degree of risk or caution involved in a decision. The second was the quality of the decision. With respect to the risk/caution dimension, it was found the group decisions can go farther toward either extreme than those made by individual members. The evidence suggests that the risky/cautious shift phenomenon is closely related to the convergence phenomenon observed by Sherif in his study of norm formation. Both seem to result from the pressures toward uniformity that are found in groups of all types. However, the risky/cautious shift experiments used groups formed under peculiar environmental conditions; thus the extent to which these findings can be generalized to naturally occurring groups is limited.

Subjects in the various risky/cautious shift experiments were interested in the positions of others primarily to assess and reevaluate their own positions. In naturally occurring committees, members may face pressures toward uniformity for the same reasons, but there is an additional factor contributing to uniformity. This is the fact that great emphasis is placed upon security, rigidity, and caution in the formal organizations within which most committees form. Thus, committees operate within a context where caution is valued and so discussions move members toward accepting cautious solutions.

It appears that pressures toward uniformity determine the quality of group decisions or solutions. According to Janis (1971), groups engage in groupthink when members attempt to stifle critical comments and suggestions in order to preserve consensus or the illusion of consensus. There are two major environmental factors that contribute to groupthink: (1) the general expectation held by members that unanimity should result from discussion; (2) the fact that members work closely together within the larger formal organization and are motivated to maintain cordial relationships.

Like other subsystems, committees are strongly influenced by an external authority, the committee chairman. The study by Kriesberg and Guetzkow (1950) shows that executives often call meetings to obtain uniform acceptance of an already formulated proposal. By assuming the chairmanship, an executive is in a position to control the discussion and thus to bring about favorable action of his solution. Berkowitz (1953) found that a chairman's failure to lead the discussion results in membership dissatisfaction which points to the degree of control in the hands of the chairman. This finding was interpreted as another example of the tendency for members to maintain status congruence, which, as we saw in Chapter 4, contributes to the power of the high status members. Also contributing to the control of the chairman, and thus the likelihood of consensus, is the fact that chairmen of committees usually hold high-ranking status within the formal organization. If members are dependent upon the chairman for salary increases and promotions, they will be disinclined to argue against solutions that he might favor.

While it is difficult to specify what type of chairman can lead committee members away from groupthink, group processes can be influenced by external factors. Hall (1971) improved the decisions made in laboratory discussion groups by reading them a list of instructions that remedy groupthink. It is argued that because of his power, a chairman who understands the dangers of and conditions leading to groupthink can steer a committee away from groupthink and extreme conflict.

ten

Environmental Changes and Solidarity

INTRODUCTION

We have seen from numerous examples that individuals in groups can be influenced by fellow members to behave in ways judged to be productive or unproductive, "good" or "bad." It is no surprise, then, that much of the interest in small-group research has come from those concerned with bringing about behavioral changes in individuals. This chapter deals with informal groups that form for the *purpose* of bringing about certain changes in the individual member. As we carry out our discussion of change-oriented groups, certain questions will be raised concerning how they resemble other types of groups. Therefore, we will, from time to time, be including in our analysis information about informal subsystems of other types.

THERAPEUTIC COMMUNITIES

In our earlier discussion of subsystems within prisons and mental hospitals, we pointed to certain inconsistencies between the organizational goals of rehabilitation and of custody. Where custody is the predominant goal, it is difficult to bring about beneficial changes in the behavior of inmates. Critics of *traditional* prisons and mental hospitals charge that inmates and patients cannot be rehabilitated when they are encouraged to be dependent upon authorities and are given no personal autonomy. They argue that the individual change that does take place involves the adoption of subsystem norms and values, which counteracts rehabilitation. Defenders of the traditional structures argue that providing

247

the greater autonomy necessary to effectively rehabilitate inmates or patients would lead them to take advantage of new privileges and to gross violations of the rules. Despite this argument, there has been a gradual acceptance of the importance of rehabilitation, and this has led to the institution of "therapeutic communities" within many traditional mental hospitals and prisons.

The concept of the therapeutic community was first introduced by Maxwell Jones (1953), who set up experimental units within mental hospitals in England in which all of a patient's time was devoted to treatment. Jones's experimental units were expected to accomplish four goals: (1) all activities in which patients participated were to be thought of as treatment; (2) the unit would be run according to democratic principles; (3) the patients were to gain a measure of freedom not found in custodial units; and (4) all staff members were to be involved in treatment and their authority deemphasized. For Jones, *group participation* allowed the patient to observe and correct his inadequacies.

The idea behind therapeutic communities is to set up an environment on a ward in which the inmate system can reach high levels of solidarity. This environment is supposed to encourage the emergence of goals and norms which, unlike those on traditional wards, are congruent with the staff's emphasis on rehabilitation and supportive of positive changes on the part of the patients. In addition to group therapy, all other activities in such communities are generally carried out in groups. Ward meetings involving both patients and staff are held on a regular basis to deal with day-to-day problems. In most cases, a patient government is set up with elected representatives who are given genuine policy-making powers.

Influenced to a great extent by the experimentation with therapeutic communities in the mental health field, reforms along similar lines have been made in many penal institutions. Either whole prisons or special units in a prison may be organized as therapeutic communities. This reform is based upon the assumption that the inmates are not responsible for their behavior, and since they have been socialized incorrectly, treatment should involve a socialization process. Therapeutic communities within prisons involve a restructuring of relations between staff and inmates to discourage antagonism and reduce inmate dependency. Authority is decentralized and inmates provided with mechanisms for influencing prison policy. All staff members, even guards, are trained to help promote treatment goals. These changes in formal organization allow inmates greater personal autonomy. This autonomy is necessary, in part, to counteract informal subsystems that discourage the inmates' acceptance of the legitimacy of the rehabilitation goal. Within therapeutic communities informal subsystems can form norms which support those of the larger structure and can exert pressure on members to change in directions consistent with rehabilitation. The intended result is that inmates will participate in the various rehabilitation programs for their intrinsic benefit rather than for extrinsic gains (e.g., information, contraband, time off the job) and without worrying about being labeled as "centermen" by fellow inmates (see Johnson, 1974).

In both mental hospitals and prisons, greater patient and inmate autonomy is of major importance in instituting therapeutic communities. Consistent with the description of the relationships between autonomy and solidarity (Chapter 8), we would expect inmate solidarity to be relatively high in treatment communities. While one of the goals of therapeutic communities is to bring about solidarity, this is not accomplished automatically or easily (Raskin, 1971; Rapoport, 1960; Friedman, 1969; Groog, 1956). A major problem facing prisons and mental hospitals in which inmates are given greater autonomy is that in deemphasizing external control the risk of escapes and other violations of rules increases. Although the subsystem members are supposed to control themselves on such matters, it takes time for group solidarity to develop to a sufficient level for this to occur. The development of solidarity is also difficult in therapeutic communities because most inmates, either because of personality characteristics or because of their adaptation to custodial procedures, are highly dependent upon authorities and lack social skills. It is necessary then, in setting up a therapeutic community, for the staff to coax, push, and teach the inmates to become a group and take advantage of their new autonomy. To provide some examples of the difficulties encountered by subsystems in the transition from autocratic to autonomous environments, we now will turn to several research studies of this process.

Changes Toward Greater Autonomy

McCleery's (1960) description of the complex process involved in the change of a traditional custodially oriented prison to one emphasizing rehabilitation illustrates how greater autonomy affects solidarity among prison inmates. To begin with, a new warden consistently worked to change the traditional authority structure set up under the old warden. First, he directed the higher officials not to automatically sign punishment orders sent to them by guards and custodial officers. Prisoners were not to be punished without a hearing and the presentation of evidence. Shortly after this, he changed the prison industrial program, which used to assign simple tasks to inmates working under close supervision, to one that allowed the inmates to take responsibility for production under less restrictive supervision. At the same time, he hired a new staff that deemphasized the custodial goal of the prison in favor of treatment and he dismissed several employees who had blatantly engaged in illegal trading with inmates. This latter action resulted in resentment among guards because much of the evidence against those fired had been obtained from inmates. At one point an inmate council was set up in which elected inmates could make policy recommendations to the prison authorities.

All of these changes taken together undermined the status and authority of the guards; and because the guards had immediate authority over the prisoners, the inmate subsystem was affected as well. Because of the close relationships between inmates and members of the treatment staff, guards often found that the inmates had more information than they about the running of the prison. Furthermore, under the new regime, guards could no longer control inmates by threatening punishment as a means of control. Throughout the liberalization process, the guards resisted and attempted to enforce old traditional values. Since they were closest to the prisoners, they observed how various prisoners took advantage of the new freedoms afforded them and therefore were convinced that the new approach would fail. In fact, at one point, some of the "old guard" initiated an investigation of the prison, but the investigative body supported the new warden, which helped push the liberalization process along to its conclusion.

The waning of the guards' power and emergence of alternative sources of rewards for prisoners threatened the authority of the old inmate elite, which derived its power through connections with the guards. The old inmate leaders rejected opportunities to develop relationships with treatment personnel and to take advantage of the new rewards system. Instead, they entered into an overt alliance with the guards and attempted to maintain their position through force. However, this was not successful for long, and many inmates began to accept and work within the new rehabilitation system. According to McCleery:

> The marginally criminal first offenders, the lowest caste in the old prison, had found a focus of interest and organization in the treatment unit and the council. As official frankness, publication of rules, and a formal orientation program made new inmates independent of indoctrination by the old, another group of tough young reform-school graduates declared their independence from the old leadership and embarked on a radical course of exploitation and trouble-making. In the following year neither the traditional "code" nor the old leadership commanded the respect that would permit them to define roles or adjust conflicts in the community. In the absence of controlling definitions, disputes were increasingly submitted to arbitration by force, and the status of the physically powerful and aggressive men rose (pp. 72–73).

With the disintegration of the old inmate system and the new permissiveness of the prison authorities, there were no effective controls over aggression and attempts to escape. At one point, machine guns had to be set up on the roof to quell further disorder. It was at this point that the legislative inquiry began, and when it was completed, order was slowly restored. The guards stopped resisting the new emphasis on treatment. Voluntary participation in treatment activities increased, and the inmate council became a legitimate body in the eyes of most inmates. Disciplinary records showed that the number of inmates who were abusing the newly instituted autonomy declined.

McCleery's analysis does not focus on a single cellblock as a subsystem but with the inmate population as a whole. The inmate system consists of interrelated cellblocks. Inmates may develop relationships between subsystems, especially with the leaders in adjoining cellblocks, but most communication is restricted within subsystems. Although McCleery does not approach the topic in this manner, there is no reason to doubt that each separate subsystem underwent similar changes in response to alterations in the formal structure. The power of the guards in each unit would have eroded, and this would have made it difficult for them to give rewards and favors to inmate leaders in cellblocks. This, in turn, would have deprived the old leaders of their sources of power, and they would have lost control over the other inmates; individualistic responses would have increased. However, as the inmates began to develop relationships with treatment personnel and became involved in activities such as the inmate council, they would find alternative bases for prestige. As a result, a new informal structure would have emerged in each cellblock whose solidarity would be based on norms and goals that supported rehabilitation and participation in the inmate council. When inmates in the various cellblocks recognized the advantages to be gained from the new reign, they, especially the leaders, would have restrained one another's individualistic responses, thus increasing solidarity.

Evidence for these changes comes from several studies of single units that were purposely governed to allow greater inmate autonomy than traditional units. Briggs (1972) describes what happened when violent offenders from a cellblock were placed in a newly developed therapeutic community. Like McCleery, Briggs reported that escapes and disruptions were common during the early phases of the program. But later, the inmate organization developed to the point where offenders of prison regulations were dealt with by the inmates themselves, which indicates a fairly high level of subsystem solidarity. Studt, Messinger, and Wilson (1968) observed the move of a representative population of inmates from a traditional unit to a treatment-oriented unit in which authorities made a conscious effort to build up the inmate system in order to get the men to accept the goal of rehabilitation. They found that the new unit was initially the scene of disorder, hostility, and anxiety. Over time, however, these problems were resolved, the inmates showed higher rates of "friendliness," and the system was described by the investigator as being relatively high in solidarity. In this case, prisoner subsystems did not exist before the transition, but the study illustrates the disruptive influence of increased autonomy.

Studies of the transition from traditional to autonomous wards in mental hospitals show similar results. Hooper (1962) reports such a transition in a ward of patients characterized by "passive obedience to the firmly fixed pattern of daily activity, with virtually no autonomy of action" (p. 112). Once the transition began, there were many patient disturbances, and staff members felt that they could not handle the patients under the new system. Eventually, however, disturbances subsided and the general activity level of patients increased. While the amount of patient-staff interaction increased, the amount of patient-patient interaction increased at an even greater rate in the more autonomous situation. This would indicate a breakdown of the patients' almost total dependence on staff members typical of traditional wards (LeBar, 1964) and the development of solidarity.

In a similar transition observed by Clark and his associates (1962), patients initially expressed anxiety, hostility, and the fear that under the new system they would be subject to "bossing" from other patients. Ward meetings called by the staff were characterized either by violent disagreements or formal silences. Many patients took advantage of the lack of formal control and refused to carry out tasks they were supposed to take over from the staff. Under the traditional system, one patient had intensive interviews with a high prestige doctor on the staff and used this relationship to dominate other patients by making them believe she could arrange for their preferential treatment. During the transition, her interviews had to be terminated, which undermined her prestige on the ward. She eventually reacted by setting fire to a portion of the ward. According to Clark, a stable social structure eventually formed on the ward. Although this study makes no direct comment on the level of patient solidarity after the resolution of the transitional crises, it is safe to assume that it was necessarily higher than before since the therapeutic community was considered a success.

Lipgar (1968), analyzing the transition of a back ward to a therapeutic community, also describes an early problematic stage. During this time, all group meetings were unsuccessful and the relationships among patients consisted of "struggles for leadership and domination." As in the other studies, Lipgar reports that patients slowly became capable of communicating effectively among themselves and managing their own affairs.

The last three studies reviewed describe the disintegration in solidarity among patients in reaction to institutionally planned increases in autonomy, but there is evidence that unplanned autonomy in mental hospitals may have similar effects. Meyer (1968) extensively reviewed the literature on the phenomena called "collective disturbances" in mental hospitals. Meyer shows that although the predisposing conditions varied, in all of the studies reviewed, collective disturbances occurred when the authorities in some way failed to exert their normal control over the patients. Meyer's study suggests that informal group control among the patients breaks down when suddenly faced with increased autonomy from the external authorities.

In Chapter 8, we reviewed studies showing that groups in more autonomous environments attain high solidarity. The studies just reviewed provide some clues as to how informal subsystems react to changes in the environment. The pattern described in this research suggests the proposition that when subsystems are provided greater autonomy, their solidarity declines temporarily but later rises to its previous level or goes even higher.

Further Evidence for the Proposition

Inmate and mental patient subsystems are not the only groups that show this pattern. Take, for instance, the groups formed for the Iowa leadership study (White and Lippitt, 1960). The groups were comprised of young boys assigned to meet under adult leader playing various predefined roles and so the leaders in this experiment really acted as external authorities for the groups. Groups meeting under autocratic leaders were tightly controlled and given no encouragement for developing solidarity. Under democratic and laissez-faire leaders the groups were afforded greater autonomy. Some groups were first exposed to autocratic leaders and then were shifted to either democratic or laissez-faire leaders in which autonomy was relatively high. The investigators found that after the change there was an initial increase in disorder and aggression in these groups. Commenting on this, White and Lippitt (1960) state that "experiments in the direction of greater freedom in any group that has been in a repressed atmosphere may at first lead to a disappointingly large amount of disorder, but this does not necessarily mean that disorder will be permanent" (1960, p. 78).

While not reliable as research evidence, one can imagine the same process at work in the bank wiring room to support the proposition that increased autonomy first leads to a decline and then a rise in solidarity in informal groups. Suppose that these men had been told they could choose whatever job they wanted in the room as long as overall productivity of the group did not suffer. Men previously assigned to particular jobs now were free to choose their own. This change would probably lead to chaos for several days. The workers would quibble over who got what job, and old informal relationships would become very tenuous. In other words, individualistic orientations would become stronger than interdependent orientations, and the solidarity of the subsystem would decline. But the primary condition of their new-found autonomy was that they had to maintain the old level of productivity. While greater than before, the new autonomy is not complete, and the men must attain some degree of solidarity to meet the production demands or lose their jobs. It is likely, then, that somehow the men would develop a method of assigning jobs that would enable them to continue as a subsystem. This might involve assigning jobs according to seniority, or rotating jobs, but the important thing is that the procedure would be under the control of the group. Given the peculiar mixture of personalities in the bank wiring room, the group might not be able to withstand the anomic forces set forth by such a change. However, if it did, it would be likely to attain a higher level of solidarity than before, since now the subsystem would have control over an area of its members' behavior that was previously controlled by the external authority. If a system of rotating jobs evolved, new norms specifying *who* should do *what* and *when* would develop. Furthermore, certain new statuses might emerge as old ones became more clearly defined as a result of the change. For example, the person who conceived the idea of rotating jobs and who is informally expected to see that it continues to work may be given a leadership status within the group.

Something like this occurred among the salesmen studied by Babchuck and Goode (1955, see page 116). The reader will recall that at one point the salesmen were provided greater autonomy by being allowed to choose their salary payment program. The change initially had a disorganizing effect on the group but the salesmen eventually overcame the anomic forces and developed sufficient internal control mechanisms (rotating customers and so on) to regain lost solidarity. In this case, the increase in autonomy was incomplete because the alternative salary programs came from the company instead of being developed by the group. However, because the group enjoyed a generally high level of autonomy, they were free to modify the choices imposed by the larger organization, and these modifications were eventually accepted and formalized by the authorities.

Changes toward greater control. Another logical question to raise at this point is: What are the effects of *decreases* in autonomy (increased control) by external authorities on subsystem solidarity? We must again rely purely on intelligent speculation because no studies have been conducted on this problem. An increase in external control, like an increase in autonomy, would certainly disrupt existing informal procedures and relationships within a subsystem. For instance, if prison guards began to punish participants in activities previously allowed and did not provide inmate leaders the opportunities to obtain scarce goods, the inmate system would be undermined. If the supervisors of the bank wiring room had demanded consistently high productivity from the workers but had enforced the rules against job trading, an essential basis of the group's solidarity would have been eliminated. It appears, then, that changes toward or away from subsystem autonomy will disrupt existing informal structures and solidarity. But there is an important difference. While subsystems moving toward greater autonomy have the opportunity to renew their solidarity, they would not have it under greater control. Thus, the decline in solidarity of subsystems exposed to greater external control over time is likely to be permanent.

GROUP DEVELOPMENT AND ENVIRONMENTAL FACTORS

In the previous section we saw that changes toward solidarity or anomie can be precipitated in *existing* groups by altering the environment. The process by which *newly* formed groups move toward higher solidarity is called *group development.* One way to analyze group development is to describe the stages through which newly formed groups progress as they become more solidary. Since group development research requires that groups under study meet regularly and be easily observed, most information about development is based upon self-analytic groups (t-groups and therapy groups) and laboratory groups. We will first look at development in self-analytic groups and then in laboratory groups.

Self-Analytic Groups

Self-analytic groups include t-groups (leadership training groups), therapy groups, and the numerous types of encounter groups. According to Back (1971), self-analytic groups offer members of a science-oriented generation intense experiences and an opportunity for self-change that was previously available only through religious ritual. Whatever the reason for their proliferation, the sheer number and variety of these groups require that social scientists pay some attention to them.

Despite their wide range, almost all self-analytic groups are under the direction of a leader who serves as an external authority. It is the leader who organizes the group meetings, sets the goals, impels members toward their goals, and guides the interaction as the group progresses. Members of self-analytic groups come together voluntarily, but they are drawn to the leader or organization sponsoring the group experience rather than to the other participants who, in most cases, are strangers. The leader may set up tasks or goals such as learning to communicate in a more honest manner, learning about group dynamics, or solving personal problems. However, stated goals of this nature are rather vague and are not accomplished in the same way that a discussion group might solve a human relations problem. The members, from the beginning, are faced with a rather paradoxical situation. The goals they come to accomplish can only be reached if they interact and become a group, yet they have no basis for interacting with one another because they have no tangible common goal. It is the leader's job to provide a basis for the future development of the group.

We shall discuss two types of self-analytic groups: t-groups and therapy groups. We shall first provide a broad overview of what occurs in these groups. Then we shall engage in a more detailed analysis of the leader-member relationship to show how development occurs in such groups.

t-Groups. It is generally agreed that Kurt Lewin was the founding father of t-groups. In 1946, Lewin and some of his students were engaged in training community leaders to be more effective in their leadership. After one of the meetings between trainers and community leaders, the trainers met alone to discuss the previous session. During this meeting several of the trainees asked if they could listen. Hearing the trainer's views of what happened during the training session induced the trainees who were present to speak up and give their own views. Lewin was so impressed by the spontaneous interchange that he implemented such discussions in the regular training session. This event illustrated the importance of members providing one another feedback about on-going group processes—a key element of t-groups, therapy groups, and other self-analytic situations. It is the information about how others view them that enables members to engage in self-analysis, and it is the members' concentration on what occurs in the group that enables them to learn, by experience, about group processes or themselves. In such groups members must necessarily confront one another with frank and honest evaluations, and as a result members experience intense emotions both positive and negative.

When the group first meets, the leader will articulate for the members the goals which he envisions their reaching but also makes it clear that they, as a group, will be responsible for accomplishing these goals. Typically, the t-group leader will define his role as that of a resource person and will admonish the members not to expect him to act as most leaders do (Mintz, 1971). Needless to say, the early sessions in such groups are anxiety-producing for most members, since they have no clear idea why they are present or how they are to proceed. The atmosphere of early sessions of most t-groups can be grasped in the following descriptive accounts. The first is taken from a participant's written observations of his t-group experience with fellow medical students:

> At the first session, participants introduced themselves and explained what they expected to gain from the experience. Topics were easily exhausted and uneasy silences ensued. Participants often sat and stared at each other, grinned embarrassed grins, or even giggled. When someone spoke, the topics were generally safe areas of common interest such as medical school. Occasionally the moderator would refocus the group's attention on itself with a question such as "I wonder what this discussion has to do with what is going on in the group?" Usually this question was followed by a dead silence. People became restless and embarrassed by the silent periods which came frequently with the elimination of external topics (McCann, 1968; quoted in Goldberg, 1970).

It can be seen from this brief description that the leader did not attempt to initiate discussions or provide much guidance or structure as a typical chairman or discussion leader might. Rather, he reminded the group, in an indirect fashion, of their goals concerning analysis of the group processes.

The second description is based on one author's fictitious account of a typical first session in a t-group comprised of business executives:

> The setting looks peaceful enough—a pinepaneled room in an isolated country resort, with a fine view from the picture window. But as the ten participants begin filing into the room, the atmosphere seems charged. One senses a kind of uneasiness, the sort of anxiety that goes with expecting something unprecedented. The newcomers contribute to it in varying ways. To what degree each will eventually join in depends on what he or she really is, not on what he or she first appears to be.
> The trainees are informally dressed. Each takes an unassigned chair. Some have an easy air, but such impressions are often deceptive. One man

looks around as though he is about to give an order for lunch and is already convinced the service will be slow.

When the t-group is assembled, the leader starts the session. He may begin with something like the following:

"Now, I'd like to say a few words. You'll find that I'm a leader who isn't doing much leading. This will be especially true during the early part of the week.

"You can organize yourself in any way you wish, deciding for yourselves what's important for you to work on. Design your program in whatever way you feel will be more advantageous to you.

"My own role for the present is mostly that of a catalyst, helping when and where I can, but in no sense directing or building your program.

"How you proceed is up to you. That's about all for now."

Silence: The silence stretches out, it grows heavier, People fidget and glance at one another. The tension builds. The select group members are quietly uneasy, and are thinking to themselves:

Chuck: This silence sure can create tension. I don't have any idea of what's going to happen next. I'll pretend I'm looking at my notes. I'm sure this silence has been carefully planned. It'll be interesting to see what we are supposed to learn from it.

Molly: Now, what should I do? If I speak first in front of these men, they'll think I'm too pushy.

Gordon: This is a bit unsettling. No agenda, no rules, no chairman, and no one leading.

Pete: What a waste of time! I would take charge and get this thing going, but I'll let someone else break the ice. Then, if nothing happens, I'll take charge.

John: I'm baffled. I don't understand what's going on! I don't see how we can learn anything when there is no agenda, no leader.

Sal: I'm a little impatient, going around in circles. I wonder if I should suggest that we start by introducing ourselves.

Finally, Pete breaks the ice.

"Well," he says, "what now? What do we do? Who's chairman? What are the assignments?"

Nobody answers. Pete stares at the leader. "How about it?"

Pete doesn't realize that whatever happens next really is up to the group. He has a powerful drive. It has brought him where he is, chief executive of a company which he built himself. He is accustomed to leadership; a competitive man, as usual he demands to get things going. At the same time, though, Pete is trying to curb his impatience. He cannily senses that is the thing to do, however difficult it usually is for him.

Even so, Pete can't help pressing on. "Then who takes over?" he asks, looking around. He sees that some others, executives like himself and accustomed to getting down to business quickly, are also impatient. Yet other members of the group appear to be at ease and relaxed, a few even seem secretly amused.

Into this vacuum, then, without an official chairman and with no set agenda or rules, our group plunges headlong. Almost immediately, we see a variety of leadership and behavioral styles, with uncertainty, impatience, and frustration on the part of some and a sense of excitement on the part of others. This unstructured way of starting the first session is important because it creates dilemmas that help uncover each person's strengths and weaknesses.

The group leader speaks up, "No one person is in charge here, really. It is up to the group."

Pete tries again. "Well, what the hell, isn't there an agenda or plan? Isn't there some kind of general procedure?"

The leader says: "The group can do whatever it wants. There are many options to choose from."

Now Gordon speaks up. He is a senior executive in a governmental agency. This is the first time that he and the others have met. But when Gordon speaks, he sounds as though he has known Pete, or people like him, all his life.

"I think he means, Pete, that we make our own rules—that is, if we're going to have any. Is that right?"

The group leader nods. "For the present, let's say that's about it."

Pete stares around at the others. He can't quite believe it. "Well, I'll be damned! Is that what my firm is paying out good money for?"

A chuckle comes from around the table. Pete's comment relieves some of the tension, but the laughter, though good-natured, is in part at his expense and he is smart enough to know it. He wonders why he is so much more disturbed by the lack of set procedures than some of the others seem to be. He wants to find out but realizes it won't be easy. But maybe that just shows the t-group process is something he really ought to know more about. (Marrow, 1975, pp. 23-26).

In this second description, it can be seen that the lack of direction and structure in the situation acts as an inducement for the members to interact with one another. This interaction provides the basis for the eventual emergence of an informal structure among members. As the group continues to meet, various other issues arise that provide opportunities for members to voice their opinions, learn about one another, evaluate one another, and learn how they are evaluated. Examples of these issues can be seen in the experiences reported by the medical student from whom we quoted earlier.

After several meetings, attempts were made to reprimand those who missed sessions. Other attempts were made to insure the participants' freedom to do as they pleased. There were attempts to say "we" and urge group action, while others said "I" and resisted regimentation.

A person who has had previous experience with such groups began attending the sessions. The original participants seemed to resent his apparent self-assurance in the group and some direct hostility was experienced and expressed.

There were appeals to be more friendly and talk about personal things. There was the continued feeling among some participants that the group was not moving fast enough, that the group wasn't going any place. Some one inquired as to whether anyone knew just where the group was supposed to go.

After a couple of months, the sessions continued to start out superficially with little reference to previous events in the group. If this superficial period became prolonged, the moderator would refocus the attention of the group on itself. However, the discussions were becoming more personal toward the end of the hour. Often personal conflict developed when one person acted contrary to what someone else deemed appropriate.

No matter what issues come up in t-groups, the discussion involves a structuring process whereby the goals, statuses and norms for behavior within the group evolve. The emergence of the structure, however, is often slow because many social-emotional problems must be solved along the way. As the above account illustrates, the leader must exert constant pressure on the members to examine what is transpiring as discussions continue. The emergence of the informal structure provides data for analysis in the group, and simultaneously provides a degree of solidarity to counteract the conflict and disharmony that inevitably result when members analyze their own behavior.

Of all of the numerous issues or problems that arise for discussion in t-groups, none appears to be more important than the "problem of the leader." Very simply, the leader is a problem for the group because he violates the member's expectations and he is seen as the cause of their anxiety. Because he does not play the usual leadership role expected of him, members are not certain as to how they should relate to him or, for that matter, to one another. Our medical student summarizes the leadership problem as follows:

The moderator's apparent right to intervene and direct the group defines for him a specific role which the other participants did not have. The contrast became sharper until one of the moderator's "I wonder how you feel about it?" questions was countered with the same question. The moderator was challenged, asked to define his position, blamed for the alleged failure of the group, and urged to take a more direct part over a period of about four sessions. There was a strong counter-protest against attacking the group's only authority reference. Some one suggested that the group was using the moderator with his defined position as a scapegoat for the participants' own frustrations which grew from the anxiety-producing situations in the group.

The leader's behavior not only forces the members to take responsibility for the emergence of the informal structure; it also provides a focus for interaction.

As the above description shows, members were not of one mind as to how to define and relate to the leader. The reactions of the various members to the leader supply information for self-analysis. In most groups, the result of this self-analysis is that the members simultaneously accept the leader's role as he defines it and continue in the direction they set for themselves without worrying about whether the leader agrees or not.

The conclusion of the medical student's written account contains some clues as to what finally is accomplished in such groups as they progress.

> There was continued resentment that some participants were violating what others believed to be the "raison d'etre" of the group. Furthermore, the individuals concerned began to show a feeling that the mysterious direction that the group was supposed to take was a more intensive consideration of themselves. The inability of many in the group to accommodate themselves to an unstructured situation seems to lead them to focus on what they perceived themselves to be. In the absence of external behavioral guidelines, a person must depend on his internal guidelines. One must know what he is, if he wishes to know what behavior is appropriate for him. That is, the group moves toward a consideration of the identities of the participants.
>
> Psychological and social processes left the shroud of academic vagaries and became an integral part of the world which I generally acknowledge as being real. The experience was rewarding. Maybe I even improved my interpersonal relations.

As the members work their way through the various issues that arise, they become more comfortable with confrontation, conflict, and self-analysis. In fact, the final group norms usually require members to engage in frank and objective evaluation of themselves, other members, and the relationships that have formed within the group. Through this process, as illustrated by the medical student's account, members come to learn about group processes through direct experience rather than through reading about them. The medical student, like most participants in t-groups, came away from the experience with the feeling that it was "rewarding" in some vague way. He was also ambivalent as to whether what was learned in the t-group was helpful in relating to others outside the group. This is interesting because the little research that has been conducted on the effectiveness of t-groups in improving the members' social relations suggests that they are not (Campbell and Dunnette, 1968). One key problem is that the new honest and objective styles of relating to others that participants learn in these situations are met with confusion or hostility when they try them out on those who have not gone through the same experience. Thus, whatever is learned from the t-group experience may not be helpful to the participant when he returns to the "real world."

Therapy groups. Group therapy, which is an outgrowth of individual psychotherapy, gained popularity toward the end of World War II when the number of patients in the Army and Veterans Administration hospitals, as well as private clinics and hospitals, became too great to treat separately (Luchins, 1964). At first, many saw group therapy as a stop-gap procedure for dealing with large numbers of patients, but the simultaneous interest in informal groups greatly helped convince therapists of the legitimacy of using groups for therapeutic purposes.

Although there are many different types, most therapy groups are run in a fashion very similar to t-groups. The most notable difference between the two involves the characteristics of the members. Group therapy is designed for individuals who have some personal or psychological problem so that the goal of therapy groups is to help each member alleviate symptoms or problems. While changes are expected in t-groups, much more radical changes are strived for in group therapy (Kaplan, 1974). As a means of resolving problems, the therapist encourages group members to become aware of how their emotional experiences and their behavior in the group are related to past experiences (Slater, 1966).

Despite these differences, therapy groups and t-groups operate on similar principles. Like the leader in the t-group, the therapist tends to remain relatively passive. The early discussions are formal and stilted, for even though the members are there to talk about themselves and their problems, they are hesitant to reveal their flaws, especially when the therapist does not compel them to (Appley and Winder, 1973). As in t-groups, members of therapy groups begin to react in various ways to the passive therapist, and these reactions tend to move the assemblage of strangers toward being a group.

In individual therapy, especially of the psychoanalytic variety, patients begin to react toward the passive therapist in ways that resemble their relations to past authority figures, most importantly the parent of the same sex as the therapist. This tendency is called *transference.* According to those who theorize about the process in group therapy (see Powdermaker and Frank, 1953; Foulker and Anthony, 1957), group members also develop transference relationships with other members. A male participant may relate to an older woman in ways that resemble his relationship to his mother and to another man as he did his brother, and so on. Many theorists view the therapy group as a reconstituted family in which each member can relive, to some extent, old problematic relationships and attempt to correct them (Foulker and Anthony, 1957).

As in any discussion group, individual talking time is limited in group therapy and may cause competitiveness. This is especially true in early sessions where most members feel that whatever they say is for the benefit of the therapist more than for other group members. A member who is perceived as capturing more than his fair share of the therapist's attention may arouse feelings of jealousy in other members and revive memories of sibling rivalry. These feelings and their associations may become a theme to which all members can relate and which can provide the basis for analysis and insight.

The orientations members form toward the leader and other members in the t-group are also based in transference. The major difference is that in the therapy group transference reactions become a major focus. The therapist encourages individuals to relate their behavior feelings in the group to past events in their lives in order to gain insight into them. Thus one member may feel abandoned and depressed by the therapist's passivity while another may express direct hostility toward him. These reactions in turn trigger reactions from others who may identify with or disagree with them. Not only do such exchanges help members analyze their own behavior but they also reveal that others have similar feelings and problems. As the group develops, this type of communication becomes easier and is in fact expected of participants, so that anyone who resists or holds back is sanctioned by the group. Furthermore, as the group progresses, the members become more accepting of each other and less oriented toward the therapist as *the* authority. For many members, the realization that they need not always be concerned about pleasing an authority figure may be a major therapeutic breakthrough.

Stages of Development in Self-Analytic Groups

Because the leader's presence and behavior heavily influences the group's development, it is useful to view the leader as an external authority and the group as a subsystem. Unlike subsystems in formal organizations, the self-analytic group's relationship to the external authority is one of constant change. First, the behavior of the leader changes as the group continues to meet. Second, the group reacts to the leader differently as time goes on because of previous experiences together. The development of self-analytic groups has been the focus of many studies and these are helpfully summarized in a review by Tuckman (1965).

Tuckman's four stages. Tuckman's paper, however, is much more than a review of developmental studies. He offers a theory of group development which hypothesizes that groups of all types move through four distinct stages of development. He then attempts to determine how many of these studies are consistent with his hypothesis. The remainder of this section will be organized around Tuckman's article because it has influenced the way many social scientists, especially those interested in self-analytic groups, have come to think about group development.

Consistent with Bales's theory, Tuckman first distinguishes between the task-oriented (instrumental) and the social-emotional activities of a group. His theory then goes on to specify how members of groups deal with task and interpersonal problems in each of the four hypothesized stages. The four stages which Haire (1967) has called dependency, conflict, cohesiveness, and work are described below.

In the realm of group structure the first hypothesized stage of the model is labeled as *testing and dependence.* The term "testing" refers to an attempt by group members to discover what interpersonal behaviors are acceptable in the group, based on the reactions of the therapist or trainer (where one is present) and on the reactions of the other group members. Coincident to discovering the boundaries of the situation by testing, one relates to the therapist, trainer, some powerful group member, or existing norms and structures in a dependent way. One looks to this person, persons, or standards for guidance and support in this new and unstructured situation.

The first stage of task-activity development is labeled as *orientation to the task,* in which group members attempt to identify the task in terms of its relevant parameters and the manner in which the group experience will be used to accomplish the task. The group must decide upon the type of information they will need in dealing with the task and how this information is to be obtained. In orienting to the task, one is essentially defining it by discovering its "ground rules." Thus, orientation, in general, characterizes behavior in both interpersonal and task realms during this stage. It is to be emphasized that orientation is a general class of behavior which cuts across settings; the specifics of orientation, that is, what one must orient to and how, will be setting-specific.

The second phase in the development of group structure is labeled as *intragroup conflict.* Group members become hostile toward one another and toward a therapist or trainer as a means of expressing their individuality and resisting the formation of group structure. Interaction is uneven and "infighting" is common. The lack of unity is an outstanding feature of this phase. There are characteristic key issues that polarize the group and boil down to the conflict over progression into the "unknown" of interpersonal relations or regression to the security of earlier dependence.

Emotional response to tasks demands is identified as the second stage of task-activity development. Group members react emotionally to the task as a form of resistance to the demands of the task on the individual, that is, the discrepancy between the individual's personal orientation and that demanded by the task. This task stage will be most evident when the task has as its goal self-understanding and self-change, namely, the therapy- and training-group tasks, and will be considerably less visible in groups working on impersonal, intellectual tasks. In both task and interpersonal realms, emotionality in response to a discrepancy characterizes this stage. However, the source of the discrepancy is different in the different realms.

The third group structure phrase is labeled as the *development of group cohesion.* Group members accept the group and accept the idiosyncracies of fellow members. The group becomes an entity by virtue of its acceptance by the members, their desire to maintain and perpetuate it, and the establishment of new group-generated norms to insure the group's existence. Harmony is of maximum importance, and task conflicts are avoided to insure harmony.

The third stage of task activity development is labeled as the *open exchange of relevant interpretations.* In the therapy- and training-group context, this takes the form of *discussing oneself and other group mem-*

bers, since self and other personal characteristics are the basic inputs. In the laboratory-task context, exchanged interpretations take the form of opinions. In all cases one sees information being acted on so that alternative interpretations of the information can be arrived at. The openness to other group members is characteristic in both realms during this stage.

The fourth and final developmental phase of group structure is labeled as *functional role-relatedness.* The group, which was established as an entity during the preceding phase, can now become a problem-solving instrument. It does this by directing itself to members as objects, since the subject relationship between members has already been established. Members can now adopt and play roles that will enhance the task activities of the group, since they have learned to relate to one another as social entities in the preceding stage. Role structure is not an issue but an instrument which can now be directed at the task. The group becomes a "sounding board" off which the task is "played."

In task-activity development, the fourth and final stage is identified as the *emergence of solutions.* It is here that we observe constructive attempts at successful task completion. In the therapy- and training-group context, these solutions are more specifically *insight* into personal and interpersonal processes and constructive self-change, while in the laboratory-group context the solutions are more intellectual and impersonal. Here, as in the three preceding stages, there is an essential correspondence between group structural and task realms over time. In both realms the emphasis is on constructive action, and the realms come together so that energy previously invested in the structural realm can be devoted to the task (pp. 386–387).

Most studies of development in therapy groups and t-groups are not based on objective data but on the impressions of individuals who have been therapists or leaders in such groups. Tuckman examined the stages of development described by these authors and determined how well they fit with his four-stage theory. For purposes of organization, studies dealing with t-groups, therapy groups, and groups forming within natural settings were each reviewed separately. By natural settings, he meant groups meeting in any situation other than t-groups or therapy group settings.

There were twenty-six published reports concerning the development processes within therapy groups. Eighteen of these reports mentioned a first stage which corresponded with Tuckman's. Thirteen of the twenty-six studies identified a second stage similar to Tuckman's second stage. Twenty-two studies identified a similar third stage, and twelve, a similar fourth stage. Of the eleven t-group studies reviewed, nine of them mentioned a first stage identical with Tuckman's first stage. Ten mentioned a similar second stage, and all eleven mentioned a similar third stage.

Tuckman does not specify the number of t-group studies which are congruent with his theory at the final stage. One reason for this was that some studies cited more than four stages, making it difficult to determine points of congruence. However, most of the studies did mention a mode of functioning late in group development that resembled Tuckman's final stage. According to Tuckman:

> There is some tendency for t-groupers as there was for therapy groupers to emphasize the task aspects of the final stage, namely the emergence of insight into the interpersonal process. In doing this, it is made implicit that the group as a social entity characterized by task-oriented role-relatedness makes the emergence of such insight possible by providing support and an opportunity for experimentation and discovery (p. 393).

This statement reiterates what was said earlier—namely that the solidarity of self-analytic groups, which develops as the group progresses through the first stages, enables the members to relate to one another in a way that allows objective self-analysis.

Slater and Mann's analyses. Tuckman's theory is based on the premise that all groups in all situations progress through the same stages of development. We will comment more on this assumption later when we examine his review of groups that develop in other environments. It is enough to say at this point that other types of groups do not fit as well into Tuckman's four stages. However, the fact that Tuckman's four stages are fairly descriptive of the development of self-analytic groups, especially t-groups, does not explain why these groups move through these stages. Since Tuckman's review was published, two important books on self-analytic groups have become available: *Microcosm* by Philip Slater (1966) and *Interpersonal Styles and Group Processes* by Richard Mann (1967). Both of these are based upon more complete data than Tuckman's, and both are more concerned with analyzing *leader-member relationships*. Fortunately, their descriptions of the stages of development are very consistent with Tuckman's four-stage theory so that by examining Slater's and Mann's work, we can gain some insight into how the development in self-analytic groups can be accounted for by the particular features of their environment—that is, the subsystem-external authority relationship.

Both of the authors led and observed groups that were part of the Human Relations 120 Course taught at Harvard University, in which students met as self-analytic groups. Slater's analysis is based on transcripts of other self-analytic groups as well. The groups differed from therapy groups and t-groups in that the students met for two semesters and received course credit for participating in and analyzing the group experience. However, the groups in this course were similar to therapy groups and t-groups in that all formed under an external authority (i.e., a leader) and all members shared the goal of developing a better understanding of themselves and group processes.

For our own purposes, then, we can assume that all self-analytic groups, t-groups, therapy groups, and the Harvard groups studied by Slater and Mann were exposed to roughly the same environmental conditions. There appears to be some agreement as to how leaders in these various groups ought to behave, and therefore, although each teacher had his own style, there was a standard leadership in these various groups. Because the leaders (or external authorities) in all these situations set up similar conditions for group development, we can speak of the *self-analytic environment.*

Both Slater (1966) and Mann (1967) characterized leaders of self-analytic groups as not filling the traditional leadership role of directing, commanding, guiding, and coordinating group action. But this is not to say that a leader's behavior does not influence the group members. In fact, it appears that it is the leader's comparatively passive role that is responsible for the nature of the development in self-analytic groups.

Mann categorized what was said by both leaders and members in four different groups observed over a period of two semesters. He classified the interaction initiated by the members according to the feeling expressed (either directly or symbolically) about the leader. Some examples of the sixteen categories were: "moving against," "resisting," "identifying," "accepting," "showing dependence," "showing independence," "showing counter-dependence," "expressing anxiety." He categorized a leader's behavior according to what feelings the leader ascribed to the members with whom he was communicating. Mann also categorized the leaders' responses as to whether they contained a positive evaluation, a nonevaluation, or a negative evaluation.

Mann found that two-thirds of the leaders' remarks were nonevaluative, indicating that the leaders did not strive to control the members as is true in most groups. By examining the types of interaction to which the leaders responded positively and negatively and the situations in which leaders attempted to interpret the members' feelings, Mann determined how the leaders affected their groups. First, Mann concluded that the group members used the leaders' performances as a model—e.g., "giving interpretations" and "testing hypotheses" about group events. Second, it appears that the leaders pressured the groups toward independent behavior by negatively evaluating members' displays of dependence upon him and ignoring their displays of independence. The ignored expressions of independence did not include "withdrawing" or "denying hostility" but did include "feelings of independence" and "feelings of the wish for independence." The types of feelings that were positively evaluated by the leader varied throughout the group's development. At the early stages, leaders supported almost any expression of feeling, but during the later stages they mostly encouraged uncommonly expressed feelings. O'Day (1974), who used Mann's categories to classify the interaction initiated by four t-group leaders, generally obtained the same results.

The primary hurdle facing the leader is removing the members' dependency upon him. What is of importance, however, is that the various expressions of dependency do not have their source in the realities of the situation. The leader in expressing his goal for the group and through his actual behavior tries not to develop a superordinate-subordinate relationship with the members that would encourage this dependency. The position of authority which the leader assumes in the eyes of the members and the resulting feelings of dependency must be caused primarily by the expectations members bring into the situation in the form of transference to past authorities. This is why much of the leader's behavior is nonevaluative and passive. If the group is to move toward autonomy, the leader must, like a psychotherapist, maintain a nonevaluative and passive stance to avoid adding fuel to the members' transference reactions.

According to Slater, the members first react to a leader who fails to act like an authority with feelings of dread and abandonment (Tuckman's dependency stage). These feelings often lead them to invent myths to explain the leader's strange behavior. According to Slater, the students leap upon the leader's every word or gesture as proof for their favorite explanation as to what the experience is all about. Although this situation is frustrating, little anger or hostility is observed at first. Slater, who frequently points to analogies between the self-analytic experience and other aspects of life, characterizes the initial reactions of members of such groups as follows:

> Frightened by the freedom and responsibility given to them, afraid that the shadowy and passive figure cannot fulfill their childhood longing, they begin to mold from early parental images a fantasy of an omniscient and omnipotent protector, who will one day step forward and lead them out of their labyrinthine confusion or give them the key or secret formula which will reveal the master design behind the apparent disorder and chaos (1966, p. 22).

Mann also reports that the early orientation of members revolve around feelings of loyalty and dependence toward a leader. However, Mann's analysis differs from the usual descriptions of developmental phases. Rather than seeing the group as a whole that manifests a common orientation at any point in time, he traces through the emergence and dominance of subgroups at various stages and shows how the interplay between these subgroups determines the development of the whole group. Thus, the early meetings of the groups observed by Mann were distinguished by the emergence of four main but noncohesive subgroups. The first of these subgroups consisted of members who had in common the fact that they initiated high rates of "dependent complaining" —interaction that expresses to the leader their feelings of abandonment and rejection. A second subgroup initiated high rates of interaction categorized as "compliance and loyalty," which seemed to be attempts to win reassurance and elicit a structure from the leader. A third group, high on expression of "counter-dependent flight," appeared to be overly concerned that they were being manipulated by the leader. Finally a small group of students showed "acceptance of the leader as a colleague," an orientation that became more widely accepted in later meetings. In general these subgroups expressed dependency (or reactions to feelings of dependency) upon the leader as an external authority.

According to Slater, the dependency upon the accompanying idealization of the leader cannot be maintained and inevitably is dissolved. This leads to Tuckman's conflict stage. In the first place, the feelings of dependency, which are caused in part by the initial lack of structure, dissolve as the group members build up experiences together over time. Also, the transference reactions, which at first were encouraged by the leader's silence and passivity, dissolve as the leader reveals himself to be an ordinary human being. As this occurs, members begin to express their feelings about the leader. According to Slater, the members fluctuate in their attitudes toward the leader; at some time they see him as omniscient, at others as incompetent, and they circulate rumors that support both ideas. Both sides of this ambivalence must be expressed and shared before any reaction against the leader by the whole group can take place. Slater states:

> There must be some feeling that both dependent and resentful feelings toward the leader are widespread in the group. As the members become more aware of the generality of one feeling, the other can be more freely voiced. There is a back and forth movement, extending the recognition and expression of both feelings in ever-widening circles until a sufficient bulk of the group (a kind of emotional quorum) is involved to enable it to act (1966, p. 44).

According to Slater, the more dependent members are reluctant to break their emotional ties to the leader for fear that chaos (unbridled aggression and sensuality) will reign. This idea is reinforced by the attacks directed at them by those advocating a revolt. However, the fact that the leader fails to impose a structure, even when members remain loyal and stick up for him, at some point pushes the dependents to join the revolt. The revolt itself usually involves a fairly free expression of hostility directed at and against the leader and culminates in some symbolic act of independence such as meeting without the leader or usurping his chair.

Mann's description of this stage is similar. According to him, the movement toward autonomy is usually precipitated by a subgroup of males "heroes," who define themselves in terms of their opposition to the dependent and compliant subgroups. Of importance to the development of the group as a whole is the leader's failure to control the crude behavior and hostile attacks of the heroes on the more sensitive members. At some point, the frustrations suffered by the members of the more compliant subgroups, caused by the attacks of the more rebellious members and the leader's passivity, lead them to express hostility toward the leader, who they feel should exert his authority. They usually express this hostility by making the paradoxical charge that the "leader is passive and weak while at the same time complaining that the leader is manipulative" (Mann, 1967, p. 167). Those responsible for such charges are usually males who see themselves as *spokesmen* for the females and the more sensitive males. Not only do they direct their complaints to the leader but counterattack the heroes for their rebellious behavior. When the expression of hostility toward the leader reaches its zenith, revolt is possible. Finally, according to Mann, the heroes and the spokesmen join forces against the leader, even though they react against him for quite different reasons.

The group revolt, according to Slater, acts as a source of uniformity for the members and is remembered by them as their first achievement as a group. Immediately after the revolt, there is a taboo on intermember conflict (cohesion stage), but this is gradually relaxed. However, any expressions of hostility toward other members after the revolt conform to the group norms that emphasize the free expression of feeling. In Mann's description of the period immediately following the revolt, he states that neither the heroes nor the spokesman are really victorious, since the group is characterized neither by uninhibited aggression or sexuality as the heroes seemed to wish nor by the serenity desired by the spokesmen and others. Intimacy, sexuality, and the group's relationships to the leader are discussed more openly and less emotionally. Since the leader was capable of absorbing the hostility of the group without striking back, the members are more willing to trust him and accept whatever he has to offer without being concerned about being manipulated. The subgroup that has all along argued for a colleaguelike relationship between members and the leader finally grows in size and becomes dominant. As Mann says:

> There is a period in which many of the members try out the interpersonal style of the leader. It is the period during which norms that legitimate and regulate the work function of the group are being developed at a rapid rate (1967, p. 121).

Thus the members, having worked out a common orientation toward the leader, become a group with enough solidarity to take on the task of self-analysis. This, of course, corresponds to Tuckman's work stage.

While the observations of Slater and Mann fit nicely into Tuckman's four stages of development, we do not get the impression from their work that these stages are somehow automatic. They do not suggest that all groups will progress through these stages if they meet together for a period of time, as Tuckman's theory predicts. Rather we see that each stage is a direct result of the changing orientation of members to the changing role adopted by the leader. We will now utilize this same view to examine developmental changes in experimental discussion groups.

DEVELOPMENT IN LABORATORY DISCUSSION GROUPS

According to Tuckman's theory groups of all types progress through common stages of development. Just as self-analytic groups become more work-oriented over time, Tuckman argued that task groups, like laboratory groups, ought to show an increase in "task-oriented" interaction over time. Thus, he interpreted Bales's (1955) finding that laboratory groups go through stages of orientation, evaluation and control as confirming his theory. But, as the reader will recall, Bales's study dealt with phases occurring within one forty-minute problem-solving session and not with long-term stages of development. Furthermore, the Heinecke and Bales study (1953), one of the few to report on changes in laboratory groups over several sessions was not included in Tuckman's review. Contrary to Tuckman's theory, Heinecke and Bales found that the early meetings heavily emphasized task-oriented interaction and that this declined in later sessions. Also not considered was a study by Morris (1966), who observed developmental changes in laboratory groups and found that rates of "task-irrelevant" interaction increase over time.

The environment facing members of laboratory groups is very different from that of self-analytic groups, and there is no reason to expect the two to show similar stages of development. In explaining how the environment affects laboratory groups we must not only account for the results of the studies by Heinecke and Bales and Morris, but also for Slater's observation that specialization tends to increase over time. These changes could not reflect the development of solidarity, for as we indicated in the previous chapter, the meeting time for such groups is really too short for this. In self-analytic groups, developmental changes are due both to changes in the leader's behavior and changes in the members' orientations to him. But it is not likely that changes in laboratory groups are due to the changing behavior of the external authority, for the experimenter's behavior as an observer remains constant over time. This suggests that it is the members' orientations toward the experimenter that shift over time.

Evidence that this can occur comes from Roethlisberger and Dickson (1947) who report that when first observed, the men in the bank wiring room remained unusually quiet and behaved in a very unnatural fashion. This is understandable, for the observer could have been an evaluator or possibly a spy for higher management. After a relatively short time, the workers realized that the observer posed no threat since he was not evaluating them. Consequently, their behavior became more natural over time. Of course, the men in the bank wiring room constituted a group before they were observed, so these changes were not developmental. But what about laboratory discussion groups in which the observer is a "built-in" feature of the environment from the beginning?

The author's (Wilson, 1969) experiment comparing observed and not-observed groups (see p. 221) indicates that members of observed groups manifested "evaluation anxiety," and behaved in ways designed to please the observer. Self-analytic groups begin the same way. However, the passivity of the leader eventually leads to the point where they realize that they are free to do as they please. Since no one is more passive than an experimenter engaged in observing a group, it is not likely that the initial evaluation anxiety of subjects will last long. Thus, the changes that occur in discussion groups can be understood as a process of habituation to external authority. By failing to evaluate, punish, or reward, the experimenter undermines his authority in the eyes of the subjects, making them less dependent upon him and providing them greater autonomy.

The decrease in "task-oriented" interaction, the increase in "task-irrelevant" interaction, and specialization over time can be understood as a result of this habituation process. Figure 10.1 compares the findings of these studies with the author's. It can be seen that in all cases the early sessions of the groups in those studies have the same characteristics of the groups in the observed condition of the author's experiment. Furthermore, the later sessions resemble the author's not-observed groups. In the observed groups "evaluation anxiety" was high as it would be in the earlier sessions. However, after several sessions, subjects would be less concerned with the observer's presence, as was the case in the not-observed groups. Concern about the observer resulted in high rates of task-oriented interaction, but this would subside and be replaced with task-irrelevant interaction over time. Specialization would emerge later when members were not uniformly task-oriented, since the subjects who initiated high rates of task interaction would be most irritating when members had become habituated to the observation process and no longer felt it necessary to remain highly task-oriented.

In line with this, Deutsch (1949) found in his study of cooperation and competition that the subjects' awareness of being observed declined as the groups met over time. However, the competitive subjects tended to be more aware of the observer's presence and were more motivated to please him than were the cooperative subjects. This is because rewards were to be gained by having one's performance directly evaluated rather than indirectly evaluated

Wilson's Experiment

Sessions in the Developmental Studies	Observed	Not Observed
Early Sessions	High task-oriented interaction Low social-emotional interaction Low specialization	
Late Sessions		Low task-oriented interaction High social-emotional interaction High specialization

Figure 10.1. The correspondence between observed and not-observed conditions and the early and late sessions of laboratory groups.

through the performance of the group. Philip and Dunphy (1959), replicating Heinecke and Bales (1953), failed to find a decrease in task-oriented interaction or an increase in task irrelevant interaction over four sessions. However, unlike Heinecke and Bales's study, which took place under laboratory conditions, this study was a part of a class where grades were contingent upon the member's performance and where the influence of the observer (instructor) would be slower to wane. A study by Gustafson (1966), also carried out within the context of a classroom, found no increase in the amount of specialization between liking and best ideas over time as did Slater (also see Gustafson and Harrell, 1970). These failures to replicate the studies in the laboratory support the idea that groups evolving within a laboratory situation have a pattern of development that is peculiar to that situation and that reflect changing reactions to the observer.

One might question whether the changes in laboratory groups that we have been discussing are really *developmental* changes. We have already stated that these changes do not seem to indicate the development of solidarity. It can only be answered that these changes *are* developmental in that they are necessary for the subsequent development of solidarity. Laboratory discussion groups apparently become habituated relatively quickly, but it required more than four forty-minute sessions for this to be manifested in higher levels of solidarity. As we have just pointed out, discussion groups meeting in classroom environments found it more difficult to overcome evaluation anxiety and the resulting dependence upon the observer. Solidarity in such situations would take even longer to develop.

SOME CONCLUDING COMMENTS

Types of Environments

The descriptions in the chapter of self-analytic groups at various stages may have had a familiar ring to some readers. This is no accident, for the relationship between self-analytic group members to their leader at various stages closely resembles that between formal organization subsystem members and their external authority (see Chapter 8). For instance, during the initial phase of development, members of self-analytic groups are low in solidarity and highly dependent upon the leader. This sounds very much like our description of subsystems within environments with extremely low levels of autonomy such as the concentration camp and the autocratic condition of the Iowa leadership study (White and Lippit, 1960). We shall call such situations *consistent autocratic environments* because control is consistently imposed at high levels by external authorities. The difference between informal groups in consistent environments and members in the first stage of self-analytic groups is that in the latter, the members' reactions to external control are more imagined than real. Self-analytic group members eventually discover that their expectations about the leader make him an external authority and they do not need to be constrained any longer by his presence. However, subsystems in consistent autocratic environments are contending with actual control and so may be said to be *arrested* from further development by these environmental features.

Self-analytic groups move on to higher solidarity because the leader does nothing to prevent it and the withering of dependency. Yet this does not occur all at once. Some members hold on to their expectations that the leader will play the role of the external authority directly by setting goals and providing structure in an anomic situation. Furthermore, much of the leader's behavior contributes to this impression. Although he remains passive, he is still in charge. He does not act like "just one of the members" but maintains an aloofness suggestive of someone who is an external authority. This inconsistent image presented by the leader contributes to the formation of subgroups: Some members argue for independence—i.e., revolting against the leader and doing what they please; others argue for continued dependence and loyalty. The result is the emergence of conflict and hostility.

Similar circumstances are found in subsystems within *inconsistent autocratic* environments. The traditional prison cellblock and the bank wiring room are examples of this type. In these cases, subsystem members were given some autonomy, but in general, it was not official and was the result of informal, often illicit, exchanges with the external authority. Members of such subsystems are confronted with demands to comply with two conflicting sources of control—the external authority and the emergent subsystem. The solidarity of subsystems in inconsistent autocratic environments is limited by the antagonism between various cliques or subgroups. As in the second stage of self-analytic groups, the issue of dependence versus independence is at the core of much of this conflict.

It is of interest that the relationships of the more independent members (the heroes) in self-analytic groups resemble those of high-ranking inmates to external authorities in the traditional prison. Those inmates enjoy a favored relationship to the external authority that enables them to control, often through brutal means, inmates of lower rank. In a real sense, the elite members, who often loudly verbalize antiauthority norms, are the most dependent upon the external authorities. This privileged relationship is often the target of suspicion and hostility from lower-ranking inmates. Similarly, the heroes in self-analytic groups are given free rein by the leader to verbally abuse other members. Mann (1967) reports that in spite of the heroes' clamor for independence, much of the hostility directed toward them involves charges that they are in collusion with the leader—i.e., that they are teachers' pets.

Despite these similarities, there are important differences. The most important is the fact that self-analytic groups have the opportunity of progressing beyond the second stage toward greater solidarity. The leader of self-analytic groups does not restrict movement toward greater independence as does the external authority in inconsistent autocratic environments, where subsystems remain arrested in a stage of low solidarity.

Another type of environment found within formal organizations is one we call *interdependent*. In such situations, subsystems are provided from the beginning with enough autonomy to avoid many of the social-emotional difficulties found in subsystems in other environments. Members of such subsystems are less dependent upon external authority and are relatively free to initiate a wide range of group products without worrying about restrictive reactions. In addition, there is likely to be more consensus about group norms since fewer members are afraid of antagonizing the external authority. In inconsistent autocratic environments, only a privileged few enjoy interdependent relationships with the external authority. This is the source of jealousy, suspicion, and unstable status structures. Within interdependent environments, rewards and resources are less scarce and are more equally distributed among all subsystem members, thus eliminating many of these barriers to high solidarity.

The miners in the gypsum plant studied by Gouldner (1954) are one example of a subsystem in this type of environment. Because of the dangers of their job and their physical separation from the rest of the plant, those miners enjoyed a degree of autonomy and solidarity not found among those working on the surface. The noncompetitive section of the employment agency studied by Blau (1961) is another example. Here, for a variety of reasons, members were given the freedom to define their own work procedures. The *strategic groups* isolated by Sayles (1958) also seem to fit this description. The members of these higher solidarity groups had relatively high-ranking positions and important jobs in their formal organization and were capable of engaging in union activities with impunity. A last example of this type is the group of salesmen in the department store studied by Babchuck and Goode (1951). Holding well-paid, high-ranking jobs, the men in this subsystem were given a great deal of autonomy; and as a result, they were able to get some of their informally derived work procedures accepted as formal policy by management.

In interdependent environments, subsystems are free, within limits, to pursue goals of their own choosing and to develop a structure for doing so—a structure not imposed by the external authorities. Members of self-analytic groups in the third stage of development are in a similar situation. They have learned through experience, especially during the revolt, that they truly have the freedom to do and become what they choose. Their relationship to the leader is interdependent in the sense that they see the leader as a specialist in group dynamics whom they can call upon for help in their endeavor.

While groups emerging within interdependent environments are capable of developing relatively high levels of solidarity, they are arrested by environmental conditions at a level resembling the third, or *cohesion*, stage in self-analytic groups. Although not impossible, the environment does not encourage self-analysis. This seems to occur only in situations that we can call *self-analytic environments,* where individuals come together especially for this purpose. Here, the group's social-emotional difficulties serve as material for analysis. In all other environments, self-analysis poses a threat to solidarity because it questions the existing norms and status structure and gives rise to expressions of hostility that might otherwise remain dormant. Resistance to analysis is also seen in the self-analytic groups, especially during the cohesive stage, but the presence of the leader exerts a pressure on members to move in this direction.

The diagram in Figure 10.2 may be of help in visualizing what we have said so far. The three different types of environments found in formal organizations are located at different points along the familiar solidarity-anomie continuum. Each point designates the maximum level of solidarity that can be attained by a subsystem in each environment. The location of each in the continuum is only an approximation. Also, there may well be other types of environments which could be added. Notice that the range of solidarity attainable within the interdependent environment is relatively wide. There is a wider range of variables that could influence a group's solidarity within interdependent environments—e.g., several groups within interdependent environments may vary in solidarity because of differences in group size, work procedures, and so on. We believe that this is much less likely to occur in autocratic environments where the external authority is the major determinant of subsystem members' behavior. Notice also that the same type of environment can be found in different kinds of formal organizations. For instance, a work organization may

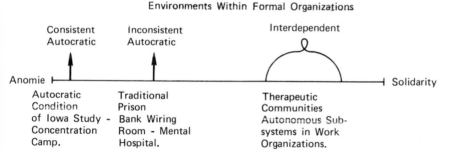

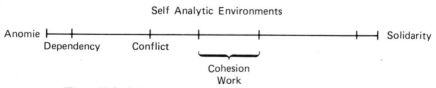

Figure 10.2. Subsystem environments within formal organizations.

contain some subsystems that operate within an inconsistent autocratic environment and others that operate within interdependent environments.

The lower continuum in Figure 10.2 depicts the advances in solidarity as the self-analytic group progresses through Tuckman's four stages. Although these groups form within a self-analytic environment, this environment is not included in the continuum above them. This is because of the differences between self-analytic groups and groups forming within formal organizations on such factors as goals and time spent together. As seen on this lower continuum, when a self-analytic group passes through the final three stages of development, there is a gradual increase in solidarity. Again the placement of the stages on the continuum is rather arbitrary and may vary from group to group. In the case of the final stage, *work,* it is not clear from Tuckman's theory or the literature that this represents an increase in group solidarity above that obtained in stage 3. For this reason, we have indicated on the continuum that a variable degree of solidarity may be attained during this last stage. It should be remembered, however, that this continuum refers only to self-analytic groups, and comparisons between the two continuums are not valid.

We have spoken of the environments on the upper continuum as arresting the development of subsystems at a stage consistent with the characteristics of the environment. On the other hand, our discussion has implied that groups automatically progress through all three stages in self-analytic environments. We must qualify this. Under ideal conditions—that is, when the leader plays his role appropriately—self-analytic groups do seem to develop along the lines suggested by Tuckman's theory. But to the extent that his behavior sets up conditions which resemble the environments located on the upper continuum, the self-analytic group may be arrested at an earlier stage. Unfortunately, there are too few studies of how differences in leaders influence the characteristics of self-analytic groups. However, both Mann (1967) and O'Day (1974) cite evidence suggesting that the development of self-analytic groups is incomplete if a leader is not capable of absorbing hostility directed toward him by the members. Whether he becomes angry, defensive, or anxious as a result of the attack, such a leader would convey through his verbal and nonverbal behavior that he is not really comfortable with the group's movement toward independence. Although much more subtle, this reaction in a self-analytic group would have the same result as the restrictive reactions of an external authority in a formal organization. That is, the self-analytic group becomes arrested at an early stage of development. For instance, if the group cannot carry out their revolt, they cannot really gain the necessary solidarity to engage in effective self-analysis.

On the other hand, while the lack of autonomy can arrest a group's development, it should not be concluded that autonomy alone is the key to the development of higher solidarity. We saw in the first section of this chapter that the autonomy built into therapeutic communities can actually cause a decline in solidarity. It appears that some subsystems, those with underdeveloped solidarity to begin with, require active participation in the role of external authorities to take advantage of this autonomy.

Similarly, it is not only the freedom that the leader of the self-analytic group gives to the members which enables them to become a group. If a collection of strangers were told that they were free to do as they pleased they would not automatically become a group. Likewise, if leaders of self-analytic groups remain too passive, it is not likely that the groups would progress very far. The leader must provide members with direct cues—by what he comments upon and what he ignores—as to what they should be doing. Although he is more passive than the usual traditional leader, he maintains his position of leader, and it is this inconsistency that compels members eventually to revolt and become a group.

Interdependence between Group and Environment

Our analysis of the relationships between groups and environments has presented a rather one-sided view of the environment as the determinant or the shaper of the group in question. The reader should remember that this is a two-way relationship, and the two strongly affect each other. However, some groups are more influenced by the structure of their environment than are others. For example, in highly dependent subsystems, members find it advantageous to form interdependent relationships to cope with a hostile environment—that is, the extreme control by the external authority. In environments of this type, the characteristics of the group (i.e., solidarity, norms, structures) can be understood as defensive reactions to anomic forces. For example, in consistent autocratic environments like the concentration camp, a norm emerged encouraging compliance or cooperation with authorities because this was seen as the most advantageous strategy. In inconsistent autocratic environments, norms emerge discouraging loyalty to the external authority but also discouraging blatant defiance of authority. Either extreme was seen as problematic by prison inmates and constituted a threat to solidarity. "Playing it cool" was valued in the traditional prison. Similarly, not producing too much or too little was valued in the bank wiring room. As mentioned in Chapter 4, the norms that emerge in such groups are formed in reaction to anomic forces. By knowing the conditions of their environments, it is easy to understand the content of the norms which emerge in these dependent subsystems.

The characteristics of subsystems in interdependent environments are less directly linked to environmental conditions. For example, the behavior of members in the more autonomous section of Blau's employment agency was less conditioned by environmental forces than that of members in the other section. Sayle's *strategic groups* were capable of exerting changes in the environment through active union participation. Therapeutic communities also have some procedures for affecting policy-making decisions. Furthermore, less dependent subsystems, those in interdependent environments, should be more capable of resisting or adapting to changes in the environment. We have seen that groups forming in autocratic environments have great difficulty in adjusting to sudden increases in autonomy. In contrast to this are the salesmen studied by Babchuck and Goode (1951). Members of this subsystem also suffered a decline in solidarity in the face of environmental changes, but they enjoyed enough autonomy to control practices which could affect group solidarity. Not only did they instigate procedures for restricting individualistic orientations but they had these procedures adopted as official policy by the external authority.

SUMMARY

By examining the research on the transition from traditional units (cell blocks or wards) to therapeutic communities, we gain some insight into how subsystems react to environmental changes. While there are no studies designed explicitly to examine this question, the existing literature points to a consistent pattern: In the transition from traditional structures to therapeutic communities, the inmate subsystem shows a temporary decline in solidarity. Furthermore, solidarity may subsequently reappear or actually move to a higher level. Studies dealing with subsystems of other kinds, that are provided greater autonomy, also report a temporary decrease in solidarity and a subsequent increase.

This pattern is understandable in terms of much of the material presented in earlier chapters. Members of subsystems are controlled from two sources: the external authority and the emergent group itself. The removal of control takes away much of the structure upon which members have come to rely. In other words, they find themselves in an anomic situation. Increased autonomy elicits forces toward anomie which the members have not faced previously. The advantages of the new freedom must be distributed among themselves, and this may raise individualistic orientations as each member attempts to increase his own rewards. In short, groups in this situation must solve the social-emotional problems that inevitably come with the emergence of a new structure. If subsystem members successfully solve the social-emotional problems of increased autonomy, they can attain a higher level of solidarity than before.

Tuckman (1965) found that the developmental changes in t-groups and therapy groups conform rather closely to his hypothesized four stages of group development: *dependency, conflict, cohesiveness,* and *work* (Haire, 1967). Tuckman's theory implies that all groups progress through these stages regardless of the nature of their immediate environment. However, the work of Slater (1966) and Mann (1967) shows how the changing relationship between the leader and members in self-analytic groups can account for this progression. The member's initial perception of the leader as an authority encourages their dependence upon him. They wait for him to lead, to set goals, to provide some structure to group discussions. Despite his refusal to lead, he does not act like just another member but rather maintains a distance from the group like an external authority. Because they see him as an authority, members are wary of proceeding without his blessing. However, some members eventually take advantage of the leader's passivity and inconsistency and set their own goals in order to become independent of him. When this occurs, the group moves into the *conflict* stage. At this point much of the discussion involves conflict between the more independent members and those who feel that it is safer to wait for the leader to provide direction. Eventually, however, the group achieves some unanimity and reacts negatively against the leader. This event is of symbolic importance because it represents a true group effort. This, together with the fact that the leader does not respond to the collective hostility directed toward him, allows the group to move toward the third stage.

During the cohesion stage members become aware of their solidarity and their potentiality for developing on their own. While members have been forced to engage in self-analysis from the initial meeting, concern about the reactions of the leader and the hostility between subgroups prevents them from being very effective. During the final stage, *work,* members can proceed with the task of self-analysis in a more open, honest, and fruitful manner. This is possible because they have developed among themselves enough solidarity to reduce the threat of social-emotional problems. Furthermore, they now relate to the leader as a resource person. He is now freer to comment on the group's proceedings without intimidating anyone or putting a damper on the discussion.

Development in laboratory discussion groups does not fit Tuckman's four stages and can best be understood by viewing the experimenter/observer as an important part of the laboratory environment. The experimenter is perceived as an external authority, and his presence as an observer has an effect on group interaction. More specifically, members of laboratory groups are concerned with behaving appropriately—in this case by initiating high rates of task-oriented interaction. However, like other groups, laboratory group members come to realize over time that the experimenter is not acting like an authority—that is, he does not do anything other than observe. This allows the members more freedom to engage in discussions not related to the task. With respect to the content of discussions and the probability of specialization, the early meetings in discussion-group experiments resemble the observed condition of Wilson's (1969) experiment in which the observer's presence was an influential factor. The later laboratory-group sessions resemble closely the groups in the not-observed condition of this experiment.

References

REFERENCES

ABEL, T., "The sociology of concentration camps." *Social Forces* 30 (1951): 150–154.

ADAMS, S., "Status congruency as a variable in small group performance." *Social Forces* 32 (1953): 16–22.

ALLPORT, F., *Social Psychology*. Boston: Houghton Mifflin, 1924.

APPLEY, D.G. and WINDER, A.E., *T-groups and Therapy Groups in a Changing Society*. San Francisco: Jossey-Bass Publishers, 1973.

ASCH, S., "Opinions and social pressure." *Scientific American* 193 (1955): 31–35.

BABCHUCK, N. and GOODE, W., "Work incentive in a self-determined group." *American Sociological Review* 16 (1951): 679–687.

BACK, K.W., "Influence through social communication." *Journal of Abnormal and Social Psychology* 46 (1951): 9–23.

BACK, K.W., *Beyond Words: The Story of Sensitivity Training and the Encounter Movement*. New York: Russell Sage Foundation, 1972.

BALES, R.F., *Interaction Process Analysis*. Reading, Mass: Addison–Wesley, 1950.

BALES, R.F., "The equilibrium problem in small groups." Pp. 111–161 in T. Parsons, R.F. Bales, and E.A. Shils, *Working Papers in the Theory of Action*. New York: Free Press, 1953.

BALES, R.F. and SLATER, P.E., "Role differentiation in small decision-making groups." Pp. 259–306 in T. Parsons, R.F. Bales, and P.E. Slater, *The Family, Socialization and Interaction Process*. New York: The Free Press, 1955.

BARTOS, O.J., "Leadership, conformity and originality." Unpublished paper presented at the 1958 Meeting of the American Sociological Society.

BASS, B.M., *The Orientation Inventory*, Palo Alto, California: Consulting Psychologists Press, 1962.

BASS, B.M., "Social behavior and the orientation inventory: a review." *Tech-*

280

nical Report No. 9. Pittsburgh, Pennsylvania: University of Pittsburgh. Contract No. 624 (14), 1965.

BAVELAS, A.A., "Communication patterns in task-oriented groups." *Journal of the Acoustical Society of America* 22 (1950): 725–730.

BAVELAS, A.A., HASTORF, A.H., GROSS, H.E., and KITE, R.H., "Experiments on the alteration of group structure." *Journal of Experimental and Social Psychology* 1 (1965): 55–70.

BELL, P.R. and JAMIESON, B.D., "Publicity of initial decisions and the risk shift phenomenon." *Journal of Experimental and Social Psychology* 6 (1970): 329–345.

BERGER, J., COHEN, B.P., and ZELDITCH, M., "Status conceptions and social interaction." *American Sociological Review* 37 (1974): 241–255.

BERKOWITZ, L., "Sharing leadership in small decision-making groups." *Journal of Abnormal and Social Psychology* 48 (1953): 231–238.

BERKOWITZ, L., "Effects of perceived dependency relationships upon conformity to group expectations." *Journal of Abnormal and Social Psychology* 55 (1957): 350–354.

BERKOWITZ, L. and HOWARD, R.C., "Reaction to opinion deviates as affected by affiliation need (n) and group member interdependence." *Sociometry* 22 (1959): 81–91.

BERTALANFFY, L. VON, *General Systems Theory: Foundation, Development, Applications.* New York: G. Braziller, 1968.

BERK, B., "Organizational goals and inmate organization." *American Journal of Sociology* 71 (1966): 523–534.

BETTELHEIM, B., "Individual mass behavior in extreme situations." *Journal of Abnormal and Social Psychology* 38 (1943): 417–452.

BLAU, P.M., *The Dynamics of Bureaucracy.* Chicago: University of Chicago Press, 1955.

BLAU, P.M. *Exchange and Power in Social Life.* New York: John Wiley & Sons, 1964.

BLAU, P.M., *Bureaucracy in Modern Society.* New York: Random House, 1971.

BLOCK, H.A., "The personality of inmates of concentration camps." *The American Journal of Sociology* 52 (1947): 338–341.

BLOCK, H.A. and NIEDERHOFFER, A., *The Gang: A Study of Adolescent Behavior.* New York: Philosophical Library, 1958.

BLOOM, S., BOYD, I., and KAPLAN, H.B. "Emotional illness and interaction process: a study of patient groups." *Social Forces* 41 (1962): 135–141.

BONACICH, "Norms and cohesion as adaptive responses to potential conflict: an experimental study." *Sociometry* 35 (1972): 357–375.

BONACICH, P. and LEWIS, G.H., "Functional specialization and sociometric judgment." *Sociometry* 36 (1972): 31–41.

BONDY, C., "Problems of internment camps." *The Journal of Abnormal and Social Psychology.* 39 (1943): 453–475.

BORGATTA, E., COUCH, A. and BALES, R.F. "Some findings relevant to the great man theory of leadership." *American Sociological Review* 19 (1954): 755–759.

BOVARD, E.W., JR., "Conformity to social norms and attraction to the group." *American Sociological Review* 19 (1953): 688–693.

BRANDON, A.C., "Status congruence and expectations." *Sociometry* 28 (1965): 272–288.

BRIGGS, D., "A transitional therapeutic community for young violent offenders." *The Howard Journal of Penology and Crime Prevention* 13 (1972): 171–183.

BROWN, R., *Social Psychology*. New York The Free Press, (1965).

BROWN, R., Further comment on the risky shift." *American Psychologist.* 29 (1974): 468–470.

BURKE, P.J. "Authority relations and disruptive behavior in small discussion groups." *Sociometry* 29 (1966): 237–250.

BURKE, P.J., "The development of task and social–emotional role differentiation." *Sociometry* 30 (1967): 379–392.

BURKE, P.J., "Role differentiation and the legitimation of task activity." *Sociometry* 39 (1968): 404–411.

BURSTEIN, E. and WOLOSIN, R.J. "The development of status distinctions under conditions of inequity." *Journal of Experimental Social Psychology* 4 (1968): 415–430.

BRYNE, D.E., *The Attraction Paradigm*. New York: Academic Press, 1971.

CAMPBELL, J.P. and DUNNETTE, M.D., "Effectiveness of *t*-group experiences in managerial training and development." *Psychological Bulletin* 70 (1968): 73–104.

CAPLOW, T.A., *Two Against One: Coalitions in Triads*. Englewoods Cliffs, N.J.: Prentice Hall, Inc., 1968.

CARTWRIGHT, D., "The nature of group cohesiveness." Pp. 91–107 in D. Cartwright and A. Zander (eds.), *Group Dynamics*. New York: Harper and Row, 1968.

CARTWRIGHT, D., "Risk taking by individuals and groups: an assessment of research employing choice dilemmas." *Journal of Personality and Social Psychology* 20 (1971): 361–378.

CARTWRIGHT, D. and ZANDER, A., *Group Dynamics*. New York: Harper and Row, 1968.

CAUDILL, W., REDLICH, F.C., GILMORE, H.R., and BRADY E., "Social structure and interaction on a psychiatric ward." *American Journal of Orthopsychiatry* 2 (1952): 314–334.

CHOWDRY, K. and NEWCOMB, T.M., "The relative abilities of leaders and non-leaders to estimate opinions of their own groups." *Journal of Abnormal and Social Psychology* 47: 51–57.

CLARK, D., Creating a therapeutic community in a psychiatric ward." *Human Relations* 15 (1962): 123–148.

CLEMMER, D., *The Prison Community*. New York: Holt, Rinehardt and Winston, Inc., 1958.

CLOWARD, R.A., "Social control in the prison." Pp. 20–48 in *Theoretical Studies in Social Organization*. New York: Social Science Research Council, Pamphlet #15, 1960.

CLOWARD, R.A. and OHLIN, L.E., *Delinquency and Opportunity: A Theory of Delinquent Gangs*. Glencoe: Free Press, 1960.

CLOYD, J.S., "Small groups as a social institution." *American Sociological Review* 30 (1965): 394–402.

COHEN, A.A., *Human Behavior in the Concentration Camp*. New York: W.W. Norton and Co., 1953.

COLLINS, B.E. and H. GUETZKOW, *A Social Psychology of Group Processes for Decision-Making*. New York: Wiley, 1964.

COOLEY, C.H., *Social Organization*. New York: Charles Scribner's, 1909.

CRESSEY, D.R. and KRASOWSKI, W., "American prisons and soviet labor camps." *Social Problems* 5 (1957): 217–229.

CRESSEY, D.R., "Limitations on organization of treatment in the modern prison." Pp. 78–90 in *Theoretical Studies in Social Organization of the Prison*. New York: Social Science Research Council, pamphlet #15, 1960.

CURRY, T.J. and EMERSON, R.M., "Balance theory: a theory of interpersonal attraction." *Sociometry* 33 (1970): 216–238.

DASHIELL, J.F., "Experimental studies of the influence of social situations on the behavior of individual human adults." Pp. 1097–1158 in C. Murchison (ed.), *A Handbook of Social Psychology*. Worcester, Mass: Clark University Press, 1935.

DAY, R.C. and HAMBLIN, R.L. "Effects of close and punitive styles of supervision." *American Journal of Sociology* 69 (1964): 499–510.

DEUTSCH, M.A., "An experimental study of the effects of cooperation and competition upon group process." *Human Relations* 2 (1949): 199–231.

DEUTSCH, M.A., "The effects of motivational orientation upon trust and suspicion." *Human Relations* 13 (1960): 123–140.

DEUTSCH, M.A. and GERARD, H.B., "A study of normative and informational social influences upon individual judgement." *Journal of Abnormal and Social Psychology* 51 (1955): 629–636.

DION, K.L., BARON, R.S., and MILLER, N., "Why do groups make riskier decisions than individuals?" Pp. 306–378 in Berkowitz, L. (ed.), *Advances in Experimental Social Psychology*. Vol. 5. New York: Academic Press, 1970.

DOWNING, J., "Cohesiveness, perceptions and values." *Human Relations* 11 (1958): 157–166.

DUNHAM, H.W. and WEINBERG, S.K., *The Culture of the State Mental Hospital*. Detroit: Wayne University Press, 1960.

DUNNETTE, M.D., CAMPBELL, J., and JAASTAD, K., "The effects of group participation on brainstorming effectiveness for two industrial samples." *Journal of Applied Psychology* 47 (1963): 30–37.

DUNPHY, D.C., *Cliques, Crowds and Gangs*. Melbourne, Australia: Cheshire Publishing Ltd, 1960.

DURKHEIM, E., *Suicide: A Study in Sociology*. Glencoe, Ill.: Free Press, 1951.

DURKHEIM, E., *Divisions of Labor in Society*. New York: The Free Press, 1964.

EISENSTADT, S.N., *From Generation to Generation: Age Groups and Social Structure*. Glencoe, Ill.: Free Press, 1956.

EISMAN, B., "Some operational measures of cohesiveness and their correlations." *Human Relations* 12 (1959): 183–189.

EMERSON, R.M., "Deviation and rejection: and experimental replication." *American Sociological Review* 19 (1954): 688–693.

ETZIONI, A., *A Comparative Analysis of Complex Organizations*. New York: The Free Press, 1961.

EXLINE, R.V. and ZILLER, R.C., "Status congruency and interpersonal conflicts in decision-making groups." *Human Relations* 12 (1959): 147–161.

FARIS, E., *The Nature of Human Nature*. New York: McGraw-Hill, Inc., 1937.

FAUNCE, W.A., "Automation in the automobile industry: some consequences for in-plant social structure." *American Sociological Review* 23 (1958): 401–407.

FELDMAN, R.A. "Interaction among three bases of group integration." *Sociometry* 31 (1968): 30–46.

FESTINGER, L., "Informal social communication." *Psychological Review* 57 (1950): 271–292.

FESTINGER, L., "A theory of social comparison processes." *Human Relations* 7 (1954): 117–140.

FESTINGER L., SCHACHTER, S., and BACK, K., *Social Pressures in Informal Groups.* New York: Harper, 1950.

FESTINGER, L., GERARD, H.B., HYMOVITCH, B., KELLEY, H.H., and RAVEN, B., "The influence process in the presence of extreme deviates." *Human Relations* 5 (1952): 327–346.

FIEDLER, F.F., *A Theory of Leadership Effectiveness.* New York: McGraw-Hill, Inc., 1967.

FISEK, H.M. and OFSHE, R., "The process of status evaluation." *Sociometry.* 33 (1970): 327–346.

FOULKER, S.H. and ANTHONY, E.J. *Group Psychotherapy: The Psychoanalytic Approach.* Middlesex, England: Penguin Books, 1957.

FOURIEZOS, N.T., HUTT, M.L., and GUETZKOW, H., "Measurement of self-oriented needs in discussion groups." *Journal of Abnormal and Social Psychology* 45 (1950): 682–690.

FREESE, L. and COHEN, B.P., "Eliminating status generalization." *Sociometry* 36 (1973): 177–193.

FREUD, S., *Group Psychology and the Analysis of the Ego.* London: Hogarth, 1960.

FRIEDMAN, H.J., "Some problems of in-patient management with borderline patients." *American Journal of Psychiatry* 126 (1969): 229–304.

GANNON, T.M. "Dimensions of current gang delinquency." *Journal of Research in Crime and Delinquency* 4 (1967): 119–131.

GIBB, C.A., "Leadership." Pp. 205–282 in G. Lindzey and E. Aronson (eds.), *Handbook of Social Psychology.* Vol. 4. Reading, Mass: Addison-Wesley Publishing Co., Inc., 1969.

GOFFMAN, E., *The Presentation of Self in Everyday Life.* Garden City, New York: Doubleday and Co., 1959.

GOFFMAN, E., *Asylums.* Garden City, New York: Doubleday and Co., 1961.

GOLDBERG, C., *Encounter: Group Sensitivity Training Experience.* New York: Science House, 1970.

GOLEMBIEWSKI, R.T., *The Small Group.* Chicago: University of Chicago Press, 1962.

GORDON, R.H., "Social level, social disability and gang interaction." *American Journal of Sociology* 73 (1967): 42–62.

GOULDNER, A.W., *Patterns of Industrial Bureaucracy.* New York: The Free Press, 1954.

GOULDNER, A.W. "Reciprocity and autonomy in functional theory." Pp. 240–270 in L. Gross (ed.), *Symposium on Sociological Theory.* New York: Harper and Row, 1959.

GOULDNER, A.W., "The norm of reciprocity; a preliminary statement." *American Sociological Review* 25 (1960): 161–177.

GREELEY, A. and CASEY, J., "An upper middle class delinquent gang." *The American Catholic Sociological Review* 24 (1963): 33–41.

GRESSLER, D.I., "Amount and intensity of interpersonal choice." Pp. 103–121 in Fairweather (ed.), *Social Psychology in Treating Mental Illness.* New York: John Wiley and Sons, Inc., 1964.

GRIFFITH, W. and VEITCH, R. "Preacquaintance attitude similarity and attraction revisited: Ten days in a fall-out shelter." *Sociometry* 37 (1974): 163–173.

GROOG, S.H., "Patient government: some aspects of participation and source background on two psychiatric wards." *Psychiatry* 19 (1956): 203–207.

GROSS, E., "Social integration and the control of competition." *The American Journal of Sociology* 67 (1961): 270–277.

GROSS, N. and MARTIN, W.E., "On groups cohesiveness." *The American Journal of Sociology* 57 (1952): 546–554.

GUETZKOW, H. and GYR, J., "An analysis of conflict in decision-making groups." *Human Relations* 7 (1954): 367–383.

GUSTAFSON, D.P., "Discussion groups with a trend away from role differentiation." Technical Report #13. Office of Naval Research. Contract NONR 225. 62 (August), 1966.

GUSTAFSON, D.P. and HARRELL, T., "A comparison of role differentiation in several situations." *Organizational Behavior and Human Performances* 5 (1970): 299–312.

HAGSTROM, W.O. and SELVIN, H.C., "The dimensions of cohesiveness in small groups." *Sociometry* 28 (1965): 30–43.

HAIRE, P., "Small group development in the relay assembly testroom." *Sociological Inquiry* 37 (1967): 169–182.

HALL, E.T., *The Silent Language*. Garden City, New York: Doubleday, 1959.

HALL, J., "Decisions, decisions, decisions." *Psychology Today* 5 (1971): 51.

HARVEY, O.J., "An experimental approach to the study of status reaction in informal groups." *American Sociological Review* 18 (1953): 357–367.

HATCH, D.L., "Changes in structure and function of a rural New England community since 1900." Ph D. Thesis, Harvard University, 1948.

HEINECKE, C. and BALES, R.F., "Developmental trends in the structure of small groups." *Sociometry* 16 (1953): 7–38.

HENRY, J., "Space and power on a psychiatric unit." Pp. 20–34 in A.F. Wesson (ed.), *The Psychiatric Hospital as a Social System*. Springfield, Ill.: Charles C. Thomas, 1964.

HEYNS, R.W., "Effects of variation in leadership on participant behavior in discussion groups." Unpublished doctoral dissertation. University of Michigan, 1948.

HINDS, W.C., "Individual and group decisions in gambling situations. Unpublished Master's Thesis. M.I.T., 1962.

HOFFMAN, R.L., "Group problem solving." Pp. 99–132 in L. Berkowitz (ed.), *Advances in Experimental Social Psychology*. Vol. 2, New York: Academic Press, 1965.

HOLLANDER, E., *Leaders, Groups and Influence*. New York: Oxford University Press, 1964.

HOLLANDER, E. and JULIAN, J.W., "Contemporary trends in the analysis of leadership processes." *Psychological Bulletin* 71 (1969): 387–397.

HOMANS, G.C., *The Human Group*. New York: Harcourt, Brace and World, 1950.

HOMANS, G.C., *Social Behavior: Its Elementary Forms*. New York: Harcourt, Brace, Jovanovich, Inc., 1974.

HOOPER, D.F., "Changing the milieu in a psychiatric ward." *Human Relations* 15 (1962): 111–122.

HOROWITZ, M., "The recall of interrupted group tasks." *Human Relations* 7 (1954): 3–38.

JANIS, I.L., "Groupthink." *Psychology Today* 5 (1971): 43.

JANSYN, L.R., "Solidarity and delinquency in a street corner group." *American Sociological Review* 31 (1966): 600–614.

JOHNSON, E.H., *Crime, Correction, and Society*. Homewood, Ill.: The Dorsey Press, 1974.

JONES, E.E., GERGEN, K.J., and DAVIS, K.E., "Tactics of ingratiation among leaders and subordinates in a status hierarchy." *Psychological Monographs* 77 (3, whole #566), 1963.

JONES, M., *The Therapeutic Community.* New York: Basic Books, Inc., 1953.

JUNGMAN, L. and BUCHER, R., "Ward structure, therapeutic ideology and patterns of patient interaction." *Archives of General Psychiatry* 17 (1967): 407-415.

KAPLAN, H., BOYD, E., and BLOOM, S."Patient culture and the evaluation of the self." *Psychiatry* 27 (1964): 116-126.

KAPLAN, S.R., "Therapy groups and training groups: similarities and differences." Pp. 94-126 in G.S. Gibbard, J.J. Hartman, and R.D. Mann (eds.), *Analysis of Groups.* San Francisco: Jossey-Bass Publishers, 1974.

KATZ, E.E., *Autonomy and Organization.* New York: Random House, 1968.

KELLEY, H.H. and THIBAUT, J.W. "Group Problem Solving," Pp. 735-785 in G. Lindzey and E. Aronson (eds.), *The Handbook of Social Psychology.* Vol. IV. Reading, Mass.: Addison-Wesley, 1969.

KLEIN, N.W. and CRAWFORD, L.Y., "Groups, gangs and cohesiveness." *Journal of Research in Crime and Delinquency* 4 (1967): 63-75.

KOBRIN, S., PUNTIL, J., and PELUSO, E., "Criteria of status among street groups." *Journal of Research in Crime and Delinquency.* 4 (1967): 98-118.

KRIESBERG, M. and GUETZKOW, H., "The use of conference in the administrative process." *Public Administration Review* 10 (1950): 93-98.

LAWLER, E. and YOUNG, G., JR. "Coalition formation: an integrative model." *Sociometry* 38 (1975): 1-17.

LEAVITT, H.J., "Some effects of certain communication patterns on group performance." *Journal of Abnormal and Social Psychology* 46 (1951): 38-50.

LeBAR, F.M., "Some implications of ward structure for enculturation of patients." Pp. 5-19 in Albert F. Wesson (ed.), *The Psychiatric Hospital as a Social System.* Springfield, Ill.: Charles C. Thomas, 1964.

LEVINGER, G. and SCHNEIDER, D.J., "Test of the 'risk is a value' hypothesis." *Journal of Personality and Social Psychology* 11 (1969): 165-169.

LEWIN, K., *Field Theory in Social Science.* New York: Harper and Row; 1951.

LEWIS, G.H., "Role differentiation." *American Sociological Review* 37 (1972): 424-434.

LEWIS, H.B., "An experimental study of the role of the ego in work, I." *Journal of Experimental Psychology* 34 (1944): 113-127.

LIKERT, D., *New Patterns of Management.* New York: McGraw-Hill, 1961.

LIPGAR, R.M., "Evolution from a locked to an open ward through therapeutically guided group meetings." *Community Mental Health Journal* 4 (1968): 221-228.

LIPSET, S.M., TROW, M.A., and COLEMAN, J.S., *Union Democracy: The Internal Politics of the International Typographical Union.* Glencoe, Ill.: Free Press, 1956.

LUCHINS, A.S., *Group Therapy, A Guide,* New York: Random House, 1964.

LUCHTERHAND, E., "Prisoner behavior and social system in the nazi concentration camps." *International Journal of Social Psychiatry* 13 (1967): 322-325.

MANN, R., *Interpersonal Styles and Group Process.* New York: Wiley, 1967.

MARQUIS, D.G., "Individual responsibility and group decisions involving risk." *Industrial Management Review* 3 (1962): 8-23.

MARROW, A.J., *The T-group Experience: An Encounter among People for Greater Self-Fulfillment.* New York: P.S. Eriksson, 1975.

MATTICK, H.W. and CAPLAN, N.S., "Stake animals, loud talking and leadership in do-nothing and do-something situations." In M.W. Klein (ed.) *Juvenile Gangs in Context: Theory, Research and Action.* Englewood Cliffs, N.J.: Prentice-Hall, Inc., 1967.

McCLEERY, R.H., "Communication patterns as basis of systems of authority." Pp. 49-77 in *Theoretical Studies in Social Organization of the Prison.* New York: Social Science Research Council Pamphlet #15, 1960.

McCLEERY, R.H., "Authoritarianism and the belief system of incorrigibles." Pp. 260-308 in D.R. Cressy (ed.), *The Prison: Studies of Institutional Organization and Change.* New York: Holt Rinehard and Winston, Inc., 1962.

MEAD, M., *Coming of Age in Samoa: A Psychological Study of Primitive Youth for Western Civilization,* New York: Morrow, 1967.

MERTON, R.K., *Social Theory and Social Structure.* Glencoe, Ill.: Free Press, 1957.

MEYER, J.W., "Collective disturbances and staff organization on psychiatric wards: a formalization." *Sociometry* 31 (1968): 180-199.

MEYERHOFF H.L. and MEYERHOFF, B.G., "Field observation of the middle class gangs." *Social Forces* 42 (1964): 328-336.

MICHENER, H.A. and TAUSIG, M., "Usurpation and perceived support as determinants of the endorsement accorded formal leadership." *Journal of Personality and Social Psychology* 18 (1971): 364-377.

MICHENER, H.A. and FOWLER, E.J., "Revolutionary coalition strength and collective failure as determinants of status reallocation." *Journal of Experimental Social Psychology* 7 (1971): 448-460.

MILGRAM, S. "Nationality and conformity." *Scientific American* 205 (1961): 45-51.

MILGRAM, S., "Behavioral study of obedience." *Journal of Abnormal and Social Psychology* 67 (1963): 371-378.

MILLS, T.M., *Sociology of Small Groups.* Englewood Cliffs, N.J.: Prentice-Hall, Inc., 1967.

MINTZ, E.E., *Marathon Groups.* New York: Appleton-Century-Croft, 1971.

MOORE, J.C., "Status and influence in small group interaction." *Sociometry* 31 (1968): 47-63.

MORENO, J.L., Who Shall Survive? Washington, D.C.: Nervous and Mental Disease Publishing Co., 1934.

MORRIS, C.G., "Task effects on group interaction." *Journal of Personality and Social Psychology* 4 (1966): 545-554.

MURRAY, E. and COHEN, M., "Mental illness: milieu therapy and social organization in ward groups." *Journal of Abnormal and Social Psychology* 58 (1956): 48-54.

NEWCOMB, T.M., *The Acquaintance Process.* New York: Holt, Rinehardt and Winston, Inc., 1961.

NORDHØY, F., "Group interaction in decision-making under risk." Unpublished Master's thesis, M.I.T., 1962.

O'DAY, R., "The T-group trainer: a study of conflict in the exercise of authority." Pp. 387-410 in G.S. Gibbard, J.J. Hartman and R.D. Mann (eds.), *Analysis of Groups.* San Francisco: Jossey-Bass Publishers, 1974.

OLMSTED, M.S. *The Small Group.* New York: Random House, 1959.

ORNE, N.T., "On the social psychology of the psychological experiment: with particular reference to demand characteristics and their implications." *American Psychologist* 17 (1962): 776-783.

OVIANKINA, M., "Die Wiederaufnakme Unterbrochener Handlungen." *Psychologische Forschung* 2 (1928): 302–379.

PARSONS, T. and BALES, R., *Family, Socialization, and Interaction Process.* Glencoe, Ill.: Free Press, 1955.

PHILIP, H., and DUMPHY, D., "Developmental Trends in Small Groups." *Sociometry* 22 (1959): 162–174.

PILKONIS, P.A. and ZANNA, M.P., "The choice-shift phenomenon in groups: replication and extension." Unpublished manuscript. Yale University, 1969.

POLANSKY, N.A., "The prison as an autocracy." *Journal of Criminal Law and Criminology* 3 (1942): 16–22.

POWDERMAKER, F. and FRANK, J., *Group psychotherapy; studies in methodology of research and therapy.* Cambridge, Mass.: Harvard University Press, 1953.

PRUITT, D.G. and TEGER, A.I., "The risky shift in group betting." *Journal of Personality and Social Psychology* 20 (1971): 339–358.

PRUITT, D.G. and TEGER, A.I., "The risky shift in group betting.: *Journal of Experimental Social Psychology* 5 (1969): 115–126.

RAPOPORT, R., *Community as Doctor.* Springfield, Ill.: Charles C. Thomas, 1960.

RASKIN, D.E., "Problems in the therapeutic community." *American Journal of Psychiatry* 128 (1971): 492–493.

REDL, F., "Group emotion and leadership." *Psychiatry.* 5 (1942): 573–596.

REISMAN, D., *The Lonely Crowd: A Study of the Changing American Character* New Haven, Connecticut; Yale University Press, 1964.

RIOCH, D. and STANTON, A., "Milieu therapy." *Psychiatry* 16 (1952): 65–72.

ROETHLISBERGER, F.J. and DICKSON, W., *Management and the Worker.* Cambridge, Mass.: Harvard University Press, 1947.

ROSENBERG, M.J., "When dissonance fails: on eliminating evaluation apprehension from attitude measurement." *Journal of Personality and Social Psychology* 1 (1965): 28–42.

ROSENBERG, S.D., "Hospital culture as collective defense." *Psychiatry* 33 (1970): 21–35.

ROSENGREN, W.R., "Structure, policy and style: Strategies of organizational control." *Administrative Science Quarterly* 12 (1967): 140–164.

ROTTER, G.S., "An experimental evaluation of group attractiveness as a determinant of conformity." *Human Relations* 20 (1967): 273–282.

ROY, D.F., "Banana time: job satisfaction and informal interaction." *Human Organization* 18 (1960): 158–168.

RUSHING, W.A., "Organizational rules and surviellance: propositions in comparative organizational analysis." *Administrative Science Quarterly* 10 (1966): 423–443.

SAMPSON, E.E., "Status congruence and cognitive consistency." *Sociometry* 26 (1963): 146–162.

SAMPSON, E. and BRANDON, A., "The effects of role and opinion deviation on small group behavior." *Sociometry* 17 (1964): 261–281.

SAYLES, L.R., *Behavior of Industrial Work Groups.* New York: John Wiley & Sons, Inc. 1958.

SCHACHTER, S., "Deviation, rejection and communication." *Journal of Abnormal and Social Psychology* 40 (1951): 190–207.

SCHROEDER, H.E., "The risky shift as a general choice shift." *Journal of Personality and Social Psychology* 27 (1973): 297–300.

SCHULMAN, G.I., "Asch conformity studies: conformity to the experimenter and/or to the groups?" *Sociometry* 30 (1967): 26–40.

SCHUTZ, W.C., "What makes groups productive?" *Human Relations* 8 (1955): 429–466.

SCOTT, R.W., "Organizational evaluation and authority." *Administrative Science Quarterly* 12 (1967): 93–117.

SEASHORE, S.E., *Group Cohesiveness in the Industrial Work Group.* Ann Arbor: Institute for Social Research, University of Michigan, 1954.

SHAW, M.E., "Some effects of unequal distribution of information upon group performance in various communication nets." *Journal of Abnormal and Social Psychology* 49 (1954): 547–553.

SHELLEY, H.P., "Focused leadership and cohesiveness in small groups." *Sociometry* 23 (1960): 209–216.

SHELLEY, H.P., "Status consensus, leadership and satisfaction with the group." *Journal of Social Psychology* 51 (1960): 157–164.

SHERIF, M., *The Psychology of Social Norms.* New York: Harper & Row, 1936.

SHERIF, M., *Social Psychology.* New York: Harper & Row, 1969.

SHERIF, M., WHITE, B.J., and HARVEY, O.J., "Status in experimentally produced groups." *American Journal of Sociology* 60 (1955): 370–379.

SHERIF, M. and SHERIF, C.W., "Group process and collective interaction in delinquent activities." *Journal of Research in Crime and Delinquency* 4 (1967): 43–62.

SHERIF, M. and SHERIF, C.W., *Groups in Harmony and Tension.* New York: Harper & Row, 1953.

SHORT, J.F. and STRODTBECK, F.L., *Group Processes and Delinquency.* Chicago, Ill.: University of Chicago Press, 1965.

SINGLETON, R., "Another look at the conformity explanation of group-induced shifts in choice." Unpublished paper, 1975.

SIMMEL, G., *The Sociology of Georg Simmel.* Glencoe, Ill.: Free Press, 1950.

SIMMEL, G., *Conflict and the Web of Group-affiliation.* Glencoe, Ill.: Free Press, 1955.

SLATER, P.E., "Role Differentiation in small groups." *American Sociological Review* 20 (1955): 300–310.

SLATER, P.E., *Microcosm.* New York: Wiley, 1966.

SMITH, H. and THRASHER, J., "Roles, cliques and sanctions: dimensions of patient society." *International Journal of Social Psychiatry* 9 (1963): 184–191.

SOMMER, R., *Personal Space.* Englewood Cliffs, N.J.: Prentice-Hall, Inc., 1969.

SOMMER, R. and OSMOND, H., "The schizophrenic no-society." *Psychiatry* 25 (1968): 244–255.

SPERGEL, I., *Racketville, Slumtown, Haulberg: An Exploratory Study of Delinquent Subcultures.* Chicago: The University of Chicago Press, 1964.

STANTON, A.H. and SCHWARTZ, M.S., *The Mental Hospital.* New York: Basic Books, 1954.

STODGILL, R.M., "Group productivity and cohesiveness." *Organizational Behavior and Human Performance* 8 (1972): 26–43.

STONER, J.A.F., "A comparison of individual and group decisions including risk." Unpublished Master's thesis. School of Industrial Management, M.I.T., 1961.

STREET, D., "The inmate group in custodial and treatment settings." *American Sociological Review* 30 (1965): 40–55.

STRODTBECK, F.L., JAMES, R.M. and HAWKINS, C. "Social status in jury deliberation." *American Sociological Review* 22 (1957): 713–719.

STUDT, E., MESSINGER, S.F., and WILSON, T., *C-Unit: Search for Community in Prison.* New York: Russell Sage Foundation, 1968.

SUMNER, W.G., *Folkways. A Study of the Sociological Importance of Usages, Manners, Customs, Mores and Morals.* New York: New York American Library, 1960.

SYKES, G.M., *The Society of Captives.* Princeton, N.J.: Princeton University Press, 1958.

SYKES, G.M. and MESSINGER, S.F., "The inmate social system." *Theoretical Studies in Social Organization.* New York: Social Science Research Council, Pamphlet #15, 1960, pp. 5–48.

TAYLOR, D.W., BERRY, P.C., and BLOCK, C.H., "Does group participation when using brainstorming facilitate or inhibit creative thinking?" *Administrative Science Quarterly* 3 (1958): 23–47.

TEGER, A.I. and PRUITT, D.G., "Components of group risk-taking." *Journal of Experimental Social Psychology* 3 (1967): 189–205.

THIBAUT, J. and FAUCHEUX, C., "The development of contractual norms in a bargaining situation under two types of stress." *Journal of Experimental and Social Psychology* 1 (1965): 89–102.

THIBAUT, J.W. and KELLEY, H.H., *The Social Psychology of Groups.* New York: John Wiley & Sons, Inc., 1959.

THOMAS, E.J. and FINK, C.F., "Models of group problem-solving." *Journal of Abnormal and Social Psychology* 63 (1961): 53–63.

THORTON, D. and ARROWOOD, A.J., "Self-evaluation, self-enhancement and focus of social comparison." *Journal of Experimental and Social Psychology* Suppl. 1 (1966): 40–48.

THRASHER, F.M., *The Gang.* Chicago: University of Chicago Press, 1926.

THRASHER, J. and SMITH, H., "Interaction contexts of psychiatric patients: some roles and organizational implications." *Psychiatry* 27 (1964): 389–398.

TONNIES, F., *Community and Society (Gemeinschaft and Gessellschaft).* East Lansing, Michigan: State University Press, 1957.

TRAPP, E.P., "Leadership and popularity as a function of behavioral predictions." *Journal of Abnormal and Social Psychology* 51 (1955): 452–457.

TUCKMAN, B., "Developmental sequence in small groups." *Psychological Bulletin* 63 (1965): 384–399.

TURK, H., "Instrumental values and the popularity of instrumental leaders." *Social Forces* 39 (1961): 252–260.

VERBA, S., *Small Groups and Political Behavior.* Princeton, N.J.: Princeton University Press, 1961.

VIDMAR, N., "Group composition and the risky-shift." *Journal of Experimental and Social Psychology* 6 (1970): 153–166.

VROOM, V.H., GRANT, L.D., and COTTON, T.S., "Consequences of social interaction in group problem-solving." *Organizational Behavior and Human Performance* 4 (1969): 77–95.

WALKER, E.L. and HEYNS, R.W., *An Anatomy for Conformity.* Englewood Cliffs, N.J.: Prentice-Hall, Inc., 1962.

WALLACH, M.A., KOGAN, N., and BEM, D.J., "Group influence on individual risktaking." *Journal of Abnormal and Social Psychology* 65 (1962): 75–86.

WALLACH, M.A., KOGAN, N., and BEM, D.J., "Diffusion of responsibility and level of risk taking in groups." *Journal of Abnormal and Social Psychology.* 68 (1964): 263–274.

WARRINER, C.K., "Groups are real: a reaffirmation." *American Sociological Review* 21 (1956): 549–554.

WHEELER, L., "Motivation as a determinant of upward comparison." *Journal of Experimental and Social Psychology* Suppl. 1 (1966): 27–31.

WHITE, R.K. and LIPPITT, R., *Autocracy and Democracy.* New York: Harper & Row, 1960.

WHYTE, W.H., *Money and Motivation.* New York: Harper & Row, 1955.

WHYTE, W.H., *Street Corner Society.* Chicago: University of Chicago Press, 1965.

WHYTE, W.H., *The Organization Man.* New York: Simon and Schuster, 1956.

WING, J.K. and BROWN, G.W., "Social treatment of chronic schizophrenia; a comparative study of three mental hospitals." *Journal of Mental Science* 107 (1961): 847–861.

WILSON, S.R., "The effects of the laboratory situation on experimental discussion groups." *Sociometry* 32 (1969): 220–235.

WILSON, S.R., "Leadership, participation and self-orientation in observed and not-observed groups." *Journal of Applied Psychology* 55 (1971): 433–438.

WILSON, S.R. and BENNER, L., "The effects of self-esteem and situation upon comparison choices during ability evaluation." *Sociometry* 34 (1971): 381–396.

WILSON, T.P., "Patterns of management and adaptation to organizational roles: a study of prison inmates." *American Journal of Sociology* 74 (1968): 146–157.

YABLONSKY, L., "The delinquent gang as a near-group." *Social Problems* 7 (1959): 108–117.

ZAJONC, R.B., *Social Psychology: An Experimental Approach.* Belmont, California: Wadsworth, 1966.

ZEIGARNIK, B., "Das begalten erledigter handlungen." *Psychologische Forschung* 9 (1927): 1–85.

Name Index

295

Subject Index